NOTEBOOKS

NOTEBOOKS

Schubert M. Ogden

CASCADE *Books* · Eugene, Oregon

NOTEBOOKS

Copyright © 2018 Schubert M. Ogden. All rights reserved. Except for brief quotations in critical publications or reviews, no part of this book may be reproduced in any manner without prior written permission from the publisher. Write: Permissions, Wipf and Stock Publishers, 199 W. 8th Ave., Suite 3, Eugene, OR 97401.

Cascade Books
An Imprint of Wipf and Stock Publishers
199 W. 8th Ave., Suite 3
Eugene, OR 97401

www.wipfandstock.com

PAPERBACK ISBN: 978-1-5326-5710-8
HARDCOVER ISBN: 978-1-5326-5711-5
EBOOK ISBN: 978-1-5326-5712-2

Cataloguing-in-Publication data:

Names: Ogden, Schubert Miles, 1928–, author.

Title: Notebooks / Schubert M. Ogden.

Description: Eugene, OR: Cascade Books, 2018. | Includes bibliographical references and index.

Identifiers: ISBN: 978-1-5326-5710-8 (PAPERBACK). | ISBN: 978-1-5326-5711-5 (HARDCOVER). | ISBN: 978-1-5326-5712-2 (EBOOK).

Subjects: LCSH: Theology.

Classification: BR118 O421 2018 (print). | BR118 (epub).

Manufactured in the U.S.A.   JANUARY 31, 2019

"The Task of Philosophical Theology: A Restatement" appeared in the *Journal of Religion* 98 (2018), copyright © by The University of Chicago and is used exercising the author's nonexclusive right of republication.

"The Criterion of Metaphysical Truth and the Senses of Metaphysics" and "*Must* God Be Really Related to Creatures?" appeared in *Process Studies* 5 (1975) and *Process Studies* 20 (1991) respectively and are used by permission of the editor.

The quotation from R. G. Collingwood, *Faith and Reason*, in "What, Exactly, Are 'Presuppositions'?" is used by permission of the editor, Lionel Rubinoff, copyright © 1968.

The quotation from Richard Rorty, "Philosophy-envy," in "On Science and the Sciences" is from *Dædalus* 133:4 (Fall 2004) 21–22 © 2004 by the American Academy of Arts and Sciences, published by the MIT Press.

The quotation from Charles Hartshorne, *Creativity in American Philosophy*, in "'The Concrete More'" is used without formal permission of the State University of New York Press.

Again, to my students, lay and professional,
whose questions deserve the best answers I can give them,
and
in grateful memory of Charles Hartshorne,
who continues to be, for me, "the Philosopher"

Contents

Preface | xi

PART 1: PHILOSOPHICAL ANALYSES

1. Basic Faith | 3
2. Experience *Of*/Thought *About* | 5
3. "Reality," or "the Real" | 8
4. Concerning the Senses of "Symbol" | 9
5. Philosophical Anthropology: Some Tentative Conclusions | 10
6. On Nonexecutive Authority | 14
7. On Questions | 17
8. On the Senses of "Theory" and "Praxis" | 20
9. "Interpretation," "Experience," and "Reason" | 21
10. Propositions, Instructions, and Performatives | 23
11. What, Exactly, Are "Presuppositions"? | 26
12. On Intrinsic and Constitutive Value | 29
13. On Science and the Sciences | 32
14. "The Love of Wisdom" | 45
15. On Philosophy | 48
16. The Two Phases of Philosophy | 57
17. Theses in the Philosophy of Religion | 59
18. What Constitutes a Religion? | 64
19. On the Difference between True and False Religion | 69
20. What Is a "Theological Interpretation of the Bible"? | 72
21. Theses on Philosophical Theology | 77
22. The Task of Philosophical Theology: A Restatement | 78
23. The Criteria of Philosophical Theology | 89
24. A Certain Confusion | 90
25. Hartshorne on Metaphysics | 92
26. Metaphysics and Logic | 95
27. Wittgenstein Says . . . | 100
28. Logical Structure, Not Metaphors | 101
29. On Seeing "More" | 101

30. Metaphysics and the Inner Aspect of Things | 102
31. Metaphysics in the Broad/Strict Senses | 103
32. Material/Formal Object | 105
33. Explicating Metaphysics—Formally and Materially | 107
34. Being and Beings | 109
35. The Aim of the Cosmos | 111
36. Metaphysical Axioms/First Principles and Necessary Presuppositions | 111
37. Metaphysical Assertions | 113
38. Metaphysics and Falsification | 114
39. Facts and Principles | 117
40. Necessary Truths | 118
41. Metaphysics and Self-Understanding | 119
42. Formulations, Assumptions, and Consequences | 122
43. On Arguing Metaphysically | 123
44. "Antifoundationalism" and Metaphysics | 125
45. "Analysis" and "Generalization" | 127
46. "The Concrete More" | 129
47. "Mind in General," Etc. | 131
48. "The Social" | 133
49. Categorial Metaphysics | 135
50. Rethinking Categorial Metaphysics | 137
51. Heidegger Speaks... | 139

PART 2: TRANSCENDENTAL METAPHYSICS

52. Meaning and Transcendental Metaphysics | 143
53. Rights and Responsibilities | 145
54. Transcendental Metaphysics as Engagement | 147
55. Transcendental Metaphysics and Transcendental Ethics | 149
56. On Transcendental Metaphysics | 157
57. Transcendental Metaphysics: A Primer | 159
58. Logical-Ontological Type Distinctions in Outline: Ten Theses | 160
59. Hartshorne on Peirce's Three Categories | 167
60. On Transcendentals | 170
61. On "Categorials" | 175
62. Critical Theory and Revisionary Metaphysics | 176
63. Events and Transcendentals | 178
64. Existentials and Transcendentals | 180
65. Whitehead's Term for "the Ultimate" | 181
66. "Concrescence" | 182
67. Concreteness and Abstractness | 184
68. On "the Aristotelian or Ontological Principle" | 188
69. Any Ordinary Abstract... | 191
70. "Existence" | 192

71. "Human Existence" | 194
72. "Existential" | 195
73. Essence and Existence | 196
74. Possibility | 196
75. Possibility Is Futurity | 197
76. Whitehead Says . . . | 200
77. "Actualization" | 201
78. The Necessary/the Possible | 202
79. The Necessary | 203
80. The Necessary and the Contingent | 205
81. Analogy | 205
82. Hartshorne's Theory of Analogy—as Unnecessary as It Is Impossible | 216
83. On "the Infinite, Qualitative Difference" | 218
84. The Scope of Metaphysics | 219

PART 3: GOD

85. Experience and God | 225
86. Ὁ Θεός/Ἡ Θειότης αὐτοῦ | 232
87. Who (or What) Is God? | 237
88. God May Be Defined as . . . | 242
89. "God Does Not Exist"/"God Exists *A Se*" | 244
90. *Res Significata/Modus Significandi* | 245
91. What Makes Theism Theism? | 246
92. What Do I Mean, Exactly, by "Radical Monotheism"? | 247
93. Is God a Being, or . . . ? | 248
94. God Is Being in Both Aspects | 249
95. "God" as a/the Transcendental Concept/Term | 250
96. On the Works of God *Ad Extra* | 252
97. God *the* Creator and God *the* Consummator | 257
98. God and the World Are at Each Other's Service | 258
99. *Must* God Be Really Related to Creatures? | 260
100. What Is the Role that Properly Belongs to God—and to Creatures? | 261
101. On Nature and Grace | 262
102. On Providence | 265
103. Qualified Pluralism/Synergism | 268
104. The Agency of God | 271
105. "The Glory of God" | 276
106. God and the Lord's Prayer | 277
107. The Incarnation: After the Fall or Before It? | 279
108. "For These Two Belong Together, Faith and God" | 282
109. "He That Made Us without Ourselves Will not Save Us without Ourselves" | 283
110. On Tillich's Dictum: "The End of Creation Is the Beginning of the Fall" | 284
111. "One Truth Is Clear: Whatever Is, Is Right" | 285

112. Human Needs and the Reality of God | 289
113. Proofs of, or Arguments for, God's Existence | 292
114. On "the *Euthyphro* 'Dilemma'" | 303
115. "Perfect Being Theology" and Christology | 306
116. The Problem of God for Christian Systematic Theology | 307
117. Reflections on Acts 10:34–35 | 317
118. On the *Optio Fundamentalis* | 322

Bibliography | 327
Index of Names | 333

Preface

Just as thinking, in my case, has always meant trying to think with the minds of others as well as my own, and therefore reading, so has it also always meant writing, for myself as well as for others. Why? Well, because "writing it out so I can read it" is the only means I've ever found by which I could be at all sure about what I wanted to think and whether I might possibly be right in thinking it. In one form or another, then, the "notebooks" in which most of my writing has been done have always had a prominent place on my desk, and writing and rewriting them, or what eventually became them, has ever claimed a large part of my time and energy as a theological scholar-teacher.

The present volume consists of some selections from these notebooks. Taken altogether, they contain many of my first thoughts—and as often as not some of my best ones—on matters with which I believe a Christian systematic theologian today most needs to be concerned. But the small selection published here neither is nor is intended to be representative in scope. It is deliberately focused instead on some of the more fundamental issues (often philosophical) now facing anyone who would do Christian theology systematically. The other criterion I have applied in making the selection is to include entries that, in one way or another, fill in or fill out the approach to the understanding of Christian faith for and from which I have argued in my other published writings.

Central at this point was my ever-deepening conviction that the metaphysics and ethics that are called for in doing theology today have to be not only materially neoclassical instead of classical in form, but also (and just as urgently) austerely transcendental rather than categorial. However, any metaphysics and ethics that are likely to be worth considering are of a piece with a whole range of other philosophical analyses; and the one issue that both philosophy and Christian theology have to deal with sooner or later is the issue of God. Whence my rationale for ordering the entries I selected into the three main parts of the book.

But this order, like that of the entries themselves, both within their respective parts and also internally, is suggested only. Most of the titles are relatively recent and now cover more than one original or independent entry, as indicated in most cases by the fleurons. I have, of course, tried to organize the book so that it can be read as a single, if many-sided, argument. But one of the values of a good notebook is that it is precisely a book of notes, each of which ideally stands on its own and can also be read as such with profit.

There are certain persons I think of with gratitude in writing this preface. One is Andrew D. Scrimgeour, Dean of Libraries Emeritus at Drew University, in whose archives the bulk of my notebooks in their form at the time have been housed since 2009. Thanks especially to his efforts, they have now all been scanned and integrated into the database, so as to be accessible to the general public online. The other persons are my literary executor, Philip E. Devenish, and his team of fellow editors, Franklin I. Gamwell, George L. Goodwin, and Alexander F. Vishio, who have all worked with Andy in the important final stages of integration. To all of you, as always, my heartiest thanks.

Westminster, Colorado
June 2018

Part 1

PHILOSOPHICAL ANALYSES

The ideal aim of philosophizing is to become reflectively at home in the full complexity of the multi-dimensional conceptual system in terms of which we suffer, think, and act.

—WILFRID SELLARS

1

Basic Faith

To live as adult human beings is to live by faith in the existence of a reality beyond, but also including, oneself and to make distinctions between what only seems to be, or is said to be, and what really is, what is appearance and what is reality, and what is false and what is true. This faith, in reality and in truth, can be understood critically, but life cannot be lived without it. No reason can ever replace faith, although faith can be understood ever more reasonably, insofar as successive understandings of it are better able to withstand relevant rational criticism. But to give up faith, as distinct from giving up this, that, or the other relatively inadequate understanding of it, would be to give up life itself.

In much the same way, to live humanly is to live by faith in a value beyond (but also including) one's own value, and to make distinctions between what only seems to be valuable and what really is so, what is good and what is evil, and what is right and what is wrong. This faith, in value, goodness, and rightness, can be understood critically, but life cannot be lived without it. No reason can ever replace faith, although faith can be understood ever more reasonably, insofar as successive understandings of it are better able to withstand relevant critical reflection. But to give up faith, as distinct from giving up this, that, or the other relatively inadequate understanding of it, would be to give up life itself.

So, too, to live as a mature human being is to live by faith in something that makes all lives, including one's own, both possible and meaningful. The ultimate question of life is never "Is living both possible and worthwhile?" but only "What is it—really and truly—that makes it so?" Affirmation of life's possibility and worthwhileness is inalienable, even though what makes life possible and worthwhile can always be more or less misunderstood. And so this faith can also always be understood more critically, more reasonably, insofar as some explicit understandings of it are better able than others to stand up to relevant rational criticism. And yet no reason can ever replace the faith. To give it up, as distinct from giving up any and all understandings of it that prove to be relatively inadequate, would be also to give up life.

This third question about the possibility and worthwhileness of life is rightly thought and spoken of as *the* existential question, and as therefore the *religious* question as well. It does not ask *whether* life is possible and meaningful, but only *what it is* that makes it so or *how we are to understand* that it is. What is the source or ground of life's possibility and meaning—and so, in a very broad, heuristic sense of "God," who or what is God?

In what I mean by "radical monotheism"—which I take to be only more or less illustrated by the traditional theistic religions of Judaism, Christianity, and Islam—the answer to the question of life's meaning is: The source or ground of life's possibility and meaning, and so "God," is the one strictly ultimate, universal reality that is *the* necessary condition of the possibility not just of human existence but of all existence. But if this answer is relatively more adequate than any other, it is only because this one strictly ultimate, universal reality is understood to be not just abstract but also concrete, and therefore a genuine individual: the one reality that is as individual as it is universal, and vice versa, because it is as internally related to all things, as all things are internally related to it. Thus it not only makes all things really possible, both in principle and in fact, but it also makes all things really real and everlastingly significant by incorporating them into its own everlasting life. As such, it is arguably the one eminent or unsurpassable (and therefore all-worshipful) reality that alone is deserving of authentic faith—meaning both unreserved trust or confidence, and unqualified loyalty or fidelity.[1]

Our basic faith as human beings includes at least the following:

1. a faith that there is a reality in which we are to believe that comprises all three modes of the actual, the possible, and the necessary, and that this reality, being independent of what we believe about it, individually and collectively, is the measure of the truth or falsity of all our beliefs;

2. a faith that there is a good and a right that we are to pursue and do, and that, being independent of what we believe to be good and right, individually and collectively, is the measure of the rightness or wrongness of all our actions, as well as of the truth or falsity of all our beliefs about them; and

3. a faith that there is a meaning of ultimate reality for us that we are to accept in obedient trust and loyalty, and that, being likewise independent of what we believe about it, individually and collectively, is the measure of the truth or falsity of whatever we believe it to be.

This third faith included in our basic faith may also be described as a faith (1) that there is a true and authentic way for each of us to understand ourselves and others as all parts of the one encompassing whole; (2) that to understand oneself in this way and to lead one's life accordingly are both really possible in fact as well as in principle

---

1. Cf. Niebuhr, "Life Is Worth Living."

and, like everything else, real and abidingly significant; and (3) that the structure of ultimate reality in itself determines its meaning for us, or determines the true and authentic way to understand oneself and others and to guarantee that this way of self-understanding and the life-praxis that accords with it are both really possible.

2

Experience *Of*/Thought *About*

Experience is always experience *of*—of reality as given to, and as independent of, our experience. Thought, or as may also be said, understanding or reason, is always included in some experience and therefore is always thought *about*—about the reality given to, and independent of, our thought as well as of our experience. More exactly, thought is always about reality; not in its concrete content, quality, or value, but in its abstract structure. Insofar as concrete reality is given to us at all, it is not given through thought but through experience, although our experience, being fragmentary, is itself so abstract as to mediate concrete reality as such only poorly.

Any concrete reality has a content, quality, or value in itself, as well as for all other concrete realities experiencing it (or otherwise really, internally relating to it); and it may have a meaning for us, as well, as beings who not only experience it, but also understand, and think and speak about, what we experience. It has this meaning for us, not in its intrinsic value as a concrete reality, but in its different abstract aspects, and thus in its constitutive or instrumental value for us.

But if any concrete reality has a content, quality, or value in itself as well as for others, and may also have a meaning for us, it also has a structure which, relative to itself as concrete, is abstract, offering different abstract aspects in which we may find it to be of constitutive or instrumental value.

Thought about reality, as distinct from experience of reality, is always either about *ultimate* reality (including *strictly* ultimate reality) as mediated by our experience in its vertical dimension or *existential* aspect, in which case it is properly distinguished as, implicitly or explicitly, *metaphysics*; or about immediate reality as mediated by our experience in its other horizontal dimension or *empirical* aspect, in which case it is properly said to be, implicitly or explicitly, *science*, i.e., one or the other of the so-called special sciences.

Thought also takes place on two closely related, but clearly distinguishable, levels: on the primary level of self-understanding and life-praxis, and on the secondary level of critical reflection/appropriation and proper theory. Thought on the primary level is already involved in normal adult "experience," which when examined closely is as truly thought *about* reality as it is experience *of* reality. On this primary level, thought consists of asking and answering our various *vital* questions, existential and also intellectual, thereby making or implying certain claims to validity, including the claim for the truth of our answers to our questions.

Thought on the secondary level, by contrast, consists in critically reflecting on/appropriating our experience and thought on the primary level. Specifically, critical reflection/appropriation includes both *critical interpretation* of the answers to our various vital questions, existential and also intellectual, and *critical validation* of the claims we make or imply in answering them as we do, especially the claim that our answers are true. In other words, the questions we ask and answer on the secondary level are not the various *vital* questions we ask and answer on the primary level, but rather the *theoretical* questions of meaning and validity—not simply as such, of course, but as oriented by, and corresponding to, our various vital questions.

Still another word closely related to "thought," along with "understanding" and "reason," is "belief." And what has been said so far about thought, understanding, and reason may be said, *mutatis mutandis*, about belief as well. Thus, for example, if we may say that thought about reality on the primary level is already a part of normal adult "experience" of reality, we may say the same concerning belief, because our ordinary "experience" of reality is shot through with beliefs about the reality we experience. Or, again, we may and must distinguish our various vital beliefs on the primary level from our corresponding theoretical beliefs on the secondary level.

In the same way, we may and must distinguish between our basic beliefs about ultimate reality as mediated by our experience in its vertical dimension, or existential aspect, and all of our other beliefs about immediate reality that necessarily presuppose our basic beliefs, but that are themselves mediated by our experience in its other dimension or aspect previously distinguished as horizontal or empirical.

If, then, the claims to truth that we make or imply for our beliefs are valid, this can only be because our beliefs about reality, like our understandings of it, or our thoughts and reasonings about it, agree with, or correspond to, reality as it is. And the only conceivable test, finally, of whether this necessary condition is satisfied, is that our beliefs, or the assertions that we believe to be true, may somehow claim the support of our experience of reality in its vertical dimension, or existential aspect, in the case of our basic beliefs; and in its horizontal dimension, or empirical aspect, in the case of our other beliefs. This is the only conceivable test, finally, because the abstract aspects or structure of concrete realities with which our beliefs, thoughts, understandings, and reasonings about them must agree, or to which they must correspond, in order to be true are mediated only by our experience of concrete realities in one or the other of its two dimensions or aspects.

Experience Of/Thought About

Experience is to the content, quality, or value of a concrete reality as thought, understanding, reason, or belief is to its abstract structure. This means that if the structure of a concrete reality can be thought, understood, reasoned, or believed about, the concrete reality itself cannot be thought about, but can only be experienced. Therefore, relative to thought, the content, quality, or value of a concrete reality remains as mysterious as its structure is intelligible, although human thought, like human experience, is also fragmentary and abstract, excluding most, if not quite all, even of the abstract reality or structure thought about.

"Reasoning," as distinct from "reason," is a synonym for "argumentation," and thus refers to the entire process of giving reasons—from the primary level of self-understanding and life-praxis to the secondary level of critical reflection/appropriation and proper theory, and with respect both to our basic beliefs and our other beliefs, as well as the purely hypothetical, necessary, but nonexistential, assertions of formal logic and mathematics. All such reasoning is rightly said to consist of discourse or argumentation somehow grounded in, and involving final (or primal) appeal to, experience in one or the other of its two dimensions or aspects.

In addition to the connections among the several distinctions previously clarified—experience and thought, concrete and abstract, mystery and intelligibility—there is also the connection between all of them, on the one hand, and the distinction between the unsurpassable and the surpassable, on the other. This distinction does not parallel the others, but cuts across them, in that the unsurpassable and the surpassable can each be said to be, in infinitely, qualitatively different ways, objects of both experience and thought and to have aspects in themselves that are both concrete and abstract, content and structure, mystery and intelligibility. "The infinite, qualitative difference" between the unsurpassable and the surpassable is the difference between "all" and "some" (in contrast to "none"), or "whole" and "part." Thus, while the unsurpassable, as much as anything surpassable, is an object of both experience and thought, it is properly distinguished as *the* object, the universal and all-inclusive object thereof, even as anything surpassable is simply *an* object, a particular and partially exclusive object among many others, both of experience and of thought. Or, again, the unsurpassable *qua* concrete and abstract, or in its content and also in its structure, is not simply *a* concrete or content, or *an* abstract or structure, but is *the* concrete or content and *the* abstract or structure. This is because the unsurpassable as all or the whole includes within itself as concrete or content all other surpassable concretes or contents, even as in its aspect as abstract or structure it is included within all other abstracts or structures, as well as all other concretes or contents. In the same way, or for the same reason, the unsurpassable *qua* concrete or content is not simply *a* mystery, but *the* mystery, all mystery compounded into one all-encompassing, impenetrable mystery, while *qua* abstract or structure, the unsurpassable is not simply *an* intelligible, but is *the* intelligible, all intelligibility united into one incomparably lucid abstract or structure.

3

"Reality," or "the Real"

What is properly meant by "reality," or "the real"?

According to William James, the real is "what we in some way find ourselves obliged to take account of."[2] Charles Hartshorne answers the question differently, but in no way contradictorily, by saying, "The real is that to which true affirmations refer." So by "reality" is properly meant, not simply "whatever happens to exist, *taken in its contingent aspects alone*," but rather "having a character of its own with reference to which opinions can be true or false." "[R]eality is the object of correct affirmations (that which measures their truth)."[3]

On this meaning, not only the contingent, or "that which *contingent* true assertions affirm," is real, but also the necessary, or what *necessary* true assertions affirm. By "the necessary" here is meant "the common element of all possibility," and so "reality as such," which "is neither a fact, nor something merely 'behind,' or additional to all facts[,] but rather something *in* them all."[4]

Hartshorne, in my judgment, is right: the best word for what contingent true assertions affirm is not "reality," or "the real," but rather "fact," in the sense of "something in nature that, having been made or produced (*factum*, fr. *facere*) might conceivably not have been as it is."

∽

Reality is what experience is experience of, and thus what is disclosed through experience—and reason based on experience.

There are two main forms of this experiential-rational disclosure of reality: empirical-rational and existential-rational.

Correspondingly, there are two main forms of the reality thus disclosed: the immediate reality disclosed empirical-rationally ("facts"); and the ultimate reality disclosed existential-rationally ("principles").

---

2. James, *Some Problems of Philosophy*, 101.
3. Hartshorne, *Wisdom as Moderation*, 65–66.
4. Hartshorne, *Wisdom as Moderation*, 63, 65–66.

4

Concerning the Senses of "Symbol"

I use "symbol" in three distinct—albeit closely related—senses:

(1) in connection with "the symbolic capacity" (Hartshorne)—i.e., our capacity to grasp and express meaning at the high level of thinking and speaking exhibited by normal adult human behavior. In this first broad sense (*sensu lato*), "symbol" is applicable to any and all expressed meaning, whether the mode or medium of its expression be language, conduct, or artifacts generally, including "sociofacts";

(2) in connection with the expression of specifically religious (or philosophical) meaning, which is analogical in a broad sense insofar as concepts and terms ordinarily used in thinking and speaking about the empirical or the merely factual existential are also applied to the transcendental. In this second strict or proper sense (*sensu stricto*), "symbol" is equivalent in meaning with "analogy," broadly understood; and

(3) in connection with a particular, historically significant kind of expression of religious (or philosophical) meaning—namely, myth—insofar as it is understood to be precisely that. In this third narrow sense (*sensu strictissimo*), "symbol" means any myth insofar as it is understood *as myth* and used accordingly. (This, by the way, is also pretty much Rudolf Bultmann's use of "symbol"; and Hartshorne uses it similarly in distinction from "analogy" in his strict, term-of-art, sense of the word.)

In my use, "myth" designates a species of "analogy," understood broadly, and hence also of "symbol," used in what I distinguish as the second, strict or proper sense of the term. Myth is not the only species of analogy in the broad sense or of symbol in the strict or proper sense, since there can be analogies or symbols in these senses whose concepts and terms are derived, not empirically, from our external sense perception, but existentially, from our internal nonsensuous perception of our own existence as related to others and the whole. But where the concepts and terms used in an analogy are not derived existentially but empirically, it is an instance of the properly mythical species of analogy, as well as of symbol in the second sense of the term. So I would not disagree with the statement that some of the things I am wont to say about myth would apply also to symbol in that second sense; for in that sense, symbol is to myth as genus is to species. But if all myth is symbol in this second strict or proper sense of "symbol," not all symbol in this sense is myth. My main objection to the way in which Paul Tillich and others talk globally of "religious symbol" without making any such distinction is that it does not clarify but only confuses relevant issues—allowing, for instance, for such popular but hopelessly misguided claims as "'Demythologizing' is really 'remythologizing.'"

It will be noticed that I have implied a further distinction between broad and strict senses of "analogy," as when I said that "symbol" *sensu stricto* is equivalent in meaning with "analogy," broadly understood. In its strict sense, "analogy" designates what is really only a particular kind of "analogy" *sensu lato*—namely, a *nonsymbolic* analogy (in the third, strictest sense of "symbolic"). Whereas "symbol" in the third sense designates religious (or philosophical) thought and speech whose concepts and terms are derived *empirically*, "analogy" in the strict sense of the term designates discourse whose concepts and terms are derived *existentially*.

5

Philosophical Anthropology: Some Tentative Conclusions

A human being is nature become spirit, or in other words, is nature become understanding of itself, others, and its ultimate ground and end. As such, a human being is continuous and also discontinuous with the rest of nature, and is to be conceived as emergent from it in accordance with its own immanent laws of evolutionary development. This implies that there is as little reason to appeal to a special creation by God to explain the appearance of human beings as to explain the appearance of any other level of natural emergence (living from nonliving, animal from living, etc.). As Hans Jonas effectively shows in *The Phenomenon of Life*, the very structures that existentialist philosophers have isolated as definitively human—freedom, creativity, self-determination, etc.—are foreshadowed or anticipated at all earlier levels of life, so that the entire process of life's emergence is one long "history of freedom" culminating in human beings. To take this view, as I see it, is to move "beyond humanism," whether in its earlier supernaturalist form or in its more recent naturalist forms. As I read it, the story of human beings' discovery of themselves as spirit distinct from the rest of nature is not without its deeply tragic side—by which I mean their self-alienation or estrangement from nature, the original counterpart of which was the estrangement they conceived to exist between God and nature as well. The accomplishment of more recent thinking, prompted by the gradual adoption of the hypothesis of human evolutionary emergence, is to have opened the way to the overcoming of this alienation from nature on the part of God as well as human beings.

As a new emergent level within nature, human beings as nature become spirit are more than simply a compound of animal with something more than animal. There is an integrity to the distinctively human structure such that even the biology of human beings is peculiarly human. This is evident from the fundamental biological conditions of human existence—notably, the lack of instinctive specialization and the presence of a greatly enlarged neocortex, together with the peculiar pattern of growth to which each human individual is subject (premature birth, extended youth, and a relatively long period of maturity). These biological characteristics directly correspond to the fact that a human being is nature become spirit, and at once condition and are conditioned by that fact. Also relevant in this connection is the conclusion of Theodosius Dobzhansky and others that there was a "feedback process" of cultural achievement on genetic endowment in the late evolution of the human brain.

The fact that a human being is nature become spirit explains the further fact that she or he is a uniquely cultural and properly historical creature. If the question is asked whether there is any such thing as a universal human nature, the answer, in my judgment, is definitely affirmative. But this does not mean that there is any good reason to understand "human nature" in the oversimplified ways in which it has often been understood. The human, I should say, is really an abstract variable, which can have any number of different concrete values, and indeed *must* have some such values, but which, as abstract, also has a constant aspect. This can be put as well by saying that, as biologically unspecialized, and yet also able and constrained somehow to specialize her- or himself, a human being is both *homo hominans* and *homo hominatus*—or, as we may translate, a human being *making* her- or himself and a human being *made by* her- or himself. *Qua* making her- or himself, a human being shares in "the human" only insofar as it is understood as an abstract variable that can have many values, contingently upon her or his exercise of the capacity to determine her- or himself. But this is just what is meant by saying that a human being is the uniquely cultural creature; for by "culture" is meant the sum total of everything that a human being has not received from nature via heredity, but has produced through her or his creative power to determine her- or himself. Strictly speaking, of course, culture exists only in plural forms: human beings create culture only in that they create cultures. And this, in turn, explains why they are also properly historical creatures, for as William H. McNeill has written, "When cultural evolution took over primacy from biological evolution, history in the strict and proper sense began."[5]

But both culture and history involve a dialectic; and a human being as nature become spirit is essentially involved in this dialectic. On the one hand, she or he is the creator of culture, the one through whose creative freedom culture first comes to be. On the other hand, she or he is also the creature of culture, the one whose life is given shape by the cultural heritage into which she or he enters precisely in being born and raised as a human being. Thus it is possible to apply to human culture generally

---

5. McNeill, *World History*, 6.

Wilhelm von Humboldt's well-known statement about that foundational element in all culture—language: "Man is man only through language; but in order to discover language he already had to be man"; von Humboldt's statement is exactly paralleled by A. N. Whitehead when he says, "the mentality of mankind and the language of mankind created each other."[6] In a similar way, one may show that a human being is at once creative of history and created by it. Thus Michael Landmann has spoken of the dialectic of subjective and objective spirit; and Peter Berger and Thomas Luckmann, in *The Social Construction of Reality*, develop a similar dialectic in working out their sociology of knowledge. As they put it, "the relationship between man, the producer, and the social world, the product, is and remains a dialectical one. That is, man ... and his social world interact with each other. The product acts back upon the producer.... *Society is a human product. Society is an objective reality. Man is a social product.*"[7]

The important point is to recognize that this dialectic is exactly that, and that, therefore, neither side can be collapsed into the other. If a human being as nature become spirit freely transcends nature, even while remaining within it, a human being as spirit expressing or externalizing itself in culture and, in turn, internalizing culture also transcends culture, even while remaining within it. This, it seems to me, is the abiding importance of existentialist anthropology, which refuses to treat a human being as simply the product of her or his cultural and social environment, just as it also refuses to treat her or him as merely an animal. One compelling reason for thinking this view true is that it alone seems able to explain how human beings can develop, as they have in fact done, such transcendental analyses as "sociology of knowledge" and "anthropology of culture." If the statement that "reality is socially constructed" applied *tout court*, and thus also to the reality putatively disclosed by the sociology of knowledge itself, we would be faced with an obvious and, I should think, unacceptable paradox. On the other hand, the value of the kind of anthropology of culture developed by Landmann and others, or the sociology developed by Arnold Gehlen and Peter Berger, is to fill in the stark abstractness of a merely existentialist understanding of human being—just as much the same may be said, *mutatis mutandis*, for more biologically oriented anthropologies.

But also implied by this, in my judgment, is the continued relevance of the kind of philosophical anthropology worked out, in effect, by Henry Nelson Wieman, although I would have to say that Wieman himself is unable to do justice to the other side of the dialectic: the freedom of a human being as nature become spirit, beyond the power even of her or his own creative accomplishments, to create her or him anew, provided she or he meets the conditions for their accumulation and integration.

Consistent with—if not, as I would wish to argue, required by—the basically existentialist understanding of a human being as nature become free, self-transcendent

---

6. Whitehead, *Modes of Thought*, 57.
7. Berger and Luckmann, *Social Construction of Reality*, 61.

spirit is the view that "the human" as abstract constant includes a human being's understanding, even if only nonreflectively or nonthematically, of self, others, and the whole; and that "the human" as abstract variable includes *subjectively* either the authentic or the inauthentic actualization of this understanding and *objectively* the externalization-internalization of this understanding in cultural and historical forms—explicitly in religion, and implicitly in all other fields of culture. In this way, one can, I believe, provide the ampler anthropological context for what I take to be the key both to philosophy and to Christian theology—namely, that any human being as nature become spirit exists by faith in the primal possibility and final worth of life. She or he can exist at all, authentically or inauthentically, only by somehow accepting the threefold reality of self, others, and the whole as really possible and abidingly significant. Hence the task of philosophy and Christian theology alike, albeit each in its own way, is the fully reflective understanding of this basic faith—by way of a methodical hermeneutic of religion and culture generally, in the case of philosophy; and, presupposing and implying this philosophical hermeneutic, a similarly methodical hermeneutic of the witness of Christian faith specifically, in the case of Christian theology.

I should like to argue, I think, that something like Wieman's analysis of the creative good as the growth of qualitative meaning (or, as I would suggest—more aptly catching what he really means—"meaningful quality"!) is an appropriate and credible way of understanding just how God works in individual human lives, creatively/emancipatively, as distinct from consummatively/redemptively, To become all that one can and should become as a distinctively human individual requires not only that one be socialized and acculturated (which I take to be a "secular" way of thinking and talking about the process of "creative good" that Wieman identifies with God), but also that one continue to be ever and again *re*socialized and *re*-acculturated—or as he would say, *re*made into a new human being.[8]

But if Wieman's analysis, for this reason, belongs to or may be critically appropriated by an adequate Christian systematic theology, it has to take its place there in the same way as such other wholly naturalistic analyses as belong to, or have been critically appropriated by, more recent political and liberation theologies. These are analyses highlighting the place and importance of social and cultural structures/orders and the corresponding need—to put it in Wieman's terms—to use all "*created* goods" to provide the conditions necessary for the working of "*creative* good," not only in his generally moral sense pertaining to the transformation of individual persons, but also in the specifically *political* sense pertaining to transforming societies and cultures by also recreating and emancipating them. These two processes,

---

8. See Wieman, *Source of Human Good*.

arguably, are significantly interdependent. The process of creating, maintaining, and (where necessary) transforming social and cultural structures/orders is necessary for providing at least some of the required conditions for creative good to do its work in individual human lives, even as the process of "creative good," as Wieman analyzes it, is necessary to providing at least some of the necessary conditions of the political process of creating, maintaining, and transforming social and cultural structures/orders in the direction of ever greater justice and more inclusive human community.

But even as I find it necessary to draw a clear and sharp distinction between creation-emancipation in its political meaning and consummation-redemption-salvation in an appropriately Christian understanding of the terms, so I would insist that just such a distinction has to be drawn between the creation-emancipation that "creative good," in Wieman's sense, is capable of producing, and what is appropriately understood by consummation-redemption-salvation in a proper Christian sense of the words. This is to say that, on my understanding, the relation between creation-emancipation, on the one hand, and consummation-redemption-salvation, on the other, is an *analogous* (or analogical) relation—such as Abraham Lincoln expresses in speaking of Americans as God's "almost chosen people." For what is his point in so speaking? Whatever else it is, it surely includes frankly acknowledging the difference as well as the similarity between biblical Isræl and America as viewed from the standpoint of Lincoln's radical monotheistic self-understanding/understanding of existence. Americans so viewed are God's "*almost* chosen people" in something like the sense in which creation-emancipation, while liberation in its own way, is not liberation *simpliciter*, because it is only *like*, and in that sense, only "almost," liberation in the other way of consummation-redemption-salvation.

6

On Nonexecutive Authority

The basis of all authority is the supremacy of fact over thought.

—ALFRED NORTH WHITEHEAD

The primal ontic source of all nonexecutive authority can only be reality itself, even as its primal noetic source can only be common human experience. What is somehow authorized by experience of reality as corresponding to it or agreeing with it is insofar authoritative; what is not thus authorized is insofar without authority.

If reality is "what we in some way find ourselves obliged to take account of" (according to William James), it may be said to include both ultimate and immediate reality, the first being everything that we have to take account of in the vertical dimension, or existential aspect, of our experience; the second, all that we must take account of in the horizontal dimension, or empirical aspect, of our experience. Thus ultimate reality includes the necessary condition of the possibility of everything that we experience nonsensuously—ourselves, others, and the whole of which we and others are all parts—while immediate reality includes everything about this threefold reality that we can also experience through our senses, however indirectly and abstractly.

Immediate reality, like ultimate reality, may be the primal ontic source of authority in two respects: (1) in respect of its structure in itself, and (2) in respect of its meaning for us. In the first respect, immediate reality is the primal ontic source authorizing *true science*, in the sense of explicit understanding of immediate reality in its structure in itself. In the second respect of its meaning for us, immediate reality is primal ontic source authorizing *true technology* and *true policy*, moral and also political, in the sense of explicit understanding of how, in fact, we are to act and what we are to do regarding means as well as ends consistently with immediate reality's having the structure in itself that true science shows it to have.

As for ultimate reality in the first respect, it is the primal ontic source authorizing *true metaphysics* and *true ethics*, the first being explicit understanding of ultimate reality in its structure in itself that corresponds to or agrees with that structure; the second, explicit understanding of how, in principle, we are to understand ourselves and lead our lives consistently with ultimate reality's having the structure that true metaphysics shows it to have. In the second respect of its meaning for us, ultimate reality is the primal ontic source authorizing *true religion*, in the sense of the explicit understanding of human existence necessarily implied by authentic self-understanding in relation to ultimate reality and necessarily implying, and, in substance, implied by, true metaphysics and true ethics.

Any religion as such makes or implies a claim to decisive authority and therefore also claims to be the true religion, in that it is not just *substantially* true in the sense clarified, but also *formally* true, in the sense that it is the formal norm or canon by which the truth-claim of any other religion has to be validated—namely, by its substantial correspondence to, or agreement with, that religion. Thus any religion understands itself to be uniquely authorized by ultimate reality itself in its meaning for us as its primal ontic source.

Of course, it is typical of religious traditions that they are heterogeneous in composition to the extent that, through special acts of self-definition, they acknowledge certain of their elements as authoritative and therefore normative for some or all of the remaining ones. Thus elements acknowledged in a religious tradition as authoritative for *all* of its other elements constitute its *primary* authority, and therefore its formal norm or "canon."

But no religious tradition is constituted as such simply by its primary authority or formal norm and whatever secondary authorities or norms it in turn authorizes or norms. Any authority, properly so called, is and must be authorized by a source beyond itself, just as any norm in the proper sense can only be, in the theological term, a "*normed* norm" (*norma normata*), even if what norms it, although the source of its normativeness, neither is nor can be itself a norm in the same proper sense. Therefore, any religious tradition is also constituted by some explicit *primal source* of authority and therefore of normativeness as well. To be sure, the primal source of a religious tradition's authority, insofar as it is authorized, is reality itself as experienced—more exactly, ultimate reality as experienced in its meaning for us. But ultimate reality in its meaning for us, even as in its structure in itself, remains merely implicit and cannot function as the primal ontic source of authority for any religious tradition except through some *explicit* primal ontic source of authority corresponding to it, or agreeing with it, in its meaning for us. This explicit primal ontic source of a tradition's authority is the explicit self-understanding/understanding of existence constituting it as a religious tradition whose claim to decisive authority, and thus also to be the formally true religion, is a valid one. As such, a religion's *explicit* primal ontic source of authority is also authorized—namely, by ultimate reality itself functioning as the *implicit* primal ontic source of all religious and existential authority. And yet, although it is indeed thus authorized, it itself is not, in the proper sense, *an* authority, not even *the* (primary) authority, for its religious tradition. Although any religious authority, properly so-called, is itself also a source of authority, the converse statement is false: not every source of authority itself either is or can be also *an* authority in the proper sense of the term.

If a religion's implicit primal ontic source of authority, being ultimate reality itself in its meaning for us, can only be *transcendental*, its explicit primal ontic source has to be *historical*. This means, among other things, that although both sources—implicit/transcendental and explicit/historical—have a constitutive significance with respect to the religion of which they are the authorizing sources, only the first has a constitutive significance with respect to human existence and its authentic possibility. In this respect, the significance of the second source is not constitutive, but representative only. Although a religion's explicit primal ontic source is uniquely constitutive of it as the religion it is, even it is at most representative of the meaning of ultimate reality for us, which is constituted solely and sufficiently by ultimate reality as such in its meaning for us, as determined by its structure in itself.

7

On Questions

[Y]ou cannot find out what a man means by simply studying his spoken or written statements.... In order to find out his meaning you must also know what the question was (a question in his own mind, and presumed by him to be in yours) to which the thing he has said or written was meant as an answer.

—R. G. COLLINGWOOD

1.0 Human beings ask two main kinds of questions: vital and theoretical.

1.1. Vital questions are the questions they ask on the primary level of living understandingly by thinking and speaking—i.e., the level of "interaction" (Jürgen Habermas), or as I usually say, the level of self-understanding and life-praxis.

1.2. Theoretical questions are the questions they ask on the secondary level of living understandingly by thinking and speaking—i.e., the level of "discourse" (Habermas), or, alternatively, the level of critical reflection/appropriation and proper theory.

2.0. The vital questions human beings ask include both existential (in a broad sense of the word) and intellectual questions.

2.1. Existential questions in a broad sense concretely ask about the meaning of reality for us: immediate, empirical-categorial reality, as well as ultimate, existential-transcendental reality.

2.2. Intellectual questions prescind from the meaning of reality for us in order to ask abstractly about the structure of reality in itself: both immediate, empirical-categorial reality and ultimate, existential-transcendental reality.

3.0. The theoretical questions human beings ask include both questions about meaning and questions about validity.

3.1. Questions about meaning ask either about only the surface (or semantic) meaning of what is thought, said, and done on the primary level of living understandingly, or also about its deep (or logical *kind* of) meaning.

3.2. Questions about validity ask about the validity of the claims made or implied by what is thought, said, and done on the primary level of living understandingly. To ask, for example, whether a claim to truth made by a constative speech act is valid is to ask a question about validity.

4.0. Human beings ask both existential questions and intellectual questions about immediate, empirical-categorial reality, and also about ultimate, existential-transcendental reality.

4.1. Existential questions (in a broad sense of the word "existential") ask about the meaning of reality for us—immediate, empirical-categorial reality as well as ultimate, existential-transcendental reality—whereas existential questions (in a strict sense of "existential") ask only about the meaning of ultimate, existential-transcendental reality for us.

4.2. Intellectual questions prescind from the meaning of reality for us in order to ask abstractly about the structure of reality in itself—immediate, empirical-categorial reality, as well as ultimate, existential-transcendental reality.

5.0. Paradigmatic for questions about the meaning of immediate, empirical-categorial reality for us are axiological and technological questions, even as scientific questions are paradigmatic for queries into the structure of immediate, empirical-categorial reality in itself.

5.1. Axiological questions ask primarily about the ends of life-praxis, whereas technological questions ask primarily about the means of attaining its ends.

5.2. Scientific questions prescind from all questions about ends and means in order to ask abstractly about the structure of immediate, empirical-categorial reality in itself, be it the reality of nature generally, as in the case of the natural sciences, or the reality of distinctively human nature and history in particular, as in the case of the human, or social, sciences.

(NB: "Scientific" is used here in the strict sense of "*empirical* scientific." In a broader sense, not only mathematics but also metaphysics and ethics could well be held to be "scientific," in that they, too, in their ways, are concerned abstractly or intellectually with *structure in itself*: mathematics, with the structure of the *possible*; metaphysics, with the structure of the *necessary*; and ethics, with the structure of the *necessary's meaning for us*. Also, there is arguably a fourth way of prescinding from meaning for us to ask abstractly about structure—namely, the way instanced by hermeneutics, as distinct from both the other human, or social, sciences, on the one hand, and the natural sciences, on the other. Cf. note 13, "On Science and the Sciences.")

6.0. Religious and philosophical questions are paradigmatic for questions about the meaning of ultimate, existential-transcendental reality for us, even as metaphysical questions are paradigmatic for questions about the structure of ultimate, existential-transcendental reality in itself, and ethical questions are paradigmatic for questions about the structure of the meaning of ultimate, existential-transcendental reality for us.

6.1. Religious questions and philosophical questions both ask about the meaning of ultimate, existential-transcendental reality for us: religious questions asking about it on the primary level of living understandingly, and by privileging some special, decisive disclosure of its meaning; and philosophical questions asking about it on the secondary level of living understandingly, and by privileging only the disclosures of religions in general, along with those of the other forms of culture.

6.2. Metaphysical questions ask about the structure of ultimate, existential-transcendental reality in itself: metaphysical questions in the strict sense, asking about the necessary conditions of the possibility of any reality as such; metaphysical questions in the broad sense asking, in addition, about the necessary conditions of the possibility of any reality that understands at the level exhibited by human thinking and speaking.

6.3. Ethical questions ask about the meaning of ultimate, existential-transcendental reality for us, but only by prescinding from its meaning as such in order to ask *abstractly* about the structure of that meaning in itself, whereas religious questions and philosophical questions, in their different ways, both ask about its meaning for us *concretely*.

7.0. Since—in the cases of immediate, empirical-categorial reality and also of ultimate, existential-transcendental reality—the meaning of reality for us and the structure of its meaning both depend on the structure of reality in itself, human beings naturally ask intellectual questions because they want only valid answers to their existential questions.

7.1. In asking existential questions, they seek know-how and wisdom (*sapientia*).

7.2. In asking intellectual questions, they seek knowledge (*scientia*).

8.0. Since validation of the answers to any of their vital questions depends on critical reflection/appropriation and proper theory, human beings naturally ask theoretical questions because they want only valid answers to their vital questions.

8.1. In asking vital questions, they seek to live, and to live well.

8.2. In asking theoretical questions, they seek to live better.

I have become increasingly uncomfortable with my use of "intellectual" and its cognates solely in the strict or proper sense in which I contrast it with "existential." Recently, I happened to think of Robert M. Hutchins's well-known definition of education generally as "the intellectual development of the population." The more I thought about it, the clearer I became that Hutchins could hardly have been using "intellectual" in the strict sense in which I have come to use it, lest he would never have given the place he gave to the liberal arts and humanities alongside the natural and social sciences in the process of formal education. Indeed, I am now confident (as confident as I can be of most things), without engaging in the close rereading that would be required to confirm it, that he almost certainly understood "intellectual development" to include the acquisition of—what I would call—"wisdom" as well as "knowledge." So I have been asking myself ever since whether I shouldn't reconsider my more recent use of "intellectual" by inquiring whether it, too, may not be systematically ambiguous in that there is another sense (or there are other senses) in which it may very well be used. I have now concluded that it is thus ambiguous and is, in fact, subject to something like the same threefold analysis of senses that I have found applicable to several other terms that function technically, or as terms-of-art, in my writings.

I would say that "intellectual" and its cognates can be understood:

1. in the *strict or proper* sense (*sensu stricto*) of understanding concerned with abstract structure in itself, and thus in contrast to "existential" in the sense of understanding concerned with concrete meaning for us;

2. in the *broad* sense (*sensu lato*) of any and all understanding, "existential" as well as "intellectual" in the strict or proper sense of the words, and at both levels of living understandingly—i.e., the primary level of self-understanding and life-praxis as well as the secondary level of critical reflection and proper theory; and

3. in the *narrow* sense (*sensu strictissimo*) of understanding concerned with abstract structure in itself and at the secondary level of critical reflection and proper theory only.

Two comments: (1) It is, of course, the first strict or proper sense of "intellectual" that is the sense in which I use it in the preceding entry; and (2) distinguishing the broad sense of the term takes account of, and is insofar warranted by, the cognation between "intellect" (*intellectus*) and "understanding" (*intelligentia*).

8

On the Senses of "Theory" and "Praxis"

To be human is not just to live, but to live understandingly, and to do so not just on one level but on two. Also, just as living understandingly on the primary level of self-understanding and life-praxis involves theory as well as praxis, so living understandingly on the secondary level of critical reflection and proper theory involves praxis as well as theory. Recognizing this, we may say that living understandingly on either level involves theory in a broad sense of the word, even as living understandingly on either level involves praxis in a correspondingly broad sense.

But this means that "theory" and "praxis" can both be understood in different senses and are therefore "systematically ambiguous." In fact, "theory" has at least three senses that can be clarified by making use of the concept/term "belief," understood as anything held to be true by one who lives understandingly and therefore leads (and must lead) her or his own life. So "theory" can be understood:

(1) in the *strict or proper* sense (*sensu stricto*), as comprising all beliefs formed on only one of the two levels of living understandingly—i.e., the secondary level of critical reflection and (yes!) proper theory;

(2) in the *broad* sense (*sensu lato*), as comprising all beliefs formed on both levels of living understandingly—i.e., the primary level of self-understanding and life-praxis, as well as the secondary level of critical reflection and proper theory; and

(3) in the *narrow* sense (*sensu strictissimo*), as comprising only some beliefs formed on the secondary level of critical reflection and proper theory—i.e., those expressed by constatives saying "So-and-so *is* the case," as distinct from prescriptives saying "So-and-so *should be* the case."

So, too, the word "praxis" has at least three senses that can be clarified by making use of the concept/term "action," understood as anything purposely done by one who lives understandingly and therefore leads (and must lead) her or his own life. Thus "praxis" can be understood:

(1) in the *strict or proper* sense (*sensu stricto*), as comprising all actions performed on only one of the two levels of living understandingly—i.e., the primary level of self-understanding and life-praxis;

(2) in the *broad* sense (*sensu lato*), as comprising all actions performed on both levels of living understandingly—i.e., the secondary level of critical reflection and proper theory, as well as the primary level of self-understanding and life-praxis; and

(3) in the *narrow* sense (*sensu strictissimo*), as comprising only some actions performed on the primary level of self-understanding and life-praxis—i.e., those that are, in Habermas's terms, "institutionally unbound," as distinct from being "institutionally bound."

9

"Interpretation," "Experience," and "Reason"

"Interpretation" may be understood in at least three different senses:

(1) in the *strict or proper* sense (*sensu stricto*), as only the first of the two main functions of critical reflection (validation being the second);

(2) in the *broad* sense (*sensu lato*), as what I also call "appropriation," and so as comprising both of the essential functions of critical reflection, validation, and interpretation in the strict or proper sense; and

(3) in the *narrow* sense (*sensu strictissimo*), as what I distinguish, in Mortimer Adler's terms, as "interpretation of contents (≡ the answer)," and so as only the second of the two steps required by interpretation in the strict or proper sense, the first step being "analysis of structure (≡ the question)."[9]

∽

I wonder whether "experience" may not be somewhat like "interpretation," in that it, too, may be analyzed in at least three different senses:

(1) in the *strict or proper* sense (*sensu stricto*), as only one of the two levels of living understandingly—i.e., the primary level of self-understanding and life-praxis;

(2) in the *broad* sense (*sensu lato*) as both levels of living understandingly—i.e., the secondary level of critical reflection and proper theory, as well as the primary level of self-understanding and life-praxis; and

(3) in the *narrow* sense (*sensu strictissimo*) as only the first of the two moments of experience in the strict or proper sense—i.e., the moment of givenness, intuition, or prehension, as distinct from the second moment of thought, belief, interpretation, theory, judgment, etc. about what is given, intuited, or prehended.

If this analysis is sound, then whether "experience" is taken to refer to the horizontal dimension or empirical aspect of experience or, rather, to its vertical dimension or existential aspect, it may be understood in all three of these different senses.

∽

If "interpretation" and "experience" may be analyzed in at least three different senses, isn't the same true of "reason," also?

Yes, "reason," too, may be analyzed in at least the following three senses:

(1) in the *strict or proper* sense (*sensu stricto*), as only one of the two levels of living understandingly—i.e., the secondary level of critical reflection and proper theory;

(2) in the *broad* sense (*sensu lato*), as both levels of living understandingly—i.e., the primary level of self-understanding and life-praxis, as well as the secondary level of critical reflection and proper theory; and

---

9. Adler, *How to Read a Book*.

(3) in the *narrow* sense (*sensu strictissimo*), as only the second of the two moments of experience in the strict or proper sense—i.e., the moment of thought, belief, interpretation, theory, judgment, etc., about what is given, intuited, or prehended, as distinct from the first moment of givenness, intuition, or prehension.

10

Propositions, Instructions, and Performatives

Joseph M. Bochenski argues the following in *Autorität, Freiheit, Glaube*:

1.0. A proposition (*ein Satz*) expresses *what is*—e.g., "It is raining," "The door is closed," "2 + 2 = 4." Therefore:

1.1. A proposition is always either *true* or *false*.

1.2. A proposition can have different degrees of *probability* with respect to our knowledge.

1.3. A proposition always refers to a so-called *state of affairs*—i.e., it expresses how things stand in relation to one another, and thus what is. (For this reason, a proposition can be *either* true *or* false: true, if things stand in relation to one another as it says they do; false, if they stand in some other relation.)

2.0. An instruction (*eine Weisung*), by contrast, expresses not what is, but *what one should do*. Therefore:

2.1. An instruction is *neither* true *nor* false. (It can be correct, right, moral, to the point, and so on; but it can never be true, any more than it can ever be false.)

2.2. An instruction *cannot* be said to be more or less probable. (Naturally, we can ask questions *about* an instruction, and the answers to them will be either true or false, and more or less probable. But these answers are not themselves instructions, but rather practical propositions [*die praktischen Sätze*] about an instruction, and as such capable of being true or false and more or less probable. The instruction itself, however, is never true, never false, and never probable.)

2.3. An instruction does not mean what is but *what should be*. (It cannot say what is because the state of affairs with which it is concerned must first be actualized by the action for which it calls.)

3.0. A performative (*ein Performativ*) *effects* what it means.

Performatives hardly seem likely to be confused with either propositions or instructions. But as clear as the difference may also seem between propositions (*die Sätze*) and instructions (*die Weisungen*), it is commonly missed or misunderstood.

One reason for this is that propositions *about* instructions, although not themselves instructions, are mistaken for such. In reality, however, propositions about instructions are a very special kind of propositions, namely, so-called *practical propositions* (*praktische Sätze*). Because a practical proposition also refers to an action, it is easily confused with the corresponding instruction.

Nevertheless, propositions and instructions are two different kinds of things, and their difference is of great significance for the theory of authority. Because there are these two kinds of relevant ideal constructs that could possibly comprise the domain of an authority, there are also two kinds of authority: the one exercised with the help of propositions, and the other with the help of instructions. The first may be called "knowledge-authority," or "*epistemic authority*," or "nonexecutive authority"; the second, "superior-authority," or "*deontic authority*," or "executive authority." The first kind of authority is the authority of one who knows; the second kind is the authority of a superior.

It should be clear that one and the same person can hold both kinds of authority with respect to the same subject(s) and in the same domain—or, actually, in two domains that are closely connected because, in this case, the domain of epistemic authority comprises the practical propositions corresponding to the instructions comprised by the domain of deontic authority. Indeed, one could say that, in this case, the practical propositions that correspond to the instructions constitute their foundation. Therefore, deontic and epistemic authority do not exclude one another.

On the other hand, the two kinds of authority are mutually independent, in that deontic authority in a domain and epistemic authority in the corresponding domain do not necessarily go together, however desirable it may be that they do so. A superior is a superior, and thus has deontic authority simply because she or he is a superior, not because she or he knows better.

One point at which I might need to take issue with Bochenski's analysis is 1.3. Judging from his examples in 1.0, I can only suppose that "2 + 2 = 4" somehow refers to what he goes on to call "a state of affairs." In that event, he would appear to allow for necessary as well as contingent states of affairs, and I would have no substantial quarrel with him, provided he allowed for *unconditionally*, in addition to conditionally, necessary (or possible) states of affairs such as mathematical propositions—being only conditionally necessary, or hypothetical—are commonly understood to refer to. But if "states of affairs," or "how things stand in relation to one another," is taken in its usual meaning, as referring only to certain *contingent* facts (as distinct from anything real necessarily) then it would follow from Bochenski's formulation either that there cannot be such a thing as a metaphysical proposition, as I understand such, or that a metaphysical proposition cannot express what necessarily is, but (being logically like a scientific proposition) can express only what contingently is. Therefore, I might need to reformulate 1.3 to read this instead: "A proposition always refers *either* to a so-called state of affairs, and thus to what *contingently* is, *or* to the strictly necessary conditions of the possibility of any state of affairs, and thus to what *necessarily* is."

∽

I infer from Bochenski's analysis that, just as certain practical propositions may be said to constitute the foundation for certain corresponding instructions, so certain (theoretical) propositions may be said to constitute the foundation for certain corresponding practical propositions.

Consider, for example, this instruction: "Calculate how much water is necessary to produce X amount of product A." The foundation of this instruction is evidently something like the practical proposition, "It is to the point to calculate how much water is necessary to produce X amount of product A before undertaking to produce it." This practical proposition is founded in turn, then, on some such (theoretical) proposition as, "The chemical reaction necessary to the production of X amount of product A requires exactly Y amount of water."

∽

If I understand Bochenski's reasoning, one could say, in his terms, that the (theoretical) propositions of metaphysics constitute the foundation for the practical propositions of ethics, even as the practical propositions of ethics, in turn, constitute the foundation for certain corresponding moral commands or instructions.

But, then, it would seem that one might also be able to say, by analogy, that the existential propositions explicating a certain understanding of existence constitute the foundation for a corresponding existential summons to a certain self-understanding. Put in other, more specifically Christian, theological terms, the constative or indicative statements comprising the indirect witness of Christian teaching constitute the foundation for the corresponding prescriptive or imperative statements that comprise the direct witness of Christian proclamation.

Since the understanding of human existence that the constative or indicative witness of Christian teaching explicates comprises *credenda* as well as *agenda*—the first constituting the foundation for the second—there is a sense in which Christian teaching is *doubly* foundational, constituting, in its one aspect as explication of *credenda*, the foundation for its other aspect as explication of *agenda*, and then indirectly constituting the foundation for the prescriptive or imperative summons to self-understanding issued by Christian proclamation.

11

What, Exactly, Are "Presuppositions"?

First of all, and most fundamentally, "presuppositions" are what has to be the case in order for any assertion of a certain logical kind to make sense, and thus to be either true or false. A presupposition expresses the strictly necessary conditions of the possibility of whatever that kind of an assertion asserts. I take it that it is in this strict and proper sense of "presuppositions" that Anders Nygren speaks, in his *Meaning and Method*, of the distinctive task of philosophy as "analysis of presuppositions," or "presuppositional analysis."[10]

But in a broader and improper sense, "presuppositions" are simply the assumptions made in making a particular assertion. Such assumptions, understandably, are also often called "presuppositions," because they are, in fact, necessary to the assertion's having the sense it has, and thus to being either true or false. On the other hand, whether or not one makes certain assumptions is optional in a way in which presupposing presuppositions, in the strict and proper sense, is not.

One may or may not take certain things for granted and, in that sense, make certain assumptions, in order to assert what one asserts. If one does make them, then they are, in the second broad and improper sense, presuppositions of one's assertion in that their truth is a necessary condition of the possible truth of the assertion one makes in assuming them. By contrast, presupposing presuppositions in the first, strict and proper, sense, is not open to choice, because "presuppositions," strictly and properly so-called, are what *must be* presupposed, willy nilly, implicitly if not explicitly, unconsciously if not consciously, if one is to say a certain kind of thing at all.

If this answer to the question is essentially sound, it would appear that "presuppositions" in the first, strict and proper, sense are precisely what philosophy is concerned with in its one purely formal phase as logical analysis, including a purely formal, or "austerely," transcendental metaphysics and transcendental ethics. On the other hand, what philosophy—in its other existential phase—has the task of critically validating, along with such assertions as may be made, are "presuppositions" only in the second, broader and improper, sense of assumptions. More exactly, philosophy has the task of critically validating any assumptions involved in making or implying properly existential and existential-historical assertions.

Thus, for example, whether or not I assume the truth of a certain kind of theism is optional, even if assuming its truth is necessary to making or implying the assertion

---

10. Nygren, *Meaning and Method*.

that Jesus is the Christ—i.e., the Messiah, or the anointed one, of God. But there is nothing optional about my presupposing, say, that something exists, or that what exists is either a contingently existing part of reality as a whole, or else the necessarily existing whole of reality itself (i.e., the strictly ultimate reality of which this or any other kind of theism is a certain interpretation).

R. G. Collingwood argues:

> 'Why do we believe that there are laws of nature?' 'Why do we believe that if conclusions follow from true premises they are themselves true?' To these questions people sometimes thoughtlessly reply, 'They are mere assumptions.' It is a thoughtless answer because it is made without reflecting on the meaning of the word 'assumption.' An assumption is an optional thing; if I assume $x = 12$, that implies that I might have assumed $x = 13$. But if we try, we shall find that we cannot assume that there are not laws of nature or that untrue conclusions follow from true premises.... The only right answer to questions of this kind is: 'Because we know that it is so.' And if we are asked 'How do you know?' we must reply: 'That is an illegitimate question, because it implies that we ought to have reasons for these pieces of knowledge, which we haven't, and, in the nature of the case, do not need.' If then we are told that this reduces them to mere matters of faith, we shall reply, 'Not at all: faith they are, but not mere faith, because the faith which they express is a rational faith in the sense that it is universal in everyone—even in you, who pretend to doubt it—and necessary to all thought, even the thought by which you pretend to criticize it.... Whatever may be said about the *details* of the world, there is always something that may be said about the world *as a whole*, namely, that it *is* a whole: a whole within which all distinctions fall, outside which there is nothing, and which, taken as a whole, is the cause of itself and of everything in it. The details of the world are the proper theme of scientific thought; but its characteristics as a whole, its unity and the implications of that unity, are not matters of scientific inquiry. They are, rather, a foundation on which all scientific inquiry rests. If it was possible to deny them—which it is not—scientific inquiry would instantly cease.... We thus possess certain pieces of knowledge about the world which we did not acquire, and cannot criticize, by scientific methods. The knowledge in question is our knowledge of the world, not in its details, but as a whole. And not only is it not acquired by scientific thought, but it is the very foundation of such thought; for only insofar as we know, for instance, that there are laws of nature, can we reasonably devise methods for discovering them.... The finite is nothing except as part of the whole.... Unless there is a whole, a universe, an infinite, there is no science; for there is no certainty beyond the certainty of mere observation and of bare particular fact; whereas science is universal or nothing, and is bankrupt unless it can discover general laws. But this discovery, as every student of logic knows, rests on presuppositions concerning the nature of the universe as a whole—laws

of thought that are at the same time laws of the real world, not scientifically discovered but embraced by an act of faith, of necessary and rational faith.[11]

Consider, also, the argument of E. M. Adams:

> [W]e need to distinguish between philosophical assumptions and presuppositions. For our purposes, we may regard an assumption as a belief taken for granted and built on as a premise or ground in one's thinking about something else; whereas a presupposition is a necessary condition for the truth or meaningfulness of some sentence. A philosophical assumption on which a scientific or normative theory is built will be presupposed by that theory. But not all philosophical presuppositions make their entry via assumption. Those that do not are the basic ones that provide the ultimate touchstone for philosophy. If a philosophical theory is assumed or taken for granted and thereby shapes the development of a given area of thought, the rejection of that theory in favor of another, whether brought about by philosophical inquiry or otherwise, would work a radical change in the cultural area concerned. On the other hand, the philosophical presuppositions of our primary ways of experiencing, thinking, and talking, those that do not enter the fabric of experience and thought via assumption, cannot be rejected by virtue of inconsistency with philosophical theory. Whenever such inconsistencies arise, so much the worse for the philosophical theory. This is why philosophy must be primarily responsible to the philosophical presuppositions of ordinary discourse rather than those of the specialized disciplines. The latter are more likely to have been influenced by philosophical assumptions pervasive in the culture. Although philosophy does not contradict specific statements in science or judgments in normative thought, it may overturn them by contradicting philosophical assumptions on which they are based.[12]

∽

The distinction is crucial between what a religion *necessarily presupposes* and what it *simply assumes* in asserting its constitutive assertion(s) (as distinct from whatever else it may assume in asserting or clearly implying any other nonconstitutive assertion[s]).

This distinction is crucial because it is, in effect, the distinction between *the one end* a religion is intended to serve and *the many* (skillful or more or less useful) *means* it happens to use in serving its one end.

---

11. Collingwood, *Faith and Reason*, 138–39, 144.
12. Adams, "Philosophical Grounds," 11–12.

To think, say, or do anything is necessarily *to presuppose* certain things, implicitly if not explicitly. But what one happens *to assume* in order to explicate, formulate, or specify the things one necessarily presupposes always remains open to rational criticism in a way that one's presuppositions do not. One's presuppositions, strictly speaking, necessarily belong to whatever one believes, asserts, or does, along with whatever it, in turn, necessarily implies. But what one happens to assume belongs, not to what one believes, asserts, or does, but only to its explication, formulation, or specification, along with whatever consequences follow therefrom.

Presuppositions, in short, are logically of a piece with *assertions/actions* and their *implications*, whereas *assumptions* belong logically with *formulations/specifications* together with their *consequences*.

12

On Intrinsic and Constitutive Value

If, according to an "objective relativist" theory of value, no being is valuable simply in itself, but has such value as it has, positive or negative, in relation to the structure of other beings, and their needs and interests, doesn't this do away with the distinction between intrinsic and constitutive value? Doesn't it imply that the only value is constitutive value, because there is no intrinsic value? My answer is, "No, it doesn't, because an 'objective relativist' theory of value allows for the distinction between intrinsic and constitutive value in the only sense in which this distinction needs to be upheld." I defend this answer as follows.

Granted that "value" in the most general sense means either the good-for-ness or the bad-for-ness of one being for some other—in this being a term that functions very much like "being," which in its most general sense means being the object for some subject—there remains a difference between beings that can only be good or bad for other beings and beings for which other beings can be good or bad. Clearly, beings for which other beings can be valuable are themselves centers of value, or primary determinants of meaning, in a way in which beings that can only be valuable for other beings are not. But to be, in this sense, a center of value for others is to be intrinsically valuable relative to those others, just as they are constitutively valuable relative to that same center of value. And this is so even though in other relationships this same center of value may itself be constitutively valuable relative to some other center(s), just as the beings that are of constitutive value for it may in other relationships be intrinsically valuable because they too are in turn centers of value for others.

In sum: the distinction between intrinsic and constitutive value is as well-founded and indispensable ontologically as the distinction between fully real, internal relations, on the one hand, and merely logical, external relations, on the other—or, alternatively, between subjects ($\equiv$ concretes) and objects ($\equiv$ abstracts). That which is not only object for subjects, but also, in some relation, subject for objects—or, in other words, is not only logically, externally related to others, but also really, internally related to others—is intrinsically, not merely constitutively, valuable in that particular relation.

Of course, a possible alternative to this would be to state an "objective relativist" theory of value more carefully to begin with. Instead of saying, simply, "'value' properly means either the good-for-ness or the bad-for-ness of one being for some other," one could say, "'value' properly means *either* the subject of the real internal relations constitutive of being as such, which subject is therefore intrinsically as well as constitutively valuable, *or else* the object of such relations, which is only constitutively valuable in these relations." Just as to be is to be related to others—if not as the subject of such relations, then at least as the object thereof—so to be of value is also a matter of being related to others—either by being the subject as well as the object of such relations, in the case of intrinsic value, or by being the object of relations only, in the case of constitutive value.

It follows that God, properly conceived as the "all-worshipful" or "unsurpassable," and therefore the universal individual, or the individual universal, is at once both: the intrinsic value for which none greater can be conceived, and the greatest conceivable constitutive value. As the subject for which all things are objects, God is both the greatest conceivable intrinsic value and the greatest conceivable constitutive value in one of the two respects in which one being can be of constitutive value for another. As the subject for which all things are objects, God is the greatest constitutive value conceivable with respect to constituting any object as both real and abidingly significant. As the object for all subjects, on the other hand, God is the greatest constitutive value conceivable with respect to constituting any subject really possible both in principle and in fact. Except for the strictly metaphysical conditions of the possibility of all things, all of which are but aspects of God's own essence or "deity" (and hence the object for all subjects), there neither would nor could be anything whatsoever. Moreover, except for the *de facto* cosmic order that it belongs only to God to impose, no other thing could ever be possible in fact as well as in principle.

For these reasons, or in these senses, God is the constitutive good than which none greater can be conceived, the one being who is unsurpassably good for all beings in both of the respects in which one being may be constitutively good for another. On the other hand, insofar as God is the being for which all other beings are valuable, either positively or negatively, God is also the greatest conceivable intrinsic good; for nothing could conceivably be of greater intrinsic value than the One for which not only all positive values, but even all negative values, are precisely constitutive values.

∾

Anything actual has at least some intrinsic value, and any difference of value between one kind of actuality and another is only a finite difference, or difference of degree, between different emergent levels or kinds of value corresponding to different emergent levels or kinds of concreteness.

As for the real uniqueness of human existence, human concreteness and value, although only finitely different, or different in degree, from those of all other levels or kinds of actual things, are nevertheless emergent properties of a distinctive level or kind that, as such, are irreducible to those of any lower level or kind.

Thus, to hold that every creature on earth has some intrinsic value and, to this extent, deserves to be respected accordingly is in no way to hold that all creatures have the same or equal value, or that there are not relevant and important differences in value between one creature and another.

∾

"Significance," like "value," calls for analysis in objective relativist terms, because it makes no sense to talk about x as being significant by itself, in entire abstraction from persons or things intrinsically valuable for whom or for which x is significant because x is constitutively valuable, because it goes toward constituting the intrinsic value of those persons or things. At the same time, the relativity essential to the meaning of the concept of "significance" cannot be merely *de facto* or subjective without making at least some prominent uses of the concept unintelligible. There's nothing odd or contradictory, for example, in a theological teacher's replying to a student's complaint at the end of term, "You don't find Rudolf Bultmann's theology significant? Well, you sure ought to find it significant!"

My thought, then, is that "significance" implies the same kind of *de jure* or *objective* relativity as "value" implies, when it is analyzed as H. Richard Niebuhr, say, analyzes it. Indeed, the two terms seem to be verbally different ways of saying essentially the same thing, if not also expressing the same concept.

As for the implications of such an analysis, events of the past are of significance for us in general because of our present interests and preoccupations. Insofar as we are interested and preoccupied in ways involving cognition, we may conclude that past events are significant for us because, or insofar as, they express or imply answers to questions arising from what presently interests and preoccupies us.

At the core of all our interests and preoccupations, arguably, is one having to do with the meaning of ultimate reality, or the ultimate setting of our lives, for us. Because this core interest or preoccupation evidently does involve cognition in a broad sense of the word, it gives rise to a question that some past event could conceivably serve to answer more or less explicitly, thereby becoming more or less significant for us in a correspondingly core or central way. Such an event, then, could even be said to be of *decisive* significance for us—*de jure* or objectively as well as *de facto* or subjectively—provided only that we so experienced it that it became the explicit authorizing source of the same answer to our core question that ultimate reality itself implicitly authorizes.

13

On Science and the Sciences

Science is concerned with structure as distinct from quality and value. One reason for this is that structure is intersubjectively observable in a sense or to a degree that quality and value are not. Another reason is that structure is precisely or mathematically expressible (even if only with certain qualifications). But, as Bertrand Russell, for one, rightly held, structures and relations logically could not exist without qualities, because structures presuppose entities distinguished in some way other than merely by their empirically observable relations, and relations of relations—i.e., by their empirically observable structures.

Science is abstract, not in that it ignores details as distinct from general properties, but in that it ignores quality and value—properties that are and must be at least as general as structure. Science uses (sensory) qualities (and values) merely as indices of abstract structures.

But it is not only science that abstracts; our sense perceptions themselves are enormous simplifications of the perceived world. Although there are billions upon billions of individuals (cells, molecules, atoms, particles), direct perception gives us only gross outlines of quasi-individual groups of these individuals. This, too, is an extreme form of abstraction, although one performed for us, rather than by us, as conscious beings—partly by our bodies, and partly by mental functions that elude conscious in(tro)spection.

Science and perception, then, are both abstract, even if in different ways. It is one thing to leave details out of account as simply special cases of some general property (as ordinary perception does); it is something else again to omit one or more general properties themselves (as science does). Although science does not simply abstract from, or omit, certain of the positive features of the observed world, but, on the contrary, enormously adds to them—e.g., by adding the subworld of microorganisms to the macroorganisms perceived as part of the rich world of daily experience (*Lebenswelt*), or by adding galaxies and island universes to the stars visible in the night sky—it nevertheless does abstract in the other way, by setting aside the entire class of what have often been called secondary and tertiary qualities, focusing entirely upon so-called primary qualities, which are really structures (of qualities), rather than qualities in the distinctive sense. Ordinary perception, on the other hand, yields quality (and value) as well as structure, although neither distinctly or with sharpness of detail.

So conscious sense experience omits and abstracts as genuinely as science does, although in a different way. Only a combination of the two, as in their different ways revelatory of the natures of things, can give us such awareness of concrete reality as we are capable of having.

Even so, most of the universe is and must ever remain qualitatively hidden and mysterious to us. Structures can be traced from experience to bodily process, and thence to extra-bodily or environmental process, far out into the universe. But qualities can reach us only by routes that at succeeding stages lose most of the individual distinctiveness of preceding ones. Consequently, science has to focus on group structures rather than individual qualities. We can know the spatiotemporal patterns of what goes on in real individuals. But how can we ever know their feeling qualities (or, as I would have to add, whether they even have such feeling qualities, as distinct from qualities that, in perceivers more or less like ourselves, become qualities constitutive of feeling)?

What we cannot know, however, we do not need to know in order to lead our lives and to play the humble role that becomes us in the creative advance that is reality itself. Moreover, we know what, in principle, it is that we're missing, and why, no matter how our knowledge may increase, we're always bound to miss it.

In sum: perception is essentially concrete in that it exhibits all the general properties of reality; but it is in detail abstract by failing to exhibit distinctly most of the individual instances of these properties. Science, on the other hand, is essentially abstract in that it systematically sets aside some properties because they are not intersubjectively measurable, but in detail it is concrete by its power to detect individual cases of the properties it studies that are otherwise hidden. Science may be used to remedy the defects of perception by expanding the inventory of individuals to be studied far beyond the disclosures of direct perception. Perception (or what perception and memory have in common) may be used to remedy the defects of science by expanding the list of cosmically general properties to include those that science systematically sets aside. The crucial question is how this is to be done: whether, as Hartshorne, for one, holds, by including generalized versions of the basic dimensions of experience as such, e.g., qualities of feeling and personal and impersonal memory (i.e., perception), or whether, as I and others hold, solely and simply by including the analyzed object-subject structure of concreteness, as disclosed by experience in its nonsensuous aspect, as distinct from its aspect as sense experience or perception.

∽

Is there not an important distinction to be made between being a form of critical reflection and proper theory, on the one hand, and being a science proper (even in a broad sense of "science"), on the other?

Nygren argues persuasively that "[w]e can only speak of science where there is a possibility of objective argumentation." In the sciences, he insists, "it is not enough . . . simply to postulate and assert. We demand reasons for the assertion."[13] But fully granting that the possibility of some mode of reasoning or objective argumentation is indeed a *necessary* condition of the possibility of speaking of science, one may well question whether it is also a *sufficient* condition—as it seems to me that Nygren either supposes or else fails to make clear that he doesn't suppose. In fact, I should want to hold that it is *not* a sufficient condition of the possibility of speaking of science, but only of speaking of critical reflection and proper theory, as distinct from science. Thus theology, for example, is arguably a special case of critical reflection and proper theory, although it is not properly a science. Why not? Because being oriented proximately as well as remotely by an *existential* question, rather than by any *intellectual* question, it is properly a form of wisdom (*sapientia*) as distinct from a form of science (*scientia*).

In other words, for a form of critical reflection and proper theory also to be a science, its proximately orienting question has to be an abstract intellectual question about *the structure of its object in itself* instead of a concrete existential question about *the meaning of its object for us*.

∽

The special sciences and the completely general science of metaphysics, properly so-called, have in common a concern for the structure of reality in itself in abstraction from the meaning of reality for us. The main difference between all of the special sciences, on the one hand, and metaphysics, on the other, is that the theories about structure developed by the first are finally empirical, and so subject to empirical falsification, whereas the theories about structure developed by the second are existential, and so incapable of being empirically falsified.

---

13. Nygren, *Meaning and Method*, 219.

On Science and the Sciences

∽

Although I have often thought and said that the special sciences and metaphysics "have in common a concern for the structure of reality in itself in abstraction from the meaning of reality for us," I have only seldom, if ever, thought (much less said) that the abstraction common to the special sciences and metaphysics is, in reality, twofold: not only of reality in its structure in itself from its meaning for us, but also of the structure of reality in itself from *its own content*—i.e., quality or value.

Of course, I have long thought *and* said that the special sciences and metaphysics are alike precisely in that they both abstract from the content (the quality or value) of things in order to concentrate on their structure. And I have usually explained their differences as due to the fact that, whereas the theories about structure developed by the special sciences are properly empirical, and so subject to empirical falsification, the theories developed by metaphysics are properly existential and transcendental, and so incapable of being empirically falsified. But what I have not said or thought clearly enough is that this abstraction is no less essential to the special sciences and metaphysics than their both abstracting—again, in their different ways—from the meaning of reality for us: the special sciences, by abstracting from the meaning of the contingent details of reality for us, and metaphysics, by abstracting from the meaning of its necessary outline for us.

I am still not altogether clear about just what to make of the two abstractions—or the two aspects of the abstraction—that the special sciences and metaphysics have in common. At first glance, it might appear, for instance, that the symbolic language of religion is by way of disclosing the content (the quality or value) of strictly ultimate reality from which metaphysics—or, at any rate, an austerely transcendental metaphysics—abstracts. But my guess is that appearance and reality in this matter are rather different.

What the symbolic language of religion may really symbolize, insofar as it has any cognitive function, is not the content (the quality or value) of strictly ultimate reality, but rather its structure—not, however, in itself, but in its meaning for us. So far as religion is concerned, what strictly ultimate reality is in itself, in its own quality and value, as distinct from its structure, is simply mystery, *the all-inclusive, unfathomable* mystery, embracing the essential mysteriousness of each and every concrete thing, which concretely as such ever remains a surd to reason. Religion's concern in appealing to some special or decisive revelation of ultimate reality is in no way to dispel *this* mystery, but only to lift the veil that keeps us from understanding its meaning for us, given what it is in itself, in its essential logical/ontological structure. *That* it is unfathomable mystery does indeed belong to its essential structure, and thus also to the meaning of its structure for us. But *what* that mystery is remains, precisely, unfathomable.

NOTEBOOKS

∾

A special science proceeds inductively, in that it seeks general ideas that will fit the empirical facts—and that would be proved false if the empirical facts were otherwise than they are. But in order to test its candidate ideas—also known as "working hypotheses"—a special science also proceeds deductively by tracing the consequences of its ideas, so as to estimate their truth or falsity by comparing their consequences as well with the relevant *empirical* evidence.

The general science of metaphysics, by contrast, proceeds analytically or transcendentally, in that it seeks ideas so general that they will fit special scientific ideas that do not fit the empirical facts as well as any that do. But in order to test its candidate ideas—also known as "working hypotheses"—metaphysics also proceeds deductively, by so tracing the consequences of its ideas as to estimate their truth or falsity by comparing their consequences as well with the relevant *existential* evidence.

∾

I long proceeded as though there are only two main kinds of science, strictly and properly so-called. But I gradually learned, thanks largely to critically appropriating the following sources, that there are in fact at least three.

 1. Charles Hartshorne's threefold division of "knowledge" into "[1] mathematics, dealing with various '*possible* worlds,' or better, various *possible* logical structures; [2] natural and social science, dealing with the one *actual* world; [and 3] metaphysics, dealing with what is common and *necessary* to all possible states of affairs and all possible truth, including adjudication of the question of whether 'there is no world at all' represents a conceivable truth or is mere nonsense or contradiction."[14]

 2. George L. Goodwin's threefold distinction of "truths" into (1) "contingent truths" that are "true in some possible worlds and *false in other possible worlds*"; (2) "conditionally necessary truths" that are "necessarily true in some possible worlds and *false in no possible worlds*" and are therefore also "nonexistential necessary truths"; and (3) "unconditionally necessary truths" whose criterion is not only "*falsity in no possible world,*" but also "*truth in all possible worlds*" and which are therefore "existential" as well as "necessary."[15]

 3. Anders Nygren's threefold distinction of forms of "scientific," or "objective," argumentation into (1) "axiomatic," where the method is "deduction"; (2) "empirical," where the method involves "induction" as well as "deduction"; and (3) "philosophical," where the method, again, is "deduction," albeit in the different sense of "analysis," as in "presuppositional analysis," or "transcendental deduction"—i.e., deduction *from x* of

---

14. Hartshorne, *Divine Relativity*, xiii.
15. Goodwin, *Ontological Argument of Charles Hartshorne*, 14, 17–18, 19–20.

its necessary presuppositions or conditions of possibility, as distinct from deduction *of x* from certain axioms that necessarily imply it.[16]

I now hold, then, that the three main kinds of science are as follows:

1. the kind represented by *the special empirical sciences*, human (or social) as well as natural;
2. the kind represented by *the axiomatic sciences* of mathematics; and
3. the kind uniquely represented by *the completely general science of metaphysics*— more exactly, *transcendental* metaphysics in the broad sense inclusive of existentialist analysis, as well as of transcendental metaphysics *sensu stricto*.

Each of these three kinds of science corresponds to one of the three main modes of logical modality, each of which in turn corresponds to a main mode of ontological time or process:

1. the kind represented by the special empirical sciences corresponding to the mode of *the actual* (including the contingently existent);
2. the kind represented by the axiomatic sciences corresponding to the mode of *the possible*; and
3. the kind represented by metaphysics corresponding to the mode of *the necessary*.

But all kinds of science are alike in that the vital question by which any science, properly so-called, is proximately oriented is some *intellectual* question, rather than any existential question; i.e., they alike abstract altogether from any concern with meaning for us to attend solely to *structure in itself*—whether that of actuality, possibility, or necessity.

∞

Another way of distinguishing the three main kinds, or types, of science, together with the presuppositions and implications of that way, is the following:

1. *The special sciences* are inductive studies of factual states of affairs involving criticism of statements that are partially restrictive and existential.
2. *Mathematics* is a deductive study of conceivable factual states of affairs involving criticism of statements that are completely nonrestrictive but also nonexistential.
3. *Metaphysics* is an analytic study of the most abstract principles of all conceivable factual states of affairs involving criticism of statements that are completely nonrestrictive but also existential.

Presuppositions have implications:

---

16. Nygren, *Meaning and Method*, 65–125.

1. Statements are to be distinguished as either (a) partially restrictive, (b) completely restrictive, or (c) completely nonrestrictive.

2. A *completely restrictive statement* (e.g., "Nothing exists") denies that any ontic possibility whatsoever is actualized.

3. A *partially restrictive statement*, if affirmative (e.g., "There is a deer in the garden"), implicitly denies that some ontic possibility is actualized (e.g., "Everything in the garden is other than a deer"), whereas a partially restrictive statement, if negative (e.g., "There is no deer in the garden"), implicitly affirms that some ontic possibility is actualized (e.g., "Everything in the garden is other than a deer").

4. A *completely nonrestrictive statement* (e.g., "Something exists") does not deny that any ontic possibility whatsoever is actualized.

5. Completely nonrestrictive statements are necessarily true: the nonexistential ones of mathematics are true negatively or hypothetically, the existential ones of metaphysics, positively or categorically. Completely restrictive statements, for the same reasons, are necessarily false. On the other hand, partially restrictive statements are true or false only contingently.

6. Statements are also to be distinguished as either (a) existential or (b) nonexistential, according to whether they do or do not assert existence in the primary sense of actual or concrete existence. (Thus the partially restrictive statements criticized by the special sciences are existential in this primary sense, as are the completely nonrestrictive statements criticized by metaphysics, while the completely nonrestrictive statements criticized by mathematics are nonexistential in that same primary sense of "existential.")

7. Possibilities are to be distinguished as either (merely) *ontological* or (also) *ontic*—this distinction roughly corresponding to the familiar distinction between (merely) "logical" and (also) "real" possibilities. (The first distinction is to be preferred because, on the view—to my mind, the correct view—that logical (*de dictu*) and real (*de re*) modality are convertible or coextensive, any possibility whatsoever is both logical and real.) An ontological possibility is any possibility that, logically, is clearly and coherently conceivable and, ontologically, is not incompatible with the strictly necessary conditions of the possibility of concrete reality as such, whereas an ontic possibility is, in addition, more or less probable given the contingent conditions of reality as of a given time and place.

∽

I agree with Nygren that all three of the basic scientific methods and modes of objective argumentation stand for something very simple and easy to understand. But my account differs from his in certain respects that may be clarified as follows.

Behind what I understand by *axiomatic argumentation* is the simple idea that, from certain axioms, certain conclusions can be inferred by logical necessity and may then be tested by being traced back to their axioms. Thus, whether or not a statement is axiomatically legitimated (i.e., is *validated* or *invalidated*, in the strict sense of the terms) depends on its place in some axiomatic system, on its coherence with other statements in the system.

Behind *empirical argumentation*, as I understand it, is the simple idea that empirical statements need to be tested by how they relate to observations made in experience, and that, in the case of the more general of them, this requires the two-step procedure of (1) deducing certain conclusions from them, and then (2) comparing these conclusions with experiential observations. Thus, whether or not a statement is empirically legitimated (i.e., is *verified* or *falsified*) depends on whether or not it corresponds with the empirical facts it is intended to express as confirmed by observations.

Similarly, the simple idea behind what I understand by *analytical (including metaphysical) argumentation* is that any statement made in the context of some form of experience has and implies certain necessary and more or less fundamental presuppositions, but for which the statement could not be meaningful and so possibly true. Beginning with such a statement, then, presuppositional analysis, or, as Nygren also calls it, "transcendental deduction," explicates the basic presuppositions that it necessarily implies. Thus, whether or not a statement is analytically legitimated (i.e., is *justified* or *unjustified*) depends on its explication of a proposition shown to be necessarily implied by analysis of presuppositions.

ɑ⃗

There is a striking convergence between Hartshorne's analysis of "reason" in his essay "Two Levels of Faith and Reason" and Nygren's analysis of the three types of "objective" or "scientific" argumentation" in his book *Meaning and Method*.[17]

True, Hartshorne does not come right out and say that the type of argumentation proper to philosophy, or philosophy *qua* metaphysics, is "transcendental deduction," or "analysis of presuppositions." But there is nothing he says that would in any way keep him from saying this, and among the different things he does say by way of characterizing metaphysics are statements such as this: "[T]he metaphysician studies the most utterly basic features of experience and thought which are presupposed by any world whatever and by any truth whatever."[18] Substitute "the philosopher" for "the metaphysician" in Hartshorne's statement, and one can find any number of exactly parallel formulations in Nygren's discussion.

Moreover, I do not doubt in the least that Hartshorne's attempt to justify metaphysics as "an expression of reason" and "a legitimate rational enterprise" would have

17. Hartshorne, *Reality as Social Process*, 163–76; Nygren, *Meaning and Method*, 66–125.
18. Hartshorne, *Reality as Social Process*, 174.

been less vague and more convincing had he managed to attain Nygren's level of clarity in distinguishing the three types of "scientific argumentation," including the philosophical type, along with the types represented respectively by the special sciences and by mathematics.

On the other hand, there is a feature of Hartshorne's discussion that goes a long way toward making up a notable lack in Nygren's—namely, the clarity and consistency with which he explains that and how philosophy and metaphysics are, in their way, not as "empirical," but as "experiential" as the special sciences. Thus he says that metaphysics is "an attempt to describe the most general aspects of experience, to abstract from all that is special in our awareness, and to report as clearly and accurately as possible upon the residuum. . . . The true role of deduction in metaphysics is . . . to bring out the meaning of tentative descriptions of the metaphysically ultimate in experience so that we shall be better able to judge if they do genuinely describe this ultimate. . . . [W]e may, if we are lucky, be able to see that one of them is evidently true to that residuum of experience, which is left when all details variable in imagination have been set aside."[19]

To be sure, Hartshorne makes no such explicit distinction as I make, between the "empirical" and the "existential" aspects of our experience. But, again, nothing that he says precludes making this distinction, and I am quite clear that his discussion could only have been more adequate if he had somehow managed to make it, if only, as Whitehead does, by arguing that "Our more direct experience groups itself into two large divisions, each capable of further analysis."[20]

∽

I have typically argued that critical reflection, and therefore science, also, includes critical interpretation as well as critical validation. But what, exactly, does critical interpretation include?

Critical interpretation includes both what is ordinarily meant by historical and hermeneutical reflection, on the one hand, and what on a strictly analytical view of philosophy is properly meant by philosophical reflection, on the other. Both forms of reflection are concerned with understanding the individual expressions of meaning that make up the self-understanding and life-praxis mediated by all forms of culture, including religion. The main difference between them is that historical and hermeneutical reflection is concerned with understanding the meaning of the individual expressions as such, whereas philosophical reflection, being focused on understanding *logical kinds* of meaning, concerns itself with understanding the individual expressions mainly, if not exclusively, as instances of such logical kinds. In the case of each form of reflection, interpretation is rightly said to be "critical" because it allows for a

---

19. Hartshorne, *Reality as Social Process*, 175.
20. Whitehead, *Modes of Thought*, 98.

certain kind of criticism: the kind I speak of as "*immanent* criticism" (which, incidentally, is all *I* mean by "*die Sachkritik*"), as distinct from the *transcendent* criticism that properly belongs to, or is identical with, critical validation. In the case of historical and hermeneutical reflection, such immanent criticism consists in criticizing individual expressions of meaning by reference to the meaning they more or less adequately express. In the case of philosophical reflection, by contrast, individual expressions of meaning are immanently criticized by reference to the *logical kind(s)* of meaning of which they are more or less adequate expressions.

Another way of explaining this same difference is to distinguish with Jürgen Habermas between "the surface level of meaning" and "the very rules that inform the production of utterances or that inform linguistic interaction"—and, correspondingly, between "the explication of meaning," which is directed to "the semantic content of the symbolic formation," and "rational reconstruction," which is directed to "the intuitive [or pretheoretical] knowledge [or foreknowledge] of competent subjects."[21]

∾

Assuming that there is a difference between the social sciences and the humanities, just what is the difference?

Even if one distinguishes, as Karl-Otto Apel does, between different types of social science, one of which includes what I mean here by "the humanities," one assumes that there is a difference between "the social sciences" and "the humanities" in the senses in which I am using the terms.[22] Broadly speaking, one may say that the social sciences study human life-praxis by bracketing all questions about the validity of the claims that such life-praxis necessarily makes or implies. In fact, one may say that the social sciences so thoroughly bracket or abstract from all questions about the validity of the claims made or implied by life-praxis that they do not seek even to understand the *what* of life-praxis, as distinct from its *that*, in the way in which one simply has to understand it if one is to pursue any questions about the validity of its claims.

By contrast, the humanities do seek to understand the *what* of life-praxis in the way in which one has to do if one is to pursue any questions about the validity of its claims to validity. In the case of some of the humanities (e.g., philology and history), the whole task of the field is limited to just such understanding, being concerned entirely with critical interpretation, as distinct from critical validation. In the case of other humanities (e.g., grammar, linguistics, or philosophy), the task of the field either is or includes critical validation as well as critical interpretation.

True, on an understanding of philosophy as strictly analytical, its concern with critical validation is limited to clarifying how such validation has to be done in all the different cases, as distinct from actually doing it in any particular case. This means

---

21. Holub, *Jürgen Habermas*, 11–12.
22. Apel, "Types of Social Science."

that a strictly analytical philosophy can be about equally well analyzed as being concerned, not with critical validation at all, but solely with critical interpretation, albeit at the level of the "deep grammar," or "deep structure," of the relevant "forms of life" and/or "language games." But on a more classical understanding, philosophy has an existential as well as a strictly analytical responsibility and therefore includes critical validation itself—not, to be sure, of all kinds of claims to validity (many of which it quite properly leaves to be validated by the several special sciences or arts), but only of the existential kind of statements that the special sciences or arts are not competent to validate.

The difference between the social sciences and the humanities, then, is that the second group are concerned with critical interpretation and, in the case of some of them, with critical validation of the claims to validity expressed or implied by human life-praxis simply as such.

∾

I recall John Dewey saying somewhere in *Experience and Nature* something to the effect that metaphysics supplies "the ground map of criticism," which is to say, I take it, the ground map of the critical reflection necessary to living better, if not also to living well, or even to living at all. I see no reason why Dewey's basic insight shouldn't be taken as applying, *mutatis mutandis*, not only to metaphysics as the unique *ontological* science, but also to the two other kinds of science properly so-called—i.e., the special *ontic*, empirical sciences, human (or social) as well as natural, and the *axiomatic* science of mathematics.

Common to all three kinds of science is that they are constituted as such, whether less or more critically, by some *intellectual* question rather than by any existential question; in other words, they abstract completely from any concern with meaning for us to attend entirely to *structure in itself*—whether the structure of *actuality*, in the case of the special, empirical sciences; the structure of *possibility*, in the case of mathematics; or the structure of *necessity*, in the case of metaphysics. But then, each plays the role of enabling or facilitating criticism in its own way: metaphysics, by explicating the structure of the necessary (including the strictly, unconditionally necessary); mathematics, by identifying the structure(s) of the possible; and the special, empirical sciences, by disclosing the structures of the actual (including the distinctive structure disclosed by the hermeneutical sciences commonly referred to as "meaning").

Structures of all three types determine the limits with which any life, and therefore any understanding and critically reflective life, must somehow come to terms. In this sense, all three kinds of science, in their different ways, supply "the ground map of criticism," in the sense of the critical reflection upon which any understanding life depends if it is not only to live and to live well, but also to live better.

On Science and the Sciences

A provocative statement about the distinctive character of modern science is Richard Rorty's:

> The books that change our moral and political convictions include sacred scriptures, philosophical treatises, intellectual and sociopolitical histories, epic poems, novels, political manifestoes, and writings of many other sorts. But scientific treatises have become increasingly irrelevant to this process of change. This is because, ever since Galileo, natural science has won its autonomy and its richly deserved prestige by telling us how things work, rather than, as Aristotle hoped to do, telling us about their intrinsic natures.
>
> Post-Galilean science does not tell us what is really real or really important. It has no metaphysical or moral implications. Instead it enables us to do things that we had not previously been able to do. When it became empirical and experimental, it lost both its metaphysical pretensions and the ability to set new ends for human beings to strive for. It gained the ability to provide new means. Most scientists are content with this trade-off. But every so often a scientist . . . tries to have it both ways, and to suggest that science can provide empirical evidence to show that some ends are preferable to others.
>
> Whereas physics-envy is a neurosis found among those whose disciplines are accused of being soft, philosophy-envy is found among those who pride themselves on the hardness of their disciplines. The latter think that their superior rigor qualifies them to take over the roles previously played by philosophers and other sorts of humanists—roles such as critic of culture, moral guide, guardian of rationality, and prophet of the new utopia.[23]

My main question is whether a somewhat different account of the reason for science having won its autonomy wouldn't be preferable. I would suggest that what characterized pre-Galilean science, and the main reason it had both the metaphysical and the moral implications that post-Galilean science does not have, is that it asked about the meaning of things for us—in Rorty's phrase, "what is really real or really important"—and only in this sense about their "intrinsic natures." This is why there is no hard and fast distinction in pre-Galilean science between "science" and "wisdom." Of course, this difference from Rorty's account in no way affects his main point, which, in my judgment, is well taken.

If metaphysics is, in its own way, a science—namely, as Heidegger says of "ontology," "*the* science," "the [one and only] *ontological* science," as distinct from any and all "ontic sciences"—it would seem in order to ask whether any more than a merely minimal

---

23. Rorty, "Philosophy-Envy," 21–22.

account of the objectivity of truth in the sciences wouldn't also have to be applicable to the objectivity of metaphysical truth. In other words, if metaphysics is properly a science, notwithstanding its differences from the "special," or "positive," sciences, shouldn't metaphysical propositions get their truth-job done in something like the same way in which the propositions of the other sciences do theirs?

According to one widely discussed account, scientific propositions that are non-metaphysical get their job of telling the truth done, and thus have the higher-level, "deeply normative," property of being true, because or insofar as they have the lower-level, merely descriptive, property of being causally responsive to reality. Assuming this account, then, one would need to ask whether metaphysical propositions, also, are thus causally responsive.

My answer is, unhesitatingly, "Yes, they are." If, as I argue, metaphysical propositions have their basis in the existential, as distinct from the empirical, aspect or dimension of our experience; and if a Whiteheadian-Hartshornean account of our experience is essentially sound, then metaphysical propositions must be, in fact, the paradigm case of propositions being causally responsive to reality. Why? Well, because the existential experience on which they are based is experience in the mode, in Whitehead's term, of "causal efficacy," as distinct from empirical experience in the mode of "presentational immediacy," which is the basis of the propositions of the special, or positive, sciences. To say, then, as Whitehead in effect does, that reality in this mode of experience is "causally efficacious" is evidently to imply that experience itself in this mode, together with any true propositions based on it, must be, in their ways, precisely causally responsive to reality. Metaphysical propositions get their truth-job done because or insofar as they respond, in their way, to the causal efficacy of ultimate reality: of the threefold ultimate reality of oneself, others, and the whole.

The same conclusion can be reached, obviously, by assuming another, at least verbally different account of the objectivity of truth. This is the account, which some take to have originated with C. S. Peirce, according to which the truth of a proposition of any type is its success in so engaging or interpreting its object by means of its symbols that whatever is real or of value in the object, given the purposes or interests of the interpreter, is carried over into her or his own belief and action. Clearly, for ultimate reality to be carried over into the belief and action of the interpreter, the interpreter, for her or his part, has to be causally responsive to ultimate reality; and the same must be true, in its way, of her or his propositions, given the type of purposes or interests underlying them.

14

"The Love of Wisdom"

Philosophy means, literally, "the love of wisdom." But what is "wisdom," or what is it to be wise?

To be wise, I submit, is to understand everything that can be understood by a purely "reflective method," and to understand everything else one understands in relation thereto, in relation to one's purely reflective understanding.[24]

But what, exactly, is "a purely 'reflective method'"? A purely reflective method is a method that presupposes as the datum for its analysis *any* human experience whatsoever, and thus requires no particular (or special) human experience(s).

☙

There was a time when I puzzled over how the "reflective method," in Lewis's sense, could ever be pursued except at the center of our experience, as distinct from its periphery, made up as it is of various special kinds of experience: religious, political, æsthetic, and so on. But then I happened to think of the classical anthropological distinction between "person" and "office," and it occurred to me that, just as there is the one central domain in which we all live simply as and because we are "persons," so there are also the many peripheral domains where at least some of us also always live as and because of our respective "office(s)." Depending on such variables as gender, race, and ethnicity, and the different stages of human life from birth to death, the roles we each play as human beings in society and culture are not one but many. In what we think, say, and do while playing our respective roles, we are guided by this, that, or the other human interest; ask this, that, or the other human question; or advert to this, that, or the other kind of human experience—in short, live in this, that, or the other particular context of meaning. But within any of these many particular contexts, even as within the one universal context in which we understand and express meaning simply as and because we are human beings, we may very well pursue the reflective method in something like Lewis's sense of the words. Insofar as we live in any particular context, we always already understand ourselves, others, and the whole in doing so and may therefore very well also understand ourselves therein reflectively and critically.

---

24. Lewis, *Mind and the World Order*.

Consequently, I have come to realize that the distinction I have learned to make between all possibilities *absolutely* and all possibilities *relatively* can be helpfully used in more than the one way in which I have used it so far: to distinguish between "transcendentals," as the (absolutely) necessary presuppositions of being as such, and "existentials" as the (relatively) necessary presuppositions of the being that thinks and speaks, and in this way understands. The distinction can also be used, namely, to distinguish between both transcendentals and existentials, on the one hand, and the respective necessary conditions of particular contexts of meaning—of what Whitehead calls the "directed activities of mankind," or Ludwig Wittgenstein, *Lebensformen/ Sprachspielen*—on the other.

∾

What, exactly, does the wisdom which philosophy loves include?

Well, it certainly includes a critically reflective understanding of authentic existence (and therefore a metaphysical understanding of self, others, and the whole that is theoretically true) and an ethical understanding of how one is to understand oneself and lead one's life that is practically true or right. But is this all that wisdom includes?

So I have sometimes supposed. And yet, a difficulty with that supposition is that it is not at all clear then why philosophy as "the love of wisdom" should be anything other or more than critical interpretation and validation of all the various answers to *the* existential question expressed or implied by human life-praxis and culture. Why philosophy should also be, in its other main phase, purely formal analysis of meaning, and of all the various kinds of meaning, is left unexplained. But what if the wisdom that is philosophy's object, or objective, includes a critically reflective understanding of *all* that we necessarily presuppose—not just in existing as human beings, but also in thinking, saying, and doing any of the many different kinds of things that we ordinarily think, say, and do in understanding ourselves and leading our lives in the various settings in which we actually live? Clearly, on *this* supposition, there would be no need to explain why the wisdom which philosophy loves necessarily includes analyzing meaning in all its various kinds.

∾

Does the wisdom which philosophy loves consist of authentic self-understanding itself, as I seem to have sometimes slipped into saying or implying? Or does it consist, rather, of a critically reflective understanding of what is, and is not, authentic self-understanding?

If philosophy is indeed a matter of critical reflection and proper theory, and thus understanding at the secondary rather than at the primary level of living understandingly, it would appear that the wisdom that is its objective would have to consist in the second, rather than the first—just as the objective of Christian theology as *sapientia eminens practica* is not Christian self-understanding itself, but rather a critically reflective understanding of what is and is not Christian self-understanding.

But if this is really so, it might be easier to understand why it is that the wisdom that is philosophy's objective includes, in addition to a critically reflective understanding of what is and is not authentic self-understanding, a critical analysis of meaning *überhaupt*, and so of any and all the logically different kinds thereof.

∾

Not so long ago, I asked myself what makes me a Christian, and as an exact parallel, what makes me a university teacher. My answers, expressed purely formally, were likewise exactly parallel. What makes me a Christian/a university teacher is a certain kind of self-understanding and life-praxis: that I understand myself, others, and the whole as I am called to do by the call to be a Christian/a university teacher; and that I then explicitly believe and actually do what is necessarily presupposed and implied by my self-understanding (as well as the call to be a Christian/a university teacher) and lead all of the rest of my life as a human being accordingly—in keeping with my self-understanding and the beliefs and actions that it necessarily presupposes and implies.

The more I reflected on these answers, the more I wondered whether they might not bear on answering my continuing question about the distinctive concern of philosophy. Couldn't it be, I asked myself, that the defining, unifying concern of philosophy, *qua* "love of wisdom," is precisely reflective understanding of self-understanding and life-praxis *überhaupt*?

Essential to an answer, I decided, is distinguishing between our self-understanding and life-praxis simply as human beings in the ultimate setting of our lives (which includes always being situated in some immediate setting[s]), and our self-understanding and life-praxis as participants in all the various undertakings that Whitehead refers to as "the directed activities of mankind," and Wittgenstein calls "*Lebensformen/Sprachspielen*." Given this distinction between two main kinds of life-settings, doing philosophy may be said to have a "center" as well as a "periphery." Although its peripheral (but, for all that, important) concern is all the different ways of understanding ourselves and leading our lives in the various domains within which they are set (some of which—notably, religion—have a direct, or explicit, connection with their ultimate setting, others of which are connected with that ultimate setting only indirectly or implicitly, their direct or explicit connection being with some domain or other of our lives' immediate setting only), philosophy's central concern is self-understanding and life-praxis in our ultimate setting simply as human beings. In either kind of setting (immediate as well as ultimate), philosophy, being concerned with wisdom, is concerned with self-understanding and life-praxis, in the sense of the normative understanding of ourselves and of leading our lives accordingly, or with our identity and action, peripherally as well as centrally, in our various possible "offices" and simply as "persons."

As for why philosophy inevitably turns to metaphysics and ethics, I concluded that it is because they are indispensable to pursuing its central concern with a normative understanding of our identity and action in the ultimate setting of our lives simply as human beings. On the other hand, I concluded that philosophy includes all of the peripheral philosophical disciplines that it is ordinarily understood to include (philosophy of religion, philosophy of science, philosophy of law, etc.), because it is also concerned with normative understanding of what it is to do any of the things that we typically do as human beings, as reflected in our "directed activities," or in "the forms of life"/"the language games" that typify our multiple engagements with reality, nondiscursive as well as discursive.

15

On Philosophy

Philosophy, understood classically, may be said to be comprehensive critical reflection oriented by *the* existential question, and therefore to centrally include both metaphysics and ethics. So understood, philosophy has the task of disclosing, at the secondary level of critical reflection and proper theory, the same truth about human existence that is always already disclosed at least implicitly on the primary level of self-understanding and life-praxis.

∾

Philosophy, in general, is a more or less critically reflective self-understanding that is comprehensive in scope and secular rather than specifically religious in constitution. As such, it centrally includes, although it is not exhausted by, both a metaphysics and an ethics—i.e., both a theory of ultimate reality in its structure in itself and a theory, accordingly, of how we therefore ought to act and what we ought to do given the structure of ultimate reality and its meaning for us, and that at both levels transcendental as well as categorial.

On Philosophy

∽

Philosophy is to be understood as the comprehensive critical reflection constituted by asking about human existence simply as such. Thus it belongs to philosophy that it should include, in one main phase, an analysis of meaning and thus of the logically different *kinds* of meaning involved in understanding ourselves and leading our lives through all the forms of culture, religious as well as secular, secondary as well as primary.

But philosophy is more than such analysis of meaning, and in its other main phase, it has the task of critically validating all the different answers to *the* existential question, implicit as well as explicit, so as to formulate its own constructive answer to this question—indirectly, at the level of critical reflection and proper theory and solely on the basis of common human experience and reason. If the claim of any such answer to be true is valid, it can only be because what it represents as the truth about human existence is the same truth that philosophy, also, is responsible for telling.

∽

Philosophy is a form of critical reflection *oriented* proximately as well as remotely by *the* existential question, which is to say, the most vital of our human questions, which we all ask about the meaning of our lives in their ultimate setting as all parts together with others of the encompassing whole. In asking this existential question, we ask, at one and the same time, about two things: about the meaning of ultimate reality for us, and about our authentic self-understanding (or the true understanding of human existence).

But philosophy is *constituted*, as distinct from being oriented, not by *the* existential question, any more than by any of our other *vital* questions, but by certain *theoretical* questions. Philosophy is constituted, specifically, by the two theoretical questions about the meaning of our various self-understandings and life-praxes and about the soundness of the claims to validity that they express or imply.

Philosophy may be succinctly defined, therefore, as critically reflective self-understanding—or, in more traditional terms, as the love of wisdom, in the sense of the search for, or critical reflection directed toward determining, what is and is not a true and authentic self-understanding.

As such, philosophy necessarily has two phases or tasks that are as distinct as they are inseparable. It has, for one, a purely analytic phase or task, which consists of explicating the necessary conditions of the possibility—or, if you will, the "principles" or the "criteria"—not only of the various domains of human life-praxis and culture, but also of human existence itself, and thus of self-understanding and life-praxis, as such, including the strictly necessary conditions of the possibility of anything whatsoever. Thus, in this one purely analytic phase or task, philosophy comprises not only all of the various peripheral philosophical disciplines—i.e., the various philosophies of law, science, religion, art, and so on—but also the central philosophical disciplines of metaphysics and ethics.

But philosophy also has another, existential, phase or task, which consists of critically validating—on the basis of its purely formal analysis of meaning and of all the different kinds of meaning—all answers to *the* existential question, religious and theological as well as philosophical, and then constructing the answer to this question warranted by appeal solely to our common human experience and reason. If, in this other phase or task, philosophy acts as a control on all religious and theological answers to *the* existential question, it is just as true, conversely, that religion and theology also act as a control on philosophy's answers to the same question.

∽

The question orienting philosophy is the most vital of our vital questions, and may therefore be called "*the* existential question." This is the question we human beings seem universally engaged in somehow asking and answering about the meaning of our own existence in its ultimate setting simply as a part, together with others, of the encompassing whole.

On closer analysis, this existential question, although a single question, has two closely related and yet clearly distinguishable aspects. In one aspect, it asks about the ultimate reality of our existence with others as parts of the whole encompassing us. And this aspect may be distinguished as its *metaphysical* aspect, because, although it is distinct from the proper question of metaphysics in asking about this ultimate reality concretely, in its meaning for us, rather than abstractly, in its structure in itself, the two questions are nonetheless closely related, in that any answer to either of them has definite implications for answering the other if the two questions are to be answered consistently.

In its other aspect, which may be distinguished as *ethical*, the existential question asks about how we are to understand ourselves authentically, or realistically, in accordance with the ultimate reality of our existence. Thus, while it is generally distinct from the proper question of ethics because it asks about our self-understanding as well as our life-praxis, the two questions, once again, are closely related, because any answer we give to one of them sets definite limits to how we have to answer the other if we are to avoid self-contradiction.

It is the existential question, thus understood, that orients philosophy as a distinct form of critical reflection. But precisely because it is "critical," philosophy is *constituted* as such, not by any vital question, not even the existential question that orients it, but only by the corresponding way of asking the properly theoretical questions about meaning and validity, about the meaning of any and all answers to *the* existential question and about the validity of their claim to express the truth about human existence.

This means, among other things, that the critical interpretation proper to philosophy is "critical existentialist interpretation," which is to say, the way of critically interpreting oriented by the existential question about the meaning of our existence and therefore constituted by the corresponding way of asking about meaning theoretically.

∽

The existential question by which philosophy is oriented is the question of the meaning of ultimate reality for us. This is to say, first of all, that the reality about which it asks is the ultimate reality of our own existence in relation to others and the whole. This reality is properly said to be "ultimate" on the assumption that, by the term "reality" used without further qualification, we mean, in William James's words, "what we in some way find ourselves obliged to take account of." Clearly, whatever else we may or may not find ourselves obliged to take account of, we can never fail to take account somehow of ourselves, others, and the whole to which we and they all belong. In this sense, the threefold reality of our existence simply as such is the ultimate reality that we all have to allow for in understanding ourselves and leading our own individual lives.

But if this is the reality that *the* existential question asks about, the second thing to note is how it does this—namely, by asking about this reality, not in its structure in itself, but in its meaning for us. In asking about ultimate reality, *the* existential question asks, at one and the same time, about our true and authentic self-understanding, about the understanding of ourselves in relation to others and the whole that is appropriate to, or authorized by, this ultimate reality itself. Thus, by its very nature, *the* existential question is a single question having two closely related and yet clearly distinguishable aspects—in one of which, its *metaphysical* aspect, it asks about the ultimate reality of our own existence in relation to others and the whole; in the other of which, its *ethical* aspect, it asks how we are to understand ourselves authentically.

This means that, by the very nature of *the* existential question, there are two main aspects to the procedures appropriate to determining the truth of any and all specific answers to it. Broadly speaking, we may say that a specific answer is true insofar as it so responds to the question of solving the problem that any answer to it purports to solve—the problem, namely, of making sense somehow of our basic faith in the possibility and meaning of life, given the reality of life as we actually experience it. But whether, or to what extent, any specific answer is capable of doing this can be determined only by verifying its necessary implications, ethical as well as metaphysical. If it is true, its implications also must be true, and unless they can be verified by procedures appropriate to verifying ethical and metaphysical claims respectively, it cannot be verified, either.

To recognize this is to understand the difficulties of validating claims to existential truth. As compared with the special sciences and technology, where there is, for the most part, extensive agreement concerning appropriate procedures of verification, metaphysics and ethics both remain profoundly controversial fields of inquiry, even at the level of the principles and procedures by which true claims are to be distinguished from false. In fact, there is not even agreement about the proper analysis of metaphysical and ethical utterances, which some philosophers construe as having a noncognitive kind of meaning that obviates even asking about their truth or falsity. Small wonder, then, that one of the standing temptations of all who make existential claims is to try to find some way of avoiding the difficulties of critically validating them, whether by simply deducing their truth from some presumed authority or by construing them as matters of sheer faith, whose truth supposedly cannot and need not be critically validated because they're "self-validating." But only a little reflection confirms the futility of all such moves, especially in a cultural situation such as ours has become today, in which the plurality of existential claims is an ever-present fact of life. Unless one is prepared to allow that one's claim to existential truth is something very different from the kind of cognitive claim that it gives every appearance of being, one is left either with reneging on the promise implied in making or implying the claim or with critically validating it in a non-question-begging way by the only procedures appropriate to doing so. Consequently, there is no avoiding the difficulties of validating existential claims if one is to be responsible in making them as claims to truth. By the very logic of such claims, the only way to validate them is to verify their necessary implications both metaphysical and ethical by the same procedures that would be appropriate for validating any other claims of the same logical type.

This is not to say that any specific answer to the existential question can be deduced simply from a true metaphysics and a true ethics, taken either singly or together. Any such answer is more than just a certain understanding of existence insofar as it is also the "cultural system," primary and secondary, through which any such understanding is explicitly represented as true. Therefore, while the truth of its understanding, insofar as it is true, must indeed be implied by a true metaphysics and a true ethics, as a particular way of conceiving and symbolizing its understanding it is also irreducibly historical. As such, it is simply given—a datum for metaphysical and ethical reflection rather than a deduction from them. And this means that validating its claim to truth also always involves certain properly historical and hermeneutical procedures.

Neither is it to be supposed that one must first have a true metaphysics and a true ethics before one can determine whether or not a specific existential answer is true. To argue that determining the truth of such an answer logically requires verifying its necessary implications for both belief and action does not imply that one must already be in possession of metaphysical and ethical truth whenever one undertakes to verify them. On the contrary, it is entirely possible that in following the procedures requisite to their verification, one will not only determine the truth of the answer implying them, but will also determine the falsity of the metaphysics and/or the ethics by which one may have first thought to judge their truth.

~

Although philosophy is definitely "a secondary activity" of more or less critical reflection, it individually, or as a whole, is not properly "a science" in the strict sense of the word. Why not?

Because philosophy is not properly intellectual, but in its own way, or at its own (secondary) level, is properly existential. Even at its most theoretical, philosophy remains ever oriented, proximately as well as remotely, not by any intellectual question, but by an existential question—indeed, *the* existential question, about how we are to understand ourselves and lead our lives in the ultimate setting in which we exist.

On the other hand, just as existential questions in general include intellectual questions, which can always be asked by a characteristic abstraction therefrom—from asking existentially about meaning for us to asking intellectually about structure in itself—so science in the strict sense is included in philosophy. But what science?

It is the science of the analysis of meaning, and thus of the contexts and presuppositions of meaning, including, above all, the strictly transcendental (and existentialist) presuppositions of any meaning simply as such. Thus, at its core or center, the science that philosophy itself is not but necessarily includes is twofold: transcendental metaphysics (in a broad sense inclusive of existentialist analysis) and transcendental ethics. On its periphery, then, in all of the so-called "philosophy of" disciplines, it is the science of analyzing the meaning and presuppositions of the several other main contexts of meaning: science, religion, art, medicine, business, and so on.

~

Philosophy is commonly reckoned to belong to the humanities. Why?

The answer is obvious if philosophy, as I argue, is critical appropriation—i.e., critical interpretation and critical validation—of self-understanding and life-praxis, including, although in no way exhausted by, our self-understanding and life-praxis simply as human beings in the ultimate setting of our lives. But doesn't philosophy include metaphysics as well as ethics, and isn't metaphysics, at least, properly reckoned a science, instead of being one of the humanities?

Yes, philosophy does include metaphysics as well as ethics, because it includes, although it is not exhausted by, critical appropriation of our self-understanding and life-praxis simply as human beings. And, yes, metaphysics, at least, is rightly reckoned to be a science, insofar as it is, in its own way, like all the special sciences, properly so-called, scientific or intellectual in its concern with the structure of reality in itself, rather than, like philosophy, sapient or existential in its concern with the meaning of reality for us. But there is also the fundamental difference that metaphysics is the one *ontological*, or properly conceptual, science of reality as such, whereas the other, special sciences are all rightly said to be, in their different ways, *ontic*, or properly factual, sciences of particular kinds of reality. Thus, whereas the special sciences are each dependent, in their way, on some special human experiences that different individual persons may or may not ever have, metaphysics (as well as ethics) depends solely on the common experience that we all have simply as and because we are human beings, whatever the extent to which it becomes explicit, and so the object, possibly, of critical reflection or appropriation.

It seems entirely fitting, therefore, that philosophy, including metaphysics and ethics, should be reckoned to belong to the humanities.

Is philosophy "hot" (religious) or "cold" (contemplative)?

I answer unhesitatingly that philosophy, being an activity on the secondary level of critical reflection and proper theory, is not "hot," but "cold," not religious, but contemplative, or, as I would prefer to say, reflective. So, if D. Z. Phillips is right, I am insofar in agreement not only with him but also with Ludwig Wittgenstein, for whom it is important that doing philosophy not be confused with, but clearly distinguished from, being religious.

But does this mean, then, that philosophy has only the one purely analytic, "descriptivist," function, as distinct from yet another properly existential, "prescriptivist," function—as Phillips at least sometimes appears to infer? Stephen Mulhall seems to me to argue convincingly that, insofar as philosophy of religion distinguishes, as it must, between "superstition," on the one hand, and "a more genuine religious attitude," on the other, it is inevitably functioning prescriptively, not merely descriptively.[25] But I see nothing in allowing this that would warrant supposing that philosophy, after all, must therefore be "hot," rather than "cold"—whether or not Mulhall would agree with Phillips in supposing this.

Philosophy has an existential as well as an analytic function with respect to all answers to the existential question, expressed or implied, and religious and theological as well as philosophical. But because, or insofar as, it performs this function, not on the primary level of self-understanding and life-praxis, but on the secondary level of critical reflection and proper theory, philosophy itself is not religious, but rather reflective.

---

25. Mulhall, "Wittgenstein and the Philosophy of Religion," 108–11.

On Philosophy

∽

I have said elsewhere that philosophy, although *oriented* by the vital question that is *the* existential question, is *constituted* by "appropriate forms of the theoretical questions of meaning and truth." But just what forms of these theoretical questions *are* appropriate to philosophy?

So far as *the question of meaning* is concerned, the form that is particularly appropriate to philosophy is the form that asks about the "deep structure," and not merely the "surface meaning," of things—i.e., about *the logical kind(s)* of meaning in question and about its (their) necessary presuppositions or conditions of possibility. Of course, philosophy can ask *this* form of the question of meaning only by also asking about "surface meaning"—i.e., the semantic meaning of the words, sentences, and paragraphs whose logical kind(s) of meaning it is concerned to analyze. If this involves, as it does, asking about the kind(s) of meaning expressed by any and all "*Sprachspielen/Lebensformen*," as Wittgenstein calls them, or what Whitehead speaks of—meaning, I think, essentially the same thing—as "the directed activities of mankind," it also involves asking about the strictly necessary presuppositions or conditions of possibility of any meaning whatsoever, which are the proper subject matter of metaphysics and ethics, with their respective concerns for the structure of ultimate reality in itself and for how we are to act and what we are to do, given the meaning of ultimate reality for us as human beings.

As for the form of *the question of truth* appropriate to philosophy, it is solely the question of *existential truth*—of truth about human existence, and thus of both metaphysical truth about the structure of ultimate reality in itself and ethical truth about how we are authorized to act and what we are authorized to do by the meaning of ultimate reality for us. Philosophy, in other words, neither asks nor answers the question of *empirical truth*, and thus of scientific truth or empirical-historical truth, nor does it ask or answer any other form of the question of truth about the merely factual or contingent things that have long since ceased to be the concern of philosophy, having become the proper subjects of the special sciences or other nonphilosophical fields or disciplines.

But this does not mean that philosophy may not quite properly integrate empirical or factual truths into its constructive account of existential truth, provided only that their claims to be true have been critically validated by such nonphilosophical criteria and procedures as are logically requisite to validating them.

∽

Philosophy begins in wonder. And at the end, when philosophic thought has done its best, the wonder remains.

—ALFRED NORTH WHITEHEAD

Philosophy begins in wonder, I should say, in that it is *oriented* by *the* existential question about the meaning of ultimate reality for us. But philosophy is *constituted* as such, as distinct from being oriented, not by this or any other *vital* question, but by a corresponding *theoretical* question—namely, about the meaning and the validity of any and all answers to *the* existential question, implicit as well as explicit.

Because the validity of any such answer can be determined only by first determining what it really means, philosophy includes a concern with analyzing and interpreting meaning. But philosophy's main concern with meaning is distinctive. Unlike other humanities whose concern is, in one way or another, with the "surface meaning," or the semantic meaning, of the expressions they analyze and interpret, its concern is not so much with that, or even with the relatively deeper meaning constituted by grammatical rules, but with the "deep structure," and so with *the logical kind(s)* of meaning, constituted with their presuppositions and necessary conditions of possibility.

But philosophy's concern with analyzing and interpreting meaning in its different logical kinds is not its only concern. Its other concern is with validating, not, to be sure, all claims to validity, but any such as is expressed or implied by any answer to *the* existential question. Essential to philosophy's validating these claims is the purely formal, transcendental metaphysics and ethics that its work as analysis and interpretation of meaning as such naturally includes. Presupposed by any meaning, and any kind of meaning, are certain necessary conditions of possibility: of the possibility of human existence insofar as it is the being that is capable both of expressing all kinds of meaning and of understanding and interpreting all such expressions; and of the possibility of anything whatsoever as the being that any kind of meaning must be directly or indirectly about. Corresponding to—indeed, necessarily implied by—the metaphysics explicating these necessary conditions of possibility is a purely formal, transcendental ethics, in the sense of completely general principles concerning both how any human being, or any other being endowed with understanding at the high level of thinking and speaking and therefore also with moral freedom and responsibility, is to act and what she, he, or it is to do. Since any answer to *the* existential question implies both a metaphysics and an ethics in this sense, whether or not it is a valid answer to the question depends on whether or not its implied metaphysics and ethics are in substantial agreement with the metaphysics and ethics necessarily implied by any meaning, and any kind of meaning, such as philosophy, in its one phase as analysis and interpretation, has the task of making explicit. In its other phase, then, as existential reflection on the validity of any and all answers to *the* existential question, philosophy has the task of determining the fact, or the extent, of such dependence—i.e., such substantial agreement.

And yet Whitehead is exactly right: even when philosophic thought—existential as well as analytic—has done its best, the wonder in which philosophy begins remains. It remains because, although philosophy is indeed *oriented* by *the* existential question, it is not *constituted* thereby, nor does or can it ever answer this question directly. Being a matter of critical reflection and proper theory, as distinct from self-understanding and life-praxis, philosophy (even in its existential phase) is always only *indirectly* addressed to the vital question by which it is oriented. In this sense, or for this reason, the wonder in which philosophy begins, as expressed by *the* existential question, "How shall I understand myself and lead my life here and now," remains even at the end—and that not only when philosophy has, in one way or another, fallen short, but even when (if ever) philosophy has done its very best. For the existential question cannot be answered intellectually, or theoretically, by howsoever adequate a theory, but only existentially, by how I actually understand myself and lead my life here and now as just this individual human being related to others and the whole.

16

The Two Phases of Philosophy

I have been clear for some time that and why the distinction I once made between the one "analytic" phase of philosophy and its other "critico-constructive" phase simply wouldn't do. But why I should have been so long in clearly recognizing the wanted alternative is, to say the least, disconcerting. Already in my essay on Hartshorne's theory of analogy, I had expressed my full agreement with him that "philosophy has 'two primary responsibilities,' only one of which is properly metaphysical, the other being rather practical or existential."[26]

So the obvious alternative is to speak of the two phases of philosophy simply as "analytic" and "existential" respectively. Philosophy's being "analytic" is its way of being "intellectual," or "scientific" (≡ "scient" or "sciential"), while its being "existential" is its way of being—yes, "existential" (≡ "sapient" or "sapiential"). In other words, its one phase is the relatively more concrete, inclusive, whereas the other phase is the relatively more abstract, included.

If at the center of its more abstract, included phase are transcendental metaphysics (in a broad sense) and the transcendental ethics determined thereby, it is the latter that is directly foundational for philosophy's other existential phase. Transcendental metaphysics, in a strict sense, has to do with the structure of being in itself, and, in a broad sense, also with the structure of being that understands being in itself (i.e., "existence" in the emphatic sense of the word). Transcendental ethics, on the other hand, has to do with the meaning of being and existence for us, although only with the

---

26. Ogden, *Doing Theology Today*, 208.

essential *structure* of this meaning, and thus with the authentic self-understanding/ true understanding of existence that being and existence authorize by their structure in itself.

∾

Let philosophy be understood as critical reflection on self-understanding and life-praxis, and therefore on ultimate reality, which is to say, on the necessary conditions of the possibility not only of human existence but also of being as such.

There should be no puzzle, then, about philosophy's being, in its one purely formal phase, analysis of presuppositions *überhaupt*—i.e., of the necessary conditions of the possibility of all the various forms of life-praxis and culture (this being the task of all the peripheral philosophical disciplines, the so-called "philosophies of," etc.) and also of the necessary conditions of the possibility of human existence and of being as such (this being the task of the central philosophical disciplines of transcendental metaphysics, including existentialist analysis, and transcendental ethics).

But in all such analysis of presuppositions, philosophy remains remotely oriented by *the* existential question, and thus is finally concerned with the meaning of ultimate reality for us, and so what it means to engage both in the various "directed activities of mankind" (Whitehead) and in existing simply as a human being; i.e., how one ought to understand oneself and lead one's life. For this reason, philosophy not only has one analytic phase, but also another existential phase, in which it seeks its own critically reflective answer to *the* existential question of the meaning of ultimate reality for us.

∾

I have come to distinguish "two phases of philosophy": analytic and existential. Heidegger, on the other hand, is said by Thomas Sheehan to distinguish—in effect, if not in so many words—not two "phases," but two "moments," of philosophy: "analytic" and "protreptic."[27] This prompts the question of whether I, too, could not just as well speak of "moments" as "phases" to designate what I have in mind. Whatever the answer, it seems clear that I could (and perhaps should) appropriate Sheehan's terminology and use the adjectives "analytic" and "protreptic," instead of "analytic" and "existential," to designate the two phases or moments of philosophy. "Existential" is already overworked in my lexicon, and "protreptic" seems well-suited to serve as a term-of-art for the kind of thinking and speaking I have in mind.

---

27. Sheehan, *Making Sense of Heidegger*.

17

Theses in the Philosophy of Religion

1. The adherents of a religion represent the possibility of self-understanding/understanding of existence decisively re-presented through their religion's explicit primal source as originally, if only implicitly, authorized by ultimate reality itself, and as therefore *the* answer to the existential question about the meaning of that reality for us. In this way, they explicitly address the question we all ask, implicitly, if not explicitly, of how we are to understand our own existence with others in the whole if we are to do so truly and authentically. Claiming to be authorized explicitly as well as implicitly by ultimate reality itself, they explicitly authorize all of us thus to understand ourselves and to lead our lives accordingly through the whole of our life-praxis, by effectively using and validly bearing the same witness they have borne to us.

2. The life-praxis necessarily implied by the self-understanding/understanding of existence explicitly authorized by a religion is basically twofold in form. There is the primary form of effectively using witness and validly bearing it, and there is the secondary form of critically reflecting on witness by doing theology.

3. "Bearing witness" is the whole life-praxis, secular as well as sacred or religious, expressive of the self-understanding/understanding of existence, explicitly authorized by a religion. It belongs to bearing witness to make or imply certain claims to validity—specifically, the claim to be adequate to its content because it is both appropriate to the explicit primal source authorizing it and credible to human existence; and the claim to be fitting to its situation. But whether these claims to adequacy and fittingness are valid is never settled simply by making or implying them. On the contrary, if and when they become sufficiently problematic, nothing is to be done, provided communication is to continue and its commitments are to be kept, but to shift from the primary level of making or implying the claims to the secondary level of critically validating them—and, in this sense, to doing theology.

4. "Doing theology," then, is critically reflecting on the self-understanding and life-praxis explicitly authorized by a religion—the life-praxis alone being actually given for critical reflection. Such reflection includes, first, critically *interpreting* the meaning of bearing witness, and second, critically *validating* the claims to validity that bearing witness makes or implies.

5. Bearing witness and doing theology are as distinct as they are inseparable, and therefore no more to be identified or confused than opposed or played off against one another. This is because the two forms of activity or praxis belong respectively on the

two different but related levels of existing understandingly—bearing witness belonging on the primary level where we somehow understand ourselves and lead our lives accordingly; doing theology, on the secondary level where we critically interpret the meaning of our life-praxis and critically validate its claims to validity.

6. Doing theology, so understood, naturally differentiates itself into doing mainly three things, all of which must be done if theology is to be done: "doing historical theology," "doing systematic theology," and "doing practical theology." To do the first is simply to do the critical interpretation of the meaning of bearing witness that is the *conditio sine qua non* of doing the critical validation of its claims to validity. To do the second and third is to do the critical validation necessary to confirming the claims of bearing witness to be respectively adequate to its content and fitting to its situation.

7. If to do systematic theology is to validate critically the claim of witness to be adequate to its content, doing it requires validating, in turn, the two further claims thereby implied: that bearing witness is appropriate to the explicit primal source authorizing it; and that bearing witness is credible to any human being simply as such.

8. But, then, critically validating the credibility of bearing witness is as integral to doing systematic theology as critically validating its appropriateness—and for exactly the same reason, because of the claims to validity made or implied by bearing witness itself.

9. Doing systematic theology, however, so as to validate critically bearing witness's claim to credibility is not possible without also doing the philosophical reflection necessary to determining our authentic self-understanding/true understanding of existence. Doing such philosophical reflection—or, more simply, "doing philosophy"—requires doing two different but closely related kinds of reflection. The reason for this is that there are two parts to determining what is to count as authentic self-understanding/true understanding of existence: an "in principle" part and an "in fact" part." Doing the first, "in principle" part requires doing the critical reflection proper to the philosophy of religion, understood as logical analysis of the "deep structure," or logical *kind* of meaning, expressed not only by religious language but also by the implicit bearing witness that religious language also explicitly authorizes. By means of such analysis, two things can be determined: (1) that it is only by its substantial agreement with the authentic self-understanding/true understanding of existence that bearing witness can be validated as credible; and (2) that a self-understanding can be authentic/an understanding of existence can be true only if it is appropriate to, and hence authorized by, ultimate reality itself, whose meaning for us, for how we are to understand ourselves and lead our lives, is determined by its structure in itself.

10. But, then, to do the second, "in fact" part of determining the self-understanding/understanding of existence that satisfies this principle requires doing the different kind of philosophical reflection that is properly meant by "doing metaphysics." By this is meant logical analysis, not of the several different kinds of meaning or "deep structures," whether separately or together, but of the necessary presuppositions of

any kind of meaning, and so, as it were, the deepest structure of all. Doing metaphysics, in other words, is logically analyzing the ultimate reality of our own existence in its structure in itself.

∞

1. The language of a religion is to be analyzed as "existential language" in three senses of the term. It is existential language, first of all, in the proper sense that it is about existence, understood simply as the property of being real in one of the two main ways in which something can be so (i.e., concretely real) as distinct from being real only abstractly. But then, being language that explicitly addresses *the* existential question about the meaning of ultimate reality for us, religious language is existential in two further senses. It is existential, secondly, in the emphatic sense that the concrete reality it is about is the threefold ultimate reality of our own existence, which is to say, ourselves, others, and the whole. And it is existential, thirdly, also in the emphatic sense that it is about this ultimate threefold reality, not abstractly, in its structure in itself, but concretely, in its meaning for us.

2. The difference between this analysis of religious language and that offered by the usual cognitivist analyses should be clear. On these analyses, religious utterances are taken to be existential in the first sense only, in that they simply assert or imply something about concrete reality. This they do as factual utterances that are meaningful, if they are, only because or insofar as they can be factually, if not empirically, falsified. But what such analyses deny or overlook is that the concrete reality religious utterances are about is not the immediate, merely factual reality of the world and ourselves as disclosed empirically through our sense experience, but rather the ultimate threefold reality of our own existence as disclosed existentially through our nonsensuous experience of ourselves, others, and the whole. This means that among the utterances foundational to a religion are some that, being about the strictly ultimate reality of the whole, logically cannot imply merely factual utterances that, as such, are factually falsifiable. Moreover, the way in which religious utterances are about ultimate reality is also existential, in that they assert something about its meaning for us, for our own self-understanding and life-praxis, as distinct, but also inseparable, from its structure in itself.

3. On the usual noncognitivist analyses, on the other hand, the point that paradigmatic religious utterances are existential is missed altogether, because they are taken as not asserting or implying anything at all about concrete reality, even if certain things can definitely be asserted or implied about them as themselves instances of such reality. They are analyzed, instead, as expressions of a certain basic human attitude or valuation in no way determined or authorized by reality, factual or otherwise, but variously characterized as "an intention to behave in a certain way," a "*blik*," or a "historical perspective."

NOTEBOOKS

1. "Religion," in the generic/specific sense, is the primary form of culture through which our existential question about the ultimate meaning of our lives is explicitly asked and answered.

2. Therefore, "the religious life," in the same generic/specific sense, is the way of understanding oneself and leading one's life that is explicitly mediated by the images/symbols, concepts/terms, of this, that, or the other specific religion. This means that the religious life, in the generic/specific sense, is always an explicitly authorized life. And this it is because it belongs to religion generically, and thus to each religion specifically, to lay claim to decisive authority: to claim to be *the* authorized re-presentation of the answer to our existential question. Because, from its standpoint, the self-understanding/understanding of existence that it re-presents is uniquely realistic, being uniquely appropriate to, or authorized by, the very structure of ultimate reality itself, it claims that its re-presentations of this understanding have decisive authority for the understanding of human existence.

3. To live the religious life, then, as a life explicitly authorized by means of some specific religion, is to make or imply a distinctive double claim for what one thinks, says, and does in so living: not only (1) that it is, in turn, *appropriate* to whatever this religion takes to be the explicit primal source of its authority, but also (2) that it is *credible* to any woman or man as re-presenting the truth about her or his own existence as a human being.

4. This double claim, however, is like all other claims to validity made or implied by human life-praxis in that it is one thing to make or imply it, something else again to do so validly. Consequently, to live the religious life at all, particularly in the pluralized social-cultural circumstances in which more and more people live in a "globalizing-globalized" world, is to anticipate having somehow, sooner or later, to make good on the claim that one makes or implies by so living.

5. In this way, living the religious life requires that one become a theologian—and this means also a philosopher, and a historian to boot. This assumes, of course, the generic/specific sense of "theology" in which, in correspondence with the generic/specific sense of "religion," it means the specific form of critical reflection constituted by asking about the meaning and the validity of some specific way of living religiously. So a theologian, in this generic/specific sense, asks more or less critically what it really means to live in this specific way and whether the distinctive double claim to appropriateness and credibility that anyone necessarily makes or implies by so living is really a valid claim.

6. But to ask about either meaning or validity is to ask questions that are, at least in part, properly philosophical. This is so, at any rate, if one understands "philosophy" likewise in a generic sense, to mean the comprehensive critical reflection constituted by asking about human existence simply as such. It belongs to philosophy,

so understood, that it should consist, in one aspect, in an analysis of *meaning*, and thus of the different *kinds* of meaning involved in understanding ourselves and leading our lives through all the forms of culture, religious as well as secular.

7. So, too, with the question about *validity*, including the validity of the double claim that living the religious life necessarily makes or implies. Although to ask whether a religious way of living is really appropriate to the explicit source of authority certifying it is to ask a question that is, in essential part, properly historical and hermeneutical, it is, in another essential part, a properly philosophical question. Insofar as one thereby asks about a certain *kind* of appropriateness, one asks a question that only philosophical reflection—whether done by philosophers or by theologians or by yet other students of religion—is capable of answering. And the same is even more obviously true of the other question of whether a particular way of living religiously is really credible, in the sense that it really re-presents the truth about every woman's or man's existence. This question can be answered affirmatively only if the necessary presuppositions and implications of this way of living, ethical as well as metaphysical, can somehow be validated as credible. But, again, actually validating them requires properly philosophical reflection.

8. If living religiously in a specific way requires one to be a theologian, and if being a theologian then requires that one also be a philosopher, and a historian as well, one has every reason to look for help from any others who, for reasons of their own, also have to be philosophers, including especially all who have to do philosophy simply because they profess to do it, because they do philosophy professionally. Indeed, the more professionally philosophers carry out their responsibility, the more likely they are to help anyone who is trying to live the religious life to do so responsibly.

9. There are two points where professional philosophers can be of particular help to any such religious person, especially today: (1) in connection with their one main task of analyzing the kind of meaning involved in asking and answering the existential question explicitly, and so religiously, they can provide a properly formal analysis of inter-religious dialogue, including a purely formal language—conceptuality/terminology—in which materially different answers to the existential/religious question can all be critically interpreted and the real issues between them somehow resolved insofar as this can be done by appropriate evidence and argument; and (2) in connection with their other main task of critically validating all the different answers to the existential question, implicit as well as explicit, secular as well as religious, so as to formulate their own constructive answer to this question, they can help to make good on the claim that a particular way of living religiously is not only appropriate but also credible. If any such way of living is really credible, it can only be because what it re-presents as the truth about human existence is the same truth that the professional philosopher bears particular responsibility for critically validating by verifying its necessary presuppositions and implications, both metaphysical and ethical.

10. There are still other respects in which professional philosophers can be helpful to anyone trying to lead a religious life in a responsible way: (1) they can decline to exempt anyone, including persons attempting to lead the religious life responsibly, from doing their own philosophical reflection; (2) they can recognize, as many philosophers in the past have not, that religion and philosophy, each in its way, are both formally normative for existential truth and that, therefore, the accountability between philosophers on the one hand, and religious persons and theologians on the other, is entirely mutual; and, more important still, (3) they can be clear, as so many have not been, that philosophy and the religious life are not competitive but complementary, because, if the second requires, among other things, the kind of critical reflection that only the first can provide, the first can at best only point to the second as a way of understanding oneself and leading one's life by which it, as philosophy, is utterly transcended.[28]

I have written that philosophy provides "[a] kind of critical reflection" that is "utterly transcended" by religion, understood as "a way of understanding oneself and leading one's life." But why *utterly* transcended?

Because religion transcends philosophy not just in one way but in two, and so in both of the ways in which philosophy could conceivably be transcended: (1) in the way in which the more particular or special always goes beyond the more universal or general; and (2) in the way in which understanding one's own individual existence here and now, in face of the concrete gift and demand of the moment, always goes beyond understanding human existence in general, even if it understands existence truly and includes, as it should, understanding this very distinction in general.

18

What Constitutes a Religion?

A religion is constituted by an explicit answer to *the* existential question of the meaning of ultimate reality for us. This means that a religion always involves not only an explicit self-understanding *through which* we understand our existence (*fides qua*

---

28. Ogden, "Philosophy and the Religious Life," 28–31.

creditur), but also an explicit understanding of existence *that is* understood as and when we so understand ourselves (*fides quæ creditur*).

Unless someone so understands her- or himself, the religion as such does not exist. But it also does not exist unless (1) what is understood by someone who understands her- or himself is *its* understanding of human existence; and (2) she or he comes to this understanding thanks to the explicit mediation of the religion, or (in the unique case of its founders) the explicit mediation of the religion's explicit primal ontic source.

In the case of the Christian religion, this explicit understanding of human existence is not made explicit, in the primal instance, verbally, as some law or teaching or wisdom, but nonverbally, in and as a human person, Jesus himself, through whom the meaning of ultimate reality for us is decisively re-presented. Jesus does not simply teach or bear witness to a word through which this meaning becomes explicit; he himself *is* this Word, in the same way in which, in our experience generally, persons and what they do and suffer can speak to us nonverbally and demand that we somehow respond to them in their meaning for us. But if Jesus thus belongs to the object side of the Christian religion, as distinct from its subject side, the religion does not exist as such unless and until there is a subject side, which is to say, unless and until the understanding of existence that is made explicit nonverbally in and as Jesus himself is also understood through the self-understanding of one or more persons and then somehow expressed through their life-praxis.

In short, the Christian religion does not exist, or is not constituted as such, unless and until there are Christians: persons who understand themselves as they are given and called to do decisively through Jesus, and who then express their self-understanding by somehow bearing witness to his decisive significance by all that they think, say, and do. Conversely, the Christian religion already exists, or is constituted as such, as soon and as long as there are Christians who do thus understand themselves and somehow give expression to their self-understanding and the understanding of existence that it explicitly mediates.

It seems clear that this answer to the original question both confirms and is confirmed by different but related understandings of "the Christ event" (or "the Christian event") as "the coming into being of the church" (John Knox); "the institution of the Christian proclamation" (Rudolf Bultmann); "the believing reception of the fact" (Paul Tillich); or "the primal datum of the church" (Willi Marxsen). According to all these understandings, this event has two essential components: "the person" and "the community" (in Knox's terms); "Christ" and "the word/ministry of reconciliation" (in Bultmann's terms, following Paul in 2 Cor 5:18); "the fact [*sc.* of the New Being in Jesus as the Christ]" and "believing reception of the fact" (in Tillich's terms); or "Jesus" and "faith," or "Jesus" and "the believer" (in Marxsen's terms).

The first component of the event, I should say, is Jesus as the *ontic* aspect of the explicit primal source of the event's decisive authority, while the second component, expressing as it does the *noetic* aspect of the explicit primal source in the faith experience of the first Christians, is the sole primary authority authorized by the explicit primal source in both of its aspects.

∾

The constitution of a religious community has a structure determined by three correlations. First, there is the correlation between the *religious object* and the *religious subject*; second, the correlation involved in the religious object itself between its *existential-transhistorical/transcendental aspect* and its *existential-historical aspect*; and third, the correlation between the *explicit primal source* authorizing the religion and the *sole primary authority* authorized by that source. The explicit primal source authorizing the religion also has two aspects: an *ontic* aspect in the existential-historical aspect of the religious object; and a *noetic* aspect in the religious subject's believing experience of the ontic aspect as of decisive existential significance.

Thus, for example, a Jew who is not a constitutive member of the Jewish religious community may be said to believe *in* God, decisively *through* the oral law/Torah, *with* Moses and the chosen people of Israel. Or, a Muslim who is a nonconstitutive member of the Islamic religious community may be said to believe *in* God, decisively *through* the Koran, *with* Mohammed and all his faithful followers. Similarly, any Christian who is not her- or himself an apostle—not a "disciple at first hand," in Kierkegaard's way of putting it, but a "disciple at second hand"—has traditionally been said to believe *in* God decisively *through* Jesus, *with* the apostles and their successors.

But in modern revisionary forms of Christianity, this traditional clear distinction between Jesus and the apostles breaks down. So far from being the existential-historical aspect of the constitutive religious *object*, Jesus is understood to be simply *a* (even if *the*) constitutive religious *subject*. He thus becomes "the founder of the Christian religion," the first Christian, the first and foremost apostle, and so no more than *a* (even if *the*) constitutive member of the Christian religious community.

Just this breakdown is the real import of distinguishing, as revisionary theology typically does, between authentic Christianity as "the religion *of* Jesus" and traditional Christianity as "the religion *about* Jesus."

∾

A religion, I hold, is what Clifford Geertz calls a "cultural system," meaning by that a system of concepts and symbols through which certain individuals are explicitly given and called to actualize a certain possibility of self-understanding, thereby understanding themselves, others, and the whole in a specific way. However, to be religious is not only, or primarily, to believe that the way of understanding existence necessarily implied by the self-understanding is intellectually true or to act as though it prescribes what is ethically right. Nor is it even so to believe intellectually and so to act ethically as to do both honestly or sincerely. No, to be religious is also, and primarily, to actualize the possibility of self-understanding that a religion gives and calls one to actualize, *and then* to lead one's life accordingly, by believing to be true what one necessarily presupposes and implies both theoretically and practically by so understanding oneself and by doing as right what it presupposes and implies one is to do.

Because the self-understanding a religion primarily gives and calls for thus goes beyond, even while necessarily implying, both intellectual belief and ethical action, the religion itself is significant in its *"that,"* as Bultmann says, as distinct from its *"what."* It is significant primarily as the actual historical event of bearing, or re-presenting, the primal historical event by which both it itself and the possibility of self-understanding it explicitly mediates are decisively authorized. In this sense, the religion itself is, above all, "a means [indeed, *the* means, the *primary* means] of ultimate transformation."[29] It at once appoints and empowers any individual encountered by it to understand her- or himself in a certain way, and then to lead her or his life by believing and acting accordingly.

ω

An analysis of "religion" more balanced and, insofar, more adequate, than the one for and from which I have usually argued would do well to orient itself more explicitly and systematically by something like John Wesley's distinction between "Christianity as a principle in the soul" (≡ "inward principle" ≡ "character" ≡ "tempers, holiness, happiness") and "Christianity as a scheme or system of doctrine," which "describes" and "commands/promises" this "character" and tells how it may be attained.[30]

Significantly, the epigraph from Wesley that I chose for *Is There Only One True Religion or Are There Many?* takes "true religion," in effect, to be "a principle in the soul," whereas the understanding of it for which I actually argue in the book takes it as, in effect, "a scheme or system of doctrine," which is to say, what Geertz calls "a cultural system"—"a system of concepts and symbols" important for, if not exactly necessary to, explicitly understanding oneself and leading one's life as a human being in a particular society and culture. Of course, I nowhere deny that a religion is a "self-understanding" as well as a "cultural system." On the contrary, I clearly imply, whatever I may or may not explicitly assert, that religion is indeed a "self-understanding." But I also insist that "I have not defined religion *simply* as self-understanding," because "religion essentially involves not only an understanding of our existence, but also, and just as essentially, the particular concepts and symbols through which the question of our existence can alone be asked and answered in an explicit way"[31]

29. Streng, *Understanding Religious Life*, 2.
30. Outler, *John Wesley*, 188.
31. Ogden, *Is There Only One*, 10; italics added.

In sum: the question is not whether, but how: how adequately have I said what I mean (and what I cannot but think any reasonably sympathetic reader would almost certainly take me to mean)? It's all too clear, I fear, that I've usually proceeded in my expositions more one-sidedly than I should have, given my own acknowledgement that "religion essentially involves" not just one thing, but two.

∽

What, exactly, do I understand by "the true religion"?

1. By "religion" I understand the primary form of culture in terms of which we human beings explicitly ask and answer *the* existential question of the meaning of ultimate reality for us.

2. This means that I do not understand "religion," following Paul Tillich and others, simply as "ultimate concern," or, as I would be more likely to put it, "(authentic) self-understanding"; on the contrary, I am concerned with clarifying it as the primary "cultural system" (Geertz) in terms of which we are given and called to understand ourselves as human beings in an explicit way.

3. "Religion," by its very meaning, always has an objective as well as a subjective reference—analogously to the way in which, on a traditional Christian theological analysis, the term "faith" refers to the "faith that is believed" (*fides quæ creditur*) as well as to the "faith through which (it) is believed" (*fides qua creditur*); accordingly, religion is not just the explicit understanding *through* which our existence is understood, but also the explicit understanding that *is* understood as and when we so understand ourselves.

4. But being in both respects *explicit* understanding, religion essentially involves two aspects: not just a self-understanding/understanding of existence, but also, and just as essentially, the particular concepts and symbols through which the question of our existence can alone be asked and answered explicitly in just this, that, or the other specific way.

5. As such, religion never exists in general or simply as such, but always and only as some specific religion or religions, any of which lays claim to decisive existential authority for its particular concepts and symbols; this it does because it holds the self-understanding/understanding of existence that they re-present to be uniquely appropriate to, or authorized by, the very nature of ultimate reality in its meaning for us.

6. But if it thus belongs to any religion to express or imply a claim to decisive existential authority for its particular concepts and symbols, the reason for this is that every religion at least implicitly claims to be the true religion—i.e., *the* true religion, and as such the formal norm with which any other religion must agree in substance if its claim to be true is to be critically validated.

7. By "the true religion," then, I understand one or more specific religions, any of whose claims to be formally true, and hence the norm for determining all other

religious or existential truth, is a valid claim, as determined by appropriate procedures for critically validating all claims to existential truth, philosophical and theological, as well as religious.

8. So the necessary condition for critically validating the claim of this, that, or the other specific religion to be the true religion is verifying its explicit understanding of existence as true and, correspondingly, its explicit self-understanding as authentic, and its life-praxis as right.

9. Such verification is always only indirect, in that it proceeds by verifying the necessary presuppositions and implications, ethical as well as metaphysical, of the religion's explicit understanding of existence and inferring therefrom that the explicit self-understanding corresponding to this understanding must be authentic, even as it itself can only be true and its life-praxis only right.

10. But it is also only indirect, and, in a way, partial, in that it can do no more than this to verify, and thus to validate critically, the particular concepts and symbols that comprise the other essential aspect of any specific religion; to this extent, there is always that about every religion which, being historical and simply given, is arbitrary and beyond critical validation, even in principle, by common human experience and reason.

19

On the Difference between True and False Religion

1. All religions have to do with the constitution of human existence.

2. This means that it belongs to the "basic *supposition*" of all religions that human existence is constituted somehow, while the "basic *question*" all religions ask and answer is the question of just how human existence is really constituted.[32]

3. The answer that any religion gives to this basic question serves, not to *constitute*, but to *declare* (or to constitute only by declaring) how human existence really is constituted.

4. The peculiar temptation of all religions is to pretend to have a constitutive, as distinct from a merely declarative, role relative to the constitution of human existence.

---

32. On the terms "basic supposition" and "basic question," see Christian, *Meaning and Truth in Religion*.

5. The peculiar temptation of all radical criticism of religion is to miss religion's declarative significance while rightly challenging its pretensions to constitutive significance.

∾

Insights I learned from Willi Marxsen once helped me to achieve a (to me) satisfying interpretation of Friedrich Schleiermacher's famous dictum about the difference between Protestant and Catholic Christianity.[33] On this interpretation, Schleiermacher's main point is, in effect, an anticipation of Marxsen's own point when he stipulates the rule that one may never make what is formulated or specified as the *consequence* of an earlier generation's faith into the *foundation* (or any part of the foundation) of a later generation's faith.

Following the same insights, I would generalize and say that any religion, Catholic, Protestant, or any other, is insofar false as it makes our relation to the meaning of strictly ultimate reality for us dependent in any way on its specific symbols of that reality: if not its secondary or its primary symbols, then at least its primal symbol(s). A true religion, conversely, makes our relation to its symbols—not only its secondary and its primary symbols, but even its primal symbol(s)—dependent on the meaning of strictly ultimate reality for us. This it does in that it asks us to accept the claim of its symbols to be credible as well as appropriate because or insofar as we experience them to be confirmed by, as well as to confirm, the original revelation always already given to us with our self-understanding simply as human beings.

∾

I have made use in the above statement of the distinction between "primal," "primary," and "secondary" symbols. But to what, exactly, do I refer by these terms?

I refer to essentially the same things as when I distinguish in other contexts between the "primal," "primary," and "secondary" means of salvation, or "means of ultimate transformation" (Streng), that I understand to be definitive of any specific religion. Common to all three types of such means is that they are not constitutive, but only declarative or re-presentative, in relation to the salvation, or ultimate transformation, to mediate which is their common end. But while even the *primal* means of any religion, being precisely means, are not constitutive, but only declarative or re-presentative, in relation to their end, they *are* constitutive of their specific religion as itself the *primary* means to that end. By the *secondary* means of a religion, then, I distinguish any means that mediates salvation, or ultimate transformation, only by

---

33. Schleiermacher, *Der christliche Glaube* §24.

also declaring, or re-presenting, the primary as well as the primal means by which it itself is constituted.

❧

In responding to the question of what, exactly, is "the fundamental decision which decides [a human being's] life on earth and in eternity" (Fransen), I explain why "even talking about faith in and love for God is but one way of formulating the fundamental decision, not that decision itself" (see note 118, "On the *Optio Fundamentalis*"). If the primary symbols, "God," "faith," and "love," are understood in their specifically Christian senses, or even in the more determinate senses characteristic of radically monotheistic religions generally, such talk is still "too narrow," and insofar false rather than true. Of course, the same symbols may well be used in different, more indeterminate, or heuristic, senses, in which case my argument would no longer have any purchase. But then, the dangers of equivocation in using the symbols would need to be guarded against.

❧

I have written that "the true religion" could be defined as the primary form of culture whose explicit declaration of how human existence as such is constituted (1) agrees with how human existence in fact is constituted; and (2) is free of any claim to be constitutive of human existence as distinct from simply explicitly declaring its constitution.

But it is clear upon reflection that the second of these two conditions is already implied by the first. If a religion's explicit declaration of how human existence as such is constituted really does agree with how human existence is in fact constituted; and if human existence is in fact constituted by strictly ultimate reality *alone*, then the religion, not being either strictly ultimate reality or an essential aspect thereof, is *eo ipso* free of any claim to constitutive, as distinct from declarative, significance for human existence.

Even so, given the tendency of all religions to lay claim, in one way or another, to constitutive rather than merely declarative religious significance, it is perhaps well to stipulate the second condition of being "the true religion" explicitly, even if it is already implied by the first.

So far as the Christian religion is concerned, it is arguable that the significance of Jesus' death—and of the fact that it is precisely the Crucified One and none other who is risen and reigns as Lord—is that it confirms Christianity's fulfillment of the second condition, even as Jesus' life confirms its fulfillment of the first. Just as his life declares human existence as such to be constituted as it is in fact constituted solely by the strictly ultimate reality of God's unconditional love, so his death—and his reigning only as the crucified Lord whom God has raised from the dead—underscores that his declaration itself is neither strictly ultimate nor an essential aspect of what alone is. It is thoroughly declarative or re-presentative only, in no way constitutive of human existence and its authentic actualization. This is why to die *with* Jesus is also, however paradoxically, to die *to* him—even as, in Paul's great vision of last things in 1 Corinthians 15, Jesus himself will finally surrender his lordship so that the God who has subjected all things to him may be "all in all."

20

What Is "a Theological Interpretation of the Bible"?

1. There is no single thing properly called "*the* interpretation" of any text, because there are different possible things that may be properly so called.

One reason for this is that a text itself may address any number of different questions and kinds of questions, any of which may provide a perfectly proper objective in questioning it with a view to understanding and/or interpreting it. Another reason is that there are any number of questions not asked and addressed by a text itself that an interpreter may nonetheless choose to put to it and that may likewise provide perfectly proper objectives for questioning it with a view to understanding and/or interpreting its meaning.

2. But not every so-called reading of a text may be properly called an "interpretation" of it, since interpreting a text differs from simply using it, in that it satisfies, and must satisfy, the following five conditions:

2.1. An interpretation is unprejudiced in that it does not presuppose its results.

This means that the interpreter silences her or his own personal wishes in interpreting the meaning of the text—such wishes, say, as that a text should agree with certain beliefs that she or he holds to be true or that it should prescribe guidelines for life-praxis that she or he finds to be right. What the interpreter believes or does not believe, prescribes or does not prescribe, is in no way a condition of her or his interpretation. Another way of saying this is that an interpretation is unprejudiced insofar as the interpreter respects the sole primary authority of the text itself by allowing that what the text says is the sole arbiter of what the text means.

2.2. An interpretation presupposes that the text is something at once historical and literary, and it therefore follows, or conforms to, the methods of historical- and literary-critical research, including the so-called hermeneutical rules of grammatical interpretation, formal analysis of structure and style, and explanation in terms of the social and cultural conditions under which the text was produced.

Whatever the question a text may address or the interpreter, for her or his part, may choose to put to it, interpreting it is a matter of understanding a piece both of history and of literature and, therefore, has to follow both historical- and literary-critical methods of questioning it. The interpretation may do this naively or unintentionally by simply doing what the relevant rules require without ever having explicitly formulated them or being aware of conforming to them. But conform to them it must if it is to be a proper interpretation.

2.3. An interpretation also presupposes the interpreter's prior life-relation to, and thus preunderstanding of, "the thing" ($\equiv$ *res* $\equiv$ *die Sache*) that somehow comes to expression in the text.

Without such a prior life-relation to, and preunderstanding of, the thing the text is about, there can be neither a motive for questioning it nor an objective in doing so, and hence no interpretation of it. On the other hand, given such a prior life-relation and preunderstanding, an interpreter can properly interpret any text, provided she or he also presupposes that it is something at once historical and literary and therefore follows, or conforms to, historical- and literary-critical methods of questioning what it says.

2.4. Once the objective of an interpretation is determined, it proceeds in a more or less critical way, which is to say, more or less deliberately, methodically, and reasonedly.

By "methodically" here is meant, following, or conforming to, the methods necessary to realizing the objective of the interpretation, including the historical- and literary-critical methods that require to be followed, or conformed to, by any interpretation, while "reasonedly" means having and giving reasons for whatever one takes the text to mean and then submitting one's interpretation to critical validation in free and full discussion with all of one's fellow interpreters.

2.5 An interpretation does not absolutize its objective in questioning the text by in any way denying, or even so much as challenging, the propriety of other interpretations having different objectives and, in part, therefore, following different methods.

This means, whatever else it may mean, that a valid interpretation does not state or imply condescendingly that some other way of interpreting the text, though valid, is really only "preparatory" ("*Vorarbeit*") for its "real" interpretation of the text.

So if anything is to be properly called a theological interpretation, as distinct from simply a certain reading, of the Bible, it must be one of the different possible ways of interpreting the biblical writings, and hence satisfy all of the preceding five conditions.

3. By this standard, what Robert Morgan with John Barton means by "a theological interpretation of the Bible" is really nothing of the kind, because it is none of the different things that may be properly called an "interpretation" of the biblical writings.

This is clear, most obviously, because "a theological interpretation of the Bible" in Morgan with Barton's sense of the words is anything but unprejudiced in presupposing its results. The sufficient evidence of this is that, if it were not so, Morgan with Barton could not claim, as they do, that Philip's teaching of the Ethiopian eunuch to read Isaiah "through the Christian master code" (Acts 8:30–35) is "a classic case" of such theological interpretation.[34] Philip's reading of Isaiah is "a classic case" of allegorical interpretation and thus of a thoroughly prejudiced reading of a text that presupposes its results—or, as we may also say, of an interpreter's *not* respecting the sole primary authority of the text itself for any attempt to interpret what it means. Philip obviously knows who the prophet Isaiah has to be speaking about before he ever reads what Isaiah actually says.

It is also clear by the same evidence and reasoning that what Morgan with Barton mean by "a theological interpretation of the Bible" does not really follow, or conform to, the methods of historical- and literary-critical research, including the so-called hermeneutical rules. To be sure, he repeatedly protests to the contrary, insisting that "a theological interpretation" in his sense must respect the integrity of the text and that, although its interpretive aims or priorities are different from those of both historians and literary critics, they nonetheless "include" their aims and follow their methods.[35] But such protest rings hollow if we simply consider again what Morgan with Barton himself represents as "a classic case" of theological interpretation. It was not by including the aims and methods of historical- and literary-critical research, but only by utterly ignoring them, that Philip could assure the Ethiopian eunuch that the one about whom the prophet Isaiah was really speaking is the same Jesus Christ to whom Philip would bear witness as God's decisive self-revelation. For these and other reasons, one can only conclude that what Morgan with Barton means by "a theological interpretation of the Bible" is not properly an "interpretation" of the Bible at all, but at best a "reading" of it that in reality simply uses it and for which, ironically, something beyond it is the real primary authority for "interpreting" its meaning, and hence is the real Bible in the sense of the real *auctoritas canonica*.

4. By the same standard, what I mean by "a theological interpretation of the Bible" is an interpretation, because it is one of the different possible ways in which the biblical writings may be properly interpreted—that way, namely, for which the objective in interpreting them is provided by the very question to which they themselves are addressed concerning our authentic self-understanding as human beings.[36]

Among the questions addressed by some texts—notably those of religion, philosophy, and (to a considerable extent) great literature—is *the* existential question about the meaning of ultimate reality for us and thus about the authentic understanding of our existence. But because all of us as human beings are unavoidably engaged at

---

34. Morgan with Barton, *Biblical Interpretation*, 274; cf. 296.
35. Morgan with Barton, *Biblical Interpretation*, 170.
36. Cf. Ogden, *Doing Theology Today*, 36–51.

some level in asking and answering this existential question, even if only implicitly, it is among the questions that an interpreter may well choose to put to any text and to which any text may be properly interpreted as somehow giving an answer if only indirectly. For both reasons, a reading of the text for which this existential question provides the objective in questioning it is an interpretation of the text in the proper sense of the words; provided, of course, that it also follows, or conforms to, the relevant historical- and literary-critical methods in questioning what the text says.

5. We need to recognize, however, that different as they may be, all proper interpretations of the Bible, as of writings generally, may take place on either of the two levels of living understandingly—i.e., either the primary level of self-understanding and life-praxis or the secondary level of critical reflection and proper theory.

Any interpretation of the biblical writings on the primary level is oriented by some *vital* question, but is constituted as such only by the *intellectual* question about meaning corresponding to that vital question. Thus, for example, what may be called "an existentialist interpretation" of the writings, although remotely oriented by our *existential* question about the meaning of ultimate reality for us, is constituted as such as well as proximately oriented only by the *intellectual* question about what the writings mean existentially—about the possibility for understanding our existence that they somehow set forth as our authentic possibility. By contrast, any interpretation of the biblical writings on the secondary level, although also remotely oriented by some vital question and proximately oriented by the corresponding intellectual question about their meaning, is constituted as such only by the properly *theoretical* question, not simply as such, of course, but in one or another of the different possible ways of asking about meaning theoretically, depending on the different vital interests and questions that may move us to do so. Thus an existentialist interpretation of the biblical writings on the secondary level, although remotely oriented by the same existential question orienting it on the primary level and proximately oriented by the same intellectual question, is constituted as such only by the theoretical question about the existential meaning of the writings. It asks, in other words, what the biblical writings *really* mean existentially about our authentic possibility, as distinct from what they may *appear* to mean or be *thought or said* to mean on the primary level of interpreting them.

6. Assuming, then, that theology is properly distinguished as a certain form of critical reflection—of more rather than less, critical reflection—and therefore takes place, not on the primary level of self-understanding and life-praxis, but on the secondary level of critical reflection and proper theory, we may say that a properly theological interpretation of the Bible can only be a certain form of critical interpretation.

It is that form, namely, that asks what the biblical writings really mean insofar as they address the existential question by which they themselves are oriented, as are all other religious and theological writings, including any proper theological interpretation of the Bible. In sum: a *theological* interpretation of the Bible is a *critical existentialist* interpretation.

NOTEBOOKS

Te totum applica ad textum; rem totum applica ad te.

—JOHANN ALBRECHT BENGEL

"Thyself apply wholly to the text; the thing apply wholly to thyself." Among the many things this pithy prescriptive may be taken to mean, two things concerning the nature and point of interpretation—not just of Scripture, but of any text—stand out.

1. If one asks why the interpreter should apply her- or himself wholly to the text, the answer is that the text alone is the criterion of any interpretation of it strictly and properly so-called. In other words, the only criticism appropriate to interpretation as such is strictly *immanent* criticism—the sole criterion for which is what the text itself actually says and means. By implication, then, acting on the first clause of Bengel's prescriptive entails following only the methods of historical- and literary-critical study, without which the meaning of the text itself cannot be determined.

2. Significantly, what the second clause of the prescriptive calls the interpreter to apply wholly to her- or himself is not the text, but "the thing" ($\equiv$ *res* $\equiv$ *die Sache*) that the text is about. This means, I take it, that, although the nature of interpretation is such that the interpreter must attend to nothing other than the text itself, the point of interpretation is such that the thing the text is about must be wholly brought home to the interpreter her- or himself. The interpreter is reminded, in a word, *tua res agitur*—this thing has to do with thee!

I have two further reflections. I ask, first of all, whether the *res* or thing of the text isn't to be thought of more exactly as its *formal* object than simply as its object. By the "formal object" of the text, I mean its material object, or the thing it is about, but only as the thing is viewed through the optic of the question to which the text itself is addressed. Thus, although the *res* of the text is to be distinguished not only from what the text says, but even from what the text means—namely, as the thing about which the text means whatever it means in saying whatever it says—still, it is this thing only through the optic of the text's own question about it.

My other reflection is that the prescriptive expressed by the second clause can be fully complied with even though one rejects, rather than accepts, what the text means about its formal object. There's not the least question that, just as what Bengel means by "the text" is Scripture, so what he means by "the thing" of the text is Jesus Christ (or, as he would likely say more exactly, the *beneficia Christi*) which he calls the interpreter to apply wholly to her- or himself. But Bultmann quite rightly reminds his readers that, even where an interpreter's response to the text's gift/demand is a disobedient "no" instead of an obedient "yes," her or his interpretation of the text's meaning can still be a valid interpretation. Why? Because a "no" as much as a "yes" involves a real existential encounter with "the thing" of the text.[37]

---

37. Bultmann, *New Testament and Mythology*, 152.

21

Theses on Philosophical Theology

1. Philosophical theology is the critical appropriation (i.e., critical interpretation and critical validation) of religion generically, which is to say, any and all specific religions.

2. The paramount concern of philosophical theology is to critically validate the claim of religion generically (i.e., any and all specific religions) to be authoritative because true, in the sense of corresponding to, and therefore being authorized by, the meaning of ultimate reality for us.

3. Done critically, or in the critical mode, philosophical theology critically appropriates all extant specific religions. Done constructively, or in the constructive mode, philosophical theology critically formulates what any religion would somehow need to express in order to warrant its claim to be authoritative because true.

4. The criteria for philosophical theology's judgments done in either mode are provided by "the 'right' philosophy," or "a correctly verbalized philosophy," and, specifically, by a valid transcendental metaphysics and ethics.

5. The task of philosophical theology done in the constructive mode is to formulate the concept, "the true religion," which is to say, the self-understanding/understanding of ultimate reality in its meaning for us that any specific religion somehow has to express if its claim to be the true religion is a valid claim.

6. "The true religion," so understood, is any specific religion whose self-understanding/understanding of existence is necessarily implied, in substance, by authentic self-understanding in relation to ultimate reality and therefore necessarily implies, even as it is in substance necessarily implied by, a valid metaphysics and ethics.

22

The Task of Philosophical Theology: A Restatement

As I use the term, "philosophical theology" designates one of two types of what I call "theology in general," distinguishing the other type as "theology in the generic/

specific sense."[38] Theology in general, then, I define as a way of appropriating more or less critically the faith and witness—or, in more formal terms, the self-understanding and life-praxis—explicitly mediated by religion. I assume, of course, that only witness, or life-praxis, is ever actually given to be critically appropriated, since faith, or self-understanding, is accessible solely through it.

By "critically appropriating," then, which I use, for the most part, synonymously with "critically reflecting on," I mean the two-step process whereby I make an expression of meaning my own in a more or less critical way, whether positively or negatively. This I do by, first, critically interpreting its meaning and then, second, critically validating at least the more distinctive claims to validity that it either makes or implies. Thus, for example, if the logical analysis required by my critical interpretation of an expression's meaning shows that it makes or implies a claim to truth in some sense, I can make it my own critically only by validating or invalidating its claim, by more or less critically following the procedures indicated for verifying or falsifying it.

The qualification, "more or less critically," is necessary because, in the theological context, as in other contexts of meaning, critical appropriation (or reflection) can and does occur on two different levels. To appropriate, or reflect, critically on either level is to make judgments using certain criteria. But whereas, on the first, less critical level, the criteria used are simply the consuetudinary criteria that have come to be established in some particular context, on the second, more critical level, they are the ultimate (or primal) criteria of experience and reason themselves, as these require to be used in *that* context of meaning. Simply to say, then, that theology in general is the way of performing the "second act" of critically appropriating the "first act" of believing and bearing witness explicitly mediated by religion obscures the fact that there can be and are less, as well as more, critical ways of doing this.

It will be noted, I trust, that I have not defined theology in general simply as critically appropriating, or reflecting on, religion in general. That theology in general indeed includes such appropriating, or reflecting on, religion is not in question. But to proceed as though this is all it includes ignores the fact—or what I take to be the fact—that religion neither is nor could be the only form of culture, or, in Clifford Geertz's sense, "cultural system," through which faith, or self-understanding, necessarily finds expression through witness, or life-praxis. Although "religion," as I understand it, is rightly said to be the *primary* system of concepts and symbols through which faith, or self-understanding, is expressed *explicitly*, theology and philosophy, each in its way, are *secondary* systems, and—even more important—faith, or self-understanding, by its very nature, also finds expression *implicitly* through all the other, so-called secular, cultural systems. In other words, the witness, or life-praxis, explicitly mediated by religion includes not only the explicit witness of religion, but also the implicit witness borne in some way by everything else that human beings think, say, and do insofar as it is mediated explicitly by religion. And this is why the data of theology, which are

---

38. Cf. Ogden, *Understanding of Christian Faith*, 2–4.

actually given for its reflection, include the life-praxis mediated by all forms of culture, secular as well as religious.

Undoubtedly privileged among these data are the explicit data provided by religion, although even they are privileged only with respect to the first step of critically interpreting the *meaning* of the data, as distinct from the second step of critically validating their claims to validity, including, especially, such claim as they may make to be true. Whether or not a religious expression is true depends on the support it receives from *all* the relevant data, secular as well as religious. And yet because the object with which theology in general is ultimately concerned first comes to expression explicitly through religion, the data religion provides are uniquely significant for critically interpreting the meaning of all the relevant data.

But just what is this object with which theology in general is ultimately concerned? My answer is that theology is ultimately concerned with the same object with which faith and witness, self-understanding and life-praxis, and therefore religion and all the other secular cultural systems, are also ultimately concerned in their several different ways—namely, ultimate reality in its meaning for us. By "ultimate reality" I refer to the threefold reality that, on my analysis, we all immediately experience and somehow understand simply by being human: our own existence as essentially related both to others more or less like ourselves and to the one encompassing whole of reality infinitely, qualitatively unlike ourselves, but of which all others, together with us, are so many integral parts. Although, at the deepest level, we all experience and understand this ultimate reality, we do so only in the way in which we experience and understand everything else: fragmentarily and fallibly, and therefore always with unanswered questions.

The most vital of these questions, I hold, is what I and others call "the *existential* question"—or, better, "*the* existential question"—by which I mean the question we all somehow ask and answer, if only implicitly, about the meaning of this ultimate reality for us, what it means for our own possibilities of existing and acting as human beings. How, given the structure of ultimate reality in itself, does it authorize us to understand ourselves, others, and the whole and to lead our lives accordingly (which is to say, authentically and truly because realistically, rather than unrealistically) in keeping with, rather than contrary to, our own deepest self-understanding and the ultimate reality it originally discloses?

It is this existential question about the meaning of ultimate reality for us that I understand to be explicitly asked and answered, in their different ways, both by religion in general, and so by any particular religion, and by what I am calling "theology in general." Religion asks and answers the question on the primary level of self-understanding and life-praxis; theology, on the secondary level of critical reflection and proper theory. This is also to say, I may add, that, on what I regard as the strict and proper use of the phrase, "theology in general" always connotes the more, rather than the less, critical way of appropriating the faith and witness, the self-understanding and life-praxis, that religion mediates explicitly by answering the existential question.

But now, if this will serve as at least a working characterization of theology in general, what is the specific difference of philosophical theology, as one of its two main types, from the other—i.e., theology in the generic/specific sense? The difference, I think, is that philosophical theology's only privileged data are those explicitly provided by religion in general, whereas any theology in the generic/specific sense always has those explicitly provided by this, that, or the other specific religion as its *twice-privileged* data. Of course, even twice-privileged data are privileged only with respect to meaning, not also to validity. Christian theology, for example, necessarily presupposes, as its twice-privileged data, the faith and witness explicitly mediated by the specifically Christian religion. Philosophical theology, by contrast, could and presumably would exist even in the absence of Christianity, or, for that matter, of any other specific religion or religions, provided only that there was at least *some* religion and/or something at least implicitly thought, said, or done about ultimate reality, and that there was at least someone able to ask, and interested in asking, about its meaning and validity in a more, rather than a less, critical way. Therefore, I define "philosophical theology," in the strict and proper sense, as the way of appropriating more, rather than less, critically the faith and witness, or the self-understanding and life-praxis, explicitly mediated by religion in general. And I characterize the task of philosophical theology, in the normative sense of the term I am seeking to clarify, accordingly—as the task of doing precisely this.

This brings us to the further question of just what philosophical theology, so understood, has to do in order to accomplish its task. Complicating this question a bit is the prevalence of the other term, "philosophy of religion." On some uses, it is but another way of saying "philosophical theology." But, on other uses, the two terms refer to different, if closely related, activities, both involved somehow in doing philosophy; and then the question is how, exactly, are the two activities related? Is their relation simply a dualism, both of them being necessary to some other, more inclusive activity, which might be called, say, "the philosophical study of religion"? Or is it better thought of as a duality, in which one of the two activities necessarily presupposes, and, in this sense, includes, the other? My position is that the two terms do indeed refer to two different, though closely related, activities, and that the second way of conceiving their relation is indeed better. And so I think of the task of philosophical theology, normatively understood, as necessarily including that of philosophy of religion.

The latter may be viewed, in fact, as what philosophical theology has to do in order to take the first step in its task of critically appropriating the faith and witness explicitly mediated by religion in general. This is the step, it will be recalled, that I have distinguished as "critical interpretation." But the critical interpretation incumbent upon philosophy generally, and therefore also on philosophy of religion, is distinctive, in that it includes not only critically interpreting the "surface meaning" of the expressions that provide its data, privileged data included, but also, and above all, critically analyzing their "depth structure," so as to clarify the logical *kind* of meaning they express, in its relation to, and its difference from, other logical kinds. On my view, this first step of critically analyzing the meaning of religious expressions is the only step that philosophy of religion, as such, has the task of taking. The further step of critically validating any claims to validity made or implied by religion in general, especially any claim it may make to be true in some sense, is the distinctive task of philosophical theology, although, in the nature of the case, taking the step necessarily presupposes that the first step has already been taken, that the task of philosophy of religion has already been done. Logically, critical validation in any case includes critical interpretation as its own necessary condition, at least if the validation is to be at all just and to have any point. And this means, in the case of philosophical theology, that it necessarily includes philosophy of religion as I have characterized it here.

An additional comment at this point may help to avoid a possible misunderstanding. It may seem natural enough to suppose that, if the task of philosophical theology, or of philosophy of religion, is properly so-designated, it has to be performed by persons who are rightly recognized as holding the office of philosophers, and only by them. But this supposition seems to me to mislead. To be recognized as holding a certain office is one thing; to take up the task of critical reflection that persons holding that office may be reasonably expected to carry out is something else. Why? Well, because one and the same task of critical reflection may often need to be taken up and carried out by persons holding different offices, if indeed they hold any relevant office. After all, we do recognize amateur philosophers as well as those who do philosophy professionally, because it belongs to their office to do it.

In my view, for example, to accomplish the constitutive task of the Christian systematic theologian is, as I have said, impossible without also performing the task of the philosophical theologian and, therefore, for the reasons given, that of the philosopher of religion as well. And I have argued, and would still argue, that the same is true, *mutatis mutandis*, of the constitutive task of religious studies. This is so, at any rate, if "religious studies" designates a single, more or less unified field of critical reflection, instead of simply a loose collection of studies of religion constituted by a number of such fields, and if, as I believe, a better explanation of what unifies them into a single field still waits to be proposed. But this in no way implies that a Christian theologian, or a student in religious studies, is really nothing but a philosopher *masqué*. It implies only that the same logically distinguishable kinds of critical reflection may well have to be done by different persons, whose constitutive tasks of critical reflection are also significantly different. The point is, firstly, to keep your eye on the task, and then to allow ungrudgingly that all who do it, and because of their own constitutive tasks may have to do it—whether philosophers or theologians or students in religious studies— are insofar engaged in doing the same thing, not different things.

There is another point I would like to make about this first thing that philosophical theology has to do in order to accomplish its task, by doing the critical analysis of meaning proper to philosophy of religion. So far as I can see, doing any task of critical appropriation on a more, rather than a less, critical level involves somehow solving what I think and speak of as certain "basic problems." If I am right, one such basic problem in doing philosophical theology more critically by first doing philosophy of religion on the same more critical level is what I call its "hermeneutical" problem, by which I mean—in the terms I used earlier—not only correctly interpreting the "surface meaning" of the expressions of religion in general, but also, and more fundamentally, correctly analyzing the "depth structure," or logical *kind* of meaning, proper to all such expressions as well as to the implicit witness they explicitly mediate.

We are all aware, I take it, that there is anything but consensus about the correct logical analysis of the meaning of religious expressions. Simply to recall such twentieth-century developments as the controversy over "demythologizing" and the "theology and falsification debate," along with more recent developments to which they have subsequently given rise, is to realize how controverted the whole problem of "meaning and truth in religion" has been—and continues to be. But if I really meant what I said earlier about any adequate understanding of the task of philosophical theology unavoidably having to take sides in this controversy, it may seem only fair that I should explicitly acknowledge the logical analysis of religious expressions on which I myself am relying in this attempt to restate my understanding.

So, in the interests of full disclosure, as it were, let me say that the analysis I am presupposing is my own version of what I take Rudolf Bultmann to mean by the "existentialist interpretation" of religious expressions. On this version, such expressions function, above all, to give some explicit answer to what I clarified earlier as *the* existential question. Therefore, they either are or necessarily imply what Bultmann distinguishes as "existential statements." This means that, like other kinds of statements, they purport to be cognitively significant, in that they are about reality in a certain sense and make or imply a certain claim to truth, and are therefore meaningful, if they are, only because they are either true or false in some way . They are distinct from statements of other logical kinds, however, in being "existential" in three senses of the word.

First, they are about existence in the general sense of reality that is concrete as distinct from anything merely abstract. Then, second, the concrete reality they are about is what I have previously distinguished as the ultimate reality of ourselves, others, and the whole. And here "existential" takes on the more specific, emphatic sense of being about concrete reality that understands, or, better, *self*-understands, together with what such self-understanding reality in turn necessarily implies. This emphatic meaning is retained, then, also in the third sense of the word, which brings out *how*, or in what way, religious expressions are about this ultimate reality—namely, concretely, in its meaning for us, as beings who must each somehow understand ourselves and lead our own lives, rather than abstractly, in its structure in itself, as is the case both with metaphysical statements about the same ultimate reality and, in a slightly different way, with the ethical statements that they in turn imply.

But if the existential statements expressed or implied by religious expressions are in this way distinct from metaphysical statements, and not to be confused with them, they are nonetheless inseparable from metaphysical statements, because they necessarily imply them. And the same is true, in its way, of the ethical statements that metaphysical statements themselves imply. This means, naturally, that the existential statements of religion can be true, as they claim to be, only if their necessary metaphysical and ethical implications are also true—or, to say the same thing slightly differently, the only true religion is the religion, or religions, that a true metaphysics and a true ethics implicitly authorize.

So much for how I myself seek to solve the basic hermenutical problem of philosophy of religion, and thus of philosophical theology. I proceed now to the second thing philosophical theology has to do in order to carry out its task of critically appropriating religion in general. This second thing is, of course, the distinctive thing that philosophical theology has to do beyond what is already done by philosophy of religion, doing which, as I have argued, it itself necessarily includes. And this is to take the second step of critically validating the claims to validity that religion in general necessarily makes or implies. This means—for reasons that should be clear, in part, from what I have just said about its basic problem of hermeneutics—that philosophical theology must be concerned, first and foremost, with the claim of religion in general to be true.

Analysis confirms that it is characteristic of a speech act in general to make or imply multiple claims to validity. Some of these claims it shares with other, logically different kinds of speech acts—some, indeed, with all kinds—whereas others are more distinctive, being made or implied just because it is the kind of speech act it is. But not all of its validity claims, even the more distinctive ones, are of equal interest or concern either to philosophy in general or to philosophical theology in particular. Whether what I say is grammatically correct, or is said sincerely, are not questions with which either needs to concern itself, even though claims to be valid in both respects are arguably made or implied by most of the statements I am given to making of whatever logical kind. Nor, I think, does philosophical theology, as such, have any interest in validating the other validity claim that I take to be equally distinctive of religious speech acts in general, along with their claim to be existentially true—namely, the claim that each religion makes or implies to be appropriate to the primal source by which it is explicitly authorized. As much as any theology of the other type, any theology in the generic/specific sense, may be held accountable for also critically validating this other claim to appropriateness, as made or implied by the religion to which it corresponds, the proper concern of philosophical theology is with the validity of the claim of religion in general to existential truth—together, of course, with the claim to cognitive significance that its truth claim necessarily implies. And this must seem all the clearer if one holds, as I do, that the truth sought by philosophy itself, and therefore also by philosophical theology, is the same existential truth that religion in general claims to express.

This is not the place to explain and argue for my normative understanding of philosophy as, in its own way, oriented by the same existential question that religion in general asks and answers explicitly, and also claims to answer truly and hence decisively. So I must settle for making a couple of brief comments simply by way of further clarifying my position.

One is that, although philosophy itself, being the search for wisdom, is distinct from any search for knowledge—is *sapientia*, if you will, as distinct from *scientia*—it nonetheless presupposes, and thus includes, the search for knowledge, and for knowledge of logically different kinds, in pursuing its own distinctive task. One instance of this, I think, is the way in which philosophical theology, as I have argued, necessarily presupposes, and so includes, the knowledge yielded by philosophy of religion. Critically analyzing a certain kind of meaning, as philosophy of religion has the task of doing, can produce a certain kind of knowledge in the strict and proper sense of the word; and this is so even though the philosophical theology that presupposes and includes this knowledge also goes beyond it, not only by also having to validate critically the claim to existential truth that the kind of meaning in question can be known to imply, but also by itself being oriented both remotely and proximately by the existential question, and therefore seeking wisdom rather than merely knowledge. But there are other instances of the same or analogous relationship, as we will learn presently when we see that philosophy and philosophical theology similarly presuppose or include the different kinds of knowledge produced by the critical analyses of metaphysics and ethics respectively.

The other comment I would make is that, although philosophy, like religion, is proximately as well as remotely oriented by, and seeks to answer, the existential question about the meaning of ultimate reality for us, it is so, and does so, in its own way, on its own level. Whereas religion asks and answers the question on the primary level of self-understanding and life-praxis, philosophy asks and answers it on the secondary level of critical reflection and proper theory. In this respect, philosophy is more like theology than religion, being constituted, as distinct from oriented, not by any vital question, not even the existential question, but by theoretical questions about the meaning and validity of primary cultural expressions in general. Still, all three activities, in their different ways, or on their different levels, are oriented by the same existential question, and so make or imply claims to one and the same existential truth. And this means, among other things, that each, in its way, acts (and quite properly should act) as a check or control on the other two in their claims to tell this truth

But we must go on now to our question about just what philosophical theology has to do in order to play its proper part in the common search for the truth about human existence. In order to critically validate the claim to existential truth that religion in general makes or implies, philosophical theology has to determine the criterion by which existential truth in any of its forms requires to be judged. After some hesitation, I have gradually come to think and speak of this criterion in terms used respectively by Rudolf Bultmann and Alfred North Whitehead.

Bultmann speaks in this connection of "the 'right' philosophy," which he describes, significantly, as "simply the philosophical work that endeavors to develop in an appropriate conceptuality the understanding of existence given with human existence."[39] But Whitehead evidently speaks in the same connection when he says, in a striking metaphor, "A correctly verbalized philosophy mobilizes [the] basic experience which all premises presuppose."[40] I find Whitehead's metaphor of mobilizing experience striking because, in any context of meaning, the experience that, in some way, is the only ultimate (or primal) criterion of critical appropriation can never actually function as the criterion unless and until it is "mobilized," by being formulated, "rightly," or "correctly." But be this as it may, the other basic problem that philosophical theology somehow has to solve in addition to its "hermeneutical" problem is what I distinguish as its "criteriological" problem, by which I mean its problem of determining both in principle and in fact what is to function as the criterion of existential truth; or, in other words, the "right," or "correctly verbalized" philosophy.

Actually, the first, "in principle," part of this problem is already solved if philosophical theology does the first thing it has to do by doing philosophy of religion. This is so, at any rate, insofar as philosophy of religion itself, simply by its critical analysis of the logical kind of meaning proper to religious statements in general, already includes, as I would maintain it does, determining two basic things: first, what any particular religion necessarily has to agree with in substance in order to be true—namely, our authentic self-understanding, or true understanding of existence, simply as human beings; and, second, just what self-understanding in principle is authentic, and just what understanding of existence in principle is true—namely, the ones that, in their respective ways, are appropriate to, and therefore authorized by, ultimate reality in its meaning for us as determined by its structure in itself.

But in order to solve the second, "in fact," part of its criteriological problem, philosophical theology has to go beyond doing the logical analysis proper to philosophy of religion to do the other kinds of logical analysis, and thus to seek the other kinds of knowledge necessarily included in philosophy's search for wisdom, or, as may also be said, in its search for existential truth. In other words, the only way philosophical theology can determine what is to function in fact as the "right," or "correctly verbalized," philosophy is to construct it. And this it does, first, by doing metaphysics, by logically analyzing the necessary conditions of the possibility, and, in that sense, the structure in itself, of the ultimate reality of human existence—of ourselves, others,

---

39. Bultmann, *New Testament and Mythology*, 107.
40. Whitehead, *Modes of Thought*, 67.

and the whole; and then, second, by doing ethics, logically analyzing the meaning of this ultimate reality for us, by explicating the first principles of the action it authorizes at both the transcendental level of self-understanding and the categorial level of life-praxis. In this way, philosophical theology determines in fact as well as in principle the criterion of existential truth by which the claim of religion in general requires to be critically validated.

But those same interests in full disclosure that I deferred to earlier require that I say at least a word more about the metaphysics and ethics that I myself am in fact presupposing in answering our question in this way. So far as the metaphysics is concerned, I can characterize it summarily as formally transcendental, rather than categorial, and as materially neoclassical, rather than classical.

It is formally transcendental, rather than categorial, in that it abjures generalizing categorial concepts/terms such as "mind" or "matter" so as to yield supposedly completely general "analogies" for understanding ultimate reality. It proceeds instead by the same logical analysis used to explicate the "depth structure" of all the different kinds of meaning, only now applying this analysis to the deepest structure of all: that of ourselves, others, and the whole, as constituting the necessary conditions of the possibility, not simply of this, that, or the other kind of meaning, but of any meaning at all. Hence the qualifier, "transcendental," which refers, in the first instance, to the utterly general and fundamental concepts/terms by which the logical structure of ultimate reality is critically analyzed and interpreted—not merely "analogically," but literally.

I also think and speak of the transcendental metaphysics I am presupposing as neoclassical, rather than classical, for two reasons: (1) because its key "transcendental" in this sense is "becoming," or "process," rather than "being," understood as the fixed and unchanging; and (2) because it understands the concept/term "God" properly to designate one of two infinitely different, but mutually implying, forms of becoming or process—namely, the eminent or unsurpassable form defining the One (i.e., the one and only *universal* individual) as distinct from the noneminent or surpassable form common to all the many (i.e., the many *particular* individuals and events). But I will say no more here by way of explaining what I mean by this, beyond remarking that, aside from such differences as are entailed by my metaphysics being austerely transcendental, and so in no way categorial, it is not essentially different from what others who have employed the distinction between classical and neoclassical metaphysics—notably, Charles Hartshorne—have already explained it to mean in some detail.

As for the ethics I presuppose, it must suffice to say, simply, that it is the ethics that is determined by, or inferable from, just such a neoclassical, transcendental metaphysics, and to which Franklin I. Gamwell has, in my judgment, contributed so singularly by developing it to illumine basic issues of moral theology and political philosophy in our time.[41]

41. See especially Gamwell, *Divine Good*.

The Task of Philosophical Theology: A Restatement

With this I must conclude my characterization of the task of philosophical theology as I have come to understand it. I now want to develop my restatement just a bit further by briefly discussing two of the more important differences between this understanding and another I have expressed or implied in previous writings, especially an earlier essay on the task of philosophical theology.[42] From my present standpoint, and given my Christian habits of thinking and speaking, it is easy to judge that earlier statement as flawed, in effect, by two intellectual sins that I very much feel the need to repent me of: a sin of commission and a sin of omission respectively.

The more serious sin of commission is expressed by statements such as these: "The task of philosophical theology . . . is integral to philosophy's central task as metaphysics." Or "[A]ll that 'philosophical theology' can properly mean [is] a metaphysics that answers the question of God affirmatively," as well as the several other statements in which I use the phrase, "philosophical theology or theistic metaphysics," as though the two terms were interchangeable. I won't go into all that pains me when I now read these statements and others like them. They all too clearly belong to the period in which I, too, still thought of metaphysics as categorial, rather than austerely transcendental, and was preoccupied with developing and defending a so-called theistic metaphysics—which meant then, of course, a categorial, more exactly, a panpsychic, or psychicalist, metaphysics—as a necessary condition of doing Christian systematic theology adequately.

But the deeper source of my pain is that these statements and others to the same effect serve only to undermine, however unintentionally, what I now take to be, and even then *thought* I took to be, the only adequate analysis of the meaning of religious statements. I refer to the analysis of them as existential statements, which I summarized earlier, it will be recalled, as yielding the conclusion that, although religious statements are inseparable from both metaphysical and ethical statements because they necessarily imply them, they are also distinct from both kinds of statements and are therefore not to be confused with them. The clear implication of this analysis, fully thought out, is that it neither is nor can be the task of *metaphysics* to which that of philosophical theology is integral, however certain it is that metaphysics' task has to be done if philosophical theology's is to be done. Rather, it is the task of *philosophy* of which philosophical theology's is an integral part, in that it, too, in its way and on its level, is supposed to answer *the* existential question that philosophy seeks to answer, as distinct from the merely intellectual questions of metaphysics and ethics. So I can only hope that, if my restatement in this entry serves to take back anything that I urgently need to take back, it will be this unfortunate weakening of one of my own most basic and, I believe, best insights—into, among other things, the task of philosophical theology.

The other sin of omission that I would also confess and repent here is my not having always been as explicit, not to say as emphatic, as I should have been, and as I

---

42. Ogden, *On Theology*, 69-93.

have tried to be in this restatement, about the irreplaceable role of ethics, along with metaphysics, in the second part of philosophical theology's task, as critical validation. By my own long-standing analysis, the existential question to which religion in general is addressed, and by which theology in general, and therefore philosophical theology in particular, also are oriented, has an essential ethical or moral, as well as an essential metaphysical, aspect. And yet, looking back over the record, I find that, for whatever reasons, I have again and again allowed myself to think and speak as though doing metaphysics alone was the sufficient, as well as a necessary, condition of doing philosophical theology. I could plead in extenuation, of course, that, in my view, as in many traditional views, ethics, after all, is (as I have said here) logically dependent on, and, in that sense, determined by, metaphysics. Moreover, I have long been in the fortunate position of always being able to count on Gamwell and others effectively pointing up the essential role of ethics, even if I neglected to do so myself. But they had a right to expect more from me than this, and, supposing that this is an appropriate context in which to do so, I want to say I am sorry I let them down. Given what I hope I have said clearly enough here, I trust there will no longer be any doubt that, on my understanding, doing ethics, as much as (or, in a way, more than) doing metaphysics belongs to philosophical theology's task of critically validating the claim of religion in general to be existentially true.

23

The Criteria of Philosophical Theology

The criteria proper to doing any critical reflection that is more, rather than less, critical are the ultimate (or primal) criteria of human experience and reason as they require to be differentiated to fit the relevant context and the particular case.

Insofar, then, as doing philosophical theology is a way of doing critical reflection more, rather than less, critically, the criteria proper to it can also only be just such ultimate (or primal) criteria—so differentiated as to fit (1) the relevant context of critical reflection oriented proximately as well as remotely by the existential question about the meaning of ultimate reality/human existence for us; and (2) the particular case of critically validating the claim of religion in general to decisive existential authority because it answers this question truly.

Since the claim of religion in general to answer the existential question decisively because truly means that its answer must be credible to human existence, the particular case of critically validating its claim means determining whether or not it really is thus credible.

To determine whether or not religion in general is credible is to determine whether or not it is authorized by common or generically human experience of existence as formulated by "the 'right' philosophy" (Rudolf Bultmann) or "mobilized" by "a correctly verbalized philosophy" (A. N. Whitehead). There are thus two basic problems of doing philosophical theology, both of which have an "in principle" part and an "in fact" part: (1) the hermeneutical problem of critically interpreting the meaning of religion in general; and (2) the criteriological problem of determining what is to count as the "right"/"correctly verbalized" philosophy.

To solve the hermeneutical problem by determining, first, what is to count in principle as the meaning of religion in general is to do philosophy, and, specifically, philosophy of religion, so as to determine the "deep structure"/logical *kind* of meaning proper to religion in general, thereby specifying the hermeneutical principle or method appropriate for critically interpreting it and also providing the conceptuality/terminology necessary to doing so. To determine, then, second, what is to count in fact as the meaning of religion in general is to do hermeneutics by actually interpreting the "surface meaning" of particular religions, reformulating it accordingly, in the conceptuality/terminology that philosophy of religion provides.

To solve the criteriological problem by determining, first, what is to count in principle as the "right"/"correctly verbalized" philosophy is to do philosophy, and, specifically, philosophy of religion, so as to determine (1) what any particular religion has to agree with in substance in order to be credible—namely, our authentic self-understanding/true understanding of existence as human beings; and (2) what self-understanding/understanding of existence is in principle authentic/true—namely, the one that is appropriate to, and therefore authorized by, ultimate reality/human existence in its structure in itself/meaning for us. To determine, then, second, what is to count in fact as the "right"/"correctly verbalized" philosophy also requires doing philosophy so as to determine which philosophy, and, specifically, which metaphysics/ethics, rightly/correctly explicates ultimate reality/human existence in its structure in itself/meaning for us and therewith our authentic self-understanding/true understanding of existence as human beings.

Thus to determine the "right"/"correctly verbalized" philosophy, however, is to do nothing other or less than to construct it, just this being the objective of doing philosophy, whether it be done by professional philosophers or by others—among them, theologians and other students of religion—whose own constitutive tasks require that they do it.

24

A Certain Confusion

There seems to have been, from very early times—as early, possibly, as Parmenides—a certain confusion in the minds of philosophers about just what metaphysics is. On the one hand, it is about the ultimate nature of things as they really are, as distinct from how they appear to be or are said to be. On the other hand, its propositions are not true merely contingently but necessarily, and they may even pretend to a "unique kind of certainty," and to be "exempt from intellectual challenge." Thus they are neither exactly a priori, having what we today would judge to be the empty, noninformative certainty of merely analytic statements, nor exactly a posteriori, having the merely empirical certainty of ordinary statements of fact. It is a fair question, indeed, whether even Whitehead, for one, doesn't still show signs of this venerable confusion—as when he can say in one passage, for example, that "there is no meaning to 'creativity' apart from its 'creatures,' and no meaning to 'God' apart from the 'creativity' and the 'temporal creatures,' and no meaning to the 'temporal creatures' apart from 'creativity' and 'God,'" only to say, just a few pages later, that "the oneness of the universe, and the oneness of each element in the universe repeat themselves to the crack of doom in the creative advance from creature to creature."[43] Whereas in the one passage, whether there are such things as "God," "temporal creatures," and "creativity" is implied to be wholly a matter of meaning, in the other passage, the implication is that it is entirely a matter of fact, contingent on whatever, exactly, is meant by "the crack of doom."

Hartshorne, by sharp contrast, has worked especially hard at clarifying the distinctive character of metaphysics so as to avoid confusing it with the sciences and empirical knowledge generally. Employing, in effect, Leibniz's distinction between "truths of fact (*vérités de fait*)" and "truths of reason (*vérités de raison*)," he has explained how the second include, in addition to the merely analytic, tautological truths of formal logic and mathematics, which, as generally understood, are necessary only conditionally or hypothetically, certain other truths. Being necessary *unconditionally*, these other truths are also existential to the first power, in that they are about concrete reality. Although they are not, strictly speaking, factual truths, they are like factual truths in referring to the concretely real and being measured by it, as it is disclosed through experience. More exactly, they refer to the concretely real as it is disclosed through the properly *existential* aspect of our experience, as distinct from its other, properly empirical aspect—"existential" here meaning existential to the second power,

---

43. Whitehead, *Process and Reality*, 225, 228.

in that the concrete reality referred to is not the immediate reality disclosed by our senses, but the threefold ultimate reality of ourselves, others, and the whole.

Of a piece with this analysis is a theory of modality sharply different from the currently popular view that it is *de dicto*, but not *de re*—a matter entirely of our language and of the rules governing our speaking and writing. As Hartshorne views it, on the contrary, modality is not thus merely grammatical or logical, but also, and in the first instance, *ontological*. Its modes are, first of all, modes of time or process: that which is eternal and so real at any time is necessary, whereas that which is temporal and so real, actually or possibly, only at or during some particular time, is contingent. Thus what is necessary, on this theory, is "the least common denominator" of "pure possibility," or the set of *all* possibilities simply as such—or, as may also be said, what is necessary is what is bound to obtain, no matter what possibility is or is not actualized. In the strict sense, then, metaphysics is to be defined simply as the theory of concreteness, "concreteness" designating the utterly abstract, "transcendental," property belonging to anything concretely real. As such, of course, metaphysics may also be said to be the theory of abstractness, "concreteness" itself being an abstraction that both implies and is implied by all other abstractions comparably (i.e., utterly) abstract, including "abstractness."

Also of a piece with this clarification of metaphysics and its unique logical differences from the other domains of human knowledge is the threefold distinction Hartshorne insists on making between "essence," "existence," and "actuality." In his view, the seemingly intractable controversy about metaphysics, its possibility and necessity, is almost certainly due, in large part, to failing to make this distinction—specifically, the distinction between "existence" and "actuality." An essence may be said to exist if it is actualized *somehow*, the particular *how* of its actualization being insofar undetermined. But, then, properties may be said to exist if they are instantiated *somehow*, the particular *how* of their instantiation being, again, unspecified. In the case, however, of properties that can be instantiated, if at all, only universally, whatever possibilities are or are not actualized, the class of things instantiating them cannot be an empty class. Although any particular member of the class is and must be contingent, the idea that there are at least *some* such members cannot be contingent, but has to be necessary.

With all this in mind, Hartshorne argues, in my judgment, rightly, that metaphysics is to be defined as having to do with, or as making explicit, properties of (contingently existing members of) classes that are necessarily nonempty and therefore exist *somehow*, as the properties of *something*, no matter what. On the other hand, metaphysics, in his view, does not, and cannot, say anything at all about just what possibilities are or are not actualized. Just as knowing that there are secrets need not make one privy to a single one of them, so knowing that all utterly abstract and universal properties cannot fail to be instantiated *somehow* need not include knowing just *how* even one of them happens to be instantiated. It follows from this that the existence of x may be necessary, even though the actuality of x, like that of any other value of the variable, can only be contingent. And this, of course, is just the point that Hartshorne's much-discussed reformulation of Anselm's ontological argument for the existence of God seeks to exploit.

25

Hartshorne on Metaphysics

In Hartshorne's view, metaphysics is understanding of the necessary aspects of being, and of nothing else. All contingent being lies outside its domain. It seeks to understand only two things: (1) the necessary aspect of the one and only necessary being, including the requirement that this being have some contingent aspects or other; and (2) what all contingent beings have in common—these common features of all the many contingent beings themselves being necessary.

The method of metaphysics, accordingly, is not a method for understanding things generally, competitive with the empirical method of science. And yet, in its proper sphere, metaphysical method is as democratic and scientific as the empirical method of science is in its. Both methods rely on common human experience and use common human reason, and so both are, in the broadest sense, "empirical" (better: "experiential") and "rational." But whereas science relies on experience of the contingent details of the world as disclosed especially through visual and tactual sensations, metaphysics relies on the experience of the completely general and essential factors of the world as disclosed by the sense of existence with, and the value of, others, the sense of belonging with others to the whole inclusive of the value of the self as well as of others, and so on. In this sense, metaphysics is the logical interpretation of those depths of experience which are our awareness of being so far as necessary. Significantly, the metaphysical method, no less than the empirical, involves reliance on experience as well as the use of reason. But whereas empirical statements are provisional or hypothetical in that they must be tested observationally against empirical facts, metaphysical statements are provisional or hypothetical in that they are attempted formulations of "ultimate but obscure intuitions." Thus the means of testing or judging in the one case is empirical observation, while in the other it is the attempt to become conscious of a priori necessity, of what is necessarily presupposed by, and is therefore to be analyzed out of, any experience or any thought whatsoever.

Metaphysics, Hartshorne says, is "the study seeking necessary truths about existence."[44] Strictly speaking, "there is but *one* metaphysical, innate, or strictly universal and necessary idea or principle, *concreteness* (containing internally its own contrast to abstractness)."[45] Accordingly, metaphysics may be defined as "the unrestricted or completely general theory of concreteness."[46] It has the task of elucidating what we can and cannot mean by any of our basic concepts. It does not concern questions such as "What are the facts?" but "What is it to be a fact?" The category of fact, not any particular application of the category, is the issue (better: the *transcendental* "fact," not any particular application of the transcendental, is the issue).

Metaphysics, Hartshorne says, asks the question, "What is it to be a fact?" My answer, as distinct from his, is, "To be a fact is not only to be included in other facts, including *the* fact, the all-inclusive fact, but also to include them—the many ordinary facts as well as the one extraordinary fact: some by a definite or determinate necessity, others by an indefinite or indeterminate necessity."

Of course, if Hartshorne is right that there is really only one metaphysical question, even as there is really only one metaphysical idea—"concreteness"—I could say just as well that the question my metaphysics answers is "What is concreteness?" or "What is it to be concrete?", which—because concreteness includes its own contrast with abstractness—also includes asking and answering these questions: "What is abstractness?" or "What is it to be abstract?" In other words, I take for granted that "factuality" is to "concreteness" as "a fact" is to "a concrete," understanding "concrete" as so used nominatively rather than adjectivally.

Metaphysics is a matter both of analyzing our most fundamental concepts and of so relating them that they are all fully taken account of and coherently related to one another. The significance of the fundamental concept "God," rightly understood, is that it is capable both of taking full account of all other fundamental concepts and of coherently relating them—indeed, unifying them into one fundamental concept. In this sense, "God" is, as Hartshorne says, "the very pinnacle of metaphysical knowledge," even while God as concretely actual, and thus as distinct from the utterly abstract essence-existence to which the concept as such refers, "utterly transcends metaphysical analysis." In this sense, I would very much want to say with Hartshorne that "we can conceive that God is greater than we can conceive. Any concrete reality whatsoever is greater than we can exhaustively conceive. This is so, in a radically unique

---

44. Hartshorne, *Anselm's Discovery*, 17.
45. Hartshorne, *Zero Fallacy*, 102.
46. Hartshorne, *Creative Synthesis and Philosophic Method*, 32, 24.

sense, with the divine actuality, for it is the adequate integration of all actuality as so far actualized."[47]

~

Hartshorne argues that we have to live and think as though the past were indestructibly real, for otherwise "fact" would have no definite meaning. "God" merely makes this necessary idea more intelligible; that's all.

I would prefer to argue slightly differently: we have to live and think as though there is an objectively real world, including the past and the future as well as the present, that is independent of our fragmentary living and thinking, because otherwise "reality" would have no objective, impartial meaning. The strictly transcendental concept of God as the one universal individual that is real for everything and for which whatever is is real in turn only makes this necessary thought more intelligible.

26

Metaphysics and Logic

Logicians generally agree that existential statements can be true only contingently rather than necessarily. But this view, arguably, needs further distinction, refinement, qualification—to the effect that *only existential statements on the lower logical levels*—i.e., those mentioning definite particulars or (more or less) special qualities of particulars (whether individual, specific, generic, or categorial proper)—*are contingently true*. By contrast, existential statements on the highest logical level, i.e., those that do *not* mention definite particulars or any (more or less) special qualities of particulars, but are about "transcendentals," are *not* contingently true, but true necessarily, or a priori.

~

It is widely held that there cannot be merely conceptual or nonempirical reasons for asserting the existence of anything, at least apart from elements in an abstract system like real numbers.

---

47. Hartshorne, *Anselm's Discovery*, 85.

But to this it may be objected that it is not existence but actuality that always and in principle transcends conceptual necessity. That the property to which a concept refers is *somehow* instantiated in concrete actuality is the "existence" of the property. But just *how*, or in *what* concrete form, it is instantiated is its actuality. Thus, for example, that the property to which the concept "concrete particularity" refers must be instantiated somehow may well be a nonempirical or merely conceptual necessity, because there could not not be some concrete particulars. And so, too, as Anselm discovered, the concept of "God" may likewise be existential a priori or by necessity. But this applies only to the *somehow* actualized, not to the *how*, or the concrete form, in which the property is actualized, whether "concrete particularity" or "God." At the level of utter abstractions rightly termed "transcendentals," merely being actualized or instantiated somehow is not contingent or empirical, but necessary or conceptual.

This, arguably, is the real issue concerning metaphysics. Again and again, controversy over the issue ignores the distinction between existence and actuality—i.e., the indefinite "*somehow* instantiated" and the definite "*how* of instantiation," as well as the related distinction between such utter abstractions as "concreteness" or "God" and all more specific abstractions that are not instantiated necessarily, but only contingently, because being instantiated excludes the instantiation of other abstractions that are similarly more specific.

That the most general classes of facts, such as "concrete actualities," are nonempty is a conceptual necessity. In no way, *pace* Wittgenstein, does this obliterate the distinction between conceptual and transconceptual truths. It simply treats the concept of "necessarily instantiated" as a conceptual truth applicable to all abstractions at the highest level of generality. Thus, in addition to the distinction, conceptual and factual, or merely contingent, there must be the distinction between utterly abstract, and so noncompetitive or nonexclusive concepts, and less abstract, and so competitive or exclusive concepts, as well as the distinction between necessarily and contingently instantiated concepts—these additional distinctions all being only verbally different ways of formulating one and the same distinction.[48]

Logic, arguably, cannot deal with a simply empty universe. Therefore, the widest class of concrete entities cannot be empty. There has to be at least this one necessarily nonempty class, even if its class properties could be instantiated in quite other instances than any in which they happen to be instantiated. But, then, properties that are universally applicable, because they are properties of this widest class, cannot be uninstantiated.

---

48. Cf. Hartshorne, *Insights and Oversights*, 297–98.

Given the necessary nonemptiness of the widest class, or the necessary instantiatedness of the universally applicable properties of this class, we have all we need for necessary existence, including the necessary existence of God. True, it is essential to the distinction of types between any property and its instances that the latter can exist or occur only contingently. But it is logically possible to distinguish between the property "deity" (≡ *deitas* ≡ ἡ θειότης) and its necessarily contingent instances, excluding polytheism even as a possibility, and affirming instead the necessary existence of one and only one universal individual.

The key to doing this is recognizing that the most concrete particular entities are not changing and enduring individuals, but becoming and perishing events, or "states" of individuals. According to this understanding, the existence of a changing and enduring individual is the actuality of a certain sort of event-sequence, which need not be defined as such extensionally, but can be defined intensionally, simply by reference to the chief defining characteristic(s) of the sequence, without needing to refer to all the particular events in it. This holds good, and (if certain well-known antinomies are to be avoided) must hold good also of the universal individual—which is to say, the property "deity," Supreme Greatness, or Unsurpassability, cannot be contingently but only necessarily instantiated, just as the class of the contingent instances of this property must be necessarily, not contingently, nonempty. Thus, although any of the instances, or "states," instantiating the property "deity" must occur contingently, the fact that there are some such instances and that any two of them are "genidentical," or in personally ordered sequence with one another as states of one and the same universal individual, can and must be necessary.

It may be objected to this that logic finds the idea of necessary instantiation valid at most of properties that can be applied universally. But although the property "deity" indeed individuates one, and only one, universal individual, there is still a definite, albeit unique, sense in which it can apply universally. Just as any entity is and must be identical with itself, so any entity is and must be related to the universal individual, or to deity, as its sole primal source and its sole final end, its Creator and its Consummator. Relativity to the universal individual in this twofold sense is as essential to the self-identity of any entity as its own individuality. And to deny this is not just to deny the existence of the universal individual, but even its possibility. The necessary nonemptiness of the class of instances of deity, or states of the universal individual, is related to the necessary nonemptiness of the only apparently wider class of events, or states, in general (i.e., concrete entities as such), such that, for any ordinary event or state of a particular individual, there must be some extraordinary event or state of the universal individual that is its only primal source and its only final end.

So, if there must be concrete entities of some kind, as logic requires, these entities must be entities that are created and consummated by the universal individual, the only alternative to this inference being rejection of the very idea of deity as either unclear or incoherent, and so only verbally, not conceptually, an idea.

Metaphysics and Logic

∽

The metaphysician does what the logician would do if she or he gave serious thought to the a priori or strictly necessary traits of her or his first-level entities. And the metaphysician does something else the logician would do if she or he were to investigate, instead of simply assuming, a completely general theory, sometimes referred to as a "cognitional theory," of what it is to experience or know anything whatsoever.[49] For these reasons, metaphysics may be thought and spoken of with Hartshorne as "'logic' in a broad sense of the word."

∽

Hartshorne speaks of metaphysical questions as being "pseudo-factual, or in a broad sense logical," and says "Not, 'Does [God] exist with some world or other[?],' but only, 'With what world?' is the empirical or observational question. The rest is logic, in a broad sense, not fact."[50]

∽

Question: What, exactly, is "logic in a broad sense," or "in a broad sense logical"?

Answer: "Logic in a broad sense," or "in a broad sense logical," is thought concerned with transcendental conditions of the possibility of fact, or of the factual.

In other words, there are certain necessary presuppositions of any fact, or of anything factual, that can be denied only at the price of incoherence or self-refutation, or, in the sense that the denial as a performance, and so itself a fact, implicitly asserts these presuppositions, even while explicitly denying them. "Logic in a broad sense," then, is a way of saying that every factual assertion necessarily presupposes a nonfactual and yet existential context, which must be asserted implicitly by any factual assertion whatsoever, even one that may explicitly deny this same context. As itself a fact, the denial implies as the necessary condition of its possibility the same existential context necessarily implied by any and all facts whatsoever, even merely conceivable facts. In this sense, "self-understanding is the issue"; "it is a conceptual question, a question of self-understanding, clarity and consistency."[51]

---

49. Hartshorne, *Creative Synthesis and Philosophic Method*, 32–33.
50. Hartshorne, *Natural Theology*, 89, 102.
51. Hartshorne, *Natural Theology*, 88, 85.

Hartshorne talks about "logical in a broad sense that includes informal as well as formal logic."[52] But what, exactly, does he mean by this?

Elsewhere he refers to "the idea of logical necessity" as allowing of "the distinction between those cases which involve [no] more than the constants of formal logic as now recognized, and those which involve meanings additional to purely logical ones." In the same vein, he distinguishes elsewhere "the sharp definition of necessary or 'analytic' used by formal logicians," according to which "a proposition, to be analytic, has to be fully stateable through the 'constants of formal logic.'" By contrast with this, there are propositions that are logically necessary given certain "meaning postulates"—i.e., given the meanings of the terms involved, which are either implicit or explicit. Thus Hartshorne says, "'God does not exist' is not contradictory in the purely formal sense in which 'P & $\sim P$' is so."[53] I take it that "God does not exist" is an example of a proposition that is contradictory and thus logically impossible in a broad, rather than in a strict, sense of "logical."

Another such proposition is "Nothing exists," whose contradictory "Something exists" is logically necessary. Significantly, however, Hartshorne claims that it is "semantically, and hence in a broad sense logically, necessary; since its denial [i.e., "Nothing exists"] violates the rules relating concepts to reality."[54] That Hartshorne distinguishes "semantically" from "purely formal or syntactical," and thus "syntactically," suggests that this is yet another way of formulating what he means by "logical in a broad sense."

∾

Concerning the whole issue of "logic(al) in a broad sense," distinctions may be made between three levels: (1) syntactic; (2) semantic; and (3) pragmatic.

Given these distinctions, one may then say, first, that the contradictories of true mathematical and logical assertions, in the usual narrow sense of "logical," are self-contradictory, even on the syntactic level; second, that the contradictories of true strictly metaphysical assertions, or, if you will, logical assertions in the by no means usual broad sense of "logic(al)," are self-contradictory on the semantic level; and third, that the contradictories of true broadly metaphysical assertions are self-contradictory on the pragmatic—even if not on the semantic—level.

Finally, one may say, in terms of John Passmore's distinction, first, that contradictories of assertions that are self-contradictory on either the syntactic level or the semantic level are, in their different ways, "*absolutely* self-refuting"; and, second, that

---

52. Hartshorne, "John Hick," 165.
53. Hartshorne, "John Hick," 160, 157.
54. Hartshorne, "John Hick," 162–63.

contradictories of assertions that are self-contradictory on the pragmatic level are "*pragmatically* self-refuting."

∾

Logic in the broad sense, as the a priori theory of reasoning or rational inference, includes:

(1) an a priori theory of reality as such, of what it is to be something thinkable and knowable; and

(2) an a priori theory of thinking and knowing as such, of what it is to think or know something.

In this way, metaphysics, as comprising just these two kinds of a priori theory, does what logic would do, were the logician to give serious thought to the a priori or strictly universal traits of her or his first-level entities and to what it is to think or know them.

27

Wittgenstein Says . . .

In one of his several different statements about metaphysics, Wittgenstein says: "Philosophical investigations: conceptual investigations. The essential thing about metaphysics: it obliterates the distinction between factual and conceptual investigations."[55] I take it that one is justified in replacing the colons in these two sentences by "are," in the case of the first, and "is that," in the case of the second. But if this does, in fact, yield a correct interpretation of his meaning, Wittgenstein's statement is, in reality, what Stephen Toulmin perceptively identifies as a "disguised comparison"—in fact, two disguised comparisons.[56]

"Philosophical investigations *are* conceptual investigations." That philosophical investigations are, in an important respect, *like* conceptual investigations seems clear enough. For whether or not a philosophical statement is true is to be decided purely conceptually, by conceptual (or logical) analysis. In this respect, philosophical statements are significantly like merely analytic or tautological statements, whose truth is similarly not a factual, but a self-answering, question. But "are like" statements,

---

55. Wittgenstein, *Zettel*, 458.
56. Toulmin, *Examination of the Place of Reason*, 190–93.

merely analytic, are one thing, simply "are" analytic statements, something else, so the comparison that Wittgenstein's first sentence invites one to make is not open, but disguised, and the statement it expresses, insofar apt to mislead.

The same is true of his second sentence: "The essential thing about metaphysics *is that* it obliterates the distinction between factual and conceptual investigations." What is it, exactly, to "obliterate" a distinction? Considering the special force of "obliterate" in comparison with synonyms such as "abolish," "exterminate," "extinguish," "eradicate," or "extirpate," one would presumably say that to obliterate is to destroy, or to do away with, so as to leave no trace of. But what does metaphysics actually do with "the distinction between factual and conceptual investigations"? Arguably, it does not destroy the distinction without a trace, but simply denies that it is exhaustive. The distinction between "factual" and "conceptual" remains just as intact as it ever was because, although metaphysical statements are, in different respects, significantly *like* both of these other kinds of statements, they are, in reality, of neither kind, but are *sui generis*.

Like factual statements, they are meaningful, if at all, only because they refer to reality beyond themselves. But their referent is not properly "fact," in the literal sense of something made or produced, and therefore merely contingently the case, but rather "factuality," in the sense of the utterly abstract structure belonging to any even conceivable fact, and therefore something never made or produced, or even producible, but strictly necessary. And this, of course, is why metaphysical statements are also significantly like conceptual statements that are merely analytic, and so true, not contingently, but necessarily. But, again, their likeness to conceptual statements in this respect in no way entails that they simply are conceptual statements. For whereas merely analytic statements are properly analyzed as only hypothetically true, or true only conditionally, metaphysical statements (if true) are true necessarily and *un*conditionally, and so are not even meaningful unless they are categorical, their reference to reality always being successful.

One final point: although Wittgenstein's comparisons *as disguised* are only too apt to mislead, *as comparisons*—and so *a fortiori* as *open* comparisons—they can be importantly illumining.

28

Logical Structure, Not Metaphors

I find it interesting that Hartshorne speaks at one point of "the rational structure apart from which no conceptions can have meaning."[57] Is it far-fetched to say that he uses "rational structure" here to the same effect that John Duns Scotus uses "*ratio formalis*"?

∾

Significantly, Hartshorne can also speak of the concrete—more exactly, of what the concrete requires and has *qua* concrete—noncategorially, without using any of his usual categorial terms: "experience," "sentience," "feeling," and so on. Thus he says, for example, "what the concrete requires and has is rich internal relatedness or relativity. Only the abstract can be independent of other things, even though it must be embodied in some concrete thing or other."[58]

29

On Seeing "More"

I have been struck by what Willi Marxsen says about the believer's "seeing," or "knowing," something "more" than the nonbeliever, although not anything "other." It suddenly occurred to me that something analogous could be said about what the metaphysician "sees" or "knows." She or he likewise "sees," or "knows," not anything "other," but rather something "more," more than what any and all of us can "see" and "know" empirically.

If, as Hartshorne says, the metaphysical is not *alongside* the physical but *in* it, and, as I would add, is to be experienced existentially and discerned, or known, by "analysis of presuppositions," or "transcendental deduction," then there is certainly an

57. Hartshorne, "Religion in Process Philosophy," 255.
58. Hartshorne, *Divine Relativity*, 100.

analogy between discerning, or knowing, the metaphysical and discerning, or knowing, the existential meaning, or significance, of a person or event. In both cases, the something "more" lies, not in what can be seen or known empirically, or empirical-historically, since if it did, it would not be something "more," after all, but merely something "other," which is to say, something alongside, although for that very reason, still on the same level—or of the same kind—as what is visible or knowable empirically, or empirical-historically.

On the other hand, the something "more" that is seen or known is, in both cases, something "real." This is so, at any rate, if the meaning or significance of things for us is, as John Post says, "nonreductively determined" by the being of things in themselves; for then it is, in its own way, real, and "practical propositions" about it, being precisely propositions, are capable of being true or false (Bochenski).[59] Similarly, the structure in itself of anything concretely real, although not itself concrete, but rather abstract—indeed, as utterly abstract as only "transcendentals" (and, in their way, "existentials") can be—is also real. And yet neither way of being real is the way in which things that can be asserted empirically, or empirical-historically, are real.

Given, then, my basic understanding of myth as involving a "category mistake," one may say that the mistake myth makes simply as and because it is myth is (mis-)representing what is, in reality, "something 'more'" in an idiom fit only for representing "something 'other.'"

30

Metaphysics and the Inner Aspect of Things

Metaphysics, in the sense in which I understand it, proceeds on the assumption that, just as we ourselves have an inner as well as an outer aspect, so also does anything else that, like ourselves, is concrete and singular, be it an event or an individual. On this assumption, then, metaphysics seeks to explicate what is necessarily presupposed and implied about this inner aspect of things by anything that we think, say, and do in somehow understanding ourselves, others, and the whole and leading our lives accordingly.

This distinction between the inner and the outer aspects of things is obviously of a piece with the distinctions I make between (1) the "existential" and the "empirical" aspects of experience and reality and their "vertical" and "horizontal" dimensions;

---

59. Post, *Faces of Existence*.

and (2) "ultimate reality" and "immediate reality," or the "ultimate" and the "immediate" settings of self-understanding and life-praxis.

31

Metaphysics in the Broad/Strict Senses

Metaphysics in the broad sense is more or less critical understanding of ultimate reality in its structure in itself, as distinct from its meaning for us.

"Ultimate reality" refers to the threefold reality of ourselves, others, and the whole, and thus to our own existence together with the necessary conditions of its possibility, which include *strictly* ultimate reality—i.e., the necessary conditions of the possibility of *any and all* existence.

Metaphysics in the strict sense is more or less critical understanding of strictly ultimate reality in its structure in itself, as distinct from its meaning for us. "Strictly ultimate reality" refers to the reality of the concrete whole and of any of its concrete parts simply as such, and thus to the necessary conditions of the possibility of any and all existence, including our own.

The necessary conditions of the possibility of our own existence as self-understanding existence, and thus as distinct from any and all (non-self-understanding) existence, may be called "existentials," even as the necessary conditions of the possibility of any and all (even non-self-understanding) existence, including our own, may be called "transcendentals."

That we exist is sufficient evidence of the existence or reality of all of the necessary conditions of the possibility of our existence as well as of any and all existence. Our existence is also sufficient evidence of our at least implicit understanding of all such necessary conditions, existence in our case being precisely existence in the emphatic sense of *existence that understands* at the high level of thinking and speaking exhibited by human behavior.

༄

Whereas "metaphysics in a *broad* sense" includes designating whatever is and must be present whenever and wherever any existent in the emphatic sense is present, and thus *existentiality* as such, "metaphysics in a *strict* sense" designates only whatever is and must be present whenever and wherever anything real in any sense whatever is present, and thus *transcendentality* as such.

What makes the strictly metaphysical *strictly* metaphysical?

The strictly metaphysical is made *strictly* metaphysical by being a necessary condition of the possibility of *anything whatsoever*. So what makes the strictly metaphysical *strictly* metaphysical is that it is properly *transcendental*.

Whitehead says:

> The many become one, and are increased by one. . . . Also there are two senses of the one—namely, the sense of the one which is all, and the sense of the one among the many. . . . We are each of us, one among others; and all of us are embraced in the unity of the whole. . . . The oneness of the universe and the oneness of each element in the universe, repeat themselves . . . in the creative advance from creature to creature, each creature including in itself the whole of history and exemplifying the self-identity of things and their mutual diversities.[60]

Hartshorne says:

> Metaphysics is the study of the necessary aspects of being, and of nothing else. All contingent being is outside the province of metaphysics. All individual beings except God are contingent, and so are all specific kinds of beings. There is even a side of God's nature that is contingent, the side which is relatively, not absolutely, perfect. Metaphysics does only two things, it describes the necessary aspect of the one and only necessary being, including the requirement that this being have some nonnecessary aspects or other, and it describes what all contingent beings have in common (for these common features are necessary and what distinguishes them generically from the necessary being, even in its contingent aspects).[61]

I say:

By "metaphysics" in his statement, Hartshorne obviously understands only what I distinguish as "metaphysics in the strict sense."[62] His delimitation of "the province of metaphysics," so understood to doing only "two things," evidently fits closely with (1) Whitehead's statement that there are "two senses" of the one—"namely, the sense of the one which is all, and the sense of the one among the many"; and (2) Whitehead's corresponding distinction between "the oneness of the universe and the oneness of each element in the universe."

---

60. Whitehead, *Process and Reality*, 21, 228; Whitehead, *Modes of Thought*, 150–51.
61. Hartshorne, "Philosophy of Democratic Defense," 164–65.
62. Cf. Ogden, "Criterion of Metaphysical Truth," 47–48.

Taking the two philosophers' statements together, I say that metaphysics in the strict sense, as "the study of the necessary aspects of being, and of nothing else," is the study of (1) concrescence, understood as designating the one strictly necessary process whereby "the many become one, and are increased by one"; and (2) the two disjunctive—indeed, "infinitely, qualitatively different"—forms of concrescence that are likewise strictly necessary—i.e., "the one . . . in the sense of the one which is all," whose "oneness" is "the oneness of the universe," and "the one . . . in the sense of the one among the many," whose "oneness" is "the oneness of each element in the universe."

As for what I distinguish as "metaphysics in the broad sense," I say that it includes, in addition to metaphysics in the strict sense just explained, study of the necessary aspects of that one among the many whose oneness is that of an "element in the universe," but who also *is* in an emphatic sense. Such a one not only exists, but also *understands* its existence at the high level instanced by the thinking and speaking—what Hartshorne calls "the symbolic capacity"—exhibited by human existence. This could also be put analogously to the way in which Hartshorne explains elsewhere what it means for an animal to have rights in a "strong," or "emphatic," sense. An animal has rights in this sense, he argues, "for whom there is such a thing as the concept of right."[63] So, too, I could say, one exists in the emphatic sense that metaphysics in the broad sense also studies for whom there is such a thing as the concept and symbol of existence in the emphatic sense, which is to say, the concept and symbol of self, others, and the whole.

32

Material/Formal Object

The scholastics commonly distinguish between two interrelated moments in any question:

(1) the material object (*objectum materiale quod* ≡ *das Befragte*): the thing asked about; and

(2) the formal object (*objectum formale quo* ≡ *das Gefragte*): the respect or aspect of the thing asked about, or the optic or viewpoint from which it is objectified.

---

63. Hartshorne, *Creativity in American Philosophy*, 233.

(In appropriating this distinction, Martin Heidegger further distinguishes the heuristic object (*das Erfragte*): what the inquirer anticipates obtaining by viewing the thing asked about in this respect or aspect, or from this viewpoint.)

In my view, similarly, while the material object of religion and metaphysics, which is to say, the ultimate reality of self, others, and the whole, is the same, their formal objects are different. Whereas religion asks about the material object concretely, or *existentially*, in its meaning for us, for our self-understanding and life-praxis, metaphysics asks about the same material object abstractly, or *intellectually*, in its structure in itself, independently of how we understand ourselves and lead our lives.

∽

The conditions necessary to the constitution of a religion and of a metaphysics are also respectively different. Whereas the constitution of a metaphysics requires nothing more than human existence simply as such, and so the original *presentation* of ultimate reality through the experience and understanding of each and every human being, the constitution of a religion requires, in addition, some human being(s) qualified in a special way—namely, through the experience and understanding of a "revelation" (i.e., a special/decisive *re-presentation* of ultimate reality in its meaning for us).

This means that the formal object of a religion, as distinct from that of a metaphysics, is duplex, in that it has an existential-*historical* aspect as well as an existential-*transcendental* aspect. The first aspect is related to the second as the explicit is related to the implicit, or as ultimate reality as specially/decisively *re-presented* is related to ultimate reality as originally *presented*.

So it is that the constitution of a religion, as distinct from that of a metaphysics, involves not only one correlation, but *two*: not only the correlation between its subject side and its (formal) object side, but also the correlation already involved in its (formal) object side, itself between its two aspects: its existential-transcendental aspect and its existential-historical aspect—or, in Clodovis Boff's terms, "the order of its *constitution*" and "the order of its *manifestation*."[64] In point of fact, the constitution of a religion, as distinct from that of a metaphysics, involves yet a third correlation: between its explicit primal source—i.e., its subject side experiencing its formal object side as such—and the primary authority, or "canon," authorized by that primal source (cf. note 18, "What Constitutes a Religion?").

---

64. Boff, *Theology and Praxis*, 97–98.

33

Explicating Metaphysics—Formally and Materially

I wonder whether I couldn't make my case more effectively if I were to distinguish more systematically, and therefore more clearly and consistently, between (1) explicating metaphysics *formally* and (2) explicating metaphysics *materially*.

The first way of explicating metaphysics would require clarifying "being," or "reality," more or less as I have done in my "Ten Theses" (note 58, "Logical-Ontological Type Distinctions in Outline: Ten Theses"), by focusing on "the ontological difference," in the sense of the difference between "a being," or "a reality" (*das Seiende, ein Seiendes*) and "being," or "reality," or "reality as such" (*das Sein, die Seiendheit*). Ideally, this would be done so as to leave room for any attempt—classical, revisionary, neoclassical, or what have you—to fill in this purely formal clarification by explicating some material answer to the question of "What *is* 'being,' or 'reality'?"

The second way, then, would require arguing for this, that, or the other material answer to this question—including my neoclassical answer, according to which "being" is either concrete or abstract, and concrete being is "becoming" (or "concrescence"), while abstract being is the necessary conditions of the possibility of "becoming" (again, "concrescence")—the most abstract of which conditions are, in the case of metaphysics in the strict sense, what I distinguish as "transcendentals," and, in the case of metaphysics in the broad sense," "existentials" as well as "transcendentals."

An instructive example of proceeding in these two ways—albeit for historical/hermeneutical rather than systematic purposes—is offered by Ivor Leclerc's introductory exposition of *Whitehead's Metaphysics*. Leclerc argues that Whitehead entirely agrees with Aristotle in understanding metaphysics as the attempt to conceive "a complete fact," or "a complete existence." "By 'a complete fact' Whitehead means precisely what Aristotle meant by the *that* which '*is* in this sense.'" Thus, "[w]hen Whitehead says the problem [*sc.* of metaphysics] is 'to conceive a complete fact' he means thereby what Aristotle meant in declaring the problem to be: 'what that is which *is* in this sense [*sc.* of οὐσία].'"[65] But, of course, as Leclerc then goes on to show at length in the rest of his book, Whitehead's *solution* to the problem materially differs from Aristotle's precisely because he takes "a complete fact," or a "fully existent entity," to be "an actual entity," as distinct from "a particular and actually existing thing," which is to say, the enduring individual or "substance" that Aristotle takes οὐσία properly to refer to. So, whether Leclerc ever explicitly makes the distinction between "formal" and "mate-

---

65. Leclerc, *Whitehead's Metaphysics*, 17–18.

rial"—and I have not confirmed that he does—he certainly employs it, or something like it, in arguing for his understanding of Whitehead's relation to "the great philosophical tradition."

∽

Hartshorne speaks in one place, significantly, of "mere being or somethingness."[66] I ask, why wouldn't it be entirely appropriate to pursue my project of an austerely transcendental metaphysics in straightforwardly Aristotelian terms as precisely the logical analysis of "being *qua* being," or "somethingness *qua* somethingness"?

This would be done on the understanding: (1) that "something exists" is an unconditionally necessary statement; (2) that "something" is to be analyzed in terms of two ultimate contrasts or disjunctions between (a) "concrete" and "abstract," and then, in the case of concrete somethings, (b) "unsurpassable" and "surpassable"; (3) that neither of these ultimate contrasts in any way involves dualism, but only duality, because, in their respective contrasts, "concrete" and "unsurpassable" are each the inclusive or "overlapping" concept, while "abstract" and "surpassable" are each the included or "overlapped"; and (4) that metaphysics, therefore, is properly pursued as the logical analysis of concreteness, unsurpassable as well as surpassable, because concreteness is the inclusive form of "mere being or somethingness," while abstractness is its included form.

Of course, the analysis of concreteness would be, in the nature of the case, the analysis of concrescence as "process": *the* process whereby, as Whitehead puts it, "the many become one, and are increased by one"—i.e., grow together into a "concrete" (*concretum*). In other words, "concreteness" is to "concrescence" somewhat as, in Whitehead's terms, "superject" is to "subject," the latter understood, in Hartshorne's phrase, as "self-relating, all-integrating." So a properly transcendental metaphysics pursued as the logical analysis of "being *qua* being," on the understanding that being in its inclusive form is precisely concreteness, would turn out to be the logical analysis of the process of "concrescence"—and, in that sense, or for that reason, would be a "process metaphysics," or as I prefer to say, a "neoclassical metaphysics."

Still and all, it would be a metaphysics squarely in the Aristotelian tradition, whose principal differences from its predecessors in that tradition, in addition to its controlling neoclassical instead of classical insights, would be (1) its clear and sharp distinction between the necessary truths sought by metaphysics and the contingent truths sought by the special sciences, scientific cosmology included; and (2) its austerely transcendental, in no way categorial, conceptuality/terminology.

---

66. Hartshorne, "God and the Meaning of Life," 167.

I could say, using my terms, that the question Aristotle addresses in his metaphysics is, "What is the concrete as concrete? Or what is meant, properly, by the abstraction 'concreteness'?"

Of course, this is to use "concrete" and "concreteness" as I use them, and as Aristotle himself uses οὐσία—namely, to refer to "a complete fact," to what, as he says, requires nothing but itself in order to exist, and what everything else requires in order to exist.

Aristotle's answer to his question is, "The concrete in the sense of 'a complete fact' is a substance," or, as I would translate in my terminology, "an individual." My answer, on the contrary, is, "The concrete in the sense of 'a complete fact' is not a substance, or an individual, but an event."

34

Being and beings

It lies in the nature of things that there cannot be Being without beings, and that there cannot be beings without both the One and the many: the one and only universal, necessarily existing being that includes all beings; and the many particular, contingently existing beings that are all included in the one. In this way, the One and the many necessarily imply one another, although this symmetry presupposes an even more fundamental asymmetry. Whereas what any of the many particular beings necessarily implies is the one and only One, what the one universal being necessarily implies is no particular being, but only *some* such beings, any of which exists, if it exists, only contingently. In other words, although the One and the many are interdependent, any of the many is *absolutely* dependent on the One, whereas the One is only *relatively* dependent on any of the many. The One could be and be essentially itself with or without any of the many. But "without the One" is ungrammatical—at the deep level of the grammar—which is to say, the logic—of the concepts involved, because to be and to be essentially oneself at all is either to *be* the One or else to be *with* the One, absolutely dependent on it for being and meaning alike.

To be either—the One that is all, or any one among the many—is also to be free, in the full libertarian sense of determining something that would otherwise be merely determinable, possible rather than actual. To be free in this sense is to be both determinative of, and determined by, others as well as self. The One that is all is determinative of, and determined by, *all* others as well as self, while any one among the many is determinative of, and determined by, itself and only *some* others.

༄

As for conceptuality/terminology and the relevant necessary contrasts/distinctions:

"Being" designates "the transcendental of transcendentals" necessarily presupposed by all other transcendentals, convertible (≡ coextensive) or disjunctive, as well as by all existentials and all categorial concepts (whether categories proper, genera, species, or individualities ≡ individual essences).[67] "Being-itself" is simply another term designating "the being," "the transcendental being," the one being constitutive of reality itself, hence also the synonymous terms "the Being" and "the One."

Alternatively, "being(s)" may be used, in logically different senses, and so disjunctively, to designate both the Being, or the One, which includes all the many, and any one among the many included in the One. "[T]here are two senses of the one—namely, the sense of the one which is all [≡ "the whole"], and the sense of the one among the many. . . . We are, each of us, one among others; and all of us are embraced in the unity of the whole."[68]

The contrast, "being in itself"/"being in its meaning for us," may be applied to any "being," whether the one being which is all or any one of the beings among the many that the all includes. So applied, it serves to distinguish between any being simply in itself and the same being in its significance for us as human beings, or as beings who understand self-understandingly, and so by thinking and speaking, by exercising "the symbolic capacity" (Hartshorne). The meaning of any being for us is thus its significance for our own belief and action, for our own possibilities of self-understanding and life-praxis, as beings who understand thinkingly and speakingly, and who therefore understand themselves, others, and the all-encompassing whole.

The closely related contrast, "the structure of being in itself"/"the meaning of being for us," allows for further distinguishing between relatively more concrete ways of encountering any being existentially in its meaning for us, for our own possibilities of understanding ourselves and leading our lives, and relatively more abstract ways of considering any being only intellectually, in its essential logical structure, as distinct from its own actual content or quality. Whereas the special sciences and metaphysics, in their different ways, are relatively more abstract in this sense, morality and religion, also in their different ways, are relatively more concrete.

---

67. Whitehead, *Process and Reality*, 21. Whitehead uses the term "the universal of universals" to define "creativity," understood as a designation for "ultimate matter of fact."

68. Whitehead, *Modes of Thought*, 150–51.

35

The Aim of the Cosmos

What is the aim of the cosmos?

The aim of the cosmos is to create being/good by creating beings/goods—not only the many (i.e., all ordinary, included beings/goods), but also the One (i.e., the one extraordinary, all-inclusive being/good).

One could also say that the aim of the cosmos is to actualize the possible, or to determine the indeterminate/determinable.

༄

What are the conditions of being/good (i.e., the conditions that make being/good possible)? These conditions are chiefly two: (1) that there is free, spontaneous self-creation of concretes, of both the many and the One; and (2) that there is universal sociality—i.e., anything concrete is partly determined by the being of other concrete things, and nothing concrete is wholly determined by the being of any other concrete thing.[69] But these very same conditions also make evil possible. When the interplay of free self-creating concretes that suffices to define sociality is harmonious, the result is good. But when their interplay is discordant, the result is evil. As it also is when discord is avoided, not by achieving harmony, but only by reducing possible variety and settling for uniformity.

36

Metaphysical Axioms/First Principles and Necessary Presuppositions

I find it interesting that, just as Whitehead distinguishes the faith on which all sciences rest from "a metaphysical premise," so R. G. Collingwood distinguishes "the

---

69. Cf. Ogden, *Faith and Freedom*, 62–68.

presuppositions of all proof whatever," or "the conditions of there being any arguments at all," from "the ultimate first principles," or "the Aristotelian axioms, which enter into particular arguments as their premises."[70]

I take it that the distinction being made by both philosophers is to be interpreted somewhat as follows: the "faith" of which Whitehead speaks, like Collingwood's "presuppositions," or "conditions," plays essentially the same role, logically, as William A. Christian's "basic supposition."[71] That is to say, it makes possible raising certain questions and conducting certain arguments—namely, the questions orienting the relevant inquiries or sciences and the arguments proper to answering them. But it does not enter into the answers to the questions, or into the conclusions of the arguments, in the way in which a premise of a syllogism enters into its conclusion.

But, then, isn't this yet another application of the distinction between "formal" and "material"? Whereas "faith," or a "presupposition," or "condition," is purely formal relative to a particular science or argument, a "premise" is, in the nature of the case, material to some science or to the argumentation proper to it.

What makes this a bit tricky is that metaphysics, properly understood as *transcendental* metaphysics, is not simply one more science like any other—as it is, in a way, for Whitehead, and even for Hartshorne, to the extent that their metaphysics is not austerely transcendental but also categorial. As analysis of the necessary presuppositions not only of this, that, or the other "form of life," or "language game," but also of life as such, or language as such, and thus of the necessary conditions of the possibility both of human existence and of any so much as conceivable existence, metaphysics can only be analysis of "faith" in Whitehead's sense, or of "presuppositions," or "conditions," in Collingwood's. But anything that could be properly called "a metaphysical premise" could only be a tentative formulation of, or a working hypothesis about, the necessary conditions of the possibility of human existence and any existence, and so would still be distinguishable from those necessary conditions themselves.

In short: even when the uniqueness of metaphysics as an "ontological science," as distinct from any "ontic science," is fully taken into account, the distinction that Whitehead and Collingwood both make has to be made, even if making it rightly is, as I say, a bit tricky.

There is a distinction to be made between even the axioms or first principles of metaphysics, on the one hand, and, the necessary presuppositions of human existence and of all existence, which it is the business of metaphysics to make explicit as its axioms or first principles, however tentatively or hypothetically, on the other.

---

70. Whitehead, *Process and Reality*, 42; Collingwood, *Faith and Reason*, 108, 115.
71. Christian, *Meaning and Truth in Religion*, 84–88.

Still, it *is* the business of metaphysics to explicate these necessary presuppositions in its axioms or first principles, even as it is the business of religion and philosophy, in their different ways, to explicate the meaning of these presuppositions for us in their respective teachings. But any such explication, whether metaphysical or religious or philosophical, is subject to rational criticism, just as, on the other hand, what any such explication has to do with—its object, if you will—is nothing contingent or merely factual, but what is necessary or transcendental, be it *metaphysical*-transcendental, because it is the *structure* of ultimate reality in itself, or rather *existential*-transcendental, because it is the *meaning* of ultimate reality for us.

37

Metaphysical Assertions

Metaphysical assertions, I have said, are "the fundamental assertions that must somehow be made by each of us and that none of us can meaningfully deny." Elsewhere I have explained what I mean by this, or why I take it to be so, by saying, for example, that "[t]hose statements are true metaphysically which I could not avoid believing to be true, at least implicitly, if I were to believe or exist at all; or, alternatively, they are the statements which would necessarily apply through any of my experiences, even my merely conceivable experiences, provided only that [any] such experience was sufficiently reflected on."[72]

Other things I have said either state or imply that metaphysical assertions or statements:

"make fully explicit and understandable the most fundamental presuppositions of all our experience and thought, or . . . the most universal principles that are the strictly necessary conditions of the possibility of anything whatever";

"make the necessary conditions of the possibility of anything whatever, and hence the first principles of all our thought and speech, fully explicit and understandable";

"[set forth] a theory of ultimate reality in its structure in itself [as distinct from its meaning for us]";

"[raise] to full self-consciousness . . . the basic beliefs that are the necessary conditions of the possibility of our existing or understanding at all";

---

72. Ogden, "Criterion of Metaphysical Truth," 47.

"[set forth] the faith by which we live and in this way [an understanding] of the nature of reality as disclosed to this faith"; and

"[explicate] our at least implicit understanding as human beings of ultimate reality, in the sense of the necessary conditions of the possibility of our own existence and [of] all existence."[73]

38

Metaphysics and Falsification

Whether a statement can be *factually* falsified is one question; whether it can be *empirically* falsified, another.

No metaphysical statement can be empirically falsified. And no strictly metaphysical statement can be factually falsified. But some broadly metaphysical statements—notably those having to do with existence as existence that understands self-understandingly—*can* be falsified factually, even though, like all other metaphysical statements, they cannot be falsified empirically.

No metaphysical statement is an empirical statement, and no empirical statement is a metaphysical statement. No strictly metaphysical statement is a factual statement, and no factual statement is a strictly metaphysical statement. But some broadly metaphysical statements—namely, those having to do with existence that understands self-understandingly—are factual statements, and some factual statements are broadly metaphysical statements.

∽

By "empirically falsifiable" is properly meant factually falsifiable with a specific difference. Any utterance may be said to be factually falsifiable if there are some at least conceivable facts that would render it false. But whether any such utterance is also *empirically* falsifiable is another and independent question. Even though all factual utterances must somehow apply, or fail to apply, through experience, experience comprises more than its merely empirical aspect, strictly and properly understood. Along with the external sense perception of ourselves and the world, which is properly

---

73. Ogden, *Faith and Freedom*, 61; Ogden, *Point of Christology*, 136; Ogden, "Process Theology," 20; Ogden, *On Theology*, 77; Ogden, *Doing Theology Today*, 254.

distinguished as "empirical," we also enjoy an inner, nonsensuous perception of our own existence as interacting with others and with the inclusive whole of reality as such. Although this other properly "existential" aspect of our experience necessarily discloses more than mere fact, being the perception as well of the metaphysically necessary, some of what it discloses, including our own existence, is indeed merely factual, with the consequence that at least some of the utterances that apply through it are themselves factually falsifiable. Even so, they are *existentially* rather than empirically falsifiable, since the experience through which they apply, or fail to apply, is not the experience we have through our senses, but our nonsensuous experience of our own existence together with others and the whole.

Among such factually falsifiable utterances are those about the primal fact of existence that understands self-understandingly, as well as about the other primal facts of the world and God as related to it or to other facts specifically as such. To be sure, even some utterances about existence that understands itself may be, in a broad sense, metaphysical. Although existence that understands itself is entirely factual or contingent, and so in principle different from the strictly necessary existence of God and, in a suitably different sense, of the world as well, it nevertheless has a unique primacy, which insofar entitles it to be included among the formal objects of metaphysical understanding. It has such primacy because, although it is certainly not constitutive of reality as such, God alone being the individual who is that, it is constitutive of any *understanding* of reality. But for the fact that we exist self-understandingly, at the high level of thinking and speaking in concepts and symbols, we would have no understanding at all, not even empirical or scientific, much less any metaphysical understanding of the inner nature of reality as such. We ourselves are the one existent whose nature we understand by being it, by understanding it, so to speak, from within as well as from without. Consequently, such knowledge as we can have of the inner nature of anything else, including its metaphysical nature, we can have only by way of analogy with whatever we are able to know of our own existence.

Because this is so, there is one sense of the word "anthropology," in which it is properly taken, along with "cosmology" and "theology," to designate the nonempirical inquiries of special metaphysics. Nevertheless, since our own existence, unlike that of God and the world, is merely factual, such utterances as we can make about it, or about the world and God as related to it or to any other facts, are merely factual claims that could conceivably be false.

Because religious utterances are typically of this kind, being about human existence and its authentic or inauthentic self-actualization, many, if not all, of them are factually falsifiable. Of course, the qualification is essential, since foundational religious utterances about God's existence and essential nature and activity are strictly metaphysical, and so in no way subject to factual falsification. But true and important as this is, it is also true—*and* important—that specifically religious utterances are in many cases the kind of utterances whose truth or falsity is entirely a matter of fact.

Given the essential content of these utterances, indeed, it could not be otherwise. Thus, from the standpoint of Christian faith, for instance, this logical truth but reflects the truth of its own witness that our creation and consummation alike are not necessary but contingent, being entirely the free gift of God's grace to be obediently received by the faith that works through love enacted in justice.

∽

Given the axioms of classical Christian theism, especially the arch-axiom of the divine "simplicity," it follows ineluctably that *no* assertion about God can be factually falsifiable unless *all* assertions about God are so. The classical theist, accordingly, can consistently construe the theistic issue as a properly metaphysical issue only by accepting the implication that it is *nothing but* a metaphysical issue—with the further implication that God is wholly irrelevant to our life in the world because it can be of no possible relevance to God.

But how different the case of the neoclassical theist, who frankly rejects the axiom of "simplicity," maintaining instead that God is not a monopolar, but a *dipolar*, God, who—although existing necessarily, and existing necessarily as God—essentially exists only as the God of some world of contingent events and individuals other than Godself, to all of which God is related internally as well as, in another respect, externally. Given these alternative axioms, the fundamental assertions that God exists and exists as God, as the one universal individual who is the all-inclusive ground and the end of all other individuals and events, are all strictly metaphysical assertions and, as such, immune to factual falsification. And yet, if these assertions are true, they necessarily imply that an infinite number of other, merely factual assertions also have to be true, even though they do not imply, of course, just which such assertions actually are true.

Furthermore, necessarily included among such assertions are certain factual assertions about God, all of which have the general form of asserting that God is somehow adequately related internally to just this, that, or the other particular world of contingent individuals and events that in fact happens to exist. Being factual, these assertions about God are so far from being immune to factual falsification as to be factually falsifiable in a perfectly straightforward sense. Had some other world in fact existed than actually exists, God would be adequately related to it instead, and any assertion that God is somehow related to the actual world would of necessity be false. This need not imply, naturally, that such factual assertions as may be made about God are also *empirically* falsifiable, in the sense, say, that their meaning is equivalent to their "empirical expectations."

Although, for a neoclassical theism, the truth that God exists and exists as God is strictly metaphysical and therefore not factually falsifiable, God's essential nature as God, as modally coextensive with all actuality and all possibility, implies that God is also the ever-growing whole of all factual truth, and therefore precisely "supremely relevant." One may also observe that, although the sheer existence of God as God is metaphysically necessary and can indeed make no conceivable factual difference, this is not at all the case, either of my belief in God's existence or of my willingness to entrust myself here and now to God's real, factual relation to me and to my world, and to live in loyalty to them—loving God and all other things in God. There are very real factual alternatives to both belief *that* God is and obedient faith *in* God, in the sense of unreserved trust in and unqualified loyalty to God; and so far as the witness of Christian faith is concerned, they make just the factual differences that are by far the most important for every single one of us as a human being.

39

Facts and Principles

For a long time now, I have reflected on our experience of, and thought about (nonmetaphysical) *facts*, on the one hand, and (metaphysical) *principles*, on the other, in connection not merely with one, but with two, other fundamental distinctions.

One such distinction is that between *the contingent* and *the necessary*, what simply happens to be or to be possible, on the one hand, and what could not conceivably not be, on the other. Thus, in my understanding, the necessary is, as it were, the least common denominator of the contingent—that which has always been bound, always is bound, and always will be bound to happen, no matter what else may or may not happen to be. Accordingly, I hold that (nonmetaphysical) facts are to (metaphysical) principles as the contingent is to the necessary.

The other distinction is that between the two main aspects of our immediate experience: our derived, external *sense perception* of ourselves and the world around us, on the one hand, and our original, internal *nonsensuous perception* of ourselves, others, and the whole, on the other. In the course of time, I have come to express this distinction by speaking of the first aspect of experience, together with the thought based on it and the reality disclosed by it as "empirical," and of the second, along with the thought about it and the reality it discloses, as "existential." I also make this distinction sometimes metaphorically by distinguishing between the "horizontal" and the "vertical" dimensions of our experience, and thus of our thought and of the reality thought about respectively.

But the important point is that these two distinctions are not to be understood as simply paralleling one another, as they would if the first had to do with the two main types of reality that we have experience of and think about, while the second had to do with corresponding ways in which we experience and think about realities of the respective types. The only truth in such an understanding of the distinction is that all of the realities experienced and thought about in the properly "empirical" aspect or "horizontal" dimension are facts or the contingent, whereas it is only in the other properly "existential" aspect or vertical dimension that any of the realities that we experience and think about are principles or the necessary.

And yet it is *not only* principles and the necessary that we experience and think about in this other aspect or dimension; for in it we experience and think about facts or the contingent as well. So, as I use terms, properly "empirical" experience and thought are strictly factual and nonmetaphysical as well as nonexistential, in that they have to do entirely with facts or the contingent. On the other hand, properly "existential" experience and thought are more than merely factual and are metaphysical as well as nonempirical, in that they have to do with principles or the necessary as well as with facts or the contingent.

40

Necessary Truths

Why are necessary truths implied by any and every contingent fact?

Because—and only because—any and every contingent fact has certain features in common with any and every other conceivable contingent fact—namely, the features designated summarily by "factuality," a concept/term formed like Martin Heidegger's "existentiality" (*die Existenzialität*).

∽

If an ordinary proposition is meaningful, it has a neutral element of meaning universally in common with every other meaningful proposition. Necessary propositions affirm this neutral universally common element.

Properly metaphysical propositions, then, being necessary not merely conditionally but unconditionally, are existential in reference as well as true or false necessarily, in that, if true, they refer to what is objectively necessary. This may be defined, correspondingly, as the neutral element of all real possibilities, what they all have in common, and so what is bound to be actualized, "no matter what" course the creative process may take.

The neutral element of all real possibilities is the creative process itself, the concepts/terms "creativity" and "concrescence" designating its essential or irreducible aspect, which is inseparable from both the necessary aspect (the essence and existence) of deity and the necessary aspect of all other individuals simply as such.

41

Metaphysics and Self-Understanding

Metaphysics is a matter of self-understanding—and that in two senses of the words.

First of all, in the sense that the understanding of ultimate reality that it is the business of metaphysics to formulate clearly and coherently, and, eventually, at the level of critical reflection and proper theory, is the understanding always already given in and with any self-understanding and life-praxis, implicit or explicit, authentic or inauthentic. But, then, secondly, in the sense that the metaphysician's objective at the level of critical reflection and proper theory is to understand her- or himself—i.e., what it is that she or he, like every other human being, always already understands, implicitly or explicitly, authentically or inauthentically, at the level of self-understanding and life-praxis.

It is in this second sense, of course, that Hartshorne can say that metaphysics is entirely a matter of self-understanding, because either the believer or the unbeliever is simply confused or deceived about what she or he, like everyone else, always already believes or does not believe at the deepest level of belief. But, aside from the fact that Hartshorne would almost certainly agree that metaphysics is a matter of self-understanding also in the first sense, this first sense is certainly no less important than the second; for at stake in so understanding metaphysics is nothing less than consistently upholding "the ontological difference," and thus an understanding of metaphysics as in every way an *ontological*, or logical, in no way an *ontic*, or merely factual, undertaking.

Any self-understanding necessarily implies an understanding of existence (≡ understanding of ultimate reality) that, like the self-understanding that implies it, is a matter of decision and risk. I do not *have* to understand myself or ultimate reality as I do when I understand either in a certain way.

The understanding of existence or of ultimate reality that any self-understanding necessarily implies may also be called a "worldview" (*Weltanschauung*). But while a self-understanding may therefore be said necessarily to *imply* a worldview, it itself is *not* a worldview.

Self-understanding and understanding of existence (or worldview) are both modes of existential understanding of the meaning of existence for us, as distinct from existentialist understanding of the structure of existence in itself. But any *existential* (*existenziell*) understanding—be it a self-understanding or an understanding of existence—necessarily implies an *existentialist* (*existenzial*) understanding.

When this necessarily implied understanding is made explicit, the result is existentialist analysis, or transcendental metaphysics in the broad sense of "metaphysics," which includes transcendental *anthropology* as well as transcendental *ontology*, and therefore transcendental *theology* and transcendental *cosmology* (i.e., transcendental metaphysics in the strict sense of the word).

Note that on this use of terms, "existentialist analysis" is not just another way of saying "(transcendental) anthropology," but is a synonym for "(transcendental) metaphysics" in the broad sense. Just as "existence" may be taken to include others and the whole as well as the self, in which case it is synonymous with "ultimate reality," so "existentialist analysis" may be understood to mean "(transcendental) metaphysics in the broad sense," as including not only "(transcendental) anthropology," but also "(transcendental) metaphysics in the strict sense" (i.e., "[transcendental] ontology," and therefore also "[transcendental] theology") and "(transcendental) cosmology."

As for whether there is any place in my understanding of metaphysics for "fundamental ontology," the answer is affirmative. But what is properly said to occupy this place, given the use of terms clarified here, is not what I have called "existentialist analysis" or "transcendental metaphysics in the broad sense," but rather what is distinguished as "transcendental anthropology." As analysis of the necessary conditions of the possibility of an existent in the emphatic sense—which is to say, a concrete that understands at the high level represented by human thinking and speaking—transcendental anthropology provides the basis for the deeper and more comprehensive analysis of the necessary conditions of the possibility of any even conceivable existence, and thus of God's existence as well as of the existence of the world of others. (Whether "transcendental anthropology" may be a misleading way of referring to such an analysis is a fair question. So, in the following entry, I will use "existentialist analysis" instead to refer to it.)

⁂

Is there any place for "fundamental ontology" in my understanding of metaphysics?

In my usual way of expounding what is meant by "metaphysics," I distinguish, with certain important provisions, between "general metaphysics," or "ontology" (*metaphysica generalis*), and the three disciplines comprising "special metaphysics" (*metaphysica specialis*)—i.e., "psychology" (better, "anthropology"), "cosmology," and "theology." Underlying this distinction is my view that always already given—implicitly if not explicitly, inauthentically if not authentically—in any self-understanding and life-praxis is an understanding of self, others, and God (or, more generally, self, others, and the whole), and therewith an understanding of ultimate reality as such. Metaphysics in the broad sense, then, I take to be the attempt, eventually at the secondary level of critical reflection and proper theory, to formulate this always already given understanding explicitly, in a conceptuality/terminology that is at once clear and coherent.

In this attempt, the discipline of anthropology—or, as it might be even better called (considering how "anthropology" has now come to be used), "existentialist analysis"—plays a peculiar role. Unlike both the whole and others—not any particular others, but *some* others, or others as such—the self is not necessary but contingent. Insofar, then, as by "ultimate reality" is meant *strictly* ultimate reality, and thus what is necessary, as distinct from everything contingent, metaphysics *in the strict sense*—as critical reflection on, and the proper theory of, strictly ultimate reality—does not include, but rather excludes, existentialist analysis. On the other hand, the self that as such is contingent *is* necessary to our *understanding* of ultimate reality—and that in two distinct but related senses of the words. It is necessary in the sense that, unless we existed as selves, we could not understand anything, implicitly or explicitly, and so metaphysics, among any number of other things, would be impossible for us. But the self is also necessary in that it is the only sample of ultimate reality that we understand in all the ways in which things can be understood, including the way of actually being it, or from the inside. Although we can never understand ourselves except by also understanding others and the whole, we *are* not others and the whole, and such understanding as we can have of either of them as they are in themselves must derive somehow from what we understand of ourselves.

But, for an austerely transcendental metaphysics, such as I am concerned with developing, our strictly ultimate reality as selves is simply our concreteness, our being products of concrescence, and so concretes-concrescents. Accordingly, the only legitimate metaphysical analogy is between two transcendentally different types of concreteness-concrescence: the fragmentary concreteness-concrescence of the self (and of all others), on the one hand, and the integral, nonfragmentary concreteness-concrescence of the whole, on the other. In other words, the self figures in the analogy, not specially as a human existent or even more generally as an existent that understands at the same high level represented by human thinking and speaking, but just as a sample of fragmentary concreteness-concrescence, even if the only clearly given and therefore privileged such sample. So what we understand metaphysically by analogy with ourselves is simply that others and the whole, also, are (in their transcendentally different ways) concretes-concrescents: either other fragmentary concretes-concrescents like ourselves, or else the one integral, nonfragmentary concrete-concrescent of which we and they are all parts.

∽

Granted that metaphysical statements are intellectual statements that are directly concerned solely with the structure of ultimate reality in itself, they nonetheless necessarily *imply* existential statements expressive of self-understanding/understanding of existence and directly concerned with the meaning of ultimate reality for us. Conversely, existential statements that themselves express self-understanding/understanding of existence (worldview) and are directly concerned with the meaning of ultimate reality for us nonetheless necessarily *imply* metaphysical statements that are intellectual and directly concerned solely with the structure of ultimate reality in itself.

42

Formulations, Assumptions, and Consequences

One has to be careful to distinguish clearly between the metaphysical/ethical presuppositions and implications of a given self-understanding/understanding of existence and the metaphysical/ethical assumptions and consequences of some particular formulation of them. Just as a self-understanding/understanding of existence is one thing, its explicit formulation in particular concepts/terms, something else, so the necessary presuppositions and implications of a self-understanding/understanding of existence ought never to be confused with either the assumptions made in formulating them, or the consequences that follow, given the concepts/terms employed in their formulation (cf. note 11, "What, Exactly, Are 'Presuppositions'?").

43

On Arguing Metaphysically

The presupposed necessary condition of the possibility of any meaningful assertion/denial *in actu*, or as a performance (≡ *ein Vollzug*), is the at least "tacit," or "subjectively implicit," assertion of oneself, others, and the whole. Thus any explicit denial of any part of this threefold necessary condition or a priori is self-refuting, in the sense that, precisely as a putatively meaningful denial, it of necessity asserts at least tacitly, or by subjective implication, the very thing it explicitly denies. Therefore, to demonstrate such self-refutation between the denial of any part of oneself, others, and the whole, and the (at least) tacit, or implicit, assertion of them as the a priori even of denying them, is effectively what Emerich Coreth means by the "methodical-systematic laying of the foundations" of "special metaphysics" (*metaphysica specialis*), as comprising (metaphysical) anthropology as well as cosmology and theology.[74]

The term "special metaphysics," however, presupposes as the necessary condition of its possibility "general metaphysics" (*metaphysica generalis*), or ontology—or, as I would say more exactly, onto-cosmo-theo-logy. Here, demonstration likewise takes the form of reducing the counterposition(s) to absurdity or self-contradiction. But in this case, the self-contradiction exhibited is not between an assertion/denial as act or performance, on the one hand, and tacit, or implicit, assertion of the necessary conditions of its possibility, on the other. Instead, the self-contradiction lies between the meanings involved in the proposition asserted/denied simply as such. So, for example, "I do not exist" is self-refuting because it explicitly denies what it itself at least implicitly asserts as act or performance, and therefore is—in terms of John Passmore's helpful distinction—"pragmatically" self-refuting. On the other hand, "Nothing exists" is not just pragmatically, but also—again in terms of Passmore's distinction—"absolutely" self-refuting, because it is also *semantically* self-contradictory. What is meant by "nothing" and what is meant by "exists" simply cannot be combined consistently in "Nothing exists," any more than what is meant by "round" and by "square" can be consistently combined in "round square."

It seems clear in retrospect that the distinction drawn here between *metaphysica generalis* and *metaphysica specialis* is functionally equivalent with, and thus anticipates, my later distinction between metaphysics in a strict sense and metaphysics in a broad sense. Of course, whether it was an altogether happy way of making the later distinction may well be questioned.

74. Coreth, *Metaphysik*.

Wherein, exactly, is the essential contradiction involved in metaphysical error?

According to Coreth, the essential contradiction involved in metaphysical error is between the manifest meaning or content of the erroneous metaphysical judgment and the latent (nonthematic) meaning or content necessarily presupposed by the act of judging itself as its transcendental condition of possibility.

Hartshorne's view, although different, is, in important respects, the same. "Metaphysical judgments," he says, "are a priori, though not formally analytic. To deny them is to utter no formal non-sense. Yet it is to utter non-sense, to contradict the intuitive content of one's idea." Thus "metaphysically erroneous beliefs are not, except verbally, conceivable. . . . [T]he most general conceptions can never be wholly inaccessible, and we must be able to judge, with whatever difficulty and danger, when we are using them in accordance with the meaning which experience, imaginatively varied, is able to give them, and when we are contradicting that meaning and talking non-sense, even though with good syntax. . . . [What is in question is] contradiction of what is and must be conceived concerning some general feature of experience."[75]

As for the difference of Hartshorne's view from Coreth's, the self-contradiction to which Hartshorne points is not merely "performative," but also—to use a term he uses elsewhere—"semantic." Thus, while both thinkers rely on something like Passmore's distinction between "pragmatic" and "absolute" self-refutation, Hartshorne's view is subtler in distinguishing between two species of the second—i.e., not just "syntactic," but also "semantic," self-refutation.

Hartshorne's view also closely converges with Coreth's in arguing that a properly metaphysical contradiction is involved in questioning or denying that human beings can attain to metaphysical knowledge of what is "really universal." Why? Because "'really universal' is itself a human concept, and cannot be used to demonstrate the necessarily nonuniversal character of human conceptions. To say that things may exist which do not correspond to our idea of existence (as entering into this assertion) is to contradict oneself." Furthermore—or, perhaps, as an aspect of the same notion—it is contradictory or meaningless to say that "non-human things possess characters that are quite outside the system of variability which experience itself discloses"; for "'characters,' or any other general concept can be defined only by reference to the system spoken of."[76]

---

75. Hartshorne, "Anthropomorphic Tendencies in Positivism," 199–200.
76. Hartshorne, "Metaphysics for Positivists," 290, 302.

"Antifoundationalism" and Metaphysics

The formulations of metaphysics are tentative, hypothetical descriptions of the immediately given, which claim to make explicit what we all already believe and know, even without ever clearly and consistently thinking and saying so. But how is the validity claim made or implied by such descriptions to be critically validated? The only convincing answer, I believe, is by following something very like, or in effect, the method of "transcendental deduction," or "analysis of presuppositions."[77] By this I understand the general philosophical method of analyzing meaning and all the various kinds thereof carried to the point of demonstrating that what such analysis yields, finally, are the most fundamental presuppositions of all that we think, say, and do. This is to say that, regardless of where we begin at the periphery of our self-understanding and life-praxis—with whichever "form of life" or "language game" (Wittgenstein), or whichever "directed activity of mankind" (Whitehead)—we are eventually led by way of this distinctive kind of "objective argumentation" back to the center, to the hub where all spokes meet, which is to say, to the very core of our self-understanding: our understanding of our own existence, and thus of ourselves and all others as parts of the encompassing whole.

44

"Antifoundationalism" and Metaphysics

To the charges commonly made by "anti-foundationalist," or relativist, philosophers, the metaphysician can reasonably reply:

1. Finding necessary truths, as metaphysics seeks to do, is in no way a matter of "escaping from time and history." The only thing that can be at once clearly and coherently said to be necessary, eternal, absolute, and ultimate is the most abstract aspect of becoming and cosmic history. Consequently, one in no way "escapes" from becoming and history in seeking it; one simply analyzes out their own utterly abstract essential structure.

2. Our human knowledge of the ultimate is not itself ultimate in the same sense. There is an important difference between "the [*logical*] necessity of the proposition" and "the [*epistemological*] certainty of our knowledge of it." Mistakes can be made even in arithmetic, all the more so in metaphysics; and so knowledge of necessary

---

77. See Nygren, *Meaning and Method*.

truths is every bit as fallible as knowledge of contingent truths. And there is the additional problem of formulating necessary truths in language that primarily evolved and is used for formulating contingent truths.

> Language is only relatively reliable; we must always be ready to reconsider formulæ, and this rule does not cease to apply merely because one is not dealing with an empirical matter. Premises are to be judged by consequences as well as consequences by premises, and this is so whether the means of judging is empirical observation or the attempt to become conscious of a priori necessity or of what is presupposed by any experience or any thought whatever.[78]

3. Since it is a logical truism that contingent truths cannot be deduced solely from necessary ones, metaphysics as the search for necessary truths cannot be "foundational" in *that* sense. Discussion of necessary truths is simply one part of the general discussion, and success or failure in this part in no way guarantees, or even could guarantee, success or failure in any of the other parts.

∾

Is there any sense in which metaphysical beliefs may be said to provide the foundation for other kinds of beliefs?

If metaphysics is justified in its claim to explicate the basic beliefs that all of our beliefs—basic as well as nonbasic—necessarily presuppose, then there is at least this sense in which metaphysical beliefs may be said to provide the foundation for all other kinds of beliefs.

But just as there can never be a valid inference from the universal to the particular, so there cannot be a valid inference from metaphysical beliefs to any other more particular kinds of beliefs. Therefore, metaphysical beliefs may not be said to be foundational for other kinds of beliefs in *this* sense. From the truth of metaphysical beliefs as such, one cannot validly infer the truth of any other more particular kinds of beliefs, save in conjunction with other true beliefs comparably particular in kind.

This means, among other things, that the distinction sometimes made between narrower and broader senses of "foundationalism," helpful as it may be in responding to anti-foundationalists in other connections, is irrelevant in this. Metaphysical beliefs do not provide the basis for all other kinds of beliefs in the sense that they explicate the basic beliefs from which all other nonbasic beliefs may somehow be derived by valid inference. Moreover, it lies in the nature of the case that no properly metaphysical belief can be, in principle, any more or less basic than any other. If, as has been argued, a whole system of metaphysical beliefs can be derived from the premise, "Something exists," clear-headed metaphysical theists contend that the same is true if one argues instead from the premise, "God exists."

78. Hartshorne, *Creativity in American Philosophy*, 43–44.

In sum: with respect to all other, nonmetaphysical kinds of beliefs, the only foundation metaphysics is in a position to provide, though necessary, is not sufficient. On the other hand, with respect to other beliefs of a metaphysical kind, no metaphysical belief is any more (if also not any less) sufficient than any other to be singled out as properly "foundational" for metaphysical beliefs themselves.

45

"Analysis" and "Generalization"

There is a difference in principle between "analysis" with a view to discerning the necessary and "generalization" with a view to understanding the necessary in concepts and terms otherwise employed to understand the contingent. By "the necessary" here I mean the least common denominator of all possibilities, and so the most abstract possible structure, or *ratio formalis*, of things.

∾

What is at stake in the denial of "vacuous actuality," "mere matter," etc.?

At stake is the insistence that all empirically observable pattern, structure, or behavior is always the pattern, structure, or behavior *of something*—and, ultimately, of something *concrete*. If the special sciences, for their part, can get along perfectly well without asking what the concrete something is that is patterned, structured, or behaves in a certain way, metaphysics cannot, for it is the theory of the concrete as such (and also, therefore, of the abstract as such). But if there is, in this respect, or to this extent, an important difference between the modes of abstraction typical of the special sciences and metaphysics respectively, metaphysics, properly so-called, is nevertheless abstract in the way in which it, too, deals with the concrete.[79] As the theory of the concrete (and the abstract) as such, it seeks nothing but the necessary, which is to say, the least common denominator, the most abstract possible structure, or *ratio formalis*, of all concrete (and abstract) things. Thus, for it, even as for the special sciences, there is a complete abstraction from all actual concrete things—in its case, so as to analyze their concreteness (and abstractness) as such, whereas in the case of the special sciences, abstraction is for the sake of observing in itself the pattern, structure, or behavior of various kinds of actual concrete things.

---

79. Cf., e.g., Hartshorne, *Insights and Oversights*, 207.

What is there for metaphysics as such to do?

Hartshorne says, "'Matter' taken as ultimate is but the shadow of our own will to exploit or use things rather than to sympathize with them or share in their life."[80] But, then, if the special sciences may fairly be said to be the development of our will to exploit or use things, while religion and morality, in their different if related ways, properly have to do with our choosing to sympathize with things or to share their life, metaphysics, for its part, would seem to have nothing to do but to understand or reflect on that which would be, no matter what, in any conceivable world—regardless of our exploitation or use, and equally regardless of our sympathy or sharing.

∾

Hartshorne's appeal to Whitehead's "reformed subjectivist principle" in defense of his psychicalism fails to carry conviction. Why? Well, because, according to Whitehead, that principle holds that "the whole universe consists of elements disclosed in the analysis of the experiences of subjects"; and I can as well appeal to *that* principle in defense of my austerely transcendental (noncategorial and, therefore, nonpsychicalist) version of neoclassical metaphysics.

In fact, I have more reason than Hartshorne does to appeal to it. In my view, metaphysical truths are discovered precisely by "the *analysis* of the experiences of subjects" so as to expose their structure, as distinct from Hartshorne's speculative procedure of "*generalizing*" subjective experiences. By this I mean that the strictly literal, purely formal truths that make up metaphysics are what one comes upon, if one is lucky, when one abstracts from everything in the experiences of subjects except their transcendental structure. Whitehead says in this connection that "the general principle which guides the constitution of the whole" is "the object-to-subject structure of experience. It can be otherwise stated as the vector-structure of nature. Or otherwise, it can be conceived as the doctrine of the immanence of the past energizing in the present."[81] Considered as the structure of a "fact," this structure of experience is the structure of a *concrete* or a *concrescent-concrete*; considered as the structure of a "principle," it is the structure of a *concrescence* or a *process*.

So, in my view, what the vaunted "turn to the subject" discloses as metaphysically ultimate is not "the subjective enjoyment of experience," but rather the variable concrete-concrescent of which such subjective enjoyment is simply the privileged value—"privileged" because it is the only value clearly given as such in our experience. At bottom, which is to say, fully analyzed, "the turn to the subject" is simply "the turn to the concrete."

80. Hartshorne, *Creativity in American Philosophy*, 152.
81. Whitehead, *Adventures of Ideas*, 241.

Perhaps it won't do simply to compare and contrast "generalization" with "analysis." What may be called for is to compare and contrast "generalization *from* (or *of*) *fact(s)*" with "analysis *of (kinds of) meaning.*"

46

"The Concrete More"

"The concrete more" in concrete things from which the formulæ of mathematical physics and other sciences abstract is some form or other of the same principle of which human experience is the only form clearly given in our experience. But my position is that the question must remain open whether, or to what extent, any of the other forms of the principle, to say nothing of the principle itself, can and should be described by the word "experience." Panpsychism, or psychicalism, as a categorial metaphysical position counter to materialism, or physicalism, begs this question.

The only proper way to conceive "the concrete more" of beings other than ourselves—so far, at any rate, as metaphysics is concerned—is as exemplifying or instantiating the same purely formal structure of concrescence-concreteness as such that is the necessary condition of the possibility of our own being as experiencing, indeed, knowing, willing, loving beings. Our being as such, as existing self-understandingly, and so emphatically, or to the second power, is given simply as an extremely special case, example, or instance, however privileged, of this purely formal structure. Moreover, anything else that we could conceive as concrete could only be yet another special case, example, or instance of this same structure of concreteness. In this sense, we may agree with psychicalism that the more that mathematics leaves out is neither mere matter, whatever that could be, nor our human experience, but a vast plurality of forms taken by a principle of which *human experience* is only one highly special form.

And yet if we are to avoid begging the question, as distinct from answering it, we dare not go on to say with the psychicalist that this principle is "experience as such or in general." All we can do is to confess frankly that not only our human experience, but—for anything we know or ever can know to the contrary—any other form of experience, is but a special case of this principle.

I take it that my position on this issue is, in all essentials, the position that Hartshorne criticizes as the "nonpsychicalist" position held by Bertrand Russell as well as Wilfrid Sellars—and, before him, his father, Roy Wood Sellars. According to Wilfrid Sellars (≡ WS),

> merely structural knowledge is incomplete, it lacks qualitative content. And 'being must have content.' [R]oy W[ood] S[ellars]'s colleague DeWitt Parker may have influenced him in this. Parker used to argue that structural notions, shapes for instance, by themselves are abstract and indeterminate. . . . The concepts of physics are determinables, not determinates. They could not be complete descriptions of anything. All three of these philosophers agree with Whitehead that there cannot be (qualitatively) 'vacuous' actuality. Russell was of the same opinion. But whereas Parker and Whitehead are psychicalists, Russell, RWS and WS are not. What then is the issue between these two groups? . . .
>
> The nonpsychicalist assumes that the structure-quality contrast, when fully generalized, permits 'quality' to have a universal meaning and that what Peirce called 'feeling-quality' is a special case of a more general meaning; whereas psychicalists, and this includes Peirce, hold that the distinction between feeling-quality and quality not that of feeling is merely verbal. Quality as contrasted to structure is knowable only by feeling, and when thus known, the species of quality and the species of feeling are one. The nonpsychicalist is making a distinction without a difference. Or he has failed to generalize 'feeling' to its limit while claiming to generalize quality still more widely. . . .
>
> The psychicalist identifies the mystery of quality with the mystery of feeling, whereas the nonpsychicalist has an additional mystery, that of qualities not those of feeling, human or nonhuman. I for one find the second mystery unintelligible. . . .
>
> Psychicalism has advantages that few of its rejectors have seemed to be conscious of. It can find, in the concept of prehension as feeling-of-feeling, clues to causality, spatial and temporal relations, God's relations to creatures, creatures' relations to God, that is, all the central problems of ontology. Of course, it is not easy to think of the feelings of an atom. Is it easier to think of the unfeeling content or quality of the atom? Are these really two mysteries, or is it only one? How other creatures feel is mystery enough for some of us. . . .
>
> If materialism means the doctrine that the whole truth about reality can be stated using only the structural concepts of physical science, then, as WS has said in his essay and elsewhere, materialism is false. But even if quality is admitted as a necessary and universally applicable concept, materialism explains nothing that psychicalism cannot explain at least as well. The explanatory power of the concept of mere insentient matter is exactly zero. There are insentient wholes in nature—rocks and trees, for examples—but the assertion

that these wholes are insentient also in their parts explains nothing whatever. It is not even needed to explain why many philosophers make the assertion. For that fact quite other reasons or causes are at hand.[82]

47

"Mind in General," Etc.

What's wrong with the term "mind in general," or "mind in the generic sense"? Either the meaning or referent of the term is unclear, or else its meaning is inconsistent—and that, either because such meaning as it has contradicts its alleged utter generality, or purely "generic" sense (because it tacitly commits the "pathetic fallacy" of treating some merely "local" variable as a "cosmic" variable), or because such meaning as it has proves to be redundant, being indistinguishable (except verbally) from the meaning of "concreteness in general," or "concreteness in a generic sense," defined purely formally, or transcendentally.

❧

> [A]s the psychicalist uses the words, mind, or the psychical, is an infinite variable, coextensive in range with 'active singular,' and what is not an active singular he takes to be an aggregate of singulars or else an abstraction therefrom. Viewed from without, or through the sense organs, the psychical appears as behavior, but from within, or in itself, it is feeling, memory, anticipation and the like. On the highest levels only does it include what we normally mean by 'thought' or 'consciousness.'[83]

What is this but a confession that the psychicalist insofar misuses the words "mind," or "the psychical," which, as ordinarily used, are precisely *not* "infinite," or "cosmic," variables, but rather more or less "local" ones, functioning to distinguish one special type of thing from things of other special types? And the same is true of the other terms Hartshorne uses, presumably by way of trying to specify further the variables of which any form of "mind," or "the psychical," is some value—i.e., "feeling,"

---

82. Hartshorne, *Creativity in American Philosophy*, 240, 241, 242–43.
83. Hartshorne, "Physics and Psychics," 94–95.

"memory," "anticipation," and the like. They, too, as ordinarily used, are precisely not "infinite," or "cosmic," variables, but only "local" ones.

What makes any term properly an "infinite variable," "coextensive in range of application with active singular," cannot be how some philosopher chooses to use words, but only the meaning the term can be shown to have by virtue of also designating clearly, consistently, and nonfallaciously some variable of which any "active singular" can be more than merely verbally said to be a value.

~

To say, as psychicalism does, that any conceivable concrete singular—event or individual—is, in some sense, psychic (≡ sentient ≡ experient, and so on) is: either to interpret the literal, metaphysical statement that the singular is concrete in a certain way, by means of a frankly pictorial, symbolic statement; or else to say nothing other or more than what is already said in the literal, metaphysical statement, but to do so by means of a verbally different, though seriously misleading, statement, insofar as it affects to be neither literal nor frankly symbolic, but to mean in some supposed, third "analogical" way distinct from both.

~

Hartshorne says that "concern for the future" is "a variable with an enormous, indeed, infinite range."

But what is this other than a confused and confusing way of saying that any concrete singular is really, internally related to the future as well as to the past, albeit related to the future indefinitely and indeterminately, rather than definitely and determinately, as it is related to the past? Or, to ask the same question somewhat differently, how could Hartshorne or anyone else specify the difference required to vindicate it as anything other than this without self-contradictorily treating some merely local variable as though it were infinite or cosmic, thereby committing the pathetic fallacy into the bargain?

~

I find it interesting that Hartshorne argues, against physicalism, that "no materialism can escape the dilemma: either its conception of the eternal is purely negative, or it is a conception some of whose positive aspects are logically arbitrary and therefore cannot be eternal."[84]

---

84. Hartshorne, *Man's Vision of God*, 263.

I find this interesting because it so clearly anticipates the way in which I have come to argue against Hartshorne's own psychicalism. No psychicalism, I hold, can escape the dilemma: either its conception of "mind in general" is merely verbal, and in that sense "purely negative," or else it is a conception some of whose positive aspects are logically arbitrary and therefore cannot be eternal. If it doesn't self-contradictorily reduce the positive features of its conception to the strictly literal, nonsymbolic, nonanalogical transcendentals that they necessarily presuppose, thereby rendering them redundant, it self-contradictorily treats certain logically arbitrary "local variables" that cannot be eternal, as though they were "cosmic variables" that have to be eternal, thereby committing the pathetic fallacy into the bargain.

∽

Hartshorne defines "the social" as "the appeal of life for life, of experience for experience. It is 'shared experience,' the echo of one experience in another. Hence nothing can be social that is without experience." And "the minimum of experience . . . is feeling. Creatures are social if they feel, and feel in relation to each others' feelings."[85]

Hartshorne speaks variously of "'mind,' 'soul,' or 'experience' in general and as such." And he defines "subject" to mean "anything that can be said to be aware of (know or feel or intuit) anything . . . in a radically broad and nonanthropomorphic sense."[86]

48

"The Social"

I agree with Hartshorne that there is no substitute for human existence itself as "a representative sample," or analogue, of reality generally. It is the only reality that we can know not only in all the ways in which we can know anything else from without, but also in an important additional way—from within, by actually being it. I further agree with him that one of the things that we know about human existence is that, as he puts it, "it is social to the core." And I, too, wish to argue that "social structure" is

85. Hartshorne, *Reality as Social Process*, 34; cf. 136, where he says that to have a "social life" is to have a "life of sympathetically responsive and at the same time creative feeling"; and "To be social is to weave one's own life out of strands taken from the lives of others and to furnish one's own life as a strand to be woven into their lives. It is giving and receiving, neither having priority over the other."

86. Hartshorne, *Reality as Social Process*, 69; on 75, he speaks specifically of "experience as such."

nothing limited to the level of human society, but, on the contrary, pervades the whole of reality.

Where I find it necessary to disagree is only with Hartshorne's, to my mind, excessively narrow definition of "the social"—or "social structure." He defines it as "the appeal of life for life, of experience for experience," so that "nothing can be social that is without experience" and, assuming, as he does, that "the minimum of experience . . . is feeling," that nothing that is without feeling can be social.[87] In my view, by contrast, "the social," as what has "social structure," is to be defined indefinitely more broadly—but, for metaphysical purposes, also sufficiently—simply as "anything concrete." Any concrete, whether the One that is all or any one among the many, is internally (as well as externally) related to other concretes. It is related to all the concretes in its past definitely and determinately, even as it is related to any concrete in its future indefinitely and indeterminately. But whether the only such internal relatedness there can be is, in some sense, "experience" or "feeling," remains a further independent question that I find Hartshorne, like other psychicalists, begging instead of answering.

∽

In one passage, in which he uses the contrast "relative"/"nonrelative" as equivalent with "dependent"/"independent," Hartshorne says: "So both 'relative' and 'nonrelative' are analogical, not univocal, in application to deity. And since 'social' is, in this reference, equivalent to the synthesis of independent and dependent, [']social['] also is analogical in its theological application."[88] The significance of this passage is to confirm that Hartshorne himself can use "social" with just that broader meaning for which I contend against his usual narrower use of it as necessarily entailing "sentience," "experience," or "feeling of feeling," and the like. Likewise significant is that, later in the same book, he can speak of the concrete—more exactly, of what the concrete requires and has *qua* concrete—without any reference whatsoever to "experience," "sentience," or "feeling." Thus he says, e.g., "what the concrete requires and has is rich internal relatedness or relativity. Only the abstract can be independent of other things, even though it must be embodied in some concrete thing or other."[89]

∽

The world in its most essential features does not imply either its contingent inhabitants or their defining characteristics. On the contrary, they do imply that the world is

---

87. Hartshorne, *Reality as Social Process*, 34.
88. Hartshorne, *Divine Relativity*, 32.
89. Hartshorne, *Divine Relativity*, 100.

essentially itself with them as its (contingently existing) parts. Without the world, they as individuals with their defining features would not be at all, not even as possible.

One's own self, no less than any other, is real relative to a measure of reality that our fragmentary relatedness precludes our being able to furnish either for ourselves or for anything else, and that only an integral, nonfragmentary center of interaction could possibly furnish. We refer all contents of our experience to more than one such center of interaction, or focus of individuality. One's own individuality is only one of the foci in one's experience, which is immediately, however dimly, social. But the only focus that is necessary to reality is deity's focus, which is always present as the point of reference for our sense that we ourselves are real on the same terms as everything else.

Solipsism can be avoided, but only if there is some focus of reality, or center of interaction, beyond ourselves. It has to be something like ourselves in being a concrete individual; but it must also be infinitely unlike ourselves in being able to constitute the reality of everything—by being internally related to all things, and to all in all things, and thus being the all-embracing register of reality itself, without any limitation on possible variety and independence.

49

Categorial Metaphysics

Categorial metaphysics is a kind of in-between thinking and speaking distinct both from myth, on the one hand, and from transcendental metaphysics, on the other. Like myth, it makes use of the concepts and terms of our ordinary experience of ourselves and the world; unlike myth, it more or less clearly recognizes "the infinite, qualitative difference" between the natural and the ultimate, even while continuing to represent the ultimate in the concepts and terms of our ordinary experience of the natural (i.e., individual) essences, species, genera, and categories proper. Still, relative to myth, categorial metaphysics is, in its way, demythologizing.

Just as myth may be said to be the thought form distinctive of archaic or pre-axial religions—whence Martin Prozesky's term, "mythological naturalism"—so categorial metaphysics may be said to be the thought form distinctive of the axial religions, whether—again, in Prozesky's terms—"spiritual monism" or "transcendental monotheism." In Prozesky's view, both of these forms of axial religion are forms of "the other-worldly hypothesis," as distinct from "the worldly hypothesis" of mythological naturalism.[90]

Modern transcendental metaphysics emerges with the insight most influentially represented by Kant, that the concepts and terms of our ordinary experience of "the natural" (i.e., ourselves and the world) are, in principle, inappropriate to our experience of the ultimate, except insofar as they are understood resolutely as symbolic or metaphorical, and hence are radically demythologized. Whereas categorial metaphysics involves the concept of analogy as essential to its thought form, as distinct from myth-symbol/metaphor, on the one hand, and existentialist-transcendental concepts and terms, on the other, transcendental metaphysics denies the possibility of analogy as such a third way of thinking and speaking about the ultimate. From its standpoint, putative "analogies" are really just misnamed symbols or metaphors.

There clearly seem to be close connections between three different tripartite analyses: (1) myth, categorial metaphysics, and transcendental metaphysics; (2) pre-axial (or archaic), axial, and post-axial (or modern secular) religions; and (3) myth/symbol, analogy, and transcendental (including existentialist) concepts and terms.

Also clear, if perhaps somewhat less so, is the pivotal role of our experience as structured into the two main divisions of external sense experience of ourselves and the world, on the one hand, and internal nonsensuous experience of ourselves, others, and the whole, on the other hand. Myth represents an objectification of our internal experience in the concepts and terms of our external experience, while categorial metaphysics represents an objectification of our internal experience in the concepts and terms of our internal experience, and transcendental metaphysics consists in an objectification of our internal experience in the transcendental (including existentialist) concepts and terms necessarily implied by, but also distinct from, the concepts and terms of our internal experience.

∽

By distinguishing between (1) an ultimate subject of predication and (2) a *kind* of ultimate subject(s) of predication, one can also distinguish, as I have done elsewhere, between *substantive* monism or pluralism and *attributive* monism, pluralism, or dualism.[91] But, then, by making this same distinction, one can also offer a more nuanced account than I have given previously of the fallacies committed, in different ways, by categorial metaphysics and myth respectively.

On this account, both modes of thinking and speaking transgress "the ontological difference" between "beings" and "being," or, as I also say, "facts" and "factuality," by representing being or factuality in concepts and terms appropriate only for representing beings or facts. But they do this in characteristically different ways. In the case

---

90. Prozesky, *Religion and Ultimate Well-Being*.
91. Ogden, "Pluralism."

of myth, it is what may be called, given my distinction, "the substantive way," in that factuality—or, really, the meaning of factuality for us—is represented as one or more facts other than or alongside all the others. In the case of categorial metaphysics, it is what we may call "the attributive way," in that factuality—or, more exactly, factuality in its structure in itself—is represented as if it were a certain *kind* of fact(s).

So, even though categorial metaphysics may observe the ontological difference substantively, by recognizing that factuality is something logically-ontologically different from either one fact or many facts alongside all the others, it still transgresses the ontological difference attributively insofar as it represents factuality as a certain *kind* of fact, whether physical, as in the case of physicalism (or materialism); or psychical, as in the case of psychicalism (or panpsychism); or, in different respects, both, as in the case of dualism.

50

Rethinking Categorial Metaphysics

I have had to rethink the whole question of the similarity as well as the difference between materialism/physicalism (and/or dualism), on the one hand, and objective idealism/psychicalism (or panpsychism), on the other, as alternative metaphysical positions.

If my argument is sound, that what Hartshorne takes the metaphysician to be saying "analogically," as distinct from both "symbolically" and "literally"—in his term-of-art senses of these three terms—cannot, in fact, be so distinguished except verbally, and that the metaphysician, therefore, must be saying something in one of these other two ways if it is to count as saying anything meaningful at all, then to speak of "mind [or psyche] in general," or "mind in some form," is utterly *nichtssagend*—not a whit less so than to speak of "matter" in the same completely generalized ("analogical") sense. In other words, if Hartshorne is right, as I agree he is, that "matter," used thus analogically as by the materialist, explains absolutely nothing that cannot be explained without it, I don't see why I'm not likewise right, that "mind" so used, as he himself uses it, explains just as little. If you cannot say, clearly and consistently, what "mind in general," or "mind in some form," *means*, you certainly cannot use it to explain anything!

I submit that the burden of explaining things metaphysically can and should be borne only by terms used neither "symbolically" nor "analogically," but strictly "literally," in the senses of this threefold distinction as Hartshorne uses it. Of course, once such a strictly literal explanation has been provided, it may also be "interpreted," for one purpose or another, in symbolic terms. But any such symbolic "interpretation" can add nothing whatsoever to the explanation itself, which can be provided, if at all, only in strictly literal terms. Thus x is the effect of y, or x is caused by y, not because x "somehow experiences" y, or y is "somehow experienced by" x, but because, or insofar as, x is really, internally related to y whereas y, in that relation, is only logically, externally related to x. Or, again, atoms act as they do, not—as Hartshorne says—because "they sense and feel as they do," but because they are really, internally related as they are (to the future as well as to the past)—i.e., as concrete singulars that, as such, instantiate in different respects all three of C. S. Peirce's three categories: Firstness, Secondness, and Thirdness.

If one claims in reply, then, that to say, "atoms act as they do because they sense and feel as they do," is to say more than that "atoms act as they do because they are internally/externally related as they are," wherein does the "more" consist? And can one specify it at once clearly and consistently, without logical fallacy? I maintain that Hartshorne, as one who makes the claim, never explains more than verbally wherein the "more" consists. And I further maintain that, in the nature of the case, neither he nor anyone else can ever sufficiently specify the "more" both clearly and consistently—and also nonfallaciously.

When I say that Hartshorne fails to explain other than verbally what the claimed "more" consists in, I mean that he never says anything about the "more" other than that it consists in "experience (sentience or feeling) in general," or "in some form." But clearly, phrases such as "experience (sentience, feeling) in some form," or "experience (sentience, feeling) in general," are inherently vague and anything but clear. *What* form, exactly? And what are the *variables* that define "experience (sentience, feeling) in general," and of which any form of experience is therefore presumably some value? Are they—or can they be—more than verbally different from the strictly literal variables that serve to define "concreteness" as a certain mode of internal/external relatedness distinct from that definitive of other logical/ontological types of reality?

Of course, unless they are—or can be—different, there is really nothing "more" said after all. But then, exactly wherein does the "more" consist, and how is it to be specified sufficiently to remove the inherent vagueness of Hartshorne's terms by being shown to be really (not merely verbally) "more"? And could it even possibly be so specified without in some way committing the "pathetic fallacy" of treating a merely particular or "local" variable as though it were universal or "cosmic"? Or—to put the same question more cautiously—how could one show that one had not committed this fallacy in so specifying it?

For all Hartshorne ever shows to the contrary, the supposed "analogical" variables defining the alleged "more" either are, in his terms, "symbolic," and so not "analogical" after all, or else remain at most only verbally distinguishable from the strictly "literal" variables that suffice to define "concreteness" in austerely transcendental metaphysical terms. They define it, namely, as a certain mode of relatedness, internal and also external, distinctive of concretes and thus different from the modes of relatedness distinctive of other logical/ontological types, such as abstracts generally and transcendentals (and also, in their way, existentials) specifically.

51

Heidegger Speaks . . .

Heidegger speaks of "the ontological difference" between "a being" (*ein Seiendes/das Seiende*) and "being" (*das Sein, die Seiendheit*). In somewhat the same way, I should wish to speak of the ontological difference between "a reality" and "reality." Any reality, whether concrete or abstract, unsurpassable or surpassable, is ontologically different from reality, in the sense of reality as such. But what, exactly, is the nature of this difference? What is meant by "reality" in the sense of "reality as such"?

My answer to the second question is that "reality as such" is "concrescence," which is my preferred name, using Whitehead's term, for the broadly natural (≡ *physis* ≡ *natura* ≡ process)—i.e., the one process of becoming, whereby, without beginning or end, the many again and again grow together (*concrescere*) in such a way as to become one and to be increased by one. This one process of becoming or concrescence is actual only in instances—in the different "concretes," each of which comes to be by instantiating concrescence, by the many's so growing together as to become one and to be increased by one—always keeping in mind that, as Whitehead puts it, "there are two senses of the one—namely, the sense of the one which is all, and the sense of the one among the many." But distinct from both the one process of concrescence and the many different concretes in which it alone is actual are the distinguishable abstract aspects of the process and of its instances. Although these aspects, being abstract rather than concrete, are not themselves actual, save as aspects of the concretes that alone are actual, they are nonetheless real, each being a reality distinct both from all other realities and from reality as such.

These "abstracts," which are realities in their own way, even as are concretes, are themselves distinguishable into two logically-ontologically different types: extraordinary abstracts, which at the higher level I call "transcendentals," meaning thereby inherent aspects of the one process of concrescence and hence of each and every concrete; and ordinary abstracts, which I distinguish as "categorials," and which include all other nontranscendental abstracts, whether these be, in my terms, "categories proper," "genera," "species," or "individualities" ≡ "individual essences." Whereas extraordinary abstracts at the higher level, or transcendentals, being inherent aspects of concrescence, are strictly necessary and incapable of noninstantiation, ordinary abstracts of all types are like concretes in being, to some extent or other, contingent and therefore capable of not being instantiated.

"Reality" in the sense of "reality as such," then, includes, and therefore is ontologically different from, all realities, abstract as well as concrete, surpassable as well as unsurpassable. The inclusion, and hence the difference, are twofold: abstract and concrete. As abstract, they are simply that any reality, concrete or abstract, unsurpassable or surpassable, is real in the same completely general sense of "reality," which contrasts with "unreality"—i.e., "mere appearance" or "fiction." In this sense, to be real is to be real both for the unsurpassable, the one extraordinary, everlasting individual, and also for the surpassable, at least some ordinary events and/or ordinary, transitory individuals that either have become or are in the process of becoming real in the same general sense. As concrete, the inclusion (and hence the difference) are simply that all realities, concrete and abstract, unsurpassable and surpassable, are included in, and so real for, the one concrete reality of the unsurpassable, the one extraordinary, everlasting individual, which, like the one process of concrescence that it eminently instantiates, is strictly necessary, an inherent aspect of this very process

Part 2

TRANSCENDENTAL METAPHYSICS

Metaphysics is essentially a question of the logical structure of concepts. The basic decisions are not as to metaphors, but as to logical structure. What depends upon what, what includes what, what is necessary to or contingent upon what?

—CHARLES HARTSHORNE

52

Meaning and Transcendental Metaphysics

Necessarily presupposed by any meaning and any kind of meaning are certain necessary conditions of possibility: of the possibility of some *subject of meaning* that is capable both of understanding and of expressing meaning of any and all kinds; and of the possibility of some *object of meaning* that is capable of being meant or referred to by any meaning and any kind of meaning—indirectly if not directly, implicitly if not explicitly.

If the necessary, speaking absolutely, is rightly defined as what is common to, or the least common denominator of, *all* possibilities, or what is bound to obtain, whatever possibility is or is not actualized, the necessary, speaking relatively, may be defined as what is common to, or the least common denominator of, *some set* of possibilities, or what is bound to obtain, whatever possibility in the set is or is not actualized. Speaking, then, relatively to human existence as such in the emphatic sense that understands at the high level evidenced by thinking and speaking, one may define the necessary as what is common to, or the least common denominator of, the set of possibilities belonging to such self-understanding existence, or what is bound to obtain, no matter which of its possibilities is actualized or not actualized.

Let the necessary, speaking absolutely, be called "transcendence," "the transcendental," or "transcendentality," and the necessary, speaking relatively to existence that understands, "existence," "the existential," or "existentiality" (in the emphatic sense of the words clarified by Martin Heidegger).

∽

I maintain that all meaning, and all kinds of meaning—as expressed and understood in all "the directed activities of mankind" (Whitehead), or in all its "forms of life"/"language games" (Wittgenstein)—necessarily presupposes what I take to be the topics of "transcendental metaphysics in a broad sense"—i.e., the thinking-speaking, and therefore morally free and responsible, *being* that is the *subject* of any meaning and any kind of meaning; and the being simply as such that is, directly or indirectly, explicitly or implicitly, the *object* of any meaning, and of any kind thereof.

I also acknowledge what some have called "the real world language game," and I fully agree with them in asserting its "primacy." But in doing so, I also insist that the real world with which this game has to do must be understood to include all three modes of reality, or being—i.e., not only the actual, but also the possible and the necessary.

Question: Is there more than a verbal difference between saying that the task of a transcendental metaphysics in a broad sense is the logical analysis of the necessary presuppositions of any meaning and of any kind of meaning, and saying that the task of such a metaphysics is to analyze logically what is common to all the possibilities of, and therefore necessary to, both the subject of the real world language game and the real world—actual, possible, or necessary—that is its object?

So far as metaphysics in the broad sense is concerned, "the subject of the real world language game" is simply "an existent in the emphatic sense of the word," i.e., a concrete part or fragment of reality, whether ordinary event or particular individual, that as such (1) understands at the high level evidenced by human thinking and speaking, or by such other ways of exercising the "symbolic capacity" as making maps, drawing pictures, reading musical notation, and so on (Charles Hartshorne); and therefore (2) is morally free and responsible, its metaphysical freedom having become distinctively moral freedom with its entailment of distinctively moral responsibility. Thus, whether an existent in this emphatic sense is also a human being, or a being of some other kind, is of no concern to metaphysics as such, even in the broad sense. Just as all cats are animals, but not all animals are cats, so too must we say that all human beings, properly so-called, are existents in the emphatic sense, but—for anything we know to the contrary—not all existents in the emphatic sense are human beings.

This raises the question, of course, of whether my long-standing recommendation to use "anthropology" instead of "psychology" for the third discipline of "special metaphysics" (along with "theology" and "cosmology") hasn't been, however unintentionally, unfortunate. *Psyche* is a much more general term than *anthropos*, and so its cognates are just as unlikely to mislead in the properly metaphysical context in question, even if the difference, after all, is not infinite, but only finite.

53

Rights and Responsibilities

I have argued elsewhere (e.g., note 52, "Meaning and Transcendental Metaphysics") that "the subject of the real world language game" is not a human being as such, but "simply 'an existent in the emphatic sense of the word.'" By this I mean "a concrete part or fragment of reality" that "(1) understands at the high level evidenced by thinking and speaking, or by such other ways of exercising the 'symbolic capacity' as making maps, drawing pictures, reading musical notation, and so on . . . and therefore (2) is morally free, its metaphysical freedom having become distinctively moral freedom with its entailment of moral responsibility. Thus, whether an existent in this emphatic sense is also a human being, or a being of some other kind, is of no concern to metaphysics as such even in the broad sense."

At the time I wrote this, the question crossed my mind, "Doesn't this imply, then, that, if "moral freedom with its entailment of moral responsibility" is what "metaphysical freedom" becomes in the case of an "an existent in the emphatic sense of the word," metaphysical freedom otherwise, *not* having become moral freedom, and therefore *not* entailing moral responsibility, nonetheless entails what may be called "*metaphysical* responsibility"? To be free in the full libertarian sense of self-determining is to be insofar responsible, although there is a difference between the "*metaphysical* (or *natural*) responsibility" of any concrete singular simply as such and the "*moral* responsibility" of a concrete singular that is "an existent in the emphatic sense of the word." I have always implied this whenever I have allowed myself to say, as I have said repeatedly, (1) that only the "free-will defense" offers any promise of solving the so-called problem of evil; but (2) that even it offers such promise only if it is so generalized that "natural evil" as well as "moral evil" can be accounted for by the exercise of freedom other than God's. But my usual way of saying this is to say that the only hope for solving the problem of evil is to establish "a division of *responsibility*" between God, on the one hand, and all other concrete singulars, on the other—thereby implying precisely "metaphysical *responsibility*" as the entailment of "metaphysical *freedom*," even as "*moral* freedom" necessarily entails "*moral* responsibility."

But what makes freedom and responsibility "moral"? From what I've said above, they're moral because they're yet other consequences of the same high level of understanding evidenced by thinking and speaking and other exercises of the "symbolic capacity." But another way of making the point is to follow Hartshorne's lead in discussing animal rights: "Those have rights in the strong sense (all animals do in a weaker sense) for whom there is such a thing as the concept of right."[1] *Mutatis mutandis*, those have responsibilities in the strong, or emphatic, sense of "moral responsibility" who have such a thing as the concept of moral responsibility.

∽

The role of God as Creator-Emancipator, I argue, is to make all things really possible, in fact as well as in principle, by so responding to all actions of the past as to establish ever and again the optimal limits of creaturely freedom. The role of God as Consummator-Redeemer, then, is to make all actions of the present really real and abidingly significant by ever and again incorporating them into God's own everlasting life. This understanding presupposes that freedom, in the sense of making fully determinate actuality what was theretofore only more or less indeterminate possibility, is a strictly transcendental concept. Thus anything concretely real, being as such self-created as well as created by others, makes itself determinate actuality and thus exercises freedom in just this sense. It is because every creature exercises such freedom in creating itself that God's role as Creator-Emancipator is not to make creatures fully actual, but only to make them really possible, in fact as well as in principle.

This means that what is commonly recognized to be true of human beings (as well as any other beings having distinctively moral freedom)—namely, that they can become themselves only through themselves and that, therefore, the most that God can do is to present them with the real possibility, in fact as well as in principle, of authentic existence—is just as true, in a generalized sense, of all (concretely real) beings. Distinctively moral freedom, in other words, is a special, high-level case of the metaphysical freedom to make what, up to then, is only more or less indeterminately possible into something determinately actual. It is *that* special case, namely, in which self-creation is mediated by understanding at the high level evidenced by thinking and speaking, and thus is, in the first instance, *self*-understanding.

---

1. Hartshorne, *Creativity in American Philosophy*, 233.

54

Transcendental Metaphysics as Engagement

One way of engaging with the world, arguably, is to do metaphysics, in the sense of inquiring, What are the necessary conditions of the possibility both of the world and of any of the different ways, actual and possible, of engaging with it, including the metaphysical way? Anything like a complete answer to this question would yield what I mean, more exactly, by a "transcendental metaphysics" in both of the senses in which I use the term—i.e., in the strict sense, in which doing it (and taking "world" in "engaging with the world" as utterly all-inclusive) inquires as to the necessary conditions of the possibility of anything whatsoever; and in the broad sense, in which doing it includes also inquiring as to the necessary conditions of the possibility of the distinctive kind of thing instanced by ourselves as existing understandingly by thinking and speaking, and as therefore able to engage with the world in the many ways in which we can and do engage with it, including engaging with it metaphysically.

So understood, doing transcendental metaphysics, as one way among others of engaging with the world, constitutes a distinct domain of discourse—and, insofar as its inquiries meet with success, a distinct domain of truth. The truths it pursues, however, are only necessary to, not sufficient for, the whole truth about anything, in that they describe nothing particular as such but only something universal about it. Even so, no description of anything particular is ever complete or fully explicit without metaphysical truths, because they are about the necessary common denominator of all possibilities, of all "possible worlds," or, better, of all conceivable kinds of world. This they are either in the strict sense excluding everything but the common core of all possibilities whatsoever, or in the broad sense including, in addition, the necessary common core of all of our own distinctive possibilities insofar as we exist understandingly at the high level of thinking and speaking and are thus able to engage with the world in all the different ways in which such engagement is either actual or possible. In this way, the truths sought by doing transcendental metaphysics in the broad sense, inclusive of existentialist analysis, describe only an abstract, all but empty, outline of reality, all of whose concrete contents are describable, if at all, only by other nontranscendental or categorial domains of discourse/truth.

Being one way among others of engaging with the world, doing transcendental metaphysics depends upon both a certain kind of interest and a choice to act on it, for which the individual so acting bears full responsibility. Therefore, in this important respect, doing it neither has nor may validly claim to have any unconditional priority over any other interests or the choices to act on them. Depending on the conditions obtaining in the context, pursuit of transcendental metaphysical inquiry, just as acting on any other interest or choice, may be everything from mandatory through permissible or indifferent to forbidden.

But if doing transcendental metaphysics cannot justly claim a unique priority over other human interests, choices, and ways of engaging with the world, there is still a sense in which its discourse or vocabulary is uniquely privileged; not simply because of the interests and choices of those who use it, but also and primarily because, or insofar as, it is uniquely transparent to the way things really are. Insofar as its inquiries are successful, its vocabulary cannot fail to be thus transparent because it merely makes explicit what Whitehead speaks of in one place as "the premises implicit in all reasoning"—which is to say, what any and all reasoning, in any and all of the various ways of representing the world and ourselves and acting to change them (in short, in any and all of our ways of engaging with the world)—is, at least implicitly, reasoning *from*.

But because the strictly necessary among these "premises implicit in all reasoning" are logically necessary, not merely conditionally, but unconditionally (on any conditions you please) any explications of them, if meaningful at all, are about the way things really are—i.e., are about "reality," or, in a broad sense, "existence," as such. This means that they would be true and could not conceivably be false, not only in this, that, or any other actual world, but also in any so-called possible world, or—less misleadingly—any conceivable kind of world.

One of the marks of such unconditionally necessary truths is that they are wholly positive, or noncompetitive, in that they exclude no other positive truth, whether necessary or contingent. But, then, there is no possible basis on which a transcendental metaphysics seeking to explicate the strictly necessary truths implicit in all reasoning could ever become "monopolistic." It could not possibly require that the vocabularies of all other domains of truth must either prove somehow reducible to its vocabulary, or else be acknowledged as in some way defective or inappropriate. Strictly necessary truths are utterly noncompetitive, and so utterly incapable of ever being or becoming a monopoly in this sense—not least because, among such necessary truths, arguably, are: "There are and must be some contingent as well as necessary truths" and "All strictly necessary truths but explicate the utterly abstract properties of anything and everything concrete, and so provide only the bare, all but empty, outline requiring to be filled in by all contingent truths."

But if transcendental metaphysical truths that are necessary unconditionally cannot, in the nature of the case, ever compete with the truths of any other domain, the converse, of course, is just as true. No other truths, and certainly not the truths explicated by an austerely analytic philosophy concerned solely with doing conceptual justice to all of our different ways of engaging with the world, can possibly compete with the truths made explicit by a transcendental metaphysics. On the contrary, such austerely analytic truths can only necessarily presuppose such metaphysical truths, together with those yielded by doing transcendental metaphysics in the broad sense inclusive of existentialist analysis. This they do most obviously when the one truth said or implied to be fundamental to all of them is that the many domains of discourse/truth of which they are the logical analysis are just that: so many ways of engaging with the world.

55

Transcendental Metaphysics and Transcendental Ethics

Foundational for philosophy's work in its one concrete, inclusive, or "existential" phase are the transcendental ethics as well as the transcendental metaphysics that are central to its work in its other abstract, included, or "analytic," phase.

Necessarily presupposed by any meaning and any kind of meaning as well as the presuppositions implied thereby are certain necessary conditions of possibility: the possibility of human existence insofar as it is the being that understands thinkingly and speakingly, and is therefore capable of expressing all kinds of meaning and also of understanding them; and the possibility of any being whatsoever insofar as it is what any meaning or any kind of meaning must somehow be about—directly or indirectly, explicitly or implicitly. Necessarily implied, then, by the transcendental metaphysics analyzing and explicating these necessary conditions of possibility is a transcendental ethics consisting of completely general first principles as to how any existent, in the emphatic sense of any being endowed, as human beings are, with the capacity of understanding thinkingly and speakingly and of moral freedom and responsibility, is to act and what she, he, or it is to do.

On the foundation of this transcendental ethics and metaphysics, philosophy's work in its existential phase consists in critically appropriating any and all answers to the existential question, implicit as well as explicit. In this indirect way, at the secondary level of critical reflection and proper theory, philosophy may be said to answer the existential question by which it is and ever remains oriented—even if only remotely so, as it is when it pursues the strictly intellectual question that constitutes and therefore proximately orients its work throughout its analytic phase.

Does it make sense to hold that transcendental ethics, in its way, is also concerned with structure, as distinct from meaning—specifically, the structure of right belief and action, transcendental as well as categorial? A positive answer presumably depends on whether it makes sense, having distinguished between the structure of ultimate reality in itself and its meaning for us, to distinguish further between the meaning of ultimate reality for us and *its* structure—i.e., the structure of the meaning of ultimate reality for us.

One reason for thinking that such a further distinction does make sense is provided by what I take to be implied by Joseph Bochenski's distinctions between "instructions" (*die Weisungen*) and "propositions" (*die Sätze*) and then between "propositions" and "practical propositions" (*die praktischen Sätze*) (cf. note 10, "Propositions, Instructions, and Performatives."). Just as, according to Bochenski, "practical propositions," although distinct from "instructions," may be understood to provide the reasons for them, so "propositions," I have inferred, may be understood to provide the reasons for "practical propositions." Assuming, then, that transcendental metaphysics consists in (a certain kind of) propositions, one may say that it provides the reasons for the (certain kind of) practical propositions in which transcendental ethics consists—even as transcendental ethics, in turn, provides the reasons for all valid instructions at the level of first principles.

Appealing, then, to the connections I have also made between Bochenski's analysis, as thus appropriated and (1) Rudolf Bultmann's distinction between "direct address" and "indirect address" and (2) the distinction made by many philosophers between "executive [or deontic] authority" and "nonexecutive [or epistemic] authority," and also the distinction made by some between "causative authority" and "normative authority"—and assuming that it makes at least analogical sense to speak of the authority of reality and reason—on the basis of all this, one could perhaps conclude as follows:

The meaning of ultimate reality for us is to its structure as instructions/direct address/executive authority/causative authority are to practical propositions/indirect address/nonexecutive authority/normative authority respectively. On the other hand, the structure of the meaning of ultimate reality for us is to the structure of ultimate reality in itself as practical propositions/indirect address/nonexecutive authority/normative authority are respectively to propositions.

The basic idea, in other words, is that it makes sense to hold that transcendental ethics, in its way, is also concerned with structure because the practical propositions in which it consists, like propositions otherwise, have to do precisely with structure—i.e., the structure of the meaning of ultimate reality for us, analogously to the way in which the propositions which transcendental metaphysics consists of have to do with the structure of ultimate reality in itself.

Transcendental Metaphysics and Transcendental Ethics

∾

I want to say that ethics, like metaphysics, is logical analysis in its own way. But whereas metaphysics is logical analysis of the *structure* of ultimate reality in itself, ethics is logical analysis of the *meaning* of ultimate reality for us. Being *logical analysis* of this meaning, however, ethics is, in its own way, also concerned with *structure*, and is therefore, more exactly, logical analysis of the meaning of ultimate reality for us in *its* structure in itself.

This implies that, in addition to the basic distinction between the being of ultimate reality in itself and the meaning of ultimate reality for us, two further distinctions must be made: (1) between the structure of ultimate reality in itself—this being the proper concern of transcendental metaphysics—and the meaning of ultimate reality for us—this being the proper concern, in their different ways, of faith, religion, theology, and philosophy; and (2) between the meaning of ultimate reality for us and the structure of this meaning in itself—this being the proper concern of transcendental ethics.

It further implies that metaphysics and ethics, so understood, are to one another as—on Bochenski's analysis—"propositions" (*die Sätze*) are to "practical propositions" (*die praktischen Sätze*). This means that metaphysics and ethics explicate, in turn, the foundations of witness—its theoretical and practical foundations respectively—in the same way in which, more generally, "propositions" and "practical propositions" in turn explicate the foundations—theoretical and practical—of what Bochenski further distinguishes from both types as "instructions" (*die Weisungen*).

∾

I have said sometimes that, just as transcendental metaphysics is the "culmination" of the abstract, included, or "analytic" phase of philosophy, so transcendental ethics is the "foundation" for its concrete, inclusive, or "existential" phase." At other times, I have relied more on a different metaphor and said that, just as I want to hold that transcendental metaphysics is rightly understood as the "core or central" task of philosophy in its "analytic" phase, so I also want to hold that transcendental ethics is rightly understood as "core or central" to the task of philosophy in its "existential" phase.

Both metaphors seem apt to me. Philosophy can answer the existential question by which it is oriented only insofar as it first asks and answers the intellectual question of analysis: analysis both of all the different kinds or contexts of meaning and of their necessary presuppositions; and analysis of being as such and of being that understands thinkingly and speakingly, and of their necessary presuppositions as disclosed through the existential aspect or vertical dimension of our experience. For this reason, transcendental metaphysics may well be thought of as the culmination of philosophy in its analytic phase, even as the transcendental ethics determined by the being that transcendental metaphysics analyzes may well be said to provide the foundation for philosophy in its existential phase. At the same time, the other metaphor of the core or center relative to the periphery conveys the important insight that transcendental metaphysics and transcendental ethics both have to do, in their different ways, with what is core or central, as distinct from any- and everything peripheral.

∽

If Hartshorne is right that philosophy, as distinct from metaphysics, can be appropriately defined as "the attempt to achieve forms of valuation, or principles of valuing, that are as little as possible *arbitrary, self-serving*, individually or collectively, and as little *merely regional or provincial*," then, clearly, philosophy must have a moral or ethical aspect just as surely as it has a metaphysical aspect. But, then, it would seem rather too simple, or one-sided, to say, as he does, that "metaphysical truth . . . is the core of philosophic truth."[2] Evidently, "the core of philosophic truth" comprises not just metaphysical truth, but moral or ethical truth as well.

Why, then, the priority (or unique centrality) again and again assigned to the metaphysical, and thus to metaphysics? The answer, it would seem, is that philosophy, being critical reflection on existence as such, and thus on all answers to the existential question, implicit as well as explicit, itself rests on the basic supposition that authentic self-understanding can only be appropriate or authorized self-understanding and therefore has to be realistic—i.e., a self-understanding that agrees, rather than disagrees, with ultimate reality in its structure in itself. In this sense, or to this extent, the moral or ethical aspect of philosophy depends on, or derives from, its metaphysical aspect. Hence the unique priority (or unique centrality) of metaphysics.

This all assumes, of course, that Hartshorne's talk about "forms of valuation, or principles of valuing" is not really, but only verbally, different from my talk about "self-understanding/understanding of existence."

∽

I want to hold that transcendental metaphysics and transcendental ethics are rightly understood as the core or central task of philosophy in its one abstract, included, or "analytic" phase. Far from being matters of "speculation," uncontrolled by "objective argumentation," metaphysics and ethics are precisely matters of logical "analysis." They are matters of logically analyzing the structure, as distinct from the content, of our core or central experience of ultimate reality, which is to say, ourselves, others, and the whole. In the case of metaphysics, this means analysis of the structure of this

---

2. Hartshorne, *Darkness and the Light*, 26–27, 362.

ultimate reality in itself, while in the case of ethics, it means analysis of the meaning of this ultimate reality for us—in *its* structure.

I also want to hold that transcendental metaphysics and transcendental ethics, so understood, are rightly taken to be foundational criteriologically for the core or central task of philosophy in its other concrete, inclusive, or "existential," phase. Philosophy critically validates the claim to existential truth made or implied by culture and religion in general by the criterion provided by "the 'right' philosophy," or "a correctly verbalized philosophy," which is to say, by the right transcendental metaphysics and the right transcendental ethics.

∾

Philosophy concretely, in its inclusive concrete phase, is existential, in that it is oriented, proximately as well as remotely, by *the* existential question about the meaning of ultimate reality for us. In asking this as well as any other existential question, human beings seek wisdom (*sapientia*). But because they want only valid answers to their existential questions, including *the* existential question, they also ask intellectual questions, thereby seeking knowledge (*scientia*) as well. So philosophy abstractly, in its included abstract phase, is intellectual and, more exactly, analytic, in that it is constituted by the intellectual questions of logical analysis, asking at its core or center (as transcendental metaphysics) about the structure of ultimate reality in itself and (as transcendental ethics) about the structure of ultimate reality's meaning for us.

∾

I have often thought and said that "existence," or "self-understanding/understanding of existence," is to "action," or "life-praxis," rather as "the transcendental" is to "the categorial." So there is a definite precedent in my thinking and writing for distinguishing, as I now do, between "transcendental-metaphysical propositions" and "transcendental-ethical propositions," understanding by the first propositions about the structure of ultimate reality in itself, and by the second, propositions about the meaning of ultimate reality for us, and more exactly about the structure of that meaning (and so, in Bochenski's terms, *die Sätze* and *die praktischen Sätze* respectively). In fact, I might fairly claim that my several discussions as a Christian theologian of "the original call to be a human being" either simply are, or are a special application of, my "transcendental ethics" as based in turn on my "transcendental metaphysics" as a philosopher.

∾

If "witness" is what "theology" in the more critical sense is both distinct from and critically appropriates/reflects on, what plays this role for "philosophy," also understood in the more critical sense? The answer, I take it, is life-praxis and culture, including religious life-praxis and culture, in general—just as "witness," properly, refers to the life-praxis and culture that includes, but is not exhausted by, the religious life-praxis and culture explicitly mediated by a specific religion. The parallel further implies that, just as witness, or some part thereof, may be thought and spoken of as "theology" in a less critical sense of the word, so life-praxis and culture/religion, or some part thereof, may be thought and spoken of as "philosophy" in a similarly less critical sense—if only under some such title as "Before Philosophy."

∾

As for how best to critically appropriate Hartshorne's thought that philosophy properly "mediates" between metaphysics (and, I would add, ethics), on the one hand, and science and religion, on the other, I incline to say something like the following:

In its one "analytic" phase, philosophy thus mediates precisely by analyzing the "deep structure," or logical *kind* of meaning, of both science and religion, as well as, I should think, of any other forms of understanding and transforming reality, nondiscursive as well as discursive. (Whitehead speaks in this connection of "the directed activities of mankind," while Wittgenstein refers to "*Lebensformen/Sprachspielen*," both meaning, I think, substantially the same thing.) This philosophy does analogously to the way in which metaphysics and ethics respectively analyze the "deep structure" and meaning of human existence/ultimate reality as such, relating the results of the two types of analysis each to the other. In its other, "existential" phase, then, philosophy thus mediates by relating the results of its metaphysical and ethical analyses, not just to its analyses of science and religion, but also to their own results, as well as to those of any other forms of understanding and transforming reality, including common sense, allowing each to inform the other. This is why "metaphysical theology," if the term has a proper use, refers to one thing, and "philosophical theology" to something else; so, too, with "metaphysical cosmology" and "philosophical cosmology," as well as "metaphysical anthropology" and "philosophical anthropology." In all three cases, the philosophical discipline is not "pure" metaphysics, but is "mixed" with other kinds of empirical knowledge, and rightly so—just as, in Heinrich Scholz's view, a "real-philosophical" metaphysics of nature, or of the actual world, is as important to philosophy, in its way, as a "transcendental-philosophical" metaphysics of all possible worlds (or kinds of world), is in its significantly different way.[3]

∾

One may say that "existentialist analysis," or "fundamental ontology," is metaphysical anthropology in something like the sense in which one may also speak of metaphysical

---

3. Cf. Scholz, *Metaphysik als strenge Wissenschaft*.

cosmology and, if the term be allowed, metaphysical theology. I say "something like the sense" because, although there can be no adequate distinction between ontology as *metaphysica generalis*, on the one hand, and metaphysical cosmology and metaphysical theology, if there be such a thing, as disciplines of *metaphysica specialis*, on the other, there can and should be an adequate distinction between ontology, on the one hand, and metaphysical anthropology (i.e., "existentialist analysis" or "fundamental ontology"), on the other. But, then, if it is correct to distinguish metaphysics from philosophy, and therefore metaphysical cosmology and metaphysical theology, insofar as it exists, from philosophical cosmology and philosophical theology, it is presumably no less correct to distinguish metaphysical anthropology from philosophical anthropology.

That this is the case is evident, first of all, from metaphysics as such being, in its way, *scientia*, even as philosophy as such is, in its way, *sapientia*. Thus, whereas metaphysical cosmology and metaphysical theology, if it exists, are both matters of knowledge, and are thus scient or intellectual rather than sapient or existential, asking, in their different but related ways, about the structure of strictly ultimate reality in itself, philosophical cosmology and philosophical theology ask about the meaning of strictly ultimate reality for us. So, too, *mutatis mutandis*, with the difference between metaphysical and philosophical anthropology: the first is concerned with the structure of human existence in itself, and the second with the meaning of human existence for us.

But there is a second, closely related reason. Much as philosophical theology differs from what is presumably referred to as "metaphysical theology" by mediating between it, on the one hand, and culture and religion as well as other forms of understanding and transforming reality, on the other, so philosophical anthropology differs from metaphysical anthropology by mediating between it, on the one hand, and culture and religion, along with these other forms of understanding and transforming reality, on the other. This means, in the case of philosophical theology, its critically appropriating the concepts/terms of religions generally so as to think/speak of ultimate reality not only literally, as metaphysics does, but also symbolically, as religion and theology do. In the case of philosophical anthropology, it means its integrating at least some of the results of the relevant special sciences, natural as well as human, with the results of metaphysical anthropology. Here the difference between philosophical and metaphysical anthropology is very similar, I believe, to that between philosophical and metaphysical cosmology.

∾

More than once in the preceding entries I signal reservations about the propriety of the term "metaphysical theology." Why do I have a problem with this term? The reason, very simply, is that "theology," as I use the word otherwise—whether to speak of "theology in general," "theology in the sense of philosophical theology," or "theology in the generic/specific sense"—I understand to refer to a matter of wisdom (*sapientia*), as distinct from a matter of knowledge (*scientia*). This it is because theology, properly, is proximately as well as remotely oriented by the existential question about the meaning of ultimate reality for us, as distinct from the intellectual question about the structure of ultimate reality in itself. "Metaphysical," on the other hand, properly qualifies, as I use it, thought and/or speech oriented proximately by this very intellectual question, as distinct from the existential question by which "theology," in the other senses in which I use the term, is proximately as well as remotely oriented. If "metaphysical theology" is used properly, then, theology can only be understood to refer to a kind of thought and/or speech about God that, like metaphysics otherwise, is intellectual rather than existential, a matter of knowledge rather than wisdom. By contrast, "philosophical theology," like philosophy otherwise, is proximately oriented by the existential question and is therefore a matter of wisdom as distinct from knowledge.

∽

I have explained why the term "metaphysical theology" is a problem for me—namely, because theology, properly, is not science, but wisdom, just as metaphysics, properly, is not wisdom, but science. I have also explained why metaphysical anthropology may well be "insofar a misleading concept/term (and that the same is true, *mutatis mutandis*, of 'metaphysical psychology,' also)" (see note 84, "The Scope of Metaphysics"). "*Anthropos*" and "*psyche*" are alike beyond the scope of metaphysics even in the broad sense as including only the analysis of existence in the emphatic sense of existence that understands and self-understands, as distinct from existence that is human specifically as such.

In the one case, the term implicitly confuses two different modes of understanding, the intellectual and existential modes; in the other, it implicitly confuses something with what—for all we know to the contrary—is only one particular kind of that something among other kinds. It would seem better, therefore, to avoid both terms, or, in any case, not to rely on either of them, the while leaving no doubt that neither philosophical theology nor philosophical anthropology can carry out its proper task unless and until metaphysics in the broad sense has done its.

56

On Transcendental Metaphysics

1. The Task

Our task is to work out just that utterly abstract, purely formal, literal (≡ transcendental) metaphysics (in the broad as well as in the strict sense of "metaphysics") that is both possible and necessary.

2. The Conceptuality/Terminology

Included in the conceptuality/terminology necessary to such a metaphysics are the following concepts/terms:

1. a concrete singular (≡ instance ≡ subject); hence also either

2. an event (or an actual state of an individual); or

3. an individual; or

4. an aggregate (≡ composite) of concrete singulars (i.e., events or individuals);

5. an abstract (≡ property ≡ object); hence also either

6. an ordinary (≡ particular ≡ ontic) abstract—i.e., an individuality,[4] a species, a genus, or a category proper; or

7. an extraordinary (≡ universal ≡ ontological) abstract; hence also either,

8. at the higher level, a transcendental, convertible or disjunctive; or,

9. at the lower level, an existential;[5]

---

4. To speak, in a very general sense, of the "individuality" of an individual is to speak of its essence, its essential (as distinct from its accidental) properties. But as used here, "individuality" has a more restricted meaning, designating the essence, or the essential properties, of an ordinary, transitory individual only. Therefore, although it is entirely proper to speak, in a very general sense, of the "individuality" of the extraordinary, everlasting individual, it must also be remembered that there is an infinite, qualitative difference between its essential properties and those of any ordinary, transitory individual. Whereas the latter are all on the lowest level of ordinary abstracts, the essential properties of the extraordinary, everlasting individual are all on the higher level of extraordinary abstracts—i.e., transcendentals, the concept of such an individual being (indeed, *the* transcendental) in which all the others are unified.

5. The term "an existential," as used here to designate a property on the lower level of extraordinary abstracts, is nominalized in the same way in which Martin Heidegger nominalizes "*eine Existenzial*" to refer to an essential property of "an existent," as understood in 2.12.

NOTEBOOKS

10. an ordinary (≡ particular ≡ ontic), transitory individual;

11. the extraordinary (≡ universal ≡ ontological), everlasting individual;

12. an existent in the emphatic sense of an ordinary, transitory individual that understands at the high level of thinking and speaking exhibited by human behavior and is therefore also morally free and responsible.

3. The Distinctions

Among the distinctions that a transcendental metaphysics would appear to require are those between:

1. concretes (≡ instances ≡ subjects) and abstracts (≡ properties ≡ objects);

2. events (or the actual states of individuals) and individuals;

3. concrete singulars (i.e., events or individuals), and aggregates (≡ composites) of concrete singulars;

4. ordinary (≡ particular ≡ ontic) abstracts—i.e., categorials (either individualities, species, genera, or categories proper)—and extraordinary (≡ universal ≡ ontological) abstracts—i.e., either, at the higher level, transcendentals, convertible or disjunctive, or, at the lower level, existentials;

5. the extraordinary (≡ universal ≡ ontological), everlasting individual and ordinary (≡ particular ≡ ontic), transitory individuals; and

6. the extraordinary events (or actual states) in which the extraordinary, everlasting individual can alone be actualized and ordinary events (or actual states) actualizing all ordinary, transitory individuals; and

7. ordinary (≡ particular ≡ ontic), transitory individuals and existents in the emphatic sense of ordinary, transitory individuals that understand at the high level of thinking and speaking exhibited by human behavior and are therefore also morally free and responsible.

57

Transcendental Metaphysics: A Primer

1.1. "Transcendental metaphysics" is to be understood in two senses.

1.2. In a strict or proper sense, it is the analysis of what it is simply to be: to be something as distinct from nothing at all.

1.3. But in a broad sense, it is also analysis of the unique type of being that is capable of, among other things, making an analysis of being simply as such.

1.4. Understood broadly, then, "transcendental metaphysics" includes what may be called, in Martin Heidegger's term, "existentialist analysis."

2.1. To be is to be for: for other things that also are, but in such a way that other things can also be for them.

2.2. To be something for other things is insofar to be *abstract,* whereas to be something that other things can be for is to be *concrete.*

2.3. Everything is abstract insofar as it is for other things, but some things are not just abstract but also concrete in that they are also things for which other things can be.

2.4. Anything concrete is either *particular* or *universal, surpassable* or *unsurpassable.*

2.5. If it is particular and surpassable, only *some* other concrete things are for it, even as it is for only *some* other concrete things.

2.6. If it is universal and unsurpassable, *all* other concrete things are for it, even as it is for *all* other concrete things.

2.7. To be, then, is to be either just abstract or also concrete, and if concrete, either particular or universal, surpassable or unsurpassable.

2.8. To be just abstract for all things is to be a *transcendental,* whereas to be just abstract for some things only is to be a *categorial* (i.e., either a category proper, or else a genus, a species, or an individuality).

2.9. To be concrete is to be, more exactly, *concrete-concrescent*, because a product of the process *concrescence*, whereby everlastingly, without beginning or end, the many again and again grow together to become one and to be increased by one.

2.10. Also, there are two senses, or levels, of the one: the One that is all, for which *all* of the many grow together and are; and any one among the many, for which only *some* of the many grow together and are—in other words, the universal and unsurpassable One, and any particular and surpassable one.

2.11. To be concrete-concrescent in the first sense, or on the first level, of the universal and unsurpassable One is also to be *singular*: whether a singular *event* or else the singular *individual* that is the everlasting sequence of such events having neither beginning nor end.

2.12. To be concrete-concrescent in the second sense, or on the second level, of any particular and surpassable one is either (1) to be a singular event or a singular individual that is a transitory sequence of such events having both beginning and end; or else (2) to be singular in neither sense, but rather *aggregate* or composite—namely, of events and/or individuals that are singular.

3.1. To be the unique type of being capable of making anything like the foregoing analysis of being simply as such—as well as, of course, the present analysis of the being that is thus capable—is to be a particular, surpassable, and transitory individual that also *exists* in the emphatic sense of the word.

3.2. To exist in the emphatic sense of the word is to exist understandingly, at the high level of thinking and speaking evident from human behavior, and thus to be capable of self-understanding, and therewith both of understanding what it is simply to be and to exist, and of the distinctively moral freedom and responsibility of leading one's own individual existence.

3.3. Thus, in addition to the abstracts required to analyze being simply as such, which is to say, *transcendentals*, transcendental metaphysics in the broad sense also includes *existentials*—that is, the abstracts required to analyze what it is to be in the emphatic sense of existing.

58

Logical-Ontological Type Distinctions in Outline: Ten Theses

1. To be real in the most general sense of "reality," which contrasts with "unreality"—i.e., "mere appearance" or "fiction"—is to be real for the one extraordinary, everlasting individual and also for at least some ordinary events and/or ordinary, transitory individuals that either have become or are in process of becoming real in the same general sense.

In this most general sense of "reality," everything is real for something—for something extraordinary and for something ordinary—and only nothing is real for nothing.

2. But there is a distinction in logical-ontological type between (1) things that are real solely and simply in the most general sense that they are objects, in that they are real for the one extraordinary, everlasting individual, and also for at least some ordinary events and/or ordinary, transitory individuals; and (2) things that are real in the fuller sense that other things either were or are also real for them as themselves processes of becoming, extraordinary or ordinary, and therefore are not only objects but also subjects.

Just as "objects" so understood is equivalent in meaning to "properties" or "abstracts," so "subjects" is equivalent in meaning to "instances" or "concretes"—more exactly, "concrete singulars" (see thesis 6). Also, the concrete singulars that are real, in the sense that things are also real for them, are one and all processes of becoming, or, in Whitehead's term, of "concrescence"—i.e., growing together. Therefore, to be real in the fuller sense in which subjects are real is not simply to be but also to become.

3. As between objects that are also subjects, there is a further logical-ontological type-distinction in that some of them can, while others cannot, also be real for themselves as processes of becoming—the first type of subjects being individuals, and the second type events.

Subjects of both types are not only real for the one extraordinary, everlasting individual and also for at least some of the many other things that either have become or are in process of becoming real, but also such that other things can be real for them as themselves processes of becoming. But events cannot be real for themselves, but only for other events and/or individuals, whereas individuals can also be real for themselves. Events become and perish but do not change and endure; individuals, by contrast, change and endure whether or not they also become and perish, as any of the many ordinary, transitory individuals do, and the one extraordinary, everlasting individual does not. Thus, as between events and individuals, there is also a distinction between types of identity—the identity proper to events being *strict*, that proper to individuals, *genetic*. The identity of an event is strict because it has, or is essentially qualified by, *all* of its properties, whereas the identity of an individual is genetic because it has, or is essentially qualified by, only *some* of its properties, having (or being qualified by) others only inessentially or accidentally.

4. There is another distinction in logical-ontological type between individuals—namely, that between the many ordinary, transitory individuals, for which only some things can be real and which themselves can be real for only some things—i.e., the many; and the one extraordinary, everlasting individual, for which all things are real and which itself is real for all things—i.e., the One.

Whereas there are and must be *many* ordinary, transitory individuals, there is and can be only the *One* extraordinary, everlasting individual, since, if it is both real for all things and such that all things are real for it, there neither is nor could be anything to distinguish any one such individual from any other. By the same token, the one and only extraordinary, everlasting individual cannot fail to be real, provided only that the concept "extraordinary, everlasting individual" is both clear and coherent. That it is both clear and coherent is evident, arguably, because all other things and concepts necessarily imply it.

5. Another logical-ontological type-distinction is between ordinary, transitory individuals themselves, in that some of them are, while others are not, capable of understanding by thinking and speaking, those who are thus capable being properly distinguished as "existents" in the emphatic sense of the term.

All ordinary, transitory individuals are such that some things are real for them and they can also be real for themselves and the extraordinary, everlasting individual as well as for at least some ordinary events and/or individuals. But only some ordinary, transitory individuals are capable of understanding themselves as well as others and the whole, and therefore also understanding what it is to be real both in the most general sense and in the various senses reflecting the logical-ontological type distinctions bridged by this most general sense of reality" (see thesis 1).

6. Of the other two distinctions in logical-ontological type that require to be clarified, one is the distinction with respect to both events and individuals between singulars and aggregates—i.e., between any one event or individual, on the one hand, and any group of events and/or individuals lacking in the subjective unity of any of its members, on the other.

An aggregate, or composite, is distinguished from a singular, whether event or individual, because it lacks the unity of the singulars composing it. It lacks their unity because such unity as it has is neither the strict identity of an event nor the genetic identity of an individual. Therefore, although all three types of concretes—events, individuals, and aggregates—are both one and many, each type of concrete is both one and many in a distinctive way. An event is one and many in the way constituted by its strict identity as an event: being essentially qualified by *all* of the many other events and properties to which it is internally related, it would be an essentially different event if even a single element in this many were otherwise. An individual, by contrast, is one and many in the way constituted by its genetic identity as an individual: being qualified essentially by only *some* of the many other events and properties to which it is internally related, it would still be essentially the same individual even if others of these events and relations were different, and it therefore had many different "accidental" properties from those it in fact has. Finally, an aggregate is one and many in any way allowed for by its having neither the strict nor the genetic identity of its members.

This difference may also be put by saying that, whereas individuals are both singular and subject to change, and events are singular even though not subject to change, aggregates are not singular even though subject to change. They are subject *to* change, however, not subjects *of* change. The only subjects *of* change so far as aggregates are concerned are the individuals that they include or that include them.

7. The other logical-ontological type-distinction is with respect to objects that are only objects and is between two different types thereof: (1) the extraordinary objects that are either transcendentals or existentials; and (2) the ordinary objects that are categorials—i.e., respectively, categories proper, genera, species, and individualities.

Transcendentals are extraordinary in that they are strictly universal and therefore such that they must be real for, and so characterize, anything coherently conceivable, either regardless of logical-ontological type-distinctions or taking such distinctions into account. Thus, for example, the transcendental property of being real events and/or ordinary, transitory individuals is itself real for, and so characterizes, anything whatsoever regardless of any distinctions of logical-ontological type. And the same is true of any other transcendental properties that are *convertible* (or coextensive) with the property of being real in this most general sense of the word—such properties, for example, as being one, good, true, and beautiful, to name only those most commonly reckoned among the convertible "transcendentals" of traditional Western metaphysics. By contrast, the transcendental property of being a subject as well as an object, and so real in the fuller sense, is *disjunctive* with the transcendental property of being merely an object. Accordingly, being a subject is real for, and so characterizes, something only insofar as one takes this distinction of logical-ontological type into account.

As for the question of how transcendentals can be real for themselves as well as for other categorial properties (i.e., individualities as well as species, genera, and categories proper), the answer is that transcendental properties, both convertible and disjunctive, are real for themselves and for other properties only insofar as they are also real for, and so characterize, the subjects, the events, and/or the individuals to which they and other properties belong. Thus the convertible property of being real is real for another property, whether transcendental or categorial, only insofar as it is real for some instance of the other property. Similarly, the disjunctive transcendental of being a property is real for a property only insofar as the disjunctive transcendental of being an instance of the property is real for some subject instantiating the property.

Existentials, also, may be classified as extraordinary objects, albeit on a lower level than transcendentals, because they are not strictly universal, but particular in their own way, being the essential properties, not of anything whatsoever, but only of any existent in the emphatic sense of the word, which is to say, any ordinary, transitory individual that understands by thinking and speaking and therefore self-understands (see thesis 5). Precisely in being able to understand itself, others, and the whole, an existent is the uniquely "ontological," or metaphysical, individual, in that it can therewith understand reality in the most general sense as well as in all the senses reflecting the logical-ontological type-distinctions outlined in these theses. Moreover, by understanding the essential structure of its own existence, as articulated by the several "existentials," an existent carries out what Martin Heidegger calls "existentialist analysis," or "fundamental ontology," meaning by this the understanding of reality necessary to all ontological, or metaphysical, understanding. Metaphysics in the broad sense, then, includes analysis of "existentials" as well as of the "transcendentals" that are the proper concern of metaphysics in the strict sense.

As for categorials, categories proper are real for, and so characterize, such fundamentally different kinds of individuals and/or events as respectively mental and material, living and nonliving, sentient and nonsentient, etc. Genera are real for, and so characterize, less fundamentally different kinds of individuals and/or events, whereas species are real for, and so characterize, still less fundamentally different kinds. Individualities are the properties defining individual members of species as just the particular individuals that each of them happens to be; as such they must be instantiated in every event (or "state") in which any of these individuals is actualized.

It is to be noted, also, that the distinctions between the four kinds of categorials—individualities, species, genera, and categories proper—are more or less arbitrary, and are therefore in principle different from any logical-ontological distinctions of type.

8. Two of the several distinctions in logical-ontological type are evidently fundamental to all the others: that between subjects and objects; and that between the one extraordinary everlasting individual and the many ordinary, transitory individuals.

Significantly, both of these fundamental differences exhibit the same structure of symmetry embraced within a still more fundamental asymmetry. Thus, while subjects and objects mutually require one another, neither being real without the other, and to this extent exhibit symmetry, subjects require at least some objects by a necessity that is definite or determinate, whereas objects require such subjects as they require only by a necessity that is indefinite or indeterminate, and in this respect exhibit asymmetry. So this individual woman, say, could not be real without the species property of being human, even though the species property of being human could very well be real without this individual woman or any other, provided only that there were at least *some* individual(s), possible if not actual, characterized by the property ("possible" here meaning not merely "possible *ontologically*" [≡ unrestrictively ≡ undifferentiatedly], but also "possible *ontically*" [≡ restrictively ≡ differentiatedly]).

In somewhat the same way, the one extraordinary, everlasting individual, on the one hand, and the many ordinary, transitory individuals, on the other, mutually require one another, neither being real without the other, and insofar exhibit symmetry. But ordinary, transitory individuals require the extraordinary, everlasting individual by a necessity that is definite or determinate, whereas the extraordinary, everlasting individual requires ordinary, transitory individuals only by a necessity that is indefinite or indeterminate, insofar exhibiting asymmetry. Whereas no ordinary, transitory individual could be real, but for the reality of the extraordinary, everlasting individual, the extraordinary, everlasting individual could and would be real without the reality of any ordinary, transitory individual whatsoever, provided only that at least *some* ordinary, transitory individuals were real.

Neither of these fundamental distinctions, however, is such as to constitute a dualism. In both cases, the two sides of the distinction do not simply stand alongside one another, but rather are so related that one side includes (or, in Hegelian terms, "overlaps") the other. Thus subjects include objects, and in the same way, the one and only extraordinary, everlasting individual includes all the many ordinary, transitory individuals.

9. Also evident from the preceding theses is that there are, in a sense, different degrees of concreteness and abstractness in between the two extremes of fully concrete events and completely abstract transcendentals.

The more abstract something is, the less it derives its reality from other things, and the more universally they derive their reality from it. Conversely, the more concrete something is, the more its reality derives from other things and the less universally they derive their reality from it. But the different degrees of abstractness allow for two distinct types of objects or properties: categorials (i.e., individualities, species, genera, and categories proper), on the one hand, and transcendentals and existentials, on the other (see thesis 7). The distinction between the two types—ordinary and extraordinary respectively—is that, in the case of ordinary properties, whether individual, specific, generic, or categorial proper, there is always the possibility of negative instances, whereas, in the case of extraordinary properties that are transcendental, there is no such possibility because they admit of positive instances only. Otherwise put, the intensional class of events and/or individuals or of other still more specific kinds that all ordinary properties imply by the same kind of indefinite or indeterminate necessity are only *contingently* nonempty classes, whereas the intensional classes implied by transcendental properties by the same kind of indefinite or indeterminate necessity are *necessarily* nonempty classes. This means that some properties must be instantiated by events and/or individuals, since otherwise there would be nothing at all to think and speak about, whether universal or particular. But, then, the ground of contingency is not simply in the contrast between being a property and being instantiated in some event and/or individual, but in the contrast between being a more and a less abstract property. Accordingly, all categorial or ordinary properties are more or less contingent, although categories proper are relatively less so than genera, genera relatively less so than species, and species relatively less so than individualities. On the other hand, all transcendental or extraordinary properties are necessary in that they are and must be instantiated somehow, in some events and/or individuals. Moreover, even existential properties, in their way, admit of positive instances only, the assertion "I do not exist" being self-refuting pragmatically, even if not absolutely.

There are also different degrees of concreteness insofar as there are logical-ontological type-distinctions between events and individuals, even as there are such distinctions between ordinary and extraordinary properties. Thus events alone are fully concrete, just as transcendentals alone are completely abstract. By the same token, there is a sense in which individuals, though concretes, are more abstract than events, even as there is a sense in which categorials (i.e., categories proper, genera, species, and individualities), though abstracts, are more concrete than transcendentals.

10. If "reality" can and must be used not only in the most general sense, but also in all the different senses reflecting the logical-ontological type-distinctions outlined in these theses, it is evidently an analogical—as distinct from either a univocal or an equivocal—concept, in that it can and must be used in different, if also similar, senses to refer to all the different types of reality.

Allowing that subjects and objects are both real, and that there are also different types of subjects—namely, singular events and individuals as well as aggregates thereof—and different types of objects—namely, transcendentals and existentials, in the one type, and categorials (i.e., categories proper, genera, species, and individualities) in the other—"reality" can only be, in some sense, an analogical term. Likewise, if the extraordinary, everlasting individual, on one level, and all ordinary, transitory individuals, on the other, are both properly individuals, "individual" is also evidently an analogical (neither a univocal nor an equivocal) term, in that it has two radically different, if also similar, senses when it is applied respectively to the one necessary, extraordinary, everlasting individual and to any of the many possible, ordinary, transitory individuals. Furthermore, the concept, "event," apart from which "individual" cannot be defined, must also be an analogical (rather than either a univocal or an equivocal) concept, since it applies to both the type of extraordinary events in which the extraordinary, everlasting individual can alone be actualized and the type of ordinary events in which any ordinary, transitory individual is and must be actualized if it is actualized at all.

In this sense, or to this extent, there has to be a place for analogy even in the austerely transcendental metaphysics outlined in these theses. Even so, because the logical-ontological type-distinctions bridged by these analogical terms are themselves purely formal and literal, in that whether something is or is not an "event" or an "individual," a "transcendental" or a "category," is not a matter of more or less, but of all or none, the different senses in which these analogical terms are used are each literal because they each apply, within their respective types, not in different senses, but in the same sense. Moreover, "reality," "individual," "event," and so on all retain a core of strictly literal meaning in any of their uses. Anything that is real in any sense whatever is so only because it is real for, and hence makes a difference to, the one extraordinary, everlasting individual, and also to at least some of the many ordinary, transitory things that either have become or are in the process of becoming real in the same general sense of "reality." And any individual whatsoever, whether the one extraordinary, everlasting individual or any of the many ordinary, transitory individuals, actualizes its individuality, and so exists, only in events that are and must be contingent rather than necessary.

So the sense in which analogy is involved even in an austerely transcendental metaphysics such as that outlined here is in no way to be confused with the very different sense in which any categorial metaphysics has to be "analogical."

59

Hartshorne on Peirce's Three Categories

On rereading Hartshorne's papers on C. S. Peirce's categories of Firstness, Secondness, and Thirdness, I am struck by the way in which the outlines of an entire neoclassical transcendental metaphysics are present in what he says.

The great merit of Peirce's categories, as Hartshorne develops them, is that they do in fact sum up the whole of metaphysics in purely formal, literal terms, without the difficulties of any categorial metaphysics, whether physicalist, psychicalist, or dualist. To be sure, the palmary instance of the categories given in experience is our experience itself, each occasion of which is, in its way, first, second, and third. But while the three categories are thus illustrated in and abstracted from or analyzed out of our experience of our own experience, they themselves are purely formal and literal, having to do entirely with the *structure* of our experience and being definable strictly and solely either as degrees of relativity (or nonrelativity) or as forms of dependence (or independence).

In one paper, Hartshorne thus speaks of "the three basic degrees of relativity." Firstness, or the monad, is the first, and in a sense the least genuine, of the three degrees, since it is "the zero case of true relativity," even as it is "the unit case of plurality of terms." Secondness, or the dyad, is "the first degree of true relativity" as well as "the second degree with respect to the number of terms implied." Thirdness, or the triad, is "the second, and in principle sufficient degree of relativity," even though it is "the third degree in number of terms."[6]

In another paper, Hartshorne defines the categories, not in terms of "degrees of *relativity*," but rather in terms of "forms of *dependence*." "[T]here are indeed three forms of dependence: (1) the positive form, strict dependence; (2) the negative form, strict independence (both holding asymmetrically among definite particulars); and (3) dependence that leaves the final particularity open and can be stated only in more or less general terms." Thus Firstness is defined as "sheer independence of at least something," Secondness as "dependence on at least something," and Thirdness as "qualified, partial, or probabilistic dependence on at least something."[7]

The other thing that is clear to me from these papers, especially the two quoted from, is that the only additional distinction that a neoclassical transcendental metaphysics requires is that between God or deity and all things other than God or nondeity.

---

6. Hartshorne, "Charles Peirce's 'One Contribution,'" 456.
7. Hartshorne, "Revision of Peirce's Categories," 282.

Of course, this distinction has to be formulated "neoclassically," and so significantly otherwise than in classical metaphysics.

> Just as we creatures are independent of some but not all concrete situations, God (in his Primordial aspect) is independent of all; so we are relative to, dependent upon, some but not all, while God [in his Consequent aspect] is relative to all. The old analysis which ran: we are relative, only God is absolute was too hasty. Not the relativity or its denial is distinctive of us or of God but the localization, the confinement to a restricted context, versus the non-localization, whether of the relativity or of the non-relativity.... What distinguishes God is not his ordinal degree of relativity (as between First, Second, and Third) but rather his being relative (in all three degrees) in every context.... God as merely Primordial is the neutral or undifferentiated Anticipation of all events, the only pure First; as 'Consequent' or World-synthesizing, [God] is the completely differentiated or all-discriminating Memory or retrospective perception [of all events]"; as 'Superject' (Whitehead), Providential or World-ordering, [God] is the differentiated (though still not wholly determinate) anticipation of events. Ordinary individuals have also these three functions, but locally, not universally, deficiently, or with vast inhibitions or abstractive omissions.... [A]ll things, from atoms to God, are really instances of First, Second, Third.[8]

It is clear, then, that all one really needs to formulate metaphysical truth is the three categories and the distinction between universal and particular quantification—i.e., *all* and *some*. All things are instances of First, Second, and Third. But whereas all things other than God are First, Second, and Third with respect only to *some* things, not to all, God instances the three categories with respect to *all* things, not merely to some.

I do wonder, however, whether *three* categories are really required—and whether having only *two* categories might not make for a more adequate conception. There is an apparent overlap between Secondness and Thirdness, at least as Hartshorne develops them. Insofar as Thirdness looks not only to the future but also to the past, it seems indistinguishable from Secondness. It might be better, then, to distinguish between Firstness as a way of talking about reality in the sense common to both abstracts and concretes and Secondness as a way of talking about reality in the sense distinctive of concretes. On this way of speaking, any entity, abstract or concrete, instances Firstness, insofar as, being real only because it is real for something else that is real, it anticipates this other thing but is not dependent on it—or, better, it anticipates being real for *some* thing, but not for any *particular* thing. Concrete entities, then, further instance Secondness, insofar as they are not only real for something else that is real, but are also the type of things for which other things, abstract as well as concrete, can be real. Thus whereas abstracts, in direct proportion to their degree of abstractness,

---

8. Hartshorne, "Charles Peirce's 'One Contribution,'" 464, 473–74.

presuppose nothing and anticipate other things only indefinitely or indeterminately, concretes, in direct proportion to the degree of their concreteness, necessarily presuppose other concretes definitely or determinately, while anticipating still others only indefinitely or indeterminately.

∽

Or, is Peirce right after all in arguing for a minimum of three categories (i.e., Firstness, Secondness, and Thirdness)?

One reason for thinking he is right is that there is a difference between the kind of indefinite or indeterminate necessity with which extraordinary abstracts (i.e., transcendentals) require at least some concretes to instantiate them and the other kind with which both ordinary abstracts (i.e., categories proper, genera, species, individualities) and concretes require concretes to instantiate them—both of these kinds being distinct from the kind of definite or determinate necessity with which concretes require the other concretes they objectify. In other words, because there are indeed three different degrees of relativity, or three forms of dependence, a case can definitely be made for a minimum of three categories.

Whereas extraordinary abstracts (i.e., transcendentals) are utterly nonrestrictive with respect to the kind(s) of concretes they require to instantiate them, this is not true either of ordinary abstracts (i.e., categories proper, genera, species, individualities) or of concretes, both of which are more or less restrictive with respect to the kind(s) of concretes they require to instantiate or objectify them.

Would it make sense, then, to distinguish between two kinds of indefinite or indeterminate necessity, one of which would be the kind with which extraordinary abstracts (i.e., transcendentals) require concretes to instantiate them, while the other would be the kind with which both ordinary abstracts (i.e., categories proper, genera, species, individualities) and concretes require concretes to instantiate them? If such a distinction would make sense, we could perhaps express it by speaking of *absolutely/ relatively* indefinite or indeterminate necessity—or, possibly, *wholly/partially* indefinite or indeterminate necessity.

Alternatively, it might be possible to distinguish between the utterly *undifferentiated* necessity with which extraordinary abstracts (i.e., transcendentals) require concretes to instantiate them, and the more or less *differentiated* necessity with which both ordinary abstracts (i.e., categories proper, genera, species, individualities) and concretes require concretes to instantiate them—both of these kinds of indefinite or indeterminate necessity being distinct from the kind of definite or determinate necessity with which concretes require the other concretes they instantiate.

Just why are Peirce's three categories all necessary?

Firstness is necessary in order to understand absoluteness or independence, whether that of abstracts, ordinary as well as extraordinary, or that of concretes functioning objectively, as objects for other concretes as subjects.

Secondness is necessary in order to understand the relativity or dependence of concretes in one of their two forms—namely, in their relation to the past in which they involve the actuality of their predecessor concretes.

Thirdness is necessary in order to understand both the relativity or dependence of concretes in the other of its two forms—namely, in their relation to the future, in which they involve (indeed, *are*) the potentiality of their successor concretes—and the relativity or dependence of ordinary, as distinct from, extraordinary abstracts

Explanation:

1. If concretes are, in their way, absolute or independent as well as relative or dependent, ordinary abstracts, in contrast with extraordinary ones, are relative or dependent in their own way, as well as absolute or independent.

2. They are relative or dependent because they are related to or dependent upon the contingent. This they are because the intensional classes of concretes in which they, as abstracts, must somehow be embodied or included are not empty necessarily, but only contingently. Extraordinary abstracts, by contrast, are not thus relative or dependent because the intensional classes of concretes in which they must somehow be embodied or included are not nonempty contingently only, but necessarily.

60

On Transcendentals

A concept is said to be "transcendent" in scholastic philosophy insofar as it goes beyond the limits of any and all class concepts, including categories or categorials, and therefore applies in some way to literally everything without restriction. Such concepts are called "transcendentals" (≡ *transcendentia*, or *transcendentalia*) and are usually understood to include "being" (≡ *esse* ≡ *das Sein* ≡ *die Seiendheit*), or "a being" (≡ *ens* ≡ *das Seiende*, or *ein Seiendes*), "thing" (≡ *res* ≡ *die Sache* ≡ *das Ding*), "something" (≡ *aliquid* ≡ *das Etwas*, or *die Etwasheit*—i.e., *die Abgegrenztheit gegenüber jedem andere*), "one" (≡ *unum* ≡ *das Eine*, or *die Einheit*—i.e., *die innere Untrennbarkeit der wesentlichen Bestimmungen*), "true" (≡ *verum* ≡ *das Wahre*, or *die Wahrheit* ≡ die

Erkennbarkeit ≡ die Geistbezogenheit), "good" (≡ *bonum ≡ das Gute*, or *die Werthaftigkeit ≡ die Erstrebbarkeit ≡ die Willensbezogenheit*). Added sometimes, especially in the Franciscan schools, is "beauty" (≡ *pulchrum ≡ das Schöne*, or *die Schönheit*—i.e., *die mühlosselbstverständliche Übereinstimmung mit dem Anschauungsvermögen*). Because all of these concepts have the same completely unrestricted scope as the concept "being," they are all said to be "convertible" (or "coextensive") with it, and it with them.

In scholastic and neoscholastic philosophy, the term "transcendental" often has the same meaning as the term "transcendent"—i.e., going beyond the limits of all classes and kinds, and hence all univocal meaning, to analogy. Hence *"transcendentia"* are also called *"transcendentalia."*

Immanuel Kant gives the term "transcendental" a new, distinctively different meaning when he calls all knowledge "transcendental" insofar as it has to do, not with objects, but with our way of knowing objects, to the extent that such knowledge is possible a priori. Thus "transcendental" does not designate something that goes beyond experience—for that, Kant simply uses "transcendent"—but rather something prior to experience that nonetheless has no purpose other than to make knowledge based on experience possible. Accordingly, the contrasting term to "transcendental," as he uses it, is "empirical." In scholastic usage, on the other hand, the contrasting term is "categorial," including "general," "special," and so on.

Of course, prominent in the background of all this is Aristotle, who defines metaphysics, or "first philosophy," as the study of being *qua* being, which is to say, the study of being as such together with its essential attributes. To say that something *is* is also to say that it is *one*, so that unity is an essential attribute of being and is therefore convertible (or coextensive) with it. But then, just as being is found in all the categories, so also is unity. In the *Nicomachean Ethics*, Aristotle remarks that goodness is also applicable in all the categories. Therefore, in the terms of the later scholastic philosophers, unity and goodness are transcendental attributes of being, since in being applicable in all categories, they are confined to none and do not constitute genera, species, and so on.

Of special interest, so far as my own metaphysical reflections are concerned, is the doctrine of *transcendentia* developed by John Duns Scotus. For him, the *passiones entis* (≡ properties or attributes of being) include both *passiones entis convertibles*, such as one, true, good, and beautiful, and *passiones entis disjunctæ*, such as necessary/contingent (*sc.* possible) and act/potency, both of which are "transcendent" properties. "Whatever [predicates] are common to God and creatures," Scotus says, "are of such kind [*sc.* transcendental and outside any genus], pertaining as they do to being in its indifference to what is infinite and finite."[9] Moreover, the concept of "being," and thus the concepts of its properties are and must be univocal, in the sense that they belong to being literally, whether "as indifferent to finite and [infinite]," in the case of the convertible properties, or as including both finite and infinite, act and potency,

---

9. Duns Scotus, *Philosophical Writings*, 2; cf. Copleston, *History of Philosophy II*, 503–4.

and so on, in the case of the disjunctive properties. Were it otherwise, Scotus insists, there could be no natural knowledge of God at all. "God cannot be known naturally unless being is univocal to the created and uncreated."[10]

~

For medieval thinkers generally, transcendental terms are said to transcend the categories in that they belong no more to one category than to another.[11] For Duns Scotus, transcendentals are so called because they transcend both the division of being into finite and infinite, and the further division of finite being into the ten Aristotelian categories. Being (≡ *ens*) is a transcendental, and so are its "proper attributes"—i.e., "one," "true," "good," and "beautiful," all of which are convertible (or coextensive) with "being." But Duns Scotus also notes an indefinite number of disjunctions that are coextensive with being disjunctively, and insofar count as, transcendentals, such as infinite-or-finite, necessary-or-contingent. He also holds that all the so-called pure perfections are transcendentals insofar as they transcend the division of being into finite and infinite, even though they are not convertible (or cotextensive) with being. Thus, e.g., God is wise and Socrates is wise, but an earthworm—although most certainly a being—is not wise.

But if Duns Scotus distinguishes "pure perfections" from both the proper properties of being—i.e., convertible (or coextensive) transcendentals (*passiones entis convertibiles*) and the disjunctive transcendentals (*passiones entis disjunctæ*)—isn't this because his metaphysics is, and is meant to be, attributively dualistic? Aren't his "pure perfections" simply the properties of spirit or mind, as other than body or matter? And isn't this why he says that wisdom is a transcendental even though an earthworm is not wise?

In any case, reckoning pure perfections as transcendentals seems incoherent. Pure perfections can be coherently called transcendentals only if they are attributes, or properties, either convertible or disjunctive, of being *qua* being. That they transcend the distinction between finite and infinite being is not sufficient to make them transcendentals, if transcendentals are also supposed to transcend the distinctions between any one finite being and any other. It seems clear that Duns Scotus's allowing pure perfections to be transcendentals means that his metaphysics is not austerely "transcendental" after all, but is, in its own way, "mixed," being somewhat like Hartshorne's, categorial as well as transcendental.

---

10. Duns Scotus, *Philosophical Writings*, 5.
11. Ashworth, "Medieval Theories of Analogy."

On Transcendentals

~

In my view, as in Scotus's, there is a fundamental distinction to be made between different *transcendentals*, or properties of reality (≡ *passiones entis*). Some of them are *convertible* (or coextensive) transcendentals, or properties of reality (≡ *passiones entis convertibiles*), that apply to anything real in any of the ways or senses in which something can be real. Others are *disjunctive* transcendentals, or properties of reality (≡ *passiones entis disjunctæ*), that apply to anything real in one or the other of the different (and disjunctive) ways or senses in which something can be real.

Thus anything *real* in any way or sense whatsoever is also *one, good, true,* and *beautiful*, these all being convertible (or coextensive) transcendentals applying to anything real regardless of the way or sense in which it is so. But also, in my view, anything real, one, good, true, and beautiful is either concrete or abstract, the transcendentals "concrete"/"abstract" constituting one of the two primary pairs of disjunctive transcendentals. This means that, if something is concrete, it neither is nor can be merely abstract, and therefore must be something real, one, good, true, and beautiful in the only way or sense in which something concrete can be any of these things, and not in the only way or sense in which something merely abstract can be any of them. Similarly, anything concrete and singular (i.e., any event or individual, including any existent in the emphatic sense of the term) must be either unsurpassable or surpassable, the transcendentals "unsurpassable"/"surpassable" constituting the other primary pair of disjunctive transcendentals, which are applicable, however, only to concrete singulars. This means that if something is unsurpassable, it neither is nor can be surpassable, and therefore must be something real, one, good, true, and beautiful in the only way or sense in which something unsurpassable can be any of these things, and not in the only way or sense in which something surpassable can be any of them.

So, although a concrete thing and a merely abstract thing are both good, a concrete thing is good in the way or sense of being *intrinsically* as well as constitutively good, whereas a merely abstract thing is good in the way or sense of being *constitutively* good only. Or, again, although an unsurpassable thing and a surpassable thing are also both good, an unsurpassable thing is good in the way or sense of being inclusive of *all* good things, actual and/or potential, as well as included in all of them, and therefore *unsurpassably* good. On the other hand, a surpassable thing is good in the way or sense of including only *some* good things, actual and/or potential, and of being included in only *some* of them, and therefore only *surpassably* good.

As for what I judge to be the primary pairs of disjunctive transcendentals, concrete/abstract and unsurpassable/surpassable, the referent of the first term in each pair *includes* or "overlaps" (Hegel) the referent of the second term, even as the referent of the second term in each pair is *included* in or "overlapped" by the referent of the first. Thus the concrete includes the abstract, even as the abstract is included in the concrete; and the unsurpassable includes the surpassable, even as the surpassable is included in the unsurpassable.

The key to the first pair, concrete/abstract, is the distinction between being internally related to other concretes *definitely* or *determinately*, in the case of anything concrete, and not being so related, in the case of anything merely abstract. Because anything merely abstract is internally related only to certain intensional *classes* of concretes, which are either necessarily or only contingently nonempty, it is internally related to concretes as such only *indefinitely* or *indeterminately*. The key to the second pair, unsurpassable/surpassable, is the distinction between being both internally and externally related, in suitably different respects, to *all* concretes and abstracts, in the case of the unsurpassable, and being both internally and externally related, in suitably different respects, to only *some* concretes and abstracts, in the case of the surpassable.

∾

A transcendental traditionally taken to be convertible (or coextensive) with "being" (≡ *esse*, *ens*), or "real," is "one" (≡ *unum*). But if one holds, as I do, following C. S. Peirce and Charles Hartshorne, that possibilities form a continuum—in Peirce's phrase, "a multitude beyond all multitude"—how can a possibility, as distinct from an actuality, really be "one" as well as "real," "true," "good," and "beautiful"?

Even granting my principle that convertible (or coextensive) transcendentals, including "one," must apply to concretes in a different way or sense from that in which they apply to abstracts, and to the one unsurpassable reality in a different way or sense from that in which they apply to any surpassable reality—even granting this, there still seems to be a problem. So far as I can see, the only way or sense in which a possibility could be one is in whatever way or sense a determinable, as distinct from a determinate, can be one. But what way or sense, exactly, is that?

In thinking about this question, I've learned I can't improve on the answer implied by Hartshorne's explanation of possibilities as determinables, rather than determinates or classes thereof.

> [P]ossibilities are determinables not determinates.... Given a determinate how[,] we can relate it to the [sc. determinable] somehow, but given only the somehow we cannot relate it to a determinate how. Determinables are not classes of determinates, but aspects of creativity relevant to such classes, so far as the latter are given.[12]

> [B]y 'possibility of particular *P*' we mean, if we understand ourselves, only that the previous phase of process defined itself as destined to be superseded somehow, within certain limits of variation, by a next phase of process. The 'somehow' is not, however, a wholly undifferentiated question mark, but

12. Hartshorne, *Creative Synthesis and Philosophic Method*, 65.

involves some modes of contrast, of 'alternative possibilities,' none of which can coincide in character with the particular which later turns up, but some one [sic] of which, or some one region [sic] of the continuum of possible quality, will later be recognizable as the nearest alternative or region, the one [sic] which with the least further definition is equivalent to the particular.¹³

According to this explanation, a determinable can be one because the "somehow" is always "within certain limits of variation," and thus "is not . . . a wholly undifferentiated question mark, but involves some modes of contrast, of 'alternative possibilities' . . . some one [sic] of which, or some one region of the continuum of possible quality, will later be recognizable as the nearest alternative or region, the one which *with the least further definition* [or determination?] is equivalent to the particular" (italics added). In other words, although the oneness of a determinable can be defined only relatively to that of some determinate, it is not at all relative to any determin-*er*, because "with the least further definition [or, better, 'determination']" is presumably as objective and nonrelative a criterion as any criterion could be.

61

On "Categorial(s)"

The term "categorial" may be used both as an adjective and as a noun. Used as an adjective, it is cognate with "category" analogously to the way in which "generic" is cognate with "genus," or "specific" with "species." Used as a noun, it functions analogously to the way in which "transcendental" and "existential" function when they, too, are used as nouns.

But, unlike "transcendental" and "existential," "categorial" can be used as a noun in more than one sense. In a strict or proper sense, it designates an ordinary abstract of the most general kind and is therefore properly used in the plural alongside such other terms as "genera," "species," and "individualities," to move from the more to the less general kinds of ordinary abstracts. So used, "categorials" is synonymous with "categories" (proper). Used in the broad sense, it includes all kinds of ordinary abstracts, from "categorials (or categories proper)" all the way down through "genera," "species," and "individualities." In this broad sense, any genus, species, or individuality is also a categorial (or category).

---

13. Hartshorne, *Reality as Social Process*, 97–99.

The reason for this is that the differences between the four kinds of categorials—i.e., categorials (or categories) proper, genera, species, and individualities—are not themselves differences of logical-ontological type, as is the difference between transcendentals and existentials, on the one hand, and categorials (or categories), on the other. They are simply differences of kind between all abstracts of the one ordinary type, somewhat as transcendentals and existentials are the two different kinds, or levels, of abstracts of the other extraordinary type.

62

Critical Theory and Revisionary Metaphysics

Significantly, the so-called transcendentals of scholastic philosophy are not formulated in complete abstraction from human interests, but are, in effect, the formal objects constituted by the unavoidable, indispensable human interests—e.g., good (*bonum*), true (*verum*), and beautiful (*pulchrum*). To this extent, the idea that reality, in the different senses in which "reality" may be used, is formally constituted by some human interest or other is not a new, Kantian, or post-Kantian idea.

But recognizing this need not imply any endorsement of "metaphysical neutralism." If, or insofar as, there are different levels of human interest, in the sense that there is a single dominating interest inherent in all interests—and this is, in the nature of the case, the claim that *the* existential, and so religious, theological, and philosophical interest makes for itself—the formal object constituted by this interest would be presupposed necessarily by the formal objects constituted by all other such interests. Metaphysics, then, understood as explicating the structure of reality in itself as formally constituted by this all-inclusive, absolutely fundamental, and overriding human interest would consist of explicating the concepts and principles necessarily presupposed in all human thinking, speaking, and acting.

I see no reason, therefore, why there cannot be to this extent an integration of "critical theory" in the sense of Jürgen Habermas and Karl-Otto Apel, and "revisionary metaphysics" in my sense of the term—i.e., "neoclassical metaphysics." Nor, for that matter, is there any reason to preclude an integration of "descriptive metaphysics" in something like P. F. Strawson's sense of the phrase with the same "revisionary" (as distinct from "revisionist") metaphysics. In this connection, I ask, what is "critical theory," or what is "descriptive metaphysics," if not simply a way of more fully explicating existentialist analysis, which in turn necessarily implies "revisionary metaphysics" in the strict sense?

∽

According to the reasoning in the preceding entry, at least some of the *passiones entis convertibiles* are constituted by the unavoidable, indispensable human interests—in the true, the good (including the just or right), and the beautiful. Necessarily presupposed by these interests is the interest in reality as such, as that which makes a difference to all of us, and to which we, in turn, may all also make a difference, along with its oneness, its whatness, its somewhatness, and so on. But this interest in reality as such is interest in *the passio entis convertibile*. The human subject is interested in, and simply has to take account of, the real; and the real includes whatever the human subject, in one way or another, is interested in or has to take account of. In the first instance, the human subject's interest in the real is *existential*, wherefore it takes account of the real in its meaning for us, for our own possibilities of self-understanding and/or life-praxis. But the human subject also has an *intellectual* interest in the real, wherefore it also takes account of the real in its structure in itself.

By "the *ultimately* real," one properly means whatever the human subject *qua* self-understanding subject has to take account of, or have some interest in, no matter what else it may or may not have to take account of, or have an interest in. And by "the *strictly ultimately* real," one properly means whatever any subject or concrete that is so much as conceivable would somehow have to take account of, no matter what else it did or did not take account of—if only in the completely general, purely formal sense of "taking account of," which is to say, being somehow really, internally related to it and insofar dependent on it and affected by it.

The *passiones entis disjunctæ*, by contrast, are constituted wholly objectively, by the modal distinctions between necessary and contingent (actual and possible) and therefore by the temporal distinctions between eternal and temporal (past, present, and future), together with the distinctions between all the different logical-ontological types—i.e., concrete and abstract, unsurpassable and surpassable, event, individual, and aggregate; categorials (i.e., individualities, species, genera, and categories proper), on the one hand, and transcendentals and existentials, on the other.

63

Events and Transcendentals

The extreme contrast between concrete(s) and abstract(s) is that between event(s) and transcendental(s). An event is more concrete than any other entity or type of reality, even as a transcendental is more abstract. Therefore, just as the most concrete entity or type of reality is an event, so the most abstract entity or type of reality is a transcendental.

Events and transcendentals are alike in that both, in their different ways, are strictly necessary and imply one another. Events necessarily imply transcendentals, which are the class characteristics of the class of events as such. This class, however, is necessarily nonempty, since transcendentals, in turn, necessarily imply *some* events in which they are instantiated. Whereas abstracts of all other types may or may not be instantiated in events, abstracts of the transcendental type cannot fail of instantiation. Some events there simply must be, and any event must of necessity instantiate transcendentals, both convertible ($\equiv$ coextensive) and disjunctive, each after its kind.

In between these extreme poles of the concrete/abstract contrast, there are other entities or types of reality that are either less concrete than events or less abstract than transcendentals, without prejudice to their being properly classified as concretes or abstracts respectively. Thus, for example, an individual is less concrete, or more abstract, than an event (or a particular state of an individual). And yet an individual is a concrete, not an abstract, even if it may be said to be a quasi-abstract. Similarly, an individuality ($\equiv$ individual essence) is significantly less abstract, or more concrete, than a transcendental (as well as a category proper, a genus, and even a species). And yet an individuality is an abstract, not a concrete, even if it may be thought of as a quasi-concrete. What, then, is the criterion of the difference between concretes and abstracts?

Concretes of all types (i.e., events, individuals, existents, and aggregates) are really, internally related to other concretes, some of which—namely, those in their past—they necessarily imply by a definite or determinate necessity, while others—namely, those in their future—they imply by only an indefinite or indeterminate necessity. On the other hand, abstracts of all types (i.e., transcendentals and existentials, categories proper, genera, species, and individualities) are not thus really, internally related to concretes that they necessarily imply by a definite or determinate necessity, but are thus related to only necessarily or only possibly nonempty *classes* of concretes, any particular members of which they necessarily imply by only an indefinite or indeterminate necessity. Thus, for example, a species necessarily implies that it is embodied in some individual, if only as an ontic possibility. But there is no definite or determinate individual as such that the species thus necessarily implies. Even if the specific essence were not to be instantiated in any individual at all—and this, in the nature of the case, must be possible, since the class constituted by any specific essence as its class characteristic is only a possibly (not necessarily) nonempty class—it could still be embodied, provided only that it was included in some individual as at least ontically possible. By clear contrast, any concrete is really, internally related to at least some other concretes definitely or determinately—namely, those in its past—that it necessarily implies as such.

The criterion, then, of the difference between concretes and abstracts is real, internal relatedness to other concretes, which in the case of all abstracts is, in one way or another, only indefinite or indeterminate—because to some necessarily or only possibly nonempty class of concretes, rather than to any concretes definitely or determinately as such. In the case of all concretes, on the other hand, their real, internal relatedness to other concretes is also, in one way or another, definite or determinate—not merely to some necessarily or only possibly nonempty class, but to concretes definitely or determinately as concretes.

∾

I said in the preceding entry that, in between events and transcendentals as the extreme poles of the concrete/abstract contrast, "there are other entities or types of reality that are either less concrete than events or less abstract than transcendentals, without prejudice to their being properly classified as concretes or abstracts respectively." But I did not argue for this statement by explaining why it is true.

The reason—to use the same examples—that an individual, although less concrete than an event, is nonetheless a concrete, not an abstract, is because it is, in its way, internally related to other concretes in *both* of the ways in which concretes as such are so related. Similarly, an individuality (≡ individual essence), although infinitely less abstract than a transcendental, is nonetheless an abstract, not a concrete, because, like other abstracts as such, including transcendentals, it is internally related to concretes in only *one* of the two ways in which it is possible to be so related to them.

At the same time—and for the same reason—it is proper to allow that an individual, although a concrete, may be said to be "a quasi-abstract," just as an individuality, although an abstract, may be said to be "a quasi-concrete."

∾

An ordinary event, as the most concrete of all types of things, exhibits zero independence of context, being spatio-temporally "located." A transcendental, by radical contrast, as the most abstract of all types of things, exhibits the greatest possible independence of context, being "timeless" or "eternal."

64

Existentials and Transcendentals

Extraordinary (≡ ontological) abstracts, both existentials and transcendentals, are experienced in the vertical dimension, or existential aspect, of human experience—i.e., experience of the *ultimate* reality of oneself, others, and the whole. And the analogy between oneself, on the one hand, and any other individual, including the universal individual that is the whole, on the other, is illuminating in both directions, our always only fragmentary experience of each shedding additional light on the other. By contrast, ordinary (≡ ontic) abstracts (from categories proper through genera and species to individualities ≡ individual essences) are experienced in the horizontal dimension, or empirical aspect, of our experience—i.e., experience of the immediate reality of oneself and others, although not of the whole, of which, in the nature of the case, there can be no empirical experience.

∞

Concrescence could not *not* exist and could not *not* produce particular concretes as products. That there is concrescence as such, then, with its two essential forms of unsurpassable and surpassable concrescence, is an unconditionally necessary truth—although it is, in a way, the *only* such truth. As such, it is inherent in all experience and in all thought that is both clear and coherent about the reality that experience discloses.

∞

Of all that exists, everything might not have existed except something and what "something exists" necessarily implies—i.e., "unsurpassable something inclusive of all surpassable somethings exists." Although all further particularization of mere somethingness—unsurpassable and surpassable—is not necessary but contingent, it is not contingent but necessary that every something that exists be further particularized *somehow*, and that further particularization of *something* should occur. Nothing is merely something without being further particularized, nor can further particularization of at least something—unsurpassable and surpassable—ever fail to take place.

65

Whitehead's Term for "the Ultimate"

Whitehead's main term for "the ultimate" is "creativity," whereas Hartshorne typically speaks of "creative synthesis," and I, for my part, prefer Whitehead's other term, "concrescence," in the sense, simply, of the process of "growing together" whereby the concrete becomes the concrete by the many becoming one and being increased by one.

I should wish to say, accordingly, that God and concrescence are distinct in that concrescence is—to use Hartshorne's terms in characterizing creativity—"the ultimate analogical universal or form of forms," or "*the* transcendental," which applies to everything concretely real, analogically though not univocally, whereas God is the eminent or unsurpassable form of concrescence, everything else concretely real being an instance of its noneminent or surpassable form. In a sense, however, this distinction between God and concrescence is not final or adequate, because all concrescence is *either* God's own self-creation *or* a datum therefor—either, in Whitehead's terms, a divine "subjective form" or a divine "objective form," either a contribution divinely made to the creatures or a contribution divinely received from them. Thus God is, in a way, "concrescence itself," concrescence being understood as "the determining of the antecedently indeterminate [but determinable]," "free growth in definiteness," "contingent production of additional definiteness"—all phrases used by Hartshorne to elucidate "creativity."[14]

Question: Would "concrete-concrescent" perhaps be an apt designation for what Whitehead calls "subject-superject"? "Concrescent" so used would, of course, be nominative, not participial/adjectival, in meaning.

---

14. Cf., e.g., Hartshorne, "Whitehead's Differences from Buddhism," 409; Hartshorne, *Insights and Oversights*, 241, 201.

66

"Concrescence"

If "concrescence" is defined, in Whitehead's phrase, as "the universal of universals characterizing ultimate matter of fact," then it does indeed refer to "*the* transcendental," or, as Heidegger puts it, "the *transcendens* pure and simple." This means that, logically considered, it is the one concept that one cannot fail to employ in thinking about anything whatsoever. Ontologically considered, it is "the indispensable minimum of what thought is about."[15]

But the abstract is never actual simply in itself; it is actual only insofar as it is included in something concrete or contingent. Therefore, while it is true that "nothing is strictly eternal save what Whitehead calls creativity," and I call, using his term, "concrescence," it is more explicit and therefore more accurate to say that "nothing is unconditionally necessary except creativity as such *with its two essential aspects of divine and nondivine becoming* (God in some possible state and some world or other)."[16]

∽

Concrescence is the only reality that is entirely self-explanatory, because it feeds on nothing other than its own products and properties—i.e., on concretes and the more or less specific abstracts instantiated by them.

As for what is wholly nonconcrete, in that it has never grown together, this is simply the universal common denominator of concrescence as such and whatever it, in turn, necessarily implies—namely, both unsurpassable and surpassable forms of concrescence, and thus also unsurpassable and surpassable concretes.

This means, among other things, that if a concept refers neither to a producible product or property of concrescence nor to some abstract aspect of concrescence itself, then it does not refer at all and is insofar void of clear and coherent meaning.

Logical modalities and, by implication, all concepts whatsoever, refer essentially to concrescence. To be "necessary" ontologically is to be inherent in concrescence

---

15. So Hartshorne, in the foreword to Goodwin, *Ontological Argument of Charles Hartshorne*, xiv.

16. Hartshorne, *Insights and Oversights*, 270, 313, italics added; cf. Hahn, *Philosophy of Charles Hartshorne*, 663: "Only deity simply in its defining traits and what is nondivine simply as such, can obtain eternally and without change."

as such, apart from which neither being "actual" ontologically nor being "potential" ontologically has any meaning.

Thought always implies reality, even if in some cases uninstantiated predicates are part (although never the whole) of what thought is about. The reality one is thinking about when one thinks about realities whose unreality is genuinely conceivable is concrescence as such, as having the two essential forms of unsurpassable and surpassable concrescence, which instead of producing the reality in question, might produce or might have produced some other realities. The indispensable minimum of the reality that thought is about is concrescence as such, as having the two essential forms of unsurpassable and surpassable concrescence (God in some possible state and some world or other).

Thought and reality in principle belong together. Thought is about reality, and reality is what is or can be thought about. Not that all thoughts represent actualities, that is, fully actualized possibilities; rather, all thought, not unclear or inconsistent, represents either something necessary, which never was merely future, or something contingent that once was or will be merely future—i.e., once was or will be a real possibility for subsequent actualization or nonactualization.

◈

Concrescence is the process whereby "the many become one and are increased by one" (Whitehead)—i.e., a concrete ≡ subject comes into being by internally relating itself to all abstracts ≡ objects, including all abstracts ≡ objects that themselves came into being as concretes ≡ subjects at some earlier stage of the same process.

The important concept here is "self-relation." A subject comes into being by internally relating itself to objects, including objects that themselves came into being earlier as subjects.

Another idea important for understanding concrescence is "self-creation"—i.e., the process of self-determination, each new instance of which internally relates itself to all previous such instances, upon which it therefore depends, but by which it is not wholly determined.

◈

Concrescence is the process by which concretes or particulars keep being made, not unilaterally by deity, but by each and every concrete or particular self-determining its response to concretes or particulars already made, including deity so far as already self-determined.

An instance of actuality must have antecedent instances as materials for its own concrescence and will be similarly used in turn by subsequent instances.

God may be said to be concrescence itself, analogously to the way in which, in traditional philosophies of being, God is being itself. True, God's concrescence is not the only concrescence, because God is not the only concrete, and each and every concrete other than God is and must be the product of its own concrescence. Even so, all concrescence is either God's own or else a datum for God's own. In Whitehead's terms, it is either an unsurpassable "subjective form," or an unsurpassable "objective form," either an unsurpassable contribution made to, or a contribution unsurpassably received from, all surpassable concrescences. So God is, in this way, concrescence itself, because God is *the* concrete, the concrete with absolutely universal functions: universal action upon all other concrescences, universal reception of the action of all other concretes.

Maybe the only proper way to refer to any instance of concrescence, or any concrete, is by the hyphenated phrase "concrete-concrescent," formed analogously to Whitehead's term, "subject-superject."

67

Concreteness and Abstractness

If concrete reality is essentially creative process with two aspects—an aspect of pastness or full determinateness and an aspect of futurity or partial determinability—then objective ("ontological") necessity is simply what creative process in either aspect has always been and will always be. It is what all that is fully determinate and all that is partially determinable have in common, their neutral element, or least common denominator, that which was, is, and will be "no matter what" course the creative process takes and can take. This neutral element is what Whitehead calls "creativity," and Hartshorne "creative synthesis"; or, as I prefer to think and say, "concrescence," in its essential, irreducible, or invariant features, which are inseparable from the necessary aspect of God as well as from the strictly necessary aspects of anything and everything other than God.

∽

If the most basic or inclusive type of reality is concrete reality, the most basic abstraction is *concreteness*—as well as, of course, *concrescence*, understood as the creative process whereby concrete reality comes to be, thereby instantiating concreteness and, in a different but related way, also instantiating abstractness—i.e., concrescence as the creative process of the many becoming one and being increased by one.

∾

Concreteness is determinateness, definiteness; abstractness, determinability, definability.

∾

All concrete things in any possible (i.e., conceivable kind of) world must react to, and be reacted to by, their environments—if not as singular wholes, as events and individuals, then as aggregates, by reacting to, and being reacted to by, their environments in their constituent parts.

∾

Concretes may be distinguished as being of three logical-ontological types: (1) events; (2) individuals (including existents in the emphatic sense); and (3) aggregates (≡ composites).

Events and individuals are each, in their way, singulars, in contrast to aggregates, which are plurals—groups or collections of singulars, whether events or individuals. An aggregate may be distinguished from the singulars composing it if, as a group or collection of individuals or events, it has relatively less unity than any of these individuals or events themselves. Put differently, the unity of an aggregate, such as it may be, is that distinctive neither of an event nor of an individual.

The unity distinctive of an event is constituted by its *strict* identity as an event. Its identity is strict because it has, or is essentially qualified by, *all* of its properties.

The unity distinctive of an individual, on the other hand, is constituted by its *genetic* identity as an individual. Its identity is genetic because it has, or is essentially qualified by, only *some* of its properties, while it has, or is qualified by, other of its properties only accidentally. Thus, even if it had many properties different from those it in fact has, it would still be the same individual.

An aggregate is distinguished from a singular, whether event or individual, because it has relatively less unity as an aggregate than any of the singulars composing it. It has relatively less unity than any of the singulars composing it because such unity as it has is constituted neither by the strict identity of an event nor by the genetic identity of an individual.

Therefore, although all three types of concretes are both one and many, each type of concrete is both one and many in its own distinctive way. An event is one and many in the distinctive way constituted by its strict identity as an event; that is to say, it so has, or is so essentially qualified by, all of the many other events and properties to which it internally relates itself that, if even a single entity in this many were otherwise, it would have different properties and would therefore be a different event. An individual, by contrast, is one and many in the distinctive way constituted by its genetic identity as an individual; that is to say, it so has, or is so essentially qualified by, only some of the many other events and properties to which it internally relates itself that it would still be the same individual even if other of these events and properties were different and it therefore had many different properties from those it in fact has. Finally, an aggregate is one and many in the distinctive way constituted by its having neither the strict identity of an event nor the genetic identity of an individual.

∽

A concrete is relative in that it involves real, internal relations not only with abstracts, or with some intensional class of concretes that it requires merely indefinitely or indeterminately, but also with other concretes that it requires definitely or determinately.

An abstract, by contrast, is relative, if it is, in that it involves real, internal relations, not with any definite or determinate concretes, but only with some intensional class thereof that it requires merely indefinitely or indeterminately.[17]

Beyond the transcendental type distinction between a concrete and an abstract, there is the further type distinction between ordinary abstracts—i.e., individualities, species, genera, and categories proper, on the one hand, and extraordinary abstracts, i.e., transcendentals, at the higher level, and existentials, at the lower, on the other.

Although an abstract of either type is relative, if it is, in that it involves real, internal relations, not with any definite or determinate concretes, but only with some intensional class thereof that it requires merely indefinitely or indeterminately, there is the important difference that the intensional class of concretes that any ordinary abstract requires is only contingently nonempty, whereas the intensional class of concretes that an extraordinary abstract at the higher level requires is nonempty necessarily. One may also say that, although the intensional class of concretes that an extraordinary abstract at the higher level requires is not determined by anything more specific or definite than "concreteness," the intensional class of concretes required by any ordinary abstract is determined, to some extent, more specifically or definitely.

Whether an abstract is relative depends on how we use terms. If "relative," even in the broadest sense, means "constituted in some way or degree by relation to the contingent" (Hartshorne), then any ordinary abstract is relative, because it is constituted

---

17. Cf. Hartshorne, *Creative Synthesis and Philosophic Method*, 264.

by relation to an intensional class of concretes that is nonempty only contingently, or is determined by something more specific or definite than "concreteness." On the other hand, an extraordinary abstract at the higher level is not relative in the same sense of the term, because the intensional class of concretes that it requires indefinitely or indeterminately is nonempty necessarily, or is determined solely and simply by "concreteness."

Whereas abstracts are causes but not effects, in that they are really, internally related to concretes in only one of the two ways in which this is possible, concretes are effects as well as causes, in that they are really, internally related to concretes in both of these ways. Causes require their effects merely indefinitely or indeterminately, whereas effects require their causes definitely or determinately, although they, too, as causes in turn, require their own effects only indefinitely or indeterminately.

～

Granted that concreteness is what makes instances of an abstract property instances, rather than abstract properties all over again; and that, by analogy, abstractness is what all abstract properties have in common as over against their instances, what, more exactly, are concreteness and abstractness respectively?

Hartshorne indicates an answer when he observes: "Whereas both individuals and abstractions (other than those of uttermost generality) can have aspects of relativity, can depend in some way and degree upon contingent relations . . . only individuals, not abstractions, can feel or think or remember."[18]

(1) Abstractions of uttermost generality (or what I mean by "transcendentals") have no aspects of relativity, in no way and degree depend upon contingent relations, which is to say, relations to the contingent; for while they must indeed be actualized *somehow*, and the *how* of all actualization is contingent, the intensional classes of contingent instances that they require only by an utterly indefinite or indeterminate necessity are not contingently nonempty, but necessarily so. And this means that the uttermost abstractions are not properly relative.

(2) Granted that only individuals can feel or think or remember, the converse need not be true, that only entities that can feel or think or remember are individuals. Indeed, this is not true without qualification even for the metaphysical psychicalist (or panpsychist) insofar, at least, as she or he is consistent in allowing that thinking, even if not feeling and remembering, can only be a local, not a cosmic, variable.

(3) But what does characterize all individuals, indeed, all concrete singulars, including events, is that their aspect of relativity is constituted not only by real, internal relations to certain abstracts, but also, in one part, by real, internal relations to other concretes, which they require by an utterly definite or determinate necessity.

---

18. Hartshorne, *Creative Synthesis and Philosophic Method*, 154.

The other part of their aspect of relativity is constituted by real, internal relations to some concretes or other, which they require by only a more or less indefinite or indeterminate necessity.

(4) By contrast, what characterizes all abstracts other than those of uttermost generality is that their aspect of relativity is wholly constituted by real, internal relations to some concretes or other, which they require by only a more or less indefinite or indeterminate necessity. Although they have to be actualized *somehow*, the *how* of their actualization is not determined. On the other hand, the intensional classes of contingent instances that they thus require by only a more or less indefinite or indeterminate necessity are not necessarily, but only contingently, nonempty; and this means that, unlike abstractions of uttermost generality, they *are* properly relative.

Considering these four points, we can say that concreteness is the transcendental property of being relative not only to certain abstracts, but also to certain concretes—both to some concretes that are required by an utterly definite or determinate necessity and to yet other concretes that are required by only a more or less indefinite or indeterminate necessity. Abstractness, by contrast, is the transcendental property of being relative to concretes, if so relative at all, solely to some concretes or other, which are required by a more or less indefinite or indeterminate necessity only.

Alternatively, abstractness may be understood simply as the transcendental property of being an object and only an object, whereas concreteness is to be understood as the transcendental property of being an object that is (or was) also a subject, whether individual or event. Although objects do indeed require subjects, just as subjects require objects, objects require subjects by only a more or less indefinite or indeterminate necessity, whereas subjects require objects, concretes as well as abstracts, by an utterly definite or determinate necessity.

68

On "the Aristotelian or Ontological Principle"

I suspect that, in earlier writings, I used the terms "to instantiate" and "to embody" more or less interchangeably. But there is good reason to use them more carefully.

Abstracts, according to Aristotle's anticipation of Whitehead's "ontological principle," require to be embodied somehow in some concrete(s). But this requirement can be satisfied if the abstract in question is at least conceived or entertained as a possibility, even though it is not instantiated as an actuality. Thus, if someone at least conceives a definitive cure for *AIDS*, the Aristotelian requirement is satisfied, even though the possibility of such a cure still has to become actual.

It clearly seems important to take account of this Aristotelian understanding in any treatment of abstracts. But for an austerely formal or transcendental metaphysics, it will not do to say with Hartshorne and other idealists that the Aristotelian requirement can be met, provided only that the abstract in question is conceived by some mind, and that it in fact is met because every abstract is conceived, at least implicitly, by the divine mind.

What can be said, then? One suggestion is to say that an abstract's being instantiated as an actuality is not the only way, but one of two ways, in which it may be embodied. It may also be embodied by being included, as a possibility for actualization or instantiation, as distinct from being actualized or instantiated. Some such distinction has to be made in any case, since any concrete singular is internally related not only to its past but also to its future—to possibility as well as to actuality—even though the internal relatedness in the two cases is different.

One way of making the distinction, then, is to say that an abstract must indeed be somehow embodied in a concrete, but that it is so embodied either by being instantiated in the concrete as actuality or included in it as possibility. Alternatively, one could allow that "included" is like "embodied," in that instantiating or actualizing an abstract is also a way of including it, and say instead that an abstract is embodied/included in a concrete provided only that it is either instantiated in the concrete as an actuality or else entertained in the concrete as a possibility.

I have argued that, for universals to be somehow "embodied" (this being required both by "the Aristotelian principle" and Whitehead's "ontological principle") is for them to be included in some actuality—being instantiated as actuality being one mode of embodiment or inclusion, being entertained as possibility being the other mode. But what is it, exactly, for a universal to be "entertained as a possibility," as distinct from being "instantiated as an actuality"? It is for the universal to belong to the aspect of an actuality relative to its future, wherein the actuality foreshadows or anticipates but does not define or determine successor actualities, as distinct from belonging to the other aspect of the actuality relative to its past, wherein an actuality further defines or determines what was but foreshadowed or anticipated by its own predecessor actualities.

Otherwise put: for a universal "to be entertained as a possibility" is for it to be required by an actuality, not by the definite or determinate necessity wherewith the actuality requires its predecessor actualities, but by the merely indefinite or indeterminate necessity wherewith the actuality requires its successor actualities. This means, among other things, that any and every universal whatsoever is always embodied or included in God, not by being instantiated as an actuality, or required by the definite or determinate necessity wherewith God requires the past, but by being entertained as a possibility, or required by the merely indefinite or indeterminate necessity wherewith God requires the future.

Still otherwise put: an actuality embodies, or includes, universals both by instantiating some among those constituting the future of the actualities preceding it and by entertaining those constituting its own future, some of which can and must be instantiated by the actualities succeeding it.

The following passage well expresses the understanding of the actual as having two aspects—relatively to the past and relatively to the future—that I presuppose in the prior explanation of what it is for a universal to be "entertained as a possibility," as distinct from being "instantiated as an actuality":

> [T]he actuality of the present is the possibility of the future. That such and such an event is here and now possible is because a suitable predecessor of such an event is here and now actual.... The actuality of the present involves the antecedent actuality of its past, but it involves merely the potentiality of later events. It *is* their potentiality.... [T]he present as a whole is the condition for later events. So one and the same event as one whole or unity is actuality, relatively to the past, and potentiality, relatively to the future. It has a retrospective face of Secondness and a prospective face of Firstness.[19]

∽

Hartshorne says, "Universals must have some embodiment (if in nothing else, in some mind thinking them)."[20] But what, exactly, does he mean by "some mind thinking them"? I take him to mean, whatever else he may mean, *God's* mind—understood as that mind, thanks to which alone possibility as well as actuality has, as he would say, an "objective or nonlinguistic" reality.

But then, if one rejects, as I do, the idea of "God's mind" as having any but a symbolic (≡ nonliteral) meaning—if it is to have any clear and coherent meaning at all—how do I account for the "some embodiment" that—on an Aristotelian-Whiteheadian-Hartshornean understanding of the "ontological principle"—universals have to have?

I account for it by thinking and speaking, not of "God's *mind*," except as a symbolic (≡ nonliteral) and therefore nonmetaphysical concept/term, but of the universal individual's modal all-inclusiveness, its unqualified inclusion of all modes of reality: possibility (both ontological and ontic) as well as actuality. Hartshorne himself says that "all-inclusiveness, non-duality, is a formal character of deity," which, as such, can

---

19. Hartshorne, "Relativity of Nonrelativity," 220.
20. Hartshorne, *Anselm's Discovery*, 56–58.

be stated formally and, therefore, literally, by saying, "God is coincident with [or, as I prefer to say, coextensive with] all truth and reality."[21] But, then, while one certainly *may* interpret such literal modal coincidence (or coextensiveness) symbolically (≡ nonliterally) by means of the psychicalist concept/term "God's mind," there is just as certainly no reason why one *must* so interpret it, since the purely formal, literal (≡ nonsymbolic) statement that the universal individual is all-inclusive of both actuality and possibility suffices to make the point—at any rate, in the only way, arguably, in which metaphysics has any business making it.

To be embodied is to be included—being instantiated as actuality being one mode of embodiment or inclusion, being entertained as possibility being the other.

69

Any Ordinary Abstract . . .

Any ordinary (≡ ontic) abstract necessarily implies, and thus is really, internally related to, all other still more abstract abstracts of which it is a specialization, including extraordinary (≡ ontological) abstracts at the higher level (otherwise known as "transcendentals"). Thus an individuality necessarily implies, and so is internally related to, some species, which in turn necessarily implies, and so is internally related to, some genus, which in turn—and so on, all the way up to and including transcendentals.

Because this is so, it would be at best misleading to say simply that abstractness is the transcendental property of being relative solely to some concretes or other, which are required by only a more or less indefinite or indeterminate necessity. This would be misleading because it might be taken to mean that abstracts are relative only to concretes and therefore are not also relative to such abstracts, if any, as they in turn necessarily imply. As true as this may be in the case of the extraordinary (≡ ontological) abstracts at the higher level that I call "transcendentals," all ordinary (≡ ontic) abstracts also necessarily imply, and therefore are really, internally related to, the still more abstract abstracts of which they are specializations.

What is valid in the misleading formulation is that abstractness is the transcendental property of being really, internally related, and so relative, to concretes in only one of the two ways in which it is possible to be so. An abstract requires concretes only by a more or less indefinite or indeterminate necessity. Concreteness, by contrast, is the transcendental property of being relative to concretes in *both ways*. Although

---

21. Hartshorne, "Idea of God," 5.

a concrete requires the concretes in its future by only a more or less indefinite or indeterminate necessity, it requires the concretes in its past by an utterly definite or determinate necessity.

∽

If by "the abstract" one generally means either an (abstract) aspect or a (concrete) constituent of the concrete, then, taking the second sense of the phrase, one may say that whatever is by definition constituent of a larger, more inclusive concrete whole is—relative to this whole, at least—abstract. All ordinary events and individuals, being by definition not all-inclusive, are, in that sense, abstract relative to God (i.e., to God's events of concrescence) as the extraordinary and hence all-inclusive individual (or events).

For this reason, science at the level of the special sciences, as the study of all ordinary events and individuals, is *doubly* abstract: first, because, as just explained, all ordinary events and individuals are themselves in a sense abstract, namely, relative to God (or to God's extraordinary events); and second, because the sciences consider only a certain aspect even of ordinary events and individuals, namely, the aspect of structure that can be experienced somehow by sense perception and therefore permits understanding control and use of the things thereby disclosed.

Actually, science may be said to be *triply* abstract insofar as the special sciences as well as metaphysics further abstract from the meaning of things for us (thereby warranting something like the distinction Heidegger makes between "what is *at* hand [*das Zuhandene*]" and "what is *on* hand [*das Vorhandene*])."

70

"Existence"

"Existence" is yet another term having different senses that can be clarified by a threefold analysis. Actually, to take account of all the relevant senses in which it may be used, *two* threefold analyses are required.

According to the first such analysis, "existence" may be understood:

1. in the *strict or proper* sense (*sensu stricto*) as the property of being real in one of two main ways in which something can be so—i.e., concretely real, as distinct from being real only abstractly;

2. in the *broad* sense (*sensu lato*) as the property of being real in either of these two main ways (i.e., either concretely real or abstractly real), as distinct from being simply unreal (i.e., merely apparent or fictitious); and

3. in the *narrow* sense (*sensu strictissimo*) as the property of being concretely real in the way of an individual, as distinct from the ways of other types of concretely real things—i.e., events and/or aggregates (≡ composites).

NB: As understood here, an *event*, being real, is real for something else; and, being concretely real, is also such that other things can be real for it. But an event is not, and cannot be, real for itself in the way in which an *individual* can be and is. Whereas the identity of an event is *strict* because it has, or is essentially qualified by, *all* of its properties, the identity of an individual is *genetic* because it has, or is essentially qualified by, only *some* of its properties, having, or being qualified by, any others, not essentially, but only accidentally. An event, in other words, becomes and perishes but does not endure and change, whereas an individual endures and changes whether or not it becomes and perishes, as an ordinary, transitory individual does, and the one extraordinary, everlasting individual does not. Both an event and an individual, however, are (in different ways) singulars, as distinct from "aggregates," which are a group or collection of events and/or individuals that has less unity than any of its several members.

Before turning to the second threefold analysis, we also note that "existence" in the narrow sense as the property of being concretely real in the way of an individual is to be defined in relation to *two* other terms: not only "essence," but also "actuality." So defined, "existence" in the narrow sense means the property of being an "essence" actualized *somehow* in *some* "actuality(-ies)," or, as may also be said in the light of the preceding clarification of terms, "existence" in the narrow sense means the property of being an "individual" whose individuality or essence is actualized *somehow* in *some* "event(s)."

Given this definition, the second threefold analysis builds on the first by further clarifying three distinct senses in which "existence" in the narrow sense can, in turn, be understood, viz.:

1. in the *ordinary* sense as the property of an individual whose individuality or essence is to be only contingently actualized in some event(s), and which therefore is a particular, transitory individual that exists contingently;

2. in the *extraordinary* sense as the property of the individual whose individuality or essence is to be necessarily actualized in some event(s), and which therefore is the universal, everlasting individual that exists necessarily; and

3. in the *emphatic* sense as the property of an individual in the ordinary sense whose individuality or essence is to be contingently actualized in some self-understanding (because thinking-speaking) event(s), which therefore is a particular, transitory individual that exists not only contingently, but also self-understandingly (because thinkingly/speakingly), and therefore as morally free and responsible.

NB: The distinctions between a particular, transitory individual, the universal, everlasting individual, and a particular, transitory, self-understanding individual—like those clarified previously between an event, an individual, and an aggregate—are all distinctions of logical-ontological type.

71

"Human Existence"

The term "human existence" obviously designates a special case. But, less obviously, it does this, not just in one sense, but in two senses. It designates a special case in one sense insofar as it designates a special case of existence "in the *proper* sense as the property of being real in one of the two main ways in which something can be so (i.e., concretely real), as distinct from being abstractly real." In this sense, "human existence" designates a special case of concrete reality, namely, a concrete reality that has the further more specific property of being human.

But "human existence" designates a special case in another sense insofar as it designates a special case of existence "in the *emphatic* sense as the property of an individual in the ordinary sense whose individuality or essence is to be contingently actualized in some self-understanding (because thinking/speaking) event(s), which therefore is a particular, transitory individual that exists only contingently, but also self-understandingly (because thinkingly/speakingly), and therefore as morally free and responsible." In this sense, "human existence" designates a special case of contingent, self-understanding, because thinking/speaking, and therefore also morally free and responsible individuality that has the further more specific property of being human.

Metaphysics in the broad sense properly concerns itself with existence in the emphatic sense, as distinct from the special case of existence in the emphatic sense properly distinguished as "human existence." And this, of course, is why "whether existence in this emphatic sense is also a human being, or a being of some other kind, is of no concern to metaphysics even in the broad sense."

(All quoted definitions of the different senses of "existence" are from note 70, "Existence").

72

"Existential"

There are three different, yet closely related, senses in which utterances may be said to be "existential."

1. in the *proper* sense that they are about reality in one of the two main ways in which something can be real—i.e., concretely real, as distinct from abstractly real;

2. in the *emphatic* sense that the concrete reality they are about is the threefold ultimate reality of our own existence insofar as it is self-understanding existence in relation to others and the whole; and

3. also in the *emphatic* sense that how, or the way in which, they are about this ultimate reality is itself concrete as distinct from abstract, in that they are about the meaning of this reality for us as distinct from being about its structure in itself.

Thus whereas paradigmatic factual utterances are "existential" in only the first of these three senses, and paradigmatic metaphysical utterances are "existential" in only the first and second senses, paradigmatic religious and philosophical utterances are, in their different ways, "existential" in all three senses. They are about concrete reality. The concrete reality they are about is the threefold ultimate reality of ourselves, others, and the whole. And they are about this threefold reality not merely abstractly, in its structure in itself, but concretely, in its meaning for us.

73

Essence and Existence

Existence in the proper sense consists of becoming/perishing *events* and enduring/changing *individuals* ("substances"), whereas *essence* consists of the characters/properties by which events or individuals are or might be qualified.

There must be one existent in the proper sense—one universal enduring/changing individual, to be exact—that has never come into existence and can never go out of existence, because all "coming into," or "going out of," existence can only be the realization of the anterior determinability, or potentiality, of this existent through its posterior determinations, or actuality.

There is thus an essence of existence as such, a character by which the necessary factor in existence is identified as the one universal enduring/changing individual in spite of all of its real changes. The necessary factor in existence, in both possibility and actuality, is the unity pervading all alternatives or ranges of possibility open to decision, and is itself, therefore, without alternative.

Every verified privation of an essence, arguably, is the observed presence of a positive though incompatible character/property. But if this principle is valid without exception, the statement "something exists" is a priori and necessarily true unconditionally. And the statement "there is no deity (or necessary factor in existence)" is just as necessarily false and therefore meaningless. For what could conceivably be the observed positive character/property incompatible with the existence of deity?

74

Possibility

On an adequate theory of modality, according to which possibility in principle is ontological as well as logical, "real possibility" and "logical possibility" are correlative, every real possibility being also a logical possibility—and vice versa. But there remains the important distinction between being possible merely *in principle* and being possible also *in fact*. Why not express this distinction by further distinguishing "*ontic* possibility" from "*ontological* possibility"?

One may then say that, although any logical possibility is also an ontological possibility (and vice versa), not every logical possibility (and, therefore, ontological possibility) is also an ontic possibility. Why not? Because whereas x is a logical possibility only if it is clear and makes coherent sense; and is an ontological possibility only if its actuality is compatible with the nature of concrescence as such, as indispensably referred to by anything that is clear and does make coherent sense, x is also an ontic possibility only if certain ontic, or factual, conditions necessary to its becoming actual make it so.

Thus I understand:

by "logical possibility," "anything that is clear and makes coherent sense";

by "ontological possibility," "anything whose actuality is compatible with the nature of concrescence as such, as the indispensable referent of all clear and coherent meaning"; and

by "ontic possibility," "anything whose actuality is made possible by certain ontic, or factual, conditions that themselves are not just ontically possible but also actual."

75

Possibility Is Futurity

The past is settled and definite, while the future is what we and others in the present are about to settle, to make more definite than it already is.

The possibility for tomorrow consists in (or is entirely determined by) the actuality of today. But the actuality of tomorrow will not add determinations in today's possibility for tomorrow, because they are not in today's determinations but will be in tomorrow's, in its possibility for the day after tomorrow. Possibilities are the properties of actualities that they will be succeeded necessarily by later actualities with new determinations, dependent on, but not fully determined by, earlier actualities.

There are two aspects of existence: possibility and actuality; and the necessarily existing existent that has both aspects in eminent or unsurpassable form is, in its unactualized possibility, unlimited and infinite, although also completely unactualized, and, in its actuality, necessarily limited and finite, although not fragmentary, but integral, the greatest conceivable actual whole.

Possibility is futurity, the indefiniteness (≡ indeterminateness) of what, given the present, not only can but also must be further defined (≡ determined) by successor presents. Thus possibility (≡ futurity) is only an aspect of actualities as such, as concretes (i.e., events and individuals), and also aggregates (≡ composites) thereof.

Every actuality (≡ concrete) is, in one aspect, definite (≡ determinate), while, in another aspect, it is indefinite (≡ indeterminate)/definable (≡ determinable). Relative to its past, an actuality is definite (≡ determinate), in that it has somehow resolved the indefiniteness (≡ indeterminateness)/definability (≡ determinability) bequeathed to it by its past for further definition (≡ determination). But relative to its future, it itself bequeaths a certain indefiniteness (≡ indeterminateness)/definability (≡ determinability) that its successors will in turn have to resolve, each by its own self-definition (≡ self-determination).

∽

Whereas actualities (≡ concretes) are *not* continuous, but discontinuous, possibilities (≡ abstracts), in the sense of the possible ways in which an actuality can be succeeded or objectified by other later actualities, *are* continuous, in that they form a continuous range. Any ontic possibility (≡ ordinary abstract), then, is simply a still wider range of continuous possibilities—a species being a wider range than an individuality (≡ individual essence), a genus being a wider range than a species, and a category proper being a still wider range than a genus.

An ontological possibility (≡ extraordinary abstract) at the higher level (≡ transcendental) is the widest range of continuous possibilities conceivable, and therefore an unlimited range. There is literally an infinite number of possible ways in which it can be succeeded or objectified, by actualities (≡ concretes) as well as by ontic possibilities (≡ ordinary abstracts)—from categories proper through genera and species to individualities (≡ individual essences).

∽

If God simply as such—as the all-worshipful and unsurpassable, and therefore universal individual—is, in Hartshorne's phrase, "modally all-inclusive," and so excludes, or is incompatible with, absolutely nothing, either actual or possible, then the range of continuous possibilities for God to be somehow succeeded or objectified *qua* existent, or actualized merely *somehow*, rather than in any particular *how*, has to be as infinite as for any other transcendental. The infinitude, in other words, of what Whitehead calls God's "primordial nature," or of God as, in Peirce's terms, "First," is a function of God's being by nature utterly non-exclusive, or non-incompatible. Thus Whitehead says, rightly, "We must conceive the Divine Eros as the active entertainment of *all* ideals, with the urge to their finite realization, each in its due season. Thus a process must be inherent in God's nature whereby [God's] infinity is acquiring realization."[22]

The reason, however, why the nature of things is, in the final analysis, tragic as well as beautiful is that, as Whitehead argues, "every occasion of actuality is in its own nature finite. There is no totality which is the harmony of all perfections. Whatever is realized in any one occasion of experience necessarily excludes the unbounded welter of contrary possibilities. There are always 'others' which might have been and are not."[23]

In other words, there is, inevitably, tragic loss: God's infinity simply *cannot* acquire realization! In this sense, Whitehead says, "At the heart of the nature of things, there are always the dream of youth and the harvest of tragedy. The Adventure of the Universe starts with the dream and reaps tragic Beauty."[24]

So, if God simply as such, as existent, and therefore actualized *somehow*, although in no particular *how*, excludes nothing and is incompatible with nothing, God *qua* actualized, and hence particularized in *this*, rather than in that or the other, particular *how*, is exclusive of, and incompatible with, some things. Consequently, the range of continuous possibilities for succeeding or objectifying God so actualized and particularized is *not* unlimited and infinite but limited and finite. It is limited and made finite, namely, by the particular *de facto* order that it lies in the nature of God—not simply as God, and as God, therefore, of some world only, but as also God of this, that, or the other particular world—to impose on every new successor world now in process of coming into being.

In this sense, or for this reason, it is not God simply as "primordial" (≡ "First"), or even as "consequent" (≡ "Second"), but God as "superject" (≡ "Third") that is rightly said to be "the principle of concretion—the principle whereby," as Whitehead says, "there is initiated a definite outcome from a situation otherwise riddled with ambiguity."[25]

∽

Hartshorne, very much like Whitehead, speaks of the "element of tragedy inherent in all existence."[26] What he means by this is that, in any possible world (or better, any possible kind of world), there are "incompossible possibilities"—possibilities that cannot be actualized together but only if other possibilities cannot. Therefore, decisions

---

22. Whitehead, *Adventures of Ideas*, 357; italics added.
23. Whitehead, *Adventures of Ideas*, 356; or, as Hartshorne puts it, "No *infima species* of possibility ever recurs" (*Reality as Social Process*, 118).
24. Whitehead, *Adventures of Ideas*, 381.
25. Whitehead, *Process and Reality*, 345.
26. Hartshorne, *Logic of Perfection*, 285.

always have to be made as to which possibilities are to be actualized, and which left unactualized. In this sense, all actualization is exclusive, in that it actualizes some possibilities only to preclude thereby the actualization of others. And therein lies "the element of tragedy" inherent in existence as such; in God's existence, no less than in the existence of anything else, because all existence entails actualization, and all actualization is exclusive.

76

Whitehead Says . . .

Whitehead says, "The initial fact [sc. to which each concrescence is to be referred as its definite free initiation] is macrocosmic, in the sense of having equal relevance to all occasions. . . . The initial fact is the primordial appetition."[27] But, surely, "the primordial appetition" as such is neither properly a "fact" ($\equiv$ *factum*—i.e., something made or produced) nor "free," in the sense of existing contingently, nonnecessarily. Rather, it is the infinitude of possibility as "a plenum," or, as may also be said, in C. S. Peirce's term, as "a multitude beyond all multitude," which, being infinite, is precisely *not* properly a "fact," any which, as such, is and must be finite. On the other hand, "the initial fact" that indeed is a fact and therefore both finite and free is neither God merely as primordial nor even God merely as consequent, but God as "superject"—or, in terms of Peirce's categories, God neither as eminent Firstness nor as eminent Secondness, but as eminent Thirdness.

In other words, "the initial fact" that is "macrocosmic" in the sense specified is God exercising God's function as "objectively immortal" in the temporal world. Included in this "fact," of course, are both God as primordial and God as consequent. So, in that sense, they, too, may be said to be—or, more correctly, to be abstract parts or aspects of—"the initial fact."

---

27. Whitehead, *Process and Reality*, 47–48.

77

"Actualization"

C. S. Peirce's view that "the eternal is a continuum of possibilities, a 'multitude beyond all multitude,' lacking, as eternal, in definiteness," implies both that "possibilities are determinables[,] not determinates" and that "determinables are not classes of determinates, but aspects of creativity relevant to such classes, so far as the latter are given.... Given a determinate how[,] we can relate it to the [*sc.* indeterminate but determinable] somehow, but given only the somehow we cannot relate it to a determinate how."[28]

The region of possibility to which a particular event can be related, or which we say it actualizes, never implies just this determinate mode of actualization. In fact, this determinate mode is not even one of the antecedent possibilities, which as such are not determinates or classes thereof, but determinables, so that any determinate mode as such must be a creation out of them, or a yet further particularization of them.

Each antecedent phase of process involves more or less well-defined alternatives for the next phase. And the particular emerging from the next phase is the actualization of one of these alternatives. But "actualization" is not a simple change from "merely possible" to "actual," whatever that could mean, but always connotes "some additional definiteness, or determinateness," not already contained in any of the antecedently obtaining alternatives. This is not to say (with Henri Bergson and others) that there are no antecedent possibilities, or that there is something absurd about the very concept of such. What we mean by "the antecedent possibility of particular *p*" is simply that the antecedent phase of process defined itself as destined to be superseded somehow, within certain alternatives, by a next phase of process. This "somehow" is not a wholly undifferentiated question mark, but involves certain more or less well-defined alternatives, none of which can coincide in character with the particular that emerges from the next phase of process, but some one of which, or some one region of the continuum of possible quality, will later be recognizable as the nearest alternative or region, the one that *with the least further definition* is equivalent to the particular once it has emerged and is given as such.[29]

A distinction must be made, therefore, between pure, or unrestrictive, potentials, on the one hand, and impure ($\equiv$ mixed), or restrictive, potentials, on the other. But, far from being either mere selections from pure potentials, or mere (re-)arrangements

---

28. Hartshorne, *Creative Synthesis and Philosophic Method*, 65.
29. Cf. Hartshorne, *Reality as Social Process*, 97–99.

of them with respect to gradations of relevance, etc., the impure potentials are really creations out of the pure potentials, further determinations of them, without which they would remain determinables, not determinates, or classes thereof.

So, granted that there must be (1) an eternal abstract ideal or purpose (something like Plato's "Form of the Good"); (2) an eternal continuum of qualitative possibilities (Peirce's "multitude beyond all multitude"); and (3) certain eternal variables, or dimensions, of value, such as "intensity," "complexity," "unity," "variety," "harmony," why is there any need that these variables involve possible values as distinct items? Why isn't the creative process such that the primordial continuum of qualitative possibilities is inexhaustibly subdivided in the course of the creative advance, but that actualization really adds something in the way of still further definiteness or determinateness?

One advantage of limiting the eternal to the strictly necessary (i.e., to the transcendental universals, and regarding all other universals as more or less impure [≡ mixed], or restrictive, and, therefore, emergent and temporal, instead of eternal) is that individuals as a type of concrete singulars might then be given a somewhat more secure ontological status in the overall scheme of things. An enduring, changing individual could then be regarded as constituted, in one aspect, by its distinctive impure (or restrictive) potentiality, its own peculiar potency of becoming as a still more determinate, and yet still only determinable, potentiality than that of any pure, or unrestrictive, potentials. The other aspect of an individual's self-identity as such, then, would be the immanence of its entire actual history in its latest present state, so that its self-identity would not be merely abstract, but also concrete.

78

The Necessary/the Possible

There may be a certain difficulty in speaking of the necessary as simply the least common denominator of the possible. Speaking so may tend to perpetuate the notion—in my view, mistaken—that properly metaphysical ideas are simply more general than other types of general ideas, from individualities to categories proper. The truth that tends to be missed thereby is that metaphysical ideas are not simply more general, but also more fundamental—lying, as it were, on a different axis or in a different dimension: the vertical, as distinct from the horizontal, dimension.

"Transcendentals" and "existentials" are both, in their different ways, properties of the necessary. But although they are therefore more universal and abstract than categories—i.e., categories proper, genera, species, and individualities (≡ individual essences)—and although they, too, are "communicable properties" in their way, they nonetheless have to do with structure, as distinct from content. And this is the difference that may get obscured by speaking of the necessary as simply "the least common denominator of the possible." That term, if it is to be used at all, may be more apt, in some ways, at least, for the plenum, or continuum, of the purely possible—in Peirce's term, "the multitude beyond all multitude."

∾

"The necessary," strictly and properly so-called, is not so much "the neutral element," or "the least common denominator," of the possible or the contingent, whether actualized or nonactualized, as it is the essential structure, the necessary conditions of the possibility, of "the neutral element," or "the least common denominator," terms that may more appropriately refer to the plenum, or continuum, of the purely possible—what Peirce calls "the multitude beyond all multitude."

This may be expressed by saying, as Hartshorne sometimes says, that "the necessary" strictly and properly refers to "the creative process itself" (i.e., "creativity," "creative synthesis," or—as I prefer to say—"concrescence") on the understanding that this creative process is inseparable from both the strictly necessary aspect of the one universal individual, on the one hand, and the strictly necessary aspect of any and all of the many particular individuals, on the other. Included in these strictly necessary aspects is the requirement that there be both: the One and the many, the universal individual and *some* particular individuals.

79

The Necessary

Hartshorne says, "the necessary is easily explicated as what all possibilities have in common (or what will obtain no matter which possibilities are actualized). It seems extravagant to suggest that they have nothing in common."[30] It seems clear from this that Hartshorne's own favored way of defining the necessary is as "what all possibilities have in common," because it seems extravagant to suggest that possibilities have nothing in common. But, as I have noted elsewhere, there is a difficulty with this

30. Hartshorne, *Creativity in American Philosophy*, 254.

definition in that it may tend to promote the illusion—or what I take to be the illusion—that the *sole* difference between transcendentals and all other abstracts is a difference of scope, that transcendentals are simply still more general than—or the most general in comparison with—categories (i.e., categories proper, genera, species, and individualities). Therefore, I strongly favor his parenthetical alternative definition, or explication, as "what will obtain no matter which possibilities are actualized." This explication in no way suggests that the *only* difference between transcendentals and less utterly universal abstracts, such as categories, genera, species, and individualities ($\equiv$ individual essences), is their greater (even infinite) degree of abstractness. It allows for their differing, not only as do greater and lesser scope, but also as do structure and content, or bare abstract outline and outline concretely filled in.

In this connection, I recall how Hartshorne explains his statement, "God's essence is an empty outline, and is infinitely less than the divine actuality."

> But this empty outline [, he says,] is still not in the most extreme sense nothing. Nothing is one of two things: either it is a mere word, with no objective designation at all; or it is the realm of primordial possibilities, apart from all particular actualizations. Objective nothing can only be pure possibility. Now this pure possibility (which is itself not possible but real) is not completely without difference, but only without actual (specific and particular) difference. It has a certain structure, and this structure is that of God-world—no particular world, and not God knowing any particular world (or with any determinate actual content of intuition), but God-as-such knowing world-as-such. Thus God in his essence is the inseparable correlate of world-in-general. If a certain world is actual, then God actually knows this world; and to say, 'such and such a world is possible,' is the same as saying, 'such and such a sort of world might be divinely intuited as a determinate actuality.' This correlation, God-as-such and world-as-such, is not 'nothing' in the sense of a phrase without designation, but is an objective abstract aspect of every actual state of God-[w]orld. God-as-such [*sc.* knowing world-as-such] is not an actuality, but yet it exists [necessarily], by virtue of some suitable actuality or other.[31]

I take this to mean that, because pure possibility is not itself possible but necessary, it is not completely without difference—there being the difference, namely, between primordial possibilities themselves and their necessarily actual ground. This difference, however, is not an "actual" (which is to say, specific and particular) difference between this possibility being actualized instead of that, but merely a real difference that obtains no matter what possibilities are or are not realized. As such, it has "a certain structure," that of "God-[w]orld," or "God-as-such knowing [w]orld-as-such." And although this structure is not actual but only real, and, as such, is indeed, an "empty outline," it is nevertheless "not 'nothing' in the sense of a phrase without

---

31. Hartshorne, "Divine Relativity and Absoluteness," 44.

objective designation," but is "an objective abstract aspect of every actual state of God-[w]orld," and so "what will obtain no matter which possibilities are actualized."

But if this interpretation catches Hartshorne's meaning, then it seems clear to me that he himself, in his way, wants to interpret the necessary as precisely "structure," as distinct from content—not only the content provided by all particular concretes (≡ actualities), but even the content signified by all less abstract and therefore contingent rather than necessary abstracts (≡ ordinary abstracts or categories)—i.e., categories proper, genera, species, and individualities.

80

The Necessary and the Contingent

To think about anything whatsoever is to think about the creative process that I call "concrescence" either directly or indirectly, explicitly or implicitly. But to think about concrescence is to think about something that is not contingent but necessary. Were it, too, contingent, and so producible, one could think about it only by thinking about the creative process by which it alone could, in turn, be produced—again, either directly or indirectly, explicitly or implicitly.

But to think about concrescence as the truly ultimate, unproducible creative process is also to think about God, not because God simply *is* this unproducible process, but because God is its eminent or unsurpassable form and, as such, "the supreme causal factor in the world." God is not the *only* causal factor, but the *supreme* causal factor, so that "anything whatever is only superficially understood if not seen as made possible by the divine existence."[32] Of course, it is just as true that to think about concrescence as the unproducible creative process is also to think about its noneminent or surpassable forms, which is to say, the world of surpassable creative processes, or causal factors, the existence of at least *some* of which is no less necessary to concrescence's being what it is than the existence of God.

༄

What is the principle of the distinction between the necessary and the contingent?

The principle of the distinction between the necessary and the contingent is the distinction between the (more) universal and the (more) particular. Every step from

32. Hartshorne, "John Hick," 156.

the more universal to the more particular involves contingency, whereas every step from the more particular to the more universal involves necessity. From "there is an animal," for example, it does not follow necessarily, but only contingently, that "there is a cat." But from "there is a cat" it does follow necessarily that "there is an animal."

Of all that exists or occurs what, if anything, might not have existed or occurred? Everything might not have existed or occurred except something and what "something exists" necessarily implies—namely, "unsurpassable something inclusive of all surpassable somethings exists."

This does not mean that there might ever be or have been nothing more particular than merely unsurpassable-something-inclusive-of-all-surpassable-somethings. It means only that, although any further particularization of mere somethingness—unsurpassable and surpassable—is not necessary because every step from the most universal idea of somethingness to any more particular idea is contingent, it is not contingent but necessary that *some* further particularization of somethingness—unsurpassable and surpassable—should take place. As Hartshorne likes to say, "It is not accidental that accidents happen." But nor is it contingent that bare somethingness is always somehow further particularized as concrete actualities, extraordinary as well as ordinary.

∽

All thought takes place in and as a part of a real experience; and this experience, by its very nature, is always, even in dreams, an experience *of*—of a reality distinct from the experience itself. Consequently, all thought, like all experience, is thought *about*, about reality. Any thought, like any experience, is necessarily connected with, and in some way refers to, the real. Do away with all such connection and reference, and there is no reason to suppose that there is any clear and coherent thought at all. Thought never thinks just itself, any more than language ever speaks just itself.

But if all clear and coherent thought, like all experience, is a relation, which, as such, necessarily requires a term in reality itself, all thought is either unclear or incoherent or else about something at least possible; and since what is properly meant by "the necessary" is "what will obtain whatever possibility" is actualized, all thought is also about something necessary. Even ideas about merely possible things make sense only because there is an always already existing reality able to produce or not to produce such things. Nor can this always already existing reality itself be clearly and coherently thought to be merely possible, rather than strictly necessary. To think of it as possible and yet not necessarily existent would be to think of some still more ultimate reality able to produce or not to produce it, and so on *ad infinitum*.

In sum: to think at all is to think about both the contingent and the necessary: the concrete producibles or products of concrescence and the abstract creative process of concrescence itself as able to produce or not to produce them. Thus, if a putatively meaningful concept explicitly refers neither to a producible concrete reality nor to the ultimate productive reality in one or another of its essential aspects, then the concept explicitly refers to nothing and, by the rule relating all clear and coherent concepts to reality, must be devoid of meaning. If, on the other hand, the concept refers to something producible, it may or may not refer to an actual concrete product, because the thing in question may or may not have already been produced. In either case, it cannot fail to refer, at least implicitly, to the strictly ultimate creative process of concrescence that is able to produce or not to produce the thing in question, as well as to the two necessary forms or levels of that process, surpassable and unsurpassable.

81

Analogy

Hartshorne insists, rightly, that analogy is unavoidable in any adequate metaphysical theism because there is a "pretension inherent in theism as such" to the effect that "God is by definition an infinite exception!" It follows, he argues, that "each category has two levels of possible meaning, the ordinary one and the extraordinary one applicable only to God." Thus if "God" means what theists say it means, God "is 'an individual' who yet is not *simply* an individual, whose 'nature' or quality is not *simply* a quality, and who 'exists,' but not *simply* as other things exist." Accordingly, "[to] take God to be simply an individual, simply having a nature or quality, simply existing, is certainly a category mistake, if ever there was one! Deity must itself be a sort of category, and the supreme category, and until *its* rules have been investigated, there can be no demonstration that any relevant rules have been violated."[33]

But if deity itself *is* a category, indeed, "the supreme category," it can hardly be true that "*each* category has two levels of possible meaning" (italics added). What Hartshorne has to mean, obviously, is that all convertible (or coextensive) categories other than "God" have these two levels of possible meaning.

In any case, the more appropriate concept-term here is not "categories," anyhow, but "transcendentals." All convertible (or coextensive) transcendental conceptions other than "God" are rightly said to be analogical because they have two levels of possible meaning: the ordinary one, whereon they are applicable to all the many particular individuals other than God; and the extraordinary one, whereon they are applicable to the one and only universal individual God. This is why God is rightly

---

33. Hartshorne, *Anselm's Discovery*, 77, 66.

taken, not simply as "*an* individual," but only as *the* individual, the universal individual; not as having just one "nature or quality" among others, but as having *the* essence, the one self-individuating essence in which all other essences are unified; and not just as "existing," as everything else exists, contingently, with the possibility of not existing at all, but as God alone exists, *necessarily*, beyond even the possibility of nonexistence.

∾

The crucial question about analogy is whether the twofold distinction between literal (≡ nonsymbolic) and symbolic (≡ nonliteral) kinds of meaning is exhaustive, or whether there is yet a third, so-called analogical kind of meaning that certain terms may have that cannot be reduced to, or simply identified with, either of the other two kinds. My position is that the twofold distinction is exhaustive, and that any third, "analogical" kind of meaning that terms may be supposed to have can be reduced to, if not simply identified with, either the literal or the symbolic kind, depending on the sense in which "analogy" and its cognates are understood. If they are understood in the broad, general sense in which they are ordinarily used, the kind of meaning so-called analogical terms have can be reduced to, if not simply identified with, the symbolic kind. If, on the contrary, "analogy" and its cognates are understood in the stricter, more specific sense explicated by a sophisticated theory of analogy—i.e., in terms of some form or other of the threefold distinction between "univocal," "equivocal," and "analogical," the kind of meaning so-called analogical terms have can be reduced to, if not simply identified with, the literal kind.

By its very logic, any convertible (or coextensive) transcendental term other than "God" can—and if radical monotheism is intelligible, and therefore true, must—be used in two infinitely different senses, both of which are literal. In being so used, however, the term does not lose but rather retains the same core of literal meaning that it has, and must have, in any of its uses as a transcendental term. Thus, if "existence," for example, is just such a term, then to say that something exists, whether God or anything else, means literally that the essence of the thing is somehow actualized, in some actual, and therefore necessarily contingent, state(s). Nor can this same literal meaning ever fail to be retained on any use of "existence" if it is to be used intelligibly. At the same time, this literal meaning of the term itself allows for (and, if radical monotheism is intelligible and true, requires) its use in both of two infinitely different senses, each of which is also literal—i.e., the sense in which it applies to anything other than God, which exists and can exist, contingently, on some conditions, only; and the sense in which it applies solely to the thing properly called "God," which alone exists and must exist necessarily, unconditionally, or on any conditions whatsoever. This is true, too, with the other transcendental term: "individual." For anything at all to be a concrete individual, as distinct from a mere ideal or abstraction, it must be literally the case that it is internally as well as externally related somehow both to itself and to others comparably concrete. And "individual" can lose this literal meaning only by no longer being used intelligibly. Still, this literal meaning itself allows for—and, yet again, if radical monotheism is intelligible and therefore true, requires—the term being used in two infinitely different senses, both of which are likewise literal—i.e., the sense in which it applies to any and all of the many particular individuals that are literally related to self and others both internally and externally only partially and inadequately; and the sense in which it applies solely to the one universal individual called "God," whose relations to self and others are just as literally utterly impartial and wholly adequate.

But if terms supposed to be used "analogically" in this stricter, more specific sense, must, by their very logic, also be used literally in both of the respects thus explained, then, clearly, their meaning is reducible to (whether or not it can be simply identified with) the literal kind of meaning.

If, on the other hand, terms are held to be used analogically only in the broad, general sense in which "analogy" and its cognates are ordinarily used, their meaning cannot be different in kind from that of any other terms that obviously have a symbolic kind of meaning—whether "metaphors," "images," "figures," etc. To be sure, not all terms having such meaning need be, in all other respects, of simply the same kind. To say, for example, "the Lord is my shepherd," or "a mighty fortress is our God," is clearly a vivid and existentially forceful way of speaking religiously of the loving care of God, or of God's utter faithfulness and reliability. But both of these expressions—"loving care" and "utter reliability"—also are themselves symbolic ways of speaking, even though, arguably, the interpersonal symbols they employ arise from another, deeper, more religiously relevant stratum of human experience than that disclosing either shepherding sheep or providing protection by being a military fortification. Nor is it, in principle, any different if the symbols employed allegedly refer to certain "pure perfections" that—so the argument goes—are better for any being to have than not to have, and that God, therefore, as the unsurpassable being, has, and must have, in an eminent, transcendent sense. Thus "mind" or "experience" is said by some to refer to just such a pure perfection, once its meaning is so generalized that it refers no longer to any specific kind of mind or experience but only to what is called "mind in general" or "experience as such." But the profound difficulty with so reasoning is that all such phrases are, for all anyone has ever shown to the contrary, merely verbal, being either hopelessly vague or not so subtly self-contradictory, in somewhat the same way as "the greatest possible number." The plain truth of the matter is that obviously categorial terms such as "mind" or "experience" cannot be intelligibly employed as though they were not categorial, but rather the transcendental terms that they most certainly are not. They clearly do not retain the same literal sense in any of their uses, nor are their senses when applied to God or to beings other than God both literal senses; unless, of course, the only intelligible, more than merely verbal, meaning that can be validly claimed for them turns out to be only that of the literal, transcendental terms that they and all other uses of language necessarily presuppose.

But these difficulties with obviously symbolic uses of terms pretending to some third kind of "analogical" meaning I have discussed at length in other places.[34] All that needs to be said here is that the kind of meaning that all such terms have, insofar as they have any meaning, is reducible to, even if it cannot be simply identified with, that of symbolic uses of terms generally.

The conclusion, then, is clear: the only kinds of meaning that "God-talk" involves, whatever the names by which they may be called, are either literal or symbolic. *Tertium non datur.*

∾

I wrote some years ago that "such knowledge as we can have of the inner nature of anything else we can have only by way of analogy with whatever we are able to know of our own existence." During the intervening years, I found good reasons to reject such a statement insofar as it is construed as it is by idealists, including psychicalists or panpsychists, and as I myself undoubtedly construed it when I made it. My question here is whether this is the only way to construe it, or whether it bears some other construction on which it can and should still be made.

It seems clear, as I have pointed out elsewhere, that, aside from ordinary, dictionary uses of "analogy," the term has and must have proper uses even in an austerely transcendental metaphysics. Take the term "real," for example. If not only concretes, but abstracts also, are properly said to be real, then, assuming the logical-ontological type distinction between abstracts and concretes, "real" as used of both of them must be used analogically. This is so, at any rate, provided it is not used merely equivocally, since, given the logical-ontological type distinctions between abstracts and concretes or between the one universal individual and the many particular individuals, it cannot be used univocally. And so, too, with the terms "abstracts" and "concretes," both of which, like "real," are applicable across fundamental differences of logical-ontological type. In the case of "abstracts," there are not only the differences between the various kinds of categorial properties—i.e., categories proper, genera, species, and individualities—but also the differences between all of them, on the one hand, and the unique type of transcendental properties, on the other. Similarly, in the case of "concretes," there are not only the type differences between events, individuals, and aggregates, but also the unique type differences between any of the many particular individuals and the one universal individual, which can only be transcendental differences (cf. note 58, "Logical-Ontological Type Distinctions in Outline: Ten Theses").

---

34. Cf., especially, Ogden, *Point of Christology*, 127–47; Ogden, *Doing Theology Today*, 187–209.

Analogy

A precedent for suggesting an alternative construction of my earlier statement is how I have long since distinguished alternative ways of construing certain parallel statements of Whitehead's and Hartshorne's. I refer to such statements of Whitehead's as that "all final individual actualities have the metaphysical character of occasions of experience," or that "the whole universe consists of elements disclosed in the analysis of the experiences of subjects."[35] As I have previously explained, my issue is not with these statements as such, but only with one of two possible ways in which they may be construed—specifically, with how the term "metaphysical character" in the first statement, and the term "elements" in the second, may be understood. If "metaphysical character" includes "experience" in some intelligible sense of the word as one of the characteristics, as Whitehead himself may be supposed to think, then I can only reject his statement, arguing instead that it includes only the "concreteness" of which "experience," as we experience our own, is (admittedly) a special case. Or, again, if the "elements" disclosed in the analysis of experience include "experience" itself in some intelligible sense or other as such an "element," as Whitehead may appear to hold, then I have to reject the statement, arguing, on the contrary, that what is "elemental" in the experiences of subjects or in any other concrete thing is not their experience, but simply their concreteness, their being products of concrescence, and so on.

Mutatis mutandis, I can reasonably construe the statement I cited at the outset so that I can still make it. The question in its case is what is to be understood by "inner nature" and "analogy." Since the only inner nature of anything to which we are privy is our own, it is truistic to say that any knowledge we can have of the inner nature of anything else is by analogy with ours. But, again, by analogy with what? What is meant by, or included in, "inner nature"? If it is equivalent to "metaphysical character," or "elements," then the issue is the same as has already been clarified above, and I have to resolve it accordingly. As for "analogy," I have good reason to allow, as I've argued already, that even "metaphysical character" is an analogical concept in that, e.g., such metaphysical knowledge as I can have of the universal individual can only be analogous to such metaphysical knowledge as I can have of myself as a particular individual.

Of course, "inner nature," as I would use the term, includes but is not exhausted by "metaphysical character." So there may well be any number of other merely factual, nonmetaphysical things that I can know about the inner nature of things other than myself by analogy with myself. But in no case can I make or imply a legitimate claim to such knowledge where I cannot give an intelligible sense to the terms employed in the analogy—as I clearly cannot in the case where "experience" is supposedly used analogically with a claim to know thereby the "metaphysical character" of things.

---

35. Whitehead, *Adventures of Ideas*, 284; Whitehead, *Process and Reality*, 166.

I contend that "analogy" has no place in metaphysics, strictly and properly so-called, if its cognate adjective is used in either of the two senses allowed for by the two-term distinction between "literal" (≡ nonsymbolic) and "symbolic" (≡ nonliteral)—i.e., either in the sense in which "analogical" is more or less synonymous with "metaphorical" and "symbolic"; or in the quasi-technical, term-of-art sense that Hartshorne tries (as I hold, unsuccessfully) to give it as distinct from both "literal" terms, on the one hand, and other kinds of "nonliteral" terms (i.e., "metaphorical" or "symbolic" terms), on the other. At the same time, I allow that "analogy" does and must have a place in metaphysics, strictly and properly so-called, provided its cognate adjective is understood as it is in the three-term distinction between "univocal," "equivocal," and "analogical."

With all this in mind, I have naturally pondered Hartshorne's statement, "on both sides, we have something literal, but inadequate, needing to be helped out by the analogy with the other." I take this to mean that, in what is originally given in our existential experience, however "inadequately," is a literal grasp of our own contingent being as such and, in strict correlation therewith, a literal grasp of God's necessary being as such. But, then, if this literal grasp on each side needs to be "helped out" by "the analogy with the other," the analogy appealed to as providing the needed help can only be analogy in the second sense clarified above, by reference to the three-term distinction between "univocal," "equivocal," and "analogical." Why? Because analogy in either of the first two senses clarified simply cannot provide such help: in the one sense, because nonliteral uses of terms, such as metaphor, symbol, and analogy, are cognitively significant only insofar as they do not help, but are themselves helped by, literal uses of terms; and in the other sense, because, as Hartshorne's failure to distinguish it demonstrates, analogy in any such quasi-technical sense cannot possibly be distinguished except verbally from such other nonliteral (≡ symbolic) uses of terms as metaphor and symbol without fallacy and/or self-contradiction.

What Hartshorne's statement comes down to, then, is that a literal grasp of either side of the—neither univocal nor equivocal but—analogical contrast between our own contingent being, on the one side, and God's necessary being, on the other, is insofar inadequate unless and until it is "helped out" by a literal grasp of the other side. We understand clearly and consistently what contingent being means only by clearly and consistently understanding what is meant by necessary being—and vice versa.

Analogy

There are two principal differences between a classical theory of analogy like Thomas Aquinas's and a neoclassical theory such as Charles Hartshorne's or my own.

1. The two types of theories are *formally* different because, or insofar as, in a neoclassical theory, there is no question that the whole superstructure of symbolic (≡ nonliteral) predications, whether merely metaphorical or "analogical" in some supposed third sense, rests (and must do so) on a substructure of strictly literal (≡ nonsymbolic) predications. They must so rest, at any rate, in the logical-ontological "order of being," even if Morris Cohen and Ernest Nagel are right, that the reverse is true in the epistemological "order of knowing"—because, as they put it, "intelligence grows from the vague and confused to the more definite by the process of discrimination."[36] Why must this be so? Because, as Hartshorne himself says, "whatever the qualification, some abstract feature or *ratio* is implied, and this common feature must not be denied if anything is to be left of the analogy."[37]

2. The two theories are *materially* different because the strictly literal (≡ nonsymbolic) predications that must be made of God if there are to be any symbolic (≡ nonliteral) predications of God at all must be partly positive, not wholly negative in meaning. In other words, God must be said literally (≡ nonsymbolically) to be eminently relative as well as eminently absolute or nonrelative, lest the symbolic (≡ nonliteral) assertions about God essential to theistic religious faith and witness be implicitly denied as necessarily false. Thus, for example, if God is asserted symbolically (≡ nonliterally) to be love, and "love" means (whatever else it means) the real, internal relatedness of the subject of love to its object(s), then this assertion about God can be symbolically true only if God can be literally (≡ nonsymbolically) asserted to be, in some respect, relative to other things, even if in an eminent, transcendent sense of "relative" applicable only to God.

The issue between Hartshorne's theory of analogy and mine is whether, as I contend, the distinction between literal (≡ nonsymbolic) predications, on the one hand, and symbolic (≡ nonliteral) predications on the other, is exhaustive, or whether, as he maintains, a further distinction needs to be made between different kinds of nonliteral predications, only some of which are "symbolic," while others are, properly, "analogical." On classical theories, such a distinction is indeed made between two kinds of nonliteral predications: metaphorical and analogical. A term is held to be predicated analogically rather than merely metaphorically because, or insofar as, it designates a so-called pure perfection. By a "pure perfection" is understood a property that is supposed to be better for a being to have than not to have, and of which God, not any creature, is the primary exemplification, or "prime analogate"—not, to be sure, according to "how the term means," but according to "what is meant by it," to translate

---

36. Cohen and Nagel, *Introduction to Logic*, 369.
37. Hartshorne, "Analogy," 19.

the well-known distinction Aquinas makes between the *modus significandi* and the *res significata* of the term.

∞

I have written elsewhere that "any supposedly 'analogical' use of psychical terms in Hartshorne's sense is either itself empty or else fallacious, and, if fallacious, self-contradictory into the bargain."[38] But I would have better written instead: "any supposedly 'analogical' use of psychical terms in Hartshorne's sense is either redundant or else fallacious, and, in either case, self-contradictory into the bargain."

This formulation would have been better, because:

1. "redundant" conveys the point better than "empty" that, if a supposedly "analogical" use of language is not fallacious, it is only because it is merely verbally different from what is already expressed by the "literal" terms that it, in any event, necessarily presupposes; and

2. it is self-contradictory not just on one, but on both, lemmas because it could be consistent on neither unless "analogical," contrary to the whole point of Hartshorne's theory, does not really designate "a *third* stratum of meaning" after all, but only refers misleadingly to one or the other of the only two strata that are to be distinguished—i.e., "literal" or "symbolic."

∞

If "analogical" is used otherwise than in its ordinary, broad, dictionary meaning, any supposedly "analogical" assertion, if valid at all, either is or can be reduced to a literal ($\equiv$ nonsymbolic) assertion. Although the sense in which it uses a term of an ordinary, non-eminent, surpassable thing is not simply the same as, but different from—indeed, infinitely, qualitatively different from—the sense in which it uses the same term of the one extraordinary, eminent, unsurpassable thing, it uses the term in both cases literally ($\equiv$ nonsymbolically), in a twofold respect: (1) in that, on each use, it uses the term in the same sense, not in different senses, of either of the two kinds of things of which it uses it; and (2) in that, on both uses, the term has a core of literal meaning that remains ever the same, whichever kind of thing it is used of. Thus, if to be an individual, for example, means to be somehow actualized in some contingent state(s), then this must be as literally ($\equiv$ nonsymbolically) asserted of the one extraordinary, eminent, unsurpassable thing referred to as "the universal individual" as of any of the many ordinary, non-eminent, surpassable things distinguished therefrom as "particular individuals."

---

38. Ogden, "Theology without Metaphysics," 154–55.

ANALOGY

I need to take particular care to clarify the sense in which "analogy" is to be rejected, as distinct from the senses in which it is to be accepted, even in or by an austerely transcendental metaphysics such as I am concerned with developing. To some extent, at least, I think I have already done this by arguing the following:

1. that, if "reality" and its cognates can and must be used in all the different literal senses reflecting the logical-ontological type distinctions, then, even in an austerely transcendental metaphysics such as mine, it can only be a broadly "analogical," as distinct from either a "univocal" or an "equivocal," concept-term, in that it can and must be used in different, if also similar, literal senses to refer to all the different logical-ontological types of reality;

2. that even properly metaphorical or symbolic uses of language based in our empirical experience can be said to be "analogical" in a broad sense, just as, conversely, so-called analogical concepts-terms based in our existential experience are, for all that, still properly said to be metaphorical or symbolic; but

3. that the distinction between these two senses in which "analogy" is to be accepted as unavoidable even in an austerely transcendental metaphysics and the sense in which it is to be rejected is perfectly clear-cut, in that the different senses in which a properly transcendental concept-term may be used are each literal, indeed, univocal, because (1) they each apply within their respective types, not in different senses, but in the same sense; and (2) at their core, they each have the same meaning in any of their different uses. Thus, for example, anything that is real in any sense whatsoever is so only because it is real for the one extraordinary, everlasting individual, and also for at least some ordinary, transitory individuals that either have become or are in the process of becoming real in the same general sense. Similarly, any individual whatsoever, whether the extraordinary, everlasting, universal, individual God, or any ordinary, transitory, particular, individual other than God, actualizes its individuality and so exists, necessarily or contingently, only in events that are and must be contingent rather than necessary.

But even if the substance of the needed clarification has, to this extent, already been worked out, I still have to see to it that it is not misunderstood as a rejection of analogy *tout court*—lest my polemic against Hartshorne's psychicalism and "categorial metaphysics" generally fail to carry the strictly logical point that alone justifies it.

82

Hartshorne's Theory of Analogy—as Unnecessary as It Is Impossible

In arguing that there is a "qualitative" as well as a "quantitative" difference between how categories apply to God, on the one hand, and to everything else, on the other, Hartshorne speaks of "[t]he uniquely excellent way in which each category applies to deity and the less excellent ways in which it applies to the non-divine."[39] I was no doubt particularly struck by his speaking in this way when I recently came across it again, because I also had freshly in mind what I have long taken to be something like his classical definition of metaphysics, especially with respect to its limits.

> Metaphysics[, he says,] is the study of the necessary aspects of being, and of nothing else. All contingent being is outside the province of metaphysics. All individual beings except God are contingent, and so are all specific kinds of beings. There is even a side of God's nature that is contingent, the side which is relatively, not absolutely, perfect. Metaphysics does only two things, it describes the necessary aspect of the one and only necessary being, including the requirement that this being have some nonnecessary aspects or other, and it describes what all contingent beings have in common (for these common features are necessary and what distinguishes them generically from the necessary being, even in its contingent aspects).[40]

To take this delimitation of "the province of metaphysics" seriously is to realize how much of Hartshorne's "metaphysics," so called, is really nothing of the kind. Had he observed the limits of metaphysics, as he himself sets them here, he could not have consistently spoken—not, at any rate, *as a metaphysician*—of "the *ways*" (plural) in which each category applies to the nondivine, but only of "the *way*" (singular) in which it so applies. By his own account, metaphysics, being "the study of the necessary aspects of being, *and of nothing else*" (italics added), could properly describe only "what all contingent beings have in common," and therefore only the *one* "less excellent" way in which each category commonly applies to all of them. Any differences of ways, if there are, or even conceivably could be, such, could only be exactly like any other differences between contingent beings and specific kinds thereof and would consequently fall outside the province of metaphysics.

39. Hartshorne, "Love and Dual Transcendence," 98.
40. Hartshorne, "Philosophy of Democratic Defense," 164–65.

But to take account of this is to realize that and why Hartshorne's whole theory of analogy is as unnecessary as it is impossible. It is impossible because it implicitly transgresses the limits of the metaphysics of which it is presumably proposed as an essential part. But it is also unnecessary because it is proposed to solve a problem that can arise only if the limits of metaphysics, as he himself sets them, are ignored. Even allowing that a category could conceivably apply in different ways to different contingent beings, or to different more or less specific kinds of such, as a metaphysician one would still have no reason to devise a theory to account for this, if the concern of metaphysics, and its *only* concern, is with the necessary, which, in the case of contingent beings, is solely what they all have in common, not wherein they are different or of different specific kinds.

∽

If metaphysics is as limited in its objective as Hartshorne expressly and repeatedly states it is—i.e., if it is "the study of the necessary aspects of being, and of nothing else"—then metaphysics properly uses the unique human analogy, or model, for understanding reality to attain *this* objective, and not some other. This means that the only thing about the unique human sample of reality on which metaphysics, in the strict sense, focuses attention is what is strictly necessary about it, not as specifically human, but simply as a sample of contingent reality in general, and therefore, as such, an analogue of the one and only necessary reality.

In other words, the question is not *whether* we are to use "the social model of reality," but only *how* we are to use it—given our objective in pursuing properly metaphysical study of the strictly necessary—"and of nothing else."

∽

Hartshorne argues: "The purely or strictly necessary can have no concrete content. The necessary is the neutral common element of all possible alternative states of reality, the empty featureless invariant in all possible variations."[41] But, then, if metaphysics, as he also argues, is limited to "the study of the necessary aspects of being, *and of nothing else*," how could he possibly take exception to my austerely transcendental metaphysics, which, in the strict sense, simply abstracts from all "concrete content" in order to study "the purely or strictly necessary"?

By his own account, "experience" is not, properly, "categorial," but only—as he puts it paradoxically—"almost categorial."[42] But then, "experience," unlike

---

41. Hartshorne, "Religious Aspects of Necessity and Contingency," 148.
42. Hartshorne, *Creative Synthesis and Philosophic Method*, 154.

"concreteness," is hardly a likely candidate for anything properly called "purely" or "strictly" necessary!

83

On "the Infinite, Qualitative Difference"

Hartshorne argues that "the uniquely excellent way in which each category applies to deity and the less excellent ways in which it applies to the non-divine have quantitative and qualitative aspects. The non-divine illustrates the category in some relationships to others [better: in relationship to some others], the divine illustrates it in all such relationships [better: in relationships to all others]. Also, the non-divine illustrates the category in a qualitatively surpassable way, the divine in a way either unsurpassable or, in some categories, surpassable only by [itself]. . . . The contrast between 'all' and 'some' might be termed the extensional import of eminence. There is also the intensional import."[43]

Granted that, if one is to join Kierkegaard in thinking and speaking of "the infinite, qualitative difference," it must indeed be possible to distinguish such aspects, or, specifically, to distinguish a "qualitative" from an "infinite" ($\equiv$ "quantitative") aspect, what is the nature of this distinction? One way of thinking about it, I suggest, is that the so-called qualitative aspect is itself quantitative, albeit at another higher level—adverbally quantitative, if you will, rather than adjectivally, or like the first "all" in the phrase "all in all."

Thus deity is eminently or unsurpassably inclusive, not only because it includes all actuality and all possibility ("quantitative" or "extensional" aspect), but also because it includes all, or everything, *in* the all of actuality and all, or everything, *in* the all of possibility ("qualitative" or "intensional" aspect). By radical contrast, anything other than deity is only noneminently or surpassably inclusive, both because it includes only some actuality and only some possibility ("quantitative" or "extensional" aspect) and because it includes only something *in* the some of actuality that it includes and only something *in* the some of possibility, while also excluding something in both of them ("qualitative" or "intensional" aspect).

---

43. Hartshorne, "Love and Dual Transcendence," 98.

I find it interesting that Hartshorne himself speaks of "a quality wholly independent of quantity" as "that apparent impossibility."[44] It would seem, then, that he might look with favor on my suggestion that the "qualitative," or "intensional," import of God's unsurpassability—as distinct from its "quantitative," or "extensional," import—may itself be thought and spoken of as quantitative, albeit "adverbally," rather than "adjectivally."

(Come to think of it, Hartshorne himself makes use of this same adverb/adjective distinction in *The Divine Relativity* in distinguishing between "relationships" and "*types* of relationships," the latter being logically equivalent in the divine case with "attributes" that are "absolute.")

84

The Scope of Metaphysics

The more I think about it, the more I realize that—and why—more of a change is involved by my move to an "austerely transcendental metaphysics" than I seem to have supposed, judging from what I have said and written. In fact, I'm having to rethink the whole question of the scope of metaphysics in the broad sense.

The scope of metaphysics in the strict sense I continue to understand essentially as Hartshorne understands it. As "the study of the necessary aspect of being, and of nothing else," metaphysics in this sense is limited to studying two things: the strictly necessary aspect of—in terms of Whitehead's distinction—"the one which is all," and the strictly necessary aspect of "the one [*sc. any* one] among the many." But if I am right in saying, as I have come to say, that it "is of no concern to metaphysics as such, even in the broad sense" whether the "existent in the emphatic sense" that is "the subject of the real world language game" is also "a human being, or a being of some other kind" (note 52, "Meaning and Transcendental Metaphysic"), then the scope of metaphysics even in the broad sense is presumably significantly more limited than appears to be implied by thinking and speaking, as I have, for example, about "the metaphysics of faith and justice."[45]

In fact, there appears to be a confusion here parallel to that involved in my once thinking and speaking of "the task of philosophical theology" as "integral to philosophy's central task as metaphysics" (cf. note 22, "The Task of Philosophical Theology:

---

44. Hartshorne, *Anselm's Discovery*, 29.
45. Cf. Ogden, *Doing Theology Today*, 109–22.

A Restatement"). As certain as it may be that metaphysics' task must be done if philosophical theology's is to be done, it is the task of *philosophy*, not of metaphysics, even in the broad sense, of which philosophical theology's is an integral part. In somewhat the same way, presumably, the task of philosophical anthropology is an integral part of *philosophy's* task, not metaphysics', even, again, in the broad sense; and this is so, even though, unless and until metaphysics's task has been done, philosophical anthropology's cannot be done, either.

Granted, then, that there is an indispensable metaphysical component to any adequate philosophical anthropology, even as to any adequate philosophical cosmology or philosophical theology, what a Christian systematic theology needs to concern itself with is not, properly, or in the first instance, "the *metaphysics* of faith and justice," but, rather, "the *philosophy* of faith and justice."

That this is so is fully borne out, I think, if one simply considers the resources I actually adduce as relevant for Christian systematic reflection on faith and justice. Taken as a group, they would clearly be more properly thought and spoken of as "philosophical" than as "metaphysical" resources.[46]

If one says, as I've said, that metaphysical anthropology is concerned with the structure of human existence in itself, whereas philosophical anthropology is concerned with the meaning of human existence for us, then how can one say, as I've also said, that metaphysical anthropology (or metaphysics in the broad sense) is indifferent to whether or not the subject of the real world language game is a human being, as distinct from some other kind of being (compare note 55, "Transcendental Metaphysics and Transcendental Ethics," with note 52, "Meaning and Transcendental Metaphysics")?

The answer, it seems clear, is that one *can't* say both of these things! There's no way in which one and the same form of critical reflection can be concerned with the structure of human existence in itself and yet also be indifferent to whether or not the material object of its concern is a human being. Either it cannot be thus indifferent, or else the structure that concerns it is something other than the structure specific to a human subject as such—namely, the structure of *any* particular, fragmentary, and so surpassable subject, human or of some other kind, that can understand at the same high level evidenced by human thinking and speaking, and therefore also act at the correspondingly high level of metaphysical freedom and responsibility (i.e., at the level of distinctively *moral* freedom and responsibility). My way of deciding this issue is to opt for the second of these alternatives and to continue to hold that metaphysics as such is indeed indifferent to whether the subject exhibiting the structure that

---

46. Cf., e.g., Ogden, *Doing Theology Today*, 116–17.

concerns it is also, properly, a human being. I would explain and support this decision by the following considerations.

For metaphysics in the strict sense, a human being is simply one among an infinite number of particular, fragmentary, and therefore surpassable concretes, privileged only in that it is the one such concrete whose structure of concreteness we can each know by being it, and thus can know in all of the ways in which we can know anything. For metaphysics in the broad sense, on the other hand, a human being is one among perhaps any number of other such particular, fragmentary, and so surpassable concretes that not only exist, but exist in the further, emphatic sense that they exist understandingly, at the high level evidenced by human thinking, speaking, and acting, privileged, again, only in the same way, or for the same reason: because it is the only such concrete that we can each know by being it, and so know in all the ways in which we are able to know things.

So far as metaphysics is concerned, then, the human subject as such is not among its formal objects. The formal object of metaphysics in the strict sense abstracts from everything, including everything in the human subject, except the utterly abstract structure of its particular or fragmentary, and therefore surpassable, concreteness, which it has in common with an infinite number of other particular, or fragmentary, and so surpassable concretes and kinds thereof. On the other hand, the formal object of metaphysics in the broad sense abstracts from everything in the human subject that is distinctively human except the utterly abstract structure that it shares with every other concrete, or kind of concrete, if there be any such, that also exists in the further, emphatic sense of the word and consequently understands itself and everything else at the same high level, evidenced by typically human thinking and speaking and therefore acting with distinctively moral freedom and responsibility.

This means that "metaphysical anthropology" may well be insofar a misleading concept/term (and that the same is true, *mutatis mutandis*, even of the traditional concept/term "metaphysical psychology," which I've suggested be replaced by "metaphysical anthropology"). Although *anthropos* (or *psyche*) is, in its way, a *material* object of metaphysical reflection, it is the *formal* object neither of metaphysics in the strict sense, whose formal object, so far as all particular, fragmentary, and so surpassable concretes as such are concerned, includes only their utterly transcendental features, nor of metaphysics in the broad sense, whose formal object includes only the emphatically existential features of all particular, fragmentary, and so surpassable concretes that understand as such, where "to understand" means, at the same high level, evidenced by typically human thinking, speaking, and acting.

"Metaphysical anthropology" in the strict sense of "metaphysics," then, does not designate one of three distinct disciplines of "special metaphysics," but only a study indistinguishable except verbally from a certain aspect of "general metaphysics," or ontology—that aspect, namely, that is concerned with the utterly transcendental features of the many particular, fragmentary, and therefore surpassable concretes, as distinct from its other aspect that studies the utterly transcendental features of the one universal, integral, and therefore unsurpassable concrete that radically monotheistic religions call "God." So if there is such a thing as a "metaphysical anthropology" that is more than verbally distinct from a certain aspect of "general metaphysics," or ontology, it can only be "metaphysical" in the broad sense of the word. But, even then, the formal object of its special concern, as distinct from its material object, cannot be *anthropos*, or even *psyche*, as such, but only *existence* as such, in the emphatic sense of particular, fragmentary, and therefore surpassable concreteness that can understand itself and everything else at the same high level known to us only in being and knowing ourselves as human beings—even though, for all we know, or even can know, to the contrary, it may be just as really present as the essential existential structure of other, nonhuman kinds of beings as well.

Question: Could considerations such as these also possibly explain why Heidegger need not have been simply quibbling in sharply distinguishing what he meant by "existentialist analysis" in *Sein und Zeit* from "anthropology"? Whatever the answer, it seems clear that if "existentialist analysis" is rightly said to be what I say it is (i.e., the conceptual explication, in terms of the "existentials" that articulate its essential structure, not of distinctively "*human* existence," but only of "existence *in the emphatic sense*") then there is every good reason for preferring the concept/term "fundamental ontology," or, simply, "existentialist analysis," to "metaphysical anthropology" in order to designate it.

Part 3

GOD

In its early stages religion means certainty about many things. But we now see that he is most religious who is certain of but one thing, the world-embracing love of God.

—CHARLES HARTSHORNE

85

Experience and God

In the depths of all of my empirical experience of myself and the world, psychical as well as physical, there is an existential experience of myself, others, and the whole. Presupposed by all of my sense experience and the claims to truth arising from it is the nonsensuous certainty of existence: the certainty that I exist as the subject of my experience and that I exist together with others, fellow creatures more or less like myself, to whom I am related and on whose actions I am dependent, even as they are thus related and dependent with respect to me. And just as fundamental is the certainty that both I and my fellow creatures all exist within, and therefore as parts of, the all-inclusive whole, the one circumambient reality on which we all depend and which, in its way, also depends on all of us: our sole primal source and our sole final end, whence we all come and whither we all go.

This complex certainty of existence—of myself, others, and the whole—is the experience out of which all religious language arises and by reference to which it is always to be understood. In this sense, all religious language is "existential" language, in which, on the primary level of self-understanding and life-praxis, we explicitly express and refer to our own existence as selves related to others and the whole as also related to us.

This becomes the more intelligible if we keep in mind that our fundamental existential certainty has a certain richness or thickness that the word "existence" may not always convey. My experience of myself, others, and the whole is not simply an experience *that* we are, in some value-neutral sense—as mere objects, if you will—but is always, precisely as the experience of existence, an experience of worth, of value, of meaning, of significance. Indeed, in experiencing my own existence in relation to others and the whole, the essence of my experience is *the sense of worth*: of my own worth for myself and others, of their worth for themselves and me, and of our common worth for the whole and its unique worth for each and all of us as our sole primal source and sole final end.

Thus the fundamental certainty underlying all of my experience is not only that I am together with others in the whole, but that what I am and what they are is significant, makes a difference, and is worthwhile. This certainty that one is and that one is significant or worthwhile grounds a basic confidence in the meaning of life. And this confidence belongs to the original faith that, being constitutive of our very lives as human beings, is (in the proper sense) the "common faith" of humankind. To exist humanly at all is to exist as one who shares this common faith, because any attempt to question it or to controvert it necessarily presupposes it. One cannot question the worth of life without presupposing the worth of questioning, and therefore the worth of life, without which such questioning cannot be done. In the same way, to look for evidence against the claim that life is worthwhile presupposes not only that there is or can be such evidence, but that it is worth spending one's time and energy trying to find it. As a matter of fact, even suicide, as the intentional act of taking one's own life, entails not just a denial of life's worth but also an affirmation of it. One can hardly choose to end one's life unless one assumes that doing so is not merely pointless but is somehow significant or makes a difference.

This explains, in turn, why it is this same existential experience that is also the fundamental datum of philosophy, understood as critical reflection on the most basic concepts and presuppositions of all our experience and understanding, oriented (although not constituted) by *the* existential question about the meaning of ultimate reality for us. Whether as logical analysis of all such concepts and presuppositions, or as critical validation of all answers to *the* existential question, implicit as well as explicit, philosophy, in both phases, also arises, in its way, out of the depths of our existential experience of ourselves, others, and the whole, and is always to be understood by reference to it, in distinction from our empirical experience, which is the concern intellectually, not of philosophy, but of the several special sciences.

But this means that there is a definite possibility distinct from those most commonly discussed of a very different and more fundamental unification, not only of all the sciences, but also of all the other domains of experiencing, understanding, and transforming the world, nondiscursive as well as discursive. There is the possibility, in a word, of a properly *philosophical* unification of all our experience and understanding, not on the basis of any empirical science, or any branch thereof, but on the basis of the transcendental metaphysics and ethics that result from doing philosophy itself, in its one phase as logical analysis of concepts and presuppositions. In this case, any claim for the ultimacy of either main branch of empirical science, psychical or physical, to the exclusion, or reduction, of the other branch, is undercut by a very different and completely nonexclusive, or nonreductive claim. This is the claim for what really and truly is ultimate, and as such is utterly noncompetitive and unifying—namely, our existential experience of ourselves, others, and the whole, and the austerely transcendental metaphysics and ethics in which the "deep structure" of this experience, theoretical and practical, is made fully explicit.

Anyone who says that she or he has no faith in God, and yet goes on living, shows thereby that she or he has faith in *something*. Let her or him explain what that something is, and I will argue that, unless it is explained to be God in an appropriate sense of the term, it will not fit the faith that she or he has in it. For any fragmentary being to think as well as to live in any world whatsoever would express, if only implicitly, some sort of faith. And I hold that this faith can become fully intelligible, and in that sense explained, only as explicit faith in God with God's essential attributes of eminent or unsurpassable power, wisdom, and goodness.

So what I would call "the global argument" for God's existence, of which all particular arguments may be regarded as simply so many phases or aspects, is that a properly formulated theistic view of life and reality is the most intelligible, self-consistent, and adequate such view that can be conceived. Any of the so-called proofs of God's existence except the ontological proof may be interpreted as showing that the idea of God, taken as true and as therefore referring to something real, is required for the most reasonable interpretation or explanation of some fundamental aspect(s) of human life and experience.

∞

God is the eminent object of experience because God is the only individual other than ourselves that we experience both directly and universally. We experience all other individuals either indirectly or not universally—or both. Such immediate experience of God, however, can become experience of God *as God*, or *knowledge* of God, only through the mediation of concepts/terms.

The concept/term "God," as used by radical monotheistic religion, implies an analogy between the eminent or unsurpassable whole of reality directly and universally experienced "in, with, and under" anything else we experience, on the one hand, and any other noneminent or surpassable reality that we either experience or conceivably could experience, on the other. Insofar as included among such noneminent or surpassable realities is the unique reality of the self and of other selves like it, there is also the possibility of a symbolic ($\equiv$ nonliteral) or pictorial interpretation of the eminent or unsurpassable reality in the concepts/terms taken from experience of the self and other selves—i.e., persons.

But there is an important difference here. The analogy between the eminent or unsurpassable reality and any noneminent or surpassable reality, including the self and other persons, involves the literal ($\equiv$ nonsymbolic) concept/term individual, together with the comparably literal (nonsymbolic) contrasting concepts/terms of a universal and particular individual. On the other hand, interpretation of the eminent or unsurpassable reality symbolically, or pictorially, involves or implies such symbolic

(≡ nonliteral) concepts/terms as "an inclusive experience," "a super-experience," "the supreme person," "the supreme psyche," or "the universal consciousness" (all terms used by Charles Hartshorne, for one, to refer to the eminent, unsurpassable reality).

∽

We always already have both a perception of, and a basic faith in, the eminent object of experience. But religions are the primary ways—the primary "cultural systems," or "systems of concepts and symbols" (Clifford Geertz)—in which this perception and this basic faith become explicit, in which the eminent object of experience is not merely somehow perceived and believed in, but is perceived *as*, or believed in *as*, God, *as* Nature, *as* Emptiness, *as* the Encompassing, and so forth. In other words, religions offer more or less different answers to the existential question about the eminent object of our experience, which itself can be asked only given the perception of, and the basic faith in, the eminent object that is always already present, if only implicitly, in all human experience.

But religions are distinctive as the primary means of explicating the meaning of this eminent object for us, as distinct from its being, or structure, in itself, which it is the proper business of metaphysics to explicate. So, too, the different theologies in the generic/specific sense corresponding to these different religions are more or less critical appropriations of their religions' primary explications. And the same is true of theologies in the other sense of philosophical theologies, or, simply, of philosophies, insofar as their more or less critical appropriations of the forms of culture generally are focused on the primary explications of the particular form of religion generally. But whereas any theology in the generic/specific sense is impossible without the "canon" explicitly provided by its corresponding religion, any philosophy (or any theology in the other sense of philosophical theology) derives its criteria of judgment solely from common human experience and reason based thereon, and, more precisely, from the metaphysical and ethical analyses of the relevant parts of such experience and reason as make up the other phase of philosophical, or philosophical theological, reflection. Notwithstanding this difference, however, theologies in both senses, and philosophy as well, are similar in being, as A. N. Whitehead says, properly "secondary activities" of more or less critical reflection relative to the primary explications of religion and those of the other forms of culture that theologies and philosophies also have the task of critically appropriating.

∽

The same question to which thought and speech about God function to give an answer may be given answers that are at least verbally different by not thinking and speaking about God at all, but about something else instead. To be sure, the term "God" itself can be used so broadly, or heuristically, that it means simply strictly ultimate reality in its meaning for us, whatever this meaning may prove to be, or—to speak less existentially and more intellectually or metaphysically—it may mean simply strictly ultimate reality in its structure in itself, however we may finally conceive this structure. But if "God" is used, as it commonly is, in some more restricted, more specifically theistic sense, the questions it serves to answer, whether existential or metaphysical, may be answered at least verbally by thinking and speaking about something other than God. One may also answer them, however adequately, by thinking and speaking, say, about Nature or the Absolute, one's Real Self or the Whole, Nirvana or the Form of the Good.

∾

Just as an experience is always an experience *of*—of something other than the experience itself—so a thought is always a thought *about*—about something other than the thought itself. In this sense, thought and reality in principle belong together. A thought is always about reality, in that it is always about something real independently both of it and of any other thought.

A thought about reality in this sense may be true or false, depending on whether or not the something thought about is as it is thought to be. Also, a thought about reality may be not merely true, but *necessarily* true, provided that the something thought about could not conceivably not be or be otherwise than it is thought to be—the sufficient proof of this being that the contradictory thought is also *self*-contradictory and therefore not merely false, but *necessarily* false or meaningless.

Among such thoughts about reality as are thus sufficiently proved to be true necessarily are those expressed by the following three statements:

1. There is something real.
2. There is something concretely real, and there is something abstractly real.
3. There is something unsurpassably real, and there is something surpassably real.

Ad 1: The thought expressed by the first statement is not only true but necessarily true because the contradictory thought expressed by the statement "there is nothing real" is also self-contradictory, and therefore not just false, but necessarily false or meaningless. This it is, in fact, twice-over. It is, at the least, in John Passmore's term, "*pragmatically* self-refuting" because any act of asserting it, even as of asserting any other statement, necessarily presupposes that there is something real: minimally that the subject who asserts the statement is real, and that the same is true of whatever object the statement is directly or indirectly about, along with anything the subject and the object in turn necessarily implies. If either of these presuppositions is valid, assertion of the statement "there is nothing real" refutes itself pragmatically. But, more than that, it is also, as Hartshorne would say, "semantically" self-contradictory, and therefore not just pragmatically, but—to use the other term of Passmore's helpful distinction—"*absolutely* self-refuting" as well. This it is because, whether or not the statement is actually asserted, what is meant by "nothing" and by "real" simply cannot be coherently combined into "there is nothing real," any more than what is meant by "round" and "square" can be coherently combined into "there is a round square." But, then, the statement "there is something real," being the contradictory of the necessarily false and meaningless statement "there is nothing real," is necessarily true as well as meaningful, not only pragmatically, but also semantically and therefore absolutely.

Ad 2: The thought expressed by the second statement is also necessarily true because the first statement, "there is something real," necessarily implies that the utterly abstract property of being something real that anything real must somehow instantiate also has to be real. Therefore, that there is something *abstractly* real is and must be as true as that there is something real, whether concretely real or abstractly real. But since everything is real for something, only nothing being real for nothing, anything real, either concretely or abstractly, is and must be real *for* something else that is real not only in the same completely general sense, but also in the further, more specific sense that other things are and must be real for it if they're to be anything real at all. To be real in this further, more specific sense is to be real not merely abstractly, but also *concretely.* Consequently, if "there is something real" expresses a thought that is necessarily true, the statements "there is something concretely real" and "there is something abstractly real" both express thoughts that could only be true as well.

This same conclusion follows, by the way, from the principle—"the Aristotelian principle," if you will, or what Whitehead, for his part, calls "the ontological principle"—that anything abstractly real, like the utterly abstract property of being something real, can never be real simply in itself, but is always real only in that it is somehow included or embodied in something concretely real as a property thereof. Thus, even as anything concretely real somehow includes or embodies, and hence requires, the utterly abstract properties of being real and of being concretely real, so these utterly abstract properties must be somehow included or embodied in, and hence in turn require, *some* concretely real thing(s), although anything(s) concretely real will do, no particular concrete thing(s) being necessary.

Ad 3: The thought expressed in the third statement prompts the prior question: what is it to be something unsurpassably real, on the one hand, and something surpassably real, on the other? I answer that the unsurpassable is to the surpassable, as "all" is to "some," or "whole" is to "part(s)." Insofar, then, as being something unsurpassably real and being something surpassably real are alike ways of being something real concretely, not merely abstractly, to be something unsurpassably real is not only to be something real for *all* other things for which other things are real, i.e., for all concretely real things, but also to be something for which *all* other things themselves are real, be they real concretely, or merely abstractly so. By radical contrast, to be something surpassably real is to be something real for only *some* other things for which other things are real, i.e., for only some concretely real things, and also to be something for which only *some* other things themselves are real, be they real concretely, or merely abstractly.

But why is it necessarily true that there is something unsurpassably real as well as something surpassably real in these senses of the terms? If, as I have said, the unsurpassably real is to the surpassably real as "all" is to "some," or "whole" is to "part(s)," then, just as there can be neither "all" without "some" nor "some" without "all," so there can be neither "whole" without "part(s)" nor "part(s)" without "whole." Thus there cannot be anything unsurpassably real unless there is something surpassably real, any more than there can be something surpassably real unless there is something unsurpassably real. And yet this symmetry is qualified by a radical asymmetry. Although the surpassably real and the unsurpassably real necessarily require one another, the unsurpassably real's requirement of the surpassably real is satisfied by there being *some* surpassably real things, no particular such thing being required. On the contrary, there can be one, and only one, thing that satisfies the surpassably real's requirement that there be something unsurpassably real—namely, the *one and only* necessarily existent all, or whole, of reality, all of whose parts exist merely contingently, even though it is not contingent but necessary that there be some such parts or other.

∾

Hartshorne seems to me to be right, that there is, with certain qualifications, a single religious idea of God. This is true if one prescinds, as he says, from fanciful mythical ideas of divine or quasi-divine gods and demons and focuses attention solely on the God of the higher religions, or, as I call them, the axial religions. Once this is done, there is a rather definite, coherent, and universal idea that may be said to provide the religious meaning of the term "God." But although the idea of God is thus religious in intuitive origin, philosophers have tried, more or less successfully, to find logical forms or patterns appropriate to explicate it conceptually—and to do so at once clearly and coherently.

The intuitive idea of God expressed more or less adequately by all religions (but always along with other logically independent ideas) is that "God is whatever is the adequate object of unstinted or wholehearted devotion, whatever could and should be loved with all of one's being" (Hartshorne). This idea may be defined logically in various ways, in essentially equivalent terms, as follows:

Worshipfulness (or the worshipful One) $\equiv$ unsurpassability (both relative, or unsurpassability by any other, and absolute, or unsurpassability even by self) $\equiv$ eminence $\equiv$ transcendence $\equiv$ nonfragmentariness $\equiv$ modal all-inclusiveness $\equiv$ modal coextensiveness $\equiv$ modal coincidence.

God is modally all-inclusive $\equiv$ modally coextensive $\equiv$ modally coincident in that God is all actuality unified into one individual actuality, and all potentiality unified into one individual potentiality, or capacity for, actuality. God as thus "the all-inclusive yet individual actuality and the all-inclusive yet individual potentiality" (Hartshorne), is also the one necessary existent—hence God's "modal all-inclusiveness" of all three basic modes of reality: actuality, potentiality, and necessity.

86

Ὁ Θεός/Ἡ Θειότης αὐτοῦ

In Romans 1:19–20, Paul distinguishes between ὁ θεός ("God"), on the one hand, and τὸ γνωστὸν τοῦ θεοῦ ("what can be known about God"), τὰ ἀόρατα αὐτοῦ ("the invisible things of him"), and ἥ τε ἀΐδιος αὐτοῦ δύναμις καὶ θειότης ("his eternal power and deity"), on the other. What, exactly, is the difference between ὁ θεός ("God"), and, for short, ἡ θειότης αὐτοῦ ("his deity"), or ἡ θειότης τοῦ θεοῦ ("the deity of God")?

First of all, the difference clearly seems to be a difference between religious or philosophical concepts/terms on both sides, as distinct from a difference between a religious or philosophical concept/term, on one side, and a metaphysical concept/term, on the other. As Paul uses it here, ἡ θειότης αὐτοῦ is not a metaphysical concept/term, but is as much a religious or philosophical concept/term as ὁ θεός.

Secondly, whereas ὁ θεός is the distinctively theistic way of re-presenting the strictly ultimate reality in its meaning for us from the standpoint of some specific theistic religion or philosophy, ἡ θειότης αὐτοῦ re-presents that strictly ultimate reality in its meaning for us in abstraction from any and all specifically theistic religious or philosophical standpoints.

Thirdly, ἡ θειότης αὐτοῦ is nevertheless as God-dependent a formulation, so to speak, as, say, ὁ υἱὸς τοῦ θεοῦ ("the Son of God"). It is arguable that theistic religions typically generate additional concepts/terms not just of one type, but of two types: one type for designating the strictly ultimate reality that any use of ὁ θεός is but one alternative way of re-presenting; and the other type for designating the realities—persons or things, such as "the Son of God"—that, in turn, re-present ὁ θεός as designating strictly ultimate reality in its meaning for us.

I could also answer the question by making use of the distinction Paul Tillich uses in clarifying the meaning of "the religious symbol":

> The first and fundamental mark of a symbol is its transparency. This means that the inner act that directs itself to the symbol doesn't mean the symbol but what is symbolized in it. Also, what is symbolized can itself become in

Ὁ Θεός/Ἡ Θειότης αὐτοῦ

turn a symbol for what is symbolized at a higher level. So the written sign can become a symbol for the word, and the word can be called a symbol for the meaning. Devotion shown to a crucifix really belongs to the crucifixion on Golgotha, and devotion shown to it is really directed to the saving action of God, which itself is a symbolic expression for an experience of the unconditioned-transcendent.[1]

All religious symbols, at whatever level, are finally symbols of what Tillich calls "an experience of the unconditioned-transcendent." So to think and speak of "the saving action of God" is a symbolic way of expressing just such an experience. In the same way, to think and speak in Paul's concept/term ὁ θεός is to think and speak symbolically of an experience of ἡ θειότης αὐτοῦ, with the important qualification that it is "his deity," or "the deity of God," not in its structure in itself, metaphysically, but in its meaning for us, religiously or philosophically. The gain in using Tillich's concepts/terms is to get beyond the God-dependence of Paul's. But the same gain may be enjoyed without suffering the loss in using Tillich's problematic ontology by substituting "the whole" or "the universal individual" for "the unconditioned-transcendent," again, with the qualification that the concept/term so used is used in the religious or philosophical sense to designate ultimate reality in its meaning for us, as distinct from using it metaphysically to designate the structure of ultimate reality in itself.

I have argued that what Paul means by ἡ θειότης τοῦ θεοῦ (and the other terms we have noted that he uses) in Romans 1:19–20 can be expressed in terms that are less God-dependent than his, either by speaking with Tillich of "the unconditioned-transcendent," or—in order to avoid the serious limitations of Tillich's highly problematic ontology—using my preferred terms "the whole" or "the universal individual." But I have insisted at the same time that these terms, when so used, are to be understood, not in their "metaphysical-transcendental" meaning, but rather in their "existential-transcendental" meaning—to refer, not to the structure of "*the* transcendental" in itself, but rather to its meaning for us.

But what is this if not to answer my old question about how to designate the ground-object of "the true religion," as distinct from the Christian religion or any other specific religion that makes or implies the claim to be the true religion? If what I have said is correct, then any religion is insofar true that, in some concepts/symbols or other, adequately re-presents the whole, or the universal individual, not metaphysically, in its structure in itself, but existentially, in its meaning for us.

By the way, a different but entirely compatible answer to the same question is implied by what I say elsewhere about the *optio fundamentalis* (see discussion in

---

1. Tillich, *Gesammelte Werke* 5, 196.

note 118). "The fundamental decision is the same for all: whether so to trust in the encompassing whole of reality that one is both free *from* all things—oneself and all others—and free *for* them; and then to be loyal to the whole by being loyal to all its parts, accepting all others as oneself and thinking and acting accordingly." In other words, the whole, or the universal individual, is unsurpassable, absolutely as well as relatively, and, in its existential meaning for us, is worthy of worship, of unreserved trust and unqualified loyalty.

∾

I once asked myself how plausible it would be to say that, when Paul refers to "what can be known about God" (i.e., "his eternal power and deity"), which he asserts to be manifest to all persons, because God has manifested it to them "ever since the creation of the world," he is referring, in effect, to God *qua* the universal individual, as distinct from God *qua* the personal God of Jewish and Christian tradition. In other words, how plausible would it be to say that Paul's distinction between ἡ θειότης and ὁ θεός in Romans 1:20 functions very much to the same end as Meister Eckhart's later distinction between *deitas* and *deus*?

After further study, I am prepared to say that it would be entirely plausible to say this. Although there are important material differences between Paul's and Eckhart's thought and speech, on the one hand, and between both of theirs and mine, on the other, they are formally parallel in that, for both, the distinction in question is, in the first instance, a properly religious or philosophical—not a properly metaphysical—distinction. So I am confident that their thought and speech at this point do indeed anticipate mine in distinguishing, in their respective ways, between the whole, or the universal individual, considered not abstractly or metaphysically in its structure in itself, but concretely or religiously in its meaning for us, and the personal God of Christian faith, witness, and theology.

∾

The conceptuality/terminology of theistic religion includes distinctive concepts/terms of two main types: one type for designating the strictly ultimate reality that "God" is not the only, but only one "optional," way of re-presenting; and the other type for designating realities—persons or things—that, in turn, re-present God (as strictly ultimate reality). Paul's ἡ θειότης or Meister Eckhart's *deitas* is an example of the first type of concept/term, and the New Testament's ὁ υἱὸς τοῦ θεοῦ of the second.

Significantly, the term ἡ θειότης is as God-dependent as ὁ υἱὸς τοῦ θεοῦ. And, so far as I can tell, something like the same may be true, *mutatis mutandis*, of the Mahayana Buddhist distinction between "*dharmakaya*-as-suchness" (*dharmata-dharmakaya*) and "*dharmakaya*-as-compassion" (*upaya-dharmakaya*). I first supposed that this

Ὁ Θεός/Ἡ Θειότης αὐτοῦ

distinction is the Buddhist way of distinguishing, somewhat as I do, between ultimate reality metaphysically in its structure in itself and ultimate reality religiously or philosophically in its meaning for us. But I later came to suspect that this is probably too simple. My distinction functions to distinguish the proper concern, question, concepts and terms of metaphysics as such from those proper to religion or philosophy as such. Recognizing this, I might do better to think that, if the Buddhist distinction is a properly religious or philosophical distinction, as I take it to be, then, while its first term, *dharmakaya*-as-suchness, certainly *implies* the properly metaphysical concept of (strictly) ultimate reality in its structure in itself, it is not so much a way of expressing *this* concept as it is a way of expressing the properly *religious* or *philosophical* concept of the implicit primal source of authority, as distinct from, though viewed in the light of, the explicit primal source of authority—i.e., the *dharma* to which Sakyamuni Buddha awakened. This means that Buddhist reference to the *dharmakaya*-as-suchness manifested as the *dharmakaya*-as-compassion is more or less closely analogous to Christian reference to the mysterious Godhead manifested as the triune God of Father, Son, and Holy Spirit (or, alternatively, perhaps, the ontological trinity manifested as the economic trinity).

Thus, even with respect to (strictly) ultimate reality, religion's or philosophy's way of referring is precisely its way, not the different way of metaphysics; and—as becomes clear from this Buddhist distinction—this may be as true of other religions as it is of Christianity. The task of the philosopher of religion in explicating the meaning of a religion, then, presumably, is to introduce just such a "novel verbal characterization, rationally coordinated" (Whitehead)—a term that is, as John Hick puts it, "less upayic" than the characteristic terms of the religion itself. I submit that "the whole," in the sense of "the One which is all," or "the universal individual," in the sense of "the one from, through, and to (or for) which are all things," is just the concept/term that is called for in order to translate both Paul's ἡ θειότης and Eckhart's *deitas*.

I have taken Paul, in Romans 1:19–20, to use both terms, ὁ θεός and ἡ θειότης, religiously, as distinct from using the first term religiously and the second metaphysically. But I would unhesitatingly allow that both terms, the first as well as the second, could also be used metaphysically. So used, ὁ θεός would designate the universal individual concretely *qua* actual, as the God of *this* (that, or the other) actual world that in fact exists, while ἡ θειότης would designate the universal individual abstractly *qua* existent, as the God of merely *some* actual world that could possibly exist.

Whitehead says that philosophy, although "mystical," is concerned "to rationalize mysticism: not by explaining it away, but by the introduction of novel verbal characterizations, rationally coordinated."[2] In other words, philosophy's mysticism, in the sense of its "direct insight into depths unspoken," is guided by a concern for the "right" conceptuality/terminology in which to think/speak about them.

With this in mind, I ask this question: Are all human beings called to love God and all things in God? Yes and no—yes, in the sense that, from a Christian (or theistic) standpoint and in Christian (or theistic) concepts/terms, all human beings are indeed called to love God and all that God loves; but no, in the sense that "God-talk," properly so-called, does not provide the only concepts/terms in which to think/speak about the universal human calling, but only one particular set of such concepts/terms among others. Recognizing this, I think one is well advised to follow Paul's lead and distinguish between "God" in the strict and proper sense, on the one hand, and "what can be known of God, "the invisible things [of God]," and "[God's] eternal power and godness" (Rom 1:19), on the other.

True, Paul provides no more than a lead here, since he is still dependent on "God-talk" on both sides of his distinction—whence the force, I take it, of Whitehead's speaking of philosophy's needing to introduce "*novel* verbal characterizations." But even Paul himself goes further elsewhere when he speaks of God as the one from whom and through whom and for whom are all things (Rom 11:36; cf. 1 Cor 8:6: "from whom are all things and for whom we exist"). Whitehead goes still further with his concepts/terms, "the whole" and "the one which is all," as distinct from "the one among the many." And comparably advanced is Hartshorne's insistence that the idea of the strictly ultimate can be formed simply by quantifying the idea of concrete individual universally, so as to yield the concept/term "universal individual." All that remains, then, so far as I am concerned, is to interpret "individual" (as well as all other strictly metaphysical concepts/terms) austerely transcendentally.

This is all that remains for *metaphysics* to do, at any rate, even if philosophy, in its existential (as distinct from its analytic) phase, is as perfectly free as religion is, to continue to think/speak in the symbolic, or "analogical," concepts/terms that provide the privileged data for philosophical and metaphysical reflection. Still, in exercising this freedom, the burden of philosophy's understanding of the universal human calling will need to be expressed in some such "secular" terms as these:

> [T]o be human is to [be called] to live as a fragment, albeit a self-conscious and, therefore, responsible fragment of the integral whole of reality as such. In other words . . . the meaning of ultimate reality for us demands that we [each] accept both our own becoming and the becomings of all others as parts of this ultimate whole and then, by serving as best we can the transient goods of all

---

2. Whitehead, *Modes of Thought*, 237.

the parts, to make the greatest possible contribution to the enduring good of the whole.³

87

Who (or What) Is God?

To say or imply that anyone or anything is without God is either ungrammatical and as such incapable of being true or false, or else "God" is being misused to designate someone or something that could never really be God anyway, but at most what Paul dismisses out of hand as "a so-called god" (1 Cor 8:5). But if it thus belongs to the identity of anything other than God to be created and consummated by God, it also belongs to the identity of God ever to have created and consummated some things other than God. "God without a world (i.e., *some* world)" is as ungrammatical and meaningless as "a world without God (i.e., *the one and only* God)."

∽

According to Paul, "even though there may be so-called gods in heaven or on earth—as in fact there are many gods and many lords—yet for us [namely, Christians] there is one God the Father, from whom are all things and for whom we exist, and one Lord Jesus Christ, through whom are all things and through whom we exist" (1 Cor 8:5–6). Elsewhere, Paul says of the one and only God, to whom glory is to be ascribed forever, that "from him and through him and for him are all things" (Rom 11:36).

But, then, who could the one God who, for Christians, is the Father possibly be except "the One which is all," as distinct from "the one among the many" (Whitehead), which is to say, precisely, the Whole, or the universal individual, from, and through, and for which are *all* things?

∽

Who is the God of whom Paul speaks in Romans 1:19–20, if not the one God of whom he speaks in 1 Corinthians 8:6 as "the Father from whom are all things and for whom

---

3. Ogden, "Process Theology," 29.

we exist," and who is clearly the same God he characterizes in the doxology in Romans 11:36 as the One from whom and through whom and for whom are all things?

In other words, the God of whom Paul speaks in Romans 1 is the One from whom are all things and for whom all things exist—their primal source and their final end. And it is what can be known about this One, its structure in itself in its meaning for us, that is manifest to all human beings because the One itself has manifested it to them. Ever since the creation of the world, the invisible nature of this One, its eternal power and deity, has been clearly perceived, being understood by or through the things that are made.

If this unquestionably warrants saying that the One is always already manifested as the *primal source* of all things—indeed, that the principle of the cosmological as well as, possibly, the teleological argument for God's existence has a clear basis in everyone's experience and understanding simply as a human being—what Paul goes on to say—namely, that, although thus knowing God, human beings did not glorify God as God and give thanks to God—necessarily implies that this One is also the *final end* of all things, and thus that the principle of the argument from the aim or purpose of life, and also of the argument for life's abiding significance, likewise has its basis in common human experience and reason.

∾

God, according to Paul's doxology in Romans 11:36, is the One from whom and through whom and for whom are all things. On my view, according to which God is said to be the Creator-Emancipator and also the Consummator-Redeemer, it may be clear enough that God is the One *from* and *for* whom are all things, but what about God's being the One *through* whom are all things?

My answer is that, whatever is, is what it really is solely through God, in the sense that God's inclusion of things is the only inclusion of *all* things and of *all in all* things, every other inclusion of things being of *some* things only, and of only *some in some* things. Therefore, my reality, and the reality of every one and everything else (including God Godself) is the reality we each have through God alone. So, while we all come to be from God and exist for God, God's all-including love, which simply *is* God's all-righteous judgment, is also the very meaning of our coming to be whatever we really are.

It is only appropriate, then, to speak of God not only as the sole primal *source* and the sole final *end* of all things, but also as their sole adequate *medium*, but for which they would not be what they really are.

Who (or What) Is God?

❧

A review of my published writings shows that recognition of the pertinence of Paul's implicit definition of God as the all-encompassing, transcendental whole is nothing new or recent—or confined solely to my *Notebooks*. Already in my essay entitled "Present Prospects for Empirical Theology," I say that "the God of Scripture is the utterly transcendent One of whom Paul says, finally, that 'from him and through him and for him are all things' (Rom 11:36)."[4] And in "On Revelation," first published six years later, I say that "[w]hen Paul confesses . . . that for Christians, 'there is one God, the Father, from whom are all things and for whom we exist' (1 Cor 8:6), or, in ascribing glory to God, attests that 'from him and through him and for him are all things' (Rom 11:36), any merely mythical or categorial understanding of God is clearly transcended."[5]

But be this as it may, the more I have continued to reflect on Paul's statements in these passages, the more I have been struck by his assigning to God in Romans 11:36 the role or function as medium that he is so careful to assign to Jesus Christ in 1 Corinthians 8:6, as distinct from the roles or functions of God the Father as the primal source of all things and the final end for which we exist. Whatever his intention in doing this may have been, I find it entirely apt. In fact, it serves to make the very point I seek to make by distinguishing (1) the being of God in itself from the meaning of God for us; and (2) the meaning of God for us as the *implicit* primal ontic source authorizing—appointing and empowering—our authentic existence, from Jesus Christ as the *explicit* primal ontic source of the same authorization. Just as we as Christians are who we are authentically through our understanding appropriation through faith of the primal authorization by God through Jesus Christ, so all things are what they are through that same primal source whether or not they understand that they are even implicitly.

❧

God is rightly conceived as creating the world freely in that God ever and again effects the transition from the more abstract, indeterminate possibility of some world or other to the more concrete, determinate possibility of just this particular world or that. This implies that there must be contingency both in God and in the world, since God's creative act could have been otherwise than it in fact is, and so, too, could the world whose more determinate possibility God creates.

Traditionally, theologians have assumed that, if God is free in having the positive freedom to create this possible world rather than that, God must also be free in having the negative freedom to create no world at all—i.e., not to create anything. But this

---

4. Ogden, "Present Prospects for Empirical Theology," 73.
5. Quoted from Ogden, *On Theology*, 25.

assumption seems counterintuitive. What's the use of a freedom not to have something that it's better to have than not to have? Since any world is better than no world at all, there being no value in nonentity, it would be wrong or foolish of God not to create if God could create. And, being all-powerful, God certainly could create, even as being all-good and all-wise, God just as certainly could not be wrong or foolish.

Of course, on some, even, perhaps, most, classical views of God, all possible value is already actual in God anyhow, no matter what else exists, or, for that matter, whether anything else exists at all. But if this means, as it certainly seems to mean, that it is no better for creatures to be than not to be, it also means that creatures really have no value at all, since by coming to exist they add absolutely nothing to the value that God already has and must have eternally. In this case, our lives as creatures are utterly pointless, and this is counterintuitive for sure!

I conclude, therefore, that, just as there is contingency both in God and in the world with respect to creation, so must there also be necessity both in God and in the world, in that God cannot not exist and not create *some* world of creatures, and therefore some world of creatures cannot not exist either.

To be sure, *I* might not have existed, *you* might not have existed, *the earth* might not have existed—and so on, for literally everything whatsoever other than God. But it in no way follows that God might have been all alone because there might have been nothing other than God. It may be—and I believe is—the case that God's unsurpassable creative power always was and is bound to create *some* world or other. Even so, it would remain utterly contingent and in no way necessary that just this, that, or the other actual world was in fact created as a more determinate possibility. God was bound to exist, and to exist as God, but not I myself, or you yourself, or any world itself. Only God and some world or other of creatures were bound to be.

By radical contrast, the necessity that I affirm in God's case is not just for some God or other, but for the one and only God there either is or could be, who is *the* Creator and *the* Consummator of *all* things. This kind of necessity cannot be affirmed for any other determinate being whatsoever. Therefore, although I maintain that there is necessity as well as contingency both in God and in the world, I also maintain this radical asymmetry between the only relative necessity of any world for God and the absolute necessity of God for any world.

∽

What Martin Chemnitz says about the rule "no accidents befall God" makes clear enough that what's at stake in it is that "neither God's essence nor God's existence is changeable either because of time or of our own wickedness."[6]

---

6. Chemnitz, *Loci Theologici II*, 61.

But, of course, if God has feelings not just "according to effect," but also "according to emotion," then, contrary to Chemnitz, "an accident *does* (and *must*) befall God." If no accident ever befell God, then God could be said to feel only according to effect, not also according to emotion. Again, if God essentially "loves us sincerely and ardently," then God's essence has to have that about it to which accidents happen. But the only way in which this makes consistent sense is that God's essence in some respect *does* undergo accidents, even though in another respect no accidents either do or can ever befall God. *That* God is, and is always and only *as* God and nothing else, is absolutely unaffected by accidents. But that God is as the God of this, that, or any other world is, in the strict and proper sense, "accidental"—for God no less than for the world.

⁂

What I am is God's gift to me; what I become is my gift to God. But this is not to say that God is any more the sole source of what I am than its sole end. What I am is the gift of others as well as God, even as what I become is my gift not only to God but to others also.

Still, God is the sole *primal* source of what I am, and of what anything else is, even as God is the sole *final* end both of myself and of everything else. And the difference between primal and not primal, like that between final and not final, is not a merely quantitative difference in degree, but a qualitative difference in principle—in Kierkegaard's phrase, "an infinite, qualitative difference."

⁂

Aquinas argues in connection with first things: "It belongs to the idea of eternity to have no principle of duration. But it does not belong to the idea of creation to have a principle of duration, but only a principle of origin."[7]

I would now restate the "exact parallel" to Aquinas' argument that I once developed in connection with last things by saying: "It belongs to the idea of eternity to have no end of duration. But it does not belong to the idea of creation to have an end of duration, but only an end of ultimate significance."[8]

In somewhat the same way, I would be willing to develop an "exact parallel" to Meister Eckhart's argument that "[i]n the same now [*sc.* of eternity] in which God the Father exists and generates [God's] coeternal Son, [God] also creates the world."[9] I would argue, in other words, In the same "now" of eternity in which "God is eternally God and the eternal emanation of the divine Persons takes place," God not only

---

7. Quoted from Ogden, *Reality of God*, 213.
8. Cf. Ogden, *Reality of God*, 214.
9. Copleston, *History of Philosophy III*, 190.

creates the world, but also consummates the world. In fact, I have already developed this argument in all essentials in *The Understanding of Christian Faith*:

> In the one act of loving all things, Godself as well as all others, God the Father both 'generates' God the Son as the integral object of God's love, *in and with* whom God loves all other things, and, through God the Son, actively 'spirates' God the Holy Spirit as the all-inclusive subject of God's love, *by* whom God loves all things.
>
> [And] this same act of love whereby internally (*ad intra*) God is triune in Godself as well as in God's self-revelation is externally (*ad extra*) God's creation and consummation of some world of creatures other than and distinct from Godself.[10]

There is, of course, a profound difference between the classical positions of Aquinas and Eckhart and the neoclassical position I would defend instead. On it, God is consistently conceived as "dipolar," or as "dual transcendence" (Hartshorne). This means, among other things, that the paradoxes generated in the classical positions by simultaneously affirming or implying the utter necessity of God's being and implying or affirming genuine contingency in God's action are at last obviated. Both God's creation of the world and God's consummation of the world can be seen, clearly and consistently, to be, in significantly different respects, as necessary as they are contingent, and as contingent as they are necessary

---

88

God May Be Defined as . . .

The abstract property of deity may be defined with no other equipment than the transcendental idea of concrete reality, which one needs only to quantify universally in order to distinguish deity from everything else as the one and only universal individual.[11]

The abstract property of deity is the only radically abstract, and yet self-individuating, property. This is because any concrete state instantiating the property must belong genidentically to one and the same universal-individual sequence of states and no other, and no concrete state or event whatsoever can fail either to instantiate this

---

10. Ogden, *Understanding of Christian Faith*, 36.
11. Cf. Hartshorne, *Anselm's Discovery*, 44–45.

property of deity or else to instantiate the property of nondeity, or particular individuality, necessarily correlative/disjunctive with it.[12]

༄

The defining characteristics, and hence the individuality, or individual essence, of the one and only universal individual are themselves all extraordinary, transcendental, properties. By contrast, the defining characteristics of any and all particular individuals must be, in part, ordinary, categorial properties (i.e., categorials or categories proper, genera, species, and individualities).

༄

God may be defined as the one modally all-inclusive individual. To be modally all-inclusive is to be eminently, or unsurpassably, inclusive of all reality—actually inclusive of all actuality and potentiality as such, and potentially inclusive of all potentiality as and when actualized—in one unimaginably valuable, all-inclusive actuality.

The phrase "eminently, or unsurpassably" here is adverbial, qualifying the basic participial adjective, "inclusive."

༄

Although I can agree with Ingolf Dalferth (interpreting Kierkegaard) that God is definable as "the actuality of the possible," I can do so only on two conditions.[13]

The first is that God is "the actuality of the possible" in *two* senses, not merely in one. God is indeed, as Dalferth says, the actual ground, or "fountainhead," of the possible, in accordance with the rule that "[t]here is no possibility without some actuality in which it is grounded." But God, being, as Hartshorne says, "modally coincident" (or coextensive), is not only all possibility as one possibility, but also all actuality (which is to say, all *actualized* possibility) as one actuality, and is therefore rightly distinguished, in Dalferth's phrase, as "the *ultimate* actuality," which, as ultimate, is "Consequent," or "Second," as well as "Primordial," or "First" (italics added).

The second condition is that God is "the actuality of the possible" in the first sense just clarified, as the actual ground of possibility, by being the ground not only of the logically-ontologically possible, but of the factually-ontically possible as well. As the second, however, God is the Creator not just of *some* world, but of *this* (that, or the other) particular world. And yet, even as the Creator of this particular world, God is still rightly thought to be "the actuality of the possible," in that all creation,

---

12. Cf. Hartshorne, *Anselm's Discovery*, 51.
13. Dalferth, "'In God We Trust,'" 150.

all actualization of possibility, is and must be also *self*-creation, *self*-actualization, of the creatures themselves, God's role as their Creator being to make their self-creation possible—in fact, or ontically, as well as in principle, or ontologically.

89

"God Does Not Exist"/"God Exists *A Se*"

God is not just a fact, but the necessary—and therefore nonfactual—condition of the possibility of any fact. So the atheist, or antitheist, who asserts that "God does not exist" is not just denying a fact, but—self-contradictorily—even the possibility of any fact.

"God does not exist" means "nothing exists." And "nothing exists" is not merely false but necessarily false, and therefore absurd, as its contradiction "something exists" is necessarily true.

∾

If, for anything to be real, it must be real for something else that is real in the same general sense of "reality," and, in any case, real for God, then if God exists or is real, God, too, must exist or be real for something else, and, in any case, real for Godself.

But, then, the traditional teaching that God exists, or is real, *a se*—from Godself—is exactly right: God is real for the same reason that anything else is real. God is real for Godself, whereas any other individual that is real is so only because it is real not just for itself or for others like itself, but is and must be real for God, whatever else it may be real for.

90

Res Significata/Modus Significandi

It occurred to me recently that Aquinas's well-known distinction between *res significata* and *modus significandi* may be aptly adapted to an important use different from his own.

In correcting, or taking back, what I came to recognize as my unfortunate use of the phrase "a symbolic metaphysical assertion," I reasoned as follows: If "metaphysical" is understood consistently with how I myself use and explain metaphysics, a metaphysical assertion can only be a literal, and therefore nonsymbolic, assertion. There may indeed be "symbolic" assertions interpreting things about which metaphysics, for its part, makes literal assertions. But, being symbolic assertions, they themselves neither are nor logically could be metaphysical assertions as well—and vice versa."

With this reasoning in mind, I have adapted Aquinas's distinction to say that, whereas the "thing signified" by the literal, nonsymbolic assertions of metaphysics about strictly ultimate reality is the same as the "thing signified" by the symbolic, nonliteral assertions about God of religion and theology (as well as philosophy), the "mode of signification" in the two cases is not the same but different. Whereas the mode proper to metaphysics is literal, the mode proper to religion and theology (as well as to philosophy insofar as it is distinct from, or "more than," metaphysics) is symbolic. Thus, if the metaphysician may properly assert literally that the strictly ultimate reality signified as "the universal individual" is internally as well as externally related to all other realities, the religious believer or the theologian (or the philosopher, as distinct from the metaphysician) may properly assert symbolically that God both loves all things and is loved by all things, in their different ways, in return.

Is this to imply, then, that "God" is not properly a metaphysical term at all, but is "only symbolic"? Certainly, if "God" is used as it commonly is in theistic religions and philosophies, in the sense of "personal God," then I should answer that "God" is only a symbolic, not a literal, term and therefore cannot be properly metaphysical. Moreover, considering the provenance of "God" in theistic religion, I would have to say that it cannot be properly used, but only abused, by any metaphysics failing to allow that the unique thing signified by it is as eminently relative as it is eminently absolute, because it is, in one respect, as really or internally related to all other realities as, in another respect, it is related to all of them only logically or externally. But provided that another, suitably different metaphysics were to meet the condition this implies, I would not object too strenuously to its using the term "God" to signify the strictly ultimate reality that is literally related to all other realities in this uniquely "dipolar" or "dually transcendent" way.

Still, my own preference, frankly, would be to reserve "God" primarily for the properly religious, theological, and philosophical uses for which, as a symbolic term, it is well suited and to use some other term that can be defined literally, such as "the whole," or "the universal individual," to signify the strictly ultimate reality that is metaphysics' proper concern.

91

What Makes Theism Theism?

On the face of it, the defining characteristics of theism would have to include, whatever else they included, the notion of a personal God, or of God conceived analogically, or symbolically, as a human self or person. But granting that theism as a *religious* (or even a philosophical) belief may have good reasons for thus conceiving God symbolically as a supreme person (and so as mind, experience, consciousness, love, etc.), one may still ask whether the same need be true of theism as a *metaphysical* belief—or, at any rate, in what sense this is true.

It seems possible that one could define theism *metaphysically*, as distinct from religiously (or philosophically), as the belief that *the* ultimate principle of all things is as unsurpassably concrete as it is unsurpassably abstract, and therefore is as individual as it is universal, and vice versa. "Individual" so used would mean a concrete singular that acts on as well as is acted on by—and thus interacts with—both itself and others. "God," then, could be said to be, in Hartshorne's words, "the most individual of universals, the most universal of individuals."[14] "Individuality," in other words, would have become an analogical transcendental concept applicable both to deity as the extraordinary case and to any individual other than deity as an ordinary case, and definable in terms of interaction—i.e., both acting on and being acted on by self and others, being both active and passive, cause and effect, and so on—either in relation to *all* others, in the extraordinary case of deity, or in relation to *some* others only, in any ordinary case.

But, then, being a person (and so mind, experience, consciousness, etc.), although certainly illustrative of individuality as a transcendental concept, would in no way need to be simply convertible, or coextensive, with it. Although all persons

14. Hartshorne, *Natural Theology for Our Time*, 36.

would need to be individuals, not all individuals would have to be persons. Being a metaphysical individual, whether ordinary or extraordinary, particular or universal, could well be something more purely formal and abstract than being a person, unless, of course, "person" had already been tacitly redefined so as to be only a verbally different way of saying "individual."

92

What Do I Mean, Exactly, by "Radical Monotheism"?

I mean, first of all, *theism*, as the assertion that strictly ultimate reality has the character of one or more individuals, an individual being a concrete center of interaction, acting on and being acted on by others. I mean, secondly, *monotheism*, as the assertion that strictly ultimate reality has the character of one individual, one concrete center of interaction, acting on and being acted on by others. I mean, thirdly, *radical monotheism*, as the assertion that the distinction between the one strictly ultimate, universal individual and all the many merely particular individuals, actual or possible, is a modal, ontological distinction, or that the difference between them is, in Søren Kierkegaard's phrase, "an infinite, qualitative difference."

What makes radical monotheism "radical," then, is its asserting, more or less clearly and consistently, that the one universal individual God alone exists necessarily, while all the many particular individuals exist, if they exist at all, merely contingently.

In my understanding, Christianity originated only after radical monotheism in something like this sense had already emerged in different forms in both of the main traditions shaping the classical Christian tradition—that is, the tradition of Israel and Judaism, on the one hand, and the tradition of Greece and Hellenism, on the other. But I say, "more or less clearly and consistently," because in both traditions, the conceptuality/terminology in which radical monotheism was typically formulated was either mythological or categorial-metaphysical, as distinct from anything like (austerely) transcendental-metaphysical. By this I mean a conceptuality/terminology capable of formulating at once clearly and consistently the modal, ontological distinction, or the infinite, qualitative difference, between the one universal individual that alone exists necessarily and all particular individuals that exist, if they do, only contingently.

93

Is God a Being, or . . . ?

In what sense, actually, do I understand God to be *a* being? I ask this because it sometimes seems to me that my way of answering it may not always have been as sophisticated as it could and should have been. Of course, my concern all along has been to preserve the genuinely social character of God's relation to us as well as of our relation to God, by insisting that God has to be conceived as a center of interaction with others as well as self and, in this sense, as *an* individual. But I have been no less concerned with insisting that the functions of God are strictly universal and therefore metaphysical, transcendental—whence my repeated statements that God is not merely *a* center of interaction, but *the* center. Even so, my guess is that speaking in this way may still not have effectively countered the presumption that my view is but one more "metaphysical" view in the bad, discredited sense—in that God, in my understanding, too, is really just another fact among facts, however extraordinary, odd, or exotic.

In truth, however, God, in my view, is not just a fact but also integral factuality, factuality so conceived that all its aspects or dimensions can be understood as aspects or dimensions of one extraordinary fact: one transcendental individuality necessarily actualized in one transcendent individual. Thus to be is either to be this individual, or one or the other aspect or dimension of its individuality, or else to be one of the many ordinary, nonuniversal, nontranscendental individuals or events included in it. On this view, it may be more misleading than accurate to say that God is *a* being. God is not, simply, *a* being, but is *Being-itself*, although Being-itself has not only one but two necessary aspects: an abstract, "primordial" aspect, in which it is the sole primal source of all things, being universally immanent in everything that is so much as possible; and a concrete, "consequent" aspect, in which it is the sole final end of all things, being that in which everything is universally immanent as and when it becomes actual. In either of these aspects, God is not, properly, *a* being because God is not just a fact alongside other facts. Rather, "God" fully explicates the factuality of all facts—what it means to be a fact—namely, both to participate in, and to be participated in by, the one universal, transcendental individual, whose individuality is constitutive of reality as such.

God is *a* concrete-concrescent—more exactly, *an* individual (because God is not just many but one).

God is *the* concrete-concrescent—more exactly, *the* individual (because God is the one individual which is all, as distinct from one individual among the many).

God is *concreteness-concrescence itself* (because any concrete-concrescent either is God as the unity of the whole in which all things are embraced or else is included in God as one among the many things embraced in God's unity).

If any one of these three statements is true, they're all true, because each is qualified in its meaning by the others.

94

God Is Being in Both Aspects

> God is being in both its opposite aspects: abstract least common denominator, and concrete de facto maximal achieved totality.
>
> —CHARLES HARTSHORNE

There are two, and only two, senses in which we can talk about "the totality of being." In one sense, "the totality of being" refers to the completeness of the potential as such, including the necessary as the least common denominator of all potentialities. To this abstract totality, nothing determinate or actual can ever be added, since it must be conceived in entire abstraction from all determination or actualization. In the other sense, "the totality of being" refers to the most inclusive actual whole that can be conceived. To this concrete totality, new determinations can be added forever, although no determination can ever be outside it.

Rightly conceived, God is "the totality of being" in both senses of the words.

"Infinity" is an ambiguous term and needs clarification.

On the one hand, it can refer to the plenum of eternal possibilities, which is in a definite sense absolutely infinite, even if also of necessity lacking in any definite actuality. On the other hand, "infinity" can refer to the beginningless totality of already created actualities, which must be *numerically* infinite, even though it does not and never can exhaustively actualize the infinity of possibility.

95

"God" as a/the Transcendental Concept/Term

If the term "God" is understood as radical monotheism understands it—as designating the one and only universal individual—the concept "God" that the term expresses can only be, properly, a transcendental concept. But if "God," so understood, is *a* transcendental concept, because there are transcendental concepts other than "God," "God" is also, in a sense, *the* transcendental concept. How so?

The answer is that, although "God" is not the *only* transcendental concept, "God" *is* the only *self-individuating* such concept. A feature of all transcendental concepts is that, if clear and consistent, they cannot fail to apply to something concretely real, because the transcendental properties they designate, whether of God or of anything other than God, allow for positive instances only. So they simply must designate an unconditionally necessary property of something concrete, whether God or something else. But with the unique exception of "God," transcendental concepts do not, of themselves, individuate anything, none of them designating one and only one "individual"—either in the proper sense of a "long-term individual" (i.e., something concretely singular that endures and changes, whether or not it also becomes and perishes, and whose identity, therefore, is not strict, but genetic), or in the improper sense of a "short-term individual," otherwise, and properly, called an "event" (i.e., something concretely singular that becomes and perishes, but does not endure and change, and whose identity, accordingly, is not genetic but strict). The term "God," by radical contrast, can express the transcendental concept of the universal individual only by being, at one and the same time, the proper name that picks out just that one individual and no other.

It is of a piece with "God" being in this sense *the* transcendental concept that it uniquely sums up all other transcendental concepts, and that all other convertible (or coextensive), as distinct from disjunctive, transcendentals are and must be properly "analogical." They must each have, not just one, but two, levels of possible meaning, the difference between the levels being, in Kierkegaard's phrase, an "infinite, qualitative difference." There is the ordinary level on which they are applicable to any- and everything other than God; and there is the extraordinary level on which they can be applied to God alone.

"God" as a/the Transcendental Concept/Term

Thus, if "existence," for example, is used as a transcendental term, then, on any of its uses, to say that something exists, whether God or anything else, means that the essence, or individual character, of the thing is somehow actualized, in some actual, and therefore necessarily contingent, event(s) that is(are) its state(s). Nor can this same meaning ever fail to be retained on any use of "existence" if the term is to be used meaningfully at all. But at the same time, this meaning itself allows for—and, if radical monotheism is meaningful and therefore true, requires—its use in both of two infinitely, qualitatively different senses: the sense in which it applies to all things other than God, which exist, and can exist, contingently, on some conditions, only; and the sense in which it applies solely to the thing properly called "God," which alone exists, and must exist, necessarily, unconditionally, on any conditions you please. This is why, *pace* Paul Tillich, "God exists" is not, or need not be, as he claimed, "an atheistic assertion," provided "exists" is understood in the unique sense of "necessary existence," which is applicable solely to God.

So, too, with the transcendental term "individual," to give another example. For anything at all to be an individual, and thus something concrete, as distinct from a mere ideal or abstraction, it must, arguably, be internally as well as externally related somehow both to itself and to others comparably concrete. And "individual" can lose this meaning only by no longer being used at all meaningfully, which is to say, at once clearly and consistently. Yet this meaning itself allows for—and, again, if radical monotheism is meaningful and therefore true, requires—the term's being used in two radically different senses: the sense in which it applies to any and all of the many particular individuals that are related to self and others both internally and externally only partially and inadequately; and the sense in which it applies solely to the one universal individual called "God," whose relations to self and others are utterly impartial and wholly adequate. Thus the assertion "God is an individual" is entirely apt and true, though only in the unique sense in which God is *the* individual, the one and only *universal* individual, individuated by including any and all possible worlds, or kinds of world, and therefore infinitely, qualitatively different from any particular individual, individuated only by being included, localized, within some world(s) that God includes.

∽

An apparent problem with the foregoing is that its claim that "God" is "*the* transcendental concept" may seem to contradict other things I say elsewhere about "*the* transcendental" concept/term. Thus I say, for example, "*the* transcendental concept for process metaphysics is precisely 'process,' in the sense that to be anything concretely and singularly real is to be either an event or an individual—either an instance of becoming or process, or an ordered sequence of such instances, each of which is an emergent unity of real, internal relatedness to all the things that have already become in the past—together with, of course, everything that they, in turn, necessarily presuppose" (cf. note 103, "Qualified Pluralism/Synergism"). Or I say, "If 'concrescence' is defined as 'the universal of universals characterizing ultimate matter of fact,' then it does indeed refer to '*the* transcendental,' or, in Heidegger's phrase, 'the *transcendens* pure and simple.' This means that, logically considered, it is the one concept that one cannot fail to employ in thinking about anything whatever. . . . Ontologically considered, it is 'the indispensable minimum of what thought is about' (so Hartshorne)." Or, again, assuming that "process," or "concrescence," not "God," is *the* transcendental concept, I argue, "[T]he basic idea of creation can be generalized so as to be a transcendental (indeed, one side of *the* transcendental) concept without prejudice to the transcendentally distinct creativity of God. [And] since consummation is simply the other side of creation, the basic idea of consummation can also be generalized so as to be a transcendental (indeed, the other side of *the* transcendental) concept without prejudice to the transcendentally distinct consummative activity of God" (note 97, "God *the* Creator and God *the* Consummator").

But if "process," or "concrescence," is "*the* transcendental concept/term," how can I say that "God" is "*the* transcendental concept/term"? We can see how this is possible by recalling the distinction made in the preceding entry between "God" as the only transcendental concept/term that is self-individuating and all other transcendental concepts/terms that are not. All convertible (or coextensive) transcendental concepts/terms other than "God," I argue, "must each have, not one, but two levels of possible meaning, the difference between the levels being . . . an 'infinite, qualitative difference.' There is the ordinary level on which they are applicable to any- and everything other than God; and there is the extraordinary level on which they can be applied to God alone." "God," in other words, is "*the* transcendental concept/term," but "process," or "concrescence," is "the *analogical* transcendental concept/term."

The apparent contradiction, in short, is only apparent, because of this distinction between transcendental concepts/terms of which the term "God" alone is self-individuating and therefore nonanalogical.

96

On the Works of God *Ad Extra*

The divine action whereby God *ad intra* is triune is the same divine action whereby God *ad extra* is Creator-Emancipator and Consummator-Redeemer of all things, as well as Savior of all human beings and of any other beings who similarly misuse their distinctively moral freedom in understanding themselves and leading their lives.

This divine action is at once one and (infinitely) many: it is one in the sense that the *way* God acts, or the *how* of God's action, considered abstractly, is always one and the same; but God's action is (infinitely) many in the sense that its one way or how is actualized again and again anew, without beginning or end, in the concrete divine acts constitutive of God's own history and of all other history

∽

God's work *ad extra* is mainly twofold, consisting of both a creative and a consummative aspect, as explained in my *Faith and Freedom* (where, however, the operative distinction is not, as here, between "creative" and "consummative," but rather "emancipative" and "redemptive."[15] We human beings are given and called—implicitly if not also explicitly and decisively—to participate in this work in both of its aspects, notwithstanding the important difference between them and, correspondingly, between our ways of participating in them.

Because consummation is God's work alone, being one and the same with God's own ever-new act of self-creation in response to the self-creative acts of all of God's creatures, we can participate in it only by bearing witness to it, explicitly and/or implicitly. On the other hand, creation cannot be God's work alone, because all creation, the creatures' as well as God's, is and must be, in part, *self*-creation. God creates creatures that create themselves and one another and, in turn, contribute toward creating something in God—not, of course, in God's essential aspect, but only in God's accidental aspect. But just as God finally creates Godself alone (that being identical with God's consummation of God's creatures), so God's creatures must all, in part, finally create themselves alone. Except for God, and for God's unique creative action in making each creature really possible, in fact as well as in principle, no creature would or could be at all. In this sense, God's unique creative activity is the necessary condition of the possibility of every creature's existence. And yet each creature also has an irreplaceable part to play in its own creation, so that not even God can be the sufficient as well as the necessary condition of the actuality, as distinct from the real possibility, in fact as well as in principle, of any creature's existence.

Insofar, however, as a creature acts conformally to God's will for it and, through it, for others, its self-creative activity implements, executes, carries out God's own purposes, and so its work, in this sense, is God's work. Broadly speaking, then, God's work includes not only God's own creative and consummative activity but also all the creaturely activity that so participates in God's as to be conformed to it.

---

15. Ogden, *Faith and Freedom*, 57–79.

In *Faith and Freedom*, I explain why it is illuminating to think and speak of God's creative work as emancipative.[16] But while I also speak there of God's redemptive work, I do not employ the concept of God's consummative work at all. Upon reflection, however, it seems clear that God's consummative work can be said to be redemptive analogously to the way in which God's creative work can be said to be emancipative. But just what way is this?

God's creative work can be said to be emancipative insofar as God's setting the fundamental limits of natural, or cosmic, order establishes the optimal conditions of all creaturely freedom, and thus sets all creatures free to create themselves and one another, and also to create something in God. But although God's emancipative work thus extends to all creatures, and all creatures can participate in it insofar as their own creative decisions realize the purpose of God's work, this work bears uniquely on human creatures who have the distinctive kind of metaphysical freedom that we distinguish as "moral freedom," and who therefore can participate in God's emancipative work in a correspondingly distinctive way. If any being as such is in some way creative, any being as such is in some way emancipative as well. But where there is the unique emergent level of freedom properly called "moral," there is a unique capacity for creative and therefore emancipative activity. Given this capacity, the divine purpose in creating and emancipating can be realized intentionally or voluntarily.

Correspondingly, one may argue, God's consummative activity, in the sense of God's incorporation of all creaturely lives into the divine life, is redemptive insofar as such incorporation delivers the creatures from their bondage to decay and thus from the meaninglessness of not making any difference to anything or anyone more enduring than themselves. But although God's redemptive work thus extends to all creatures, and all creatures can participate in it insofar as they are incorporated into the divine life, this work bears uniquely on human creatures having the distinctive kind of metaphysical freedom properly called "moral," and therefore being able to participate in God's redemptive work in a correspondingly distinctive way. Given the unique emergent level of moral freedom, there is a unique capacity for consummative and therefore redemptive activity. With this capacity, one can so love others as thereby to bear witness to them and still others of God's love for them.

Actuality as such, we may say, is self-creative response to other self-creative actuality, which as thus responded to is also creative of others or other-creative. Relatively, then, to the antecedent self-creativity to which our own self-creativity responds, any actuality is consummative and, as such, redemptive, just as relatively to the subsequent self-creativity of which it is other-creative, any actuality is creative and, as such, emancipative. But, then, the uniqueness or unsurpassability of God as *the* Creator, and hence *the* Emancipator, on the one hand, and as *the* Consummator, and hence

---

16. Ogden, *Faith and Freedom*, 88–89.

the Redeemer, on the other, lies in the universal scope—the "modal all-inclusiveness" (Hartshorne)—of God's self-creative response to all other self-creativity, and all other self-creativity's response to God's. Although we, too, both create and consummate, emancipate and redeem, we do so always in a radically fragmentary, non-all-inclusive way with respect to *some* things only. By an infinite, qualitative difference, God both creates and consummates, emancipates and redeems, *all* things in a radically, all-inclusive, nonfragmentary way.

But while both God's emancipative and redemptive works thus bear uniquely on human beings, who can participate in them in a correspondingly unique way, both are in their respective ways *God's* work with which human beings cooperate. God's properly *saving work*, however, is different. Salvation, by contrast with both emancipation and redemption, is not thus cooperative or synergistic, even if it is not exactly monergistic, either. Because we are saved *by* grace, *through* faith, the proper formula for salvation is "by grace alone but not without ourselves." Thus salvation is the process initiated by God's redemptive work, but actualized only through our faithful response to God's work. This response then involves, in turn, our unique participation in the emancipative as well as the redemptive work of God.

As for God's providential work, I understand it, in a broad sense, to comprehend all of God's works *ad extra*, from creation and emancipation to redemption and consummation, and also salvation. But, again, it has a unique bearing on the emergent level of human freedom, because human beings have the capacity both to experience God's providence toward themselves and to cooperate with it intentionally or voluntarily, whether in the form of God's creative and emancipative work or in the form of God's consummative and redemptive work.

༄

The question may be asked whether the works of God *ad extra* can be adequately distinguished. I answer by briefly stating and developing one basic idea:

Any, however inadequate, distinction between God's creative and God's emancipative (or, in a narrow sense, providential) activity, on the one hand, and between God's consummative and God's redemptive activity, on the other, depends on a certain metaphysical distinction that may be made with respect to what Whitehead calls a "society" in his technical use of the term. Whether a society in the sense of a singular individual or an aggregate thereof exists at all, in *some* actual state or other, is one question; whether it exists in just this, that, or some other *particular* actual state, is a different question. God's creative activity, then, can be adequately distinguished from God's consummative activity insofar as they each have to do with existence as such, in some state or other, relative to its beginning and its end respectively. God's emancipative (or, in a narrow sense, providential) activity can also be adequately distinguished from God's redemptive activity insofar as they each have to do with existence in just this, that, or the other particular actual state relative to its beginning and its end respectively.

This basic idea, then, may be developed in three steps by:

(1) distinguishing between God's creative activity, on the one hand, and God's consummative activity, on the other;

(2) allowing that, just as there cannot be an adequate distinction between God's creative activity and God's emancipative (or, in a narrow sense, providential) activity, so there cannot be an adequate distinction between God's consummative activity and God's redemptive activity; and

(3) by maintaining, nevertheless, that one can and should distinguish, even if only inadequately, both between God's creative activity and God's emancipative (or, in a narrow sense, providential) activity and between God's consummative activity and God's redemptive activity.

Two explanatory comments:

Ad 2: There cannot be an adequate distinction in either case for the same reason: neither creation nor consummation is a single unique event on a timeline, running from the beginning of the line to the end, with emancipation following creation and redemption preceding consummation. Although everything other than God has its sole primal source and its sole final end in God, that there is *something* other than God, some world of creatures, has neither beginning nor end. "Evermore from his store, new-born worlds rise and adore!"

Ad 3: These distinctions can be made at least inadequately insofar as everything other than God exists, if it exists at all, contingently, not necessarily. Considered, then, with respect to anything's existence as such, in *some* actual state or other, God's creative activity may be said to be the sole primal source of the thing's existence, even as God's emancipative (or, in a narrow sense, providential) activity may be said to be the sole primal source of its existing in just this, that, or the other *particular* actual state. *Mutatis mutandis*, God's consummative activity may be said to be the sole final end of anything considered with respect to its existence as such, in *some* actual state or other, even as God's redemptive activity may be said to be the sole final end of its existing in just this, that, or the other *particular* actual state.

97

God *the* Creator and God *the* Consummator

Hartshorne has shown long since how the basic idea of creation can be generalized so as to be a transcendental (indeed, one side of *the* transcendental) concept without prejudice to the unique, transcendentally distinct creativity of God. But since consummation is simply the other side of creation, the basic idea of consummation, also, can be generalized so as to be a transcendental (indeed, the other side of *the* transcendental) concept without prejudice to the unique, transcendentally distinct consummative activity of God.

Just as God is *the* Creator because God's creative activity is unsurpassable, doing all that could conceivably be done to create both God's self and all others, so God is also *the* Consummator because God's consummative activity is likewise unsurpassable, doing all that could conceivably be done to allow both God's self and all others to contribute to God's own self-creation. But, then, God is not *the* Consummator because God alone consummates the past, but because God alone consummates the past *unsurpassably*, all other consummators being in principle surpassable—just as God is not *the* Creator because God alone creates the future, but, rather, because God alone creates the future *unsurpassably*—all other creators in principle creating it surpassably.

If our experience in what Whitehead speaks of as the first and most fundamental division is formed by "the sense of qualitative experience derived from antecedent fact, enjoyed in the personal unity of present fact, and conditioning future fact," so that "it carries with it the placing of our immediate experience as a fact in history, derivative, actual, and effective," then our experience is an experience of "transcendence" not only in one respect but in *two*: not only the transcendence of the past actualities from which our present experience is derived, but also the transcendence of the future actualities on which our present experience is destined to be effective.[17] In short: we experience the other actualities transcending our own as not only creating it, but also consummating it, as both transcendent creators and transcendent consummators.

If it is also true, then, that our experience in this first and most fundamental division further involves experiencing that "[w]e are, each of us, one among others; and all of us are embraced in the unity of the whole," then the transcendent creators

---

17. Whitehead, *Modes of Thought*, 98.

and consummators we experience include both "many which are one" and "one which includes the many"; and also experiencing that "there are two senses of the one—namely, the sense of the one which is all and the sense of the one among the many"—we may say that, just as every "one among the many" (i.e., the self and all others) is both *a* creator and *a* consummator, "the one which is all" (i.e., "the whole") is precisely *the* Creator and *the* Consummator.[18]

98

God and the World Are at Each Other's Service

God and the world are at each other's service—God doing for the world as well as for Godself what only God can do; and the world doing for God as well as for itself what only the world can do.

But if this mutual service belongs to the symmetry between God and the world, this symmetry in turn involves a more fundamental and inclusive asymmetry. Although God does indeed require a world in order to be God, what God requires is not this, that, or any other particular world, but only *some* world of which, as of any other world, or kind of world, God is at once the sole primal source and the sole final end. What the world requires, on the other hand, is not simply *some* God—the idea of "some God" being self-contradictory and absurd—but rather the one and only God that there either is or could be, whose nonexistence is as inconceivable as the nonexistence of some world.

Because the nonexistence of God is thus inconceivable, provided only that "God" is properly conceived as naming the concrete whole of reality, and so the one universal individual from whom and through whom and to whom are all things (cf. Rom 11:36; 1 Cor 8:6), there can be a sound so-called ontological argument for God's existence simply from the concept of God itself. Assuming only that the concept is at once clear and coherent, one cannot consistently deny or even doubt that God exists.

And there are at least two other valid arguments for God's existence if "God" is thus properly defined and the concept of God can be clearly and consistently conceived. There is, first, the argument for God as the primal source of all things, but for whose existence no world sufficiently ordered to be a world at all could be so much as possible. Depending on what is stressed in the argument—whether the sheer "that" of the world's existence or the sheer "what" of its existence as somehow necessarily

---

18. Whitehead, *Modes of Thought*, 149–51.

ordered—this first argument can take the form of either a sound cosmological argument for God's existence as the ground of being or a sound argument for God's existence as the principle of world order. Then, second, there is the argument for God's existence as the final end of all things, which—again, depending on how it is developed—can take the form of either a sound teleological argument for God's existence as the all-inclusive consequence of all things or a sound argument that God is the ground of the ultimate significance of all things.

John Dewey speaks, rightly, of two conceits relevant to religion. "There is a conceit," he says, "fostered by perversion of religion which assimilates the universe to our personal desires; but there is also a conceit of carrying the load of the universe from which religion liberates us."[19] It seems to me that there must be a connection between this insight and the notion that God and the world each serves the other, albeit each in its own irreplaceable way. The unique function of God is to liberate us from the "conceit of carrying the load of the universe," whether this load be to provide either the ordered being of the universe or else its final meaning. Because God is both the primal source and the final end of *all* things, we can entrust unreservedly both their being and their meaning to God and live in unqualified loyalty to God and to all things in God. At the same time, if true religion, as distinct from its perversion, means that we are to assimilate our personal desires to the universe instead of the other way around, part of what it means to be religious is to look, not to God, but to ourselves and our fellow creatures to do whatever can be done to realize such of our personal desires as can and should be realized. This is to abstract, of course, from our deepest desire for an ordered world in which we can be and become ourselves in solidarity with all our fellows and for an ultimate meaning or significance to ourselves and our world that neither we nor any other creature could conceivably provide.

The other connection I think I dimly see, but am less confident about, is with Wittgenstein's perceptive distinction between faith and superstition. Faith in the sense of authentic faith based in trust is allowing God to be God (i.e., the sole primal source and the sole final end of all things), while superstition in the sense of a false science based in fear is expecting God to do what we and our fellow creatures can and must do for ourselves and one another if it is to be done at all.

What remain clear beyond any question, however, are the ideas of mutual service between God and the world, and of the asymmetry and symmetry that such service exhibits.

---

19. Dewey, *Human Nature and Conduct*, 331.

99

Must God Be Really Related to Creatures?

1.0. There are Christian theologians and philosophers who allow that God *can* be really related to creatures, even while denying that God *must* be so related.[20] But I judge this to be an untenable position—first of all, for the properly philosophical reason that it is incoherent. Consider the following argument:

1.1. If God can be really related to creatures, creatures can make a value difference to God (analysis of "being really related").

1.2. If creatures can make a value difference to God, God can not be unsurpassable in value without being really related to creatures (analysis of "making a value difference" and of "being surpassable/unsurpassable in value").

1.3. But if God need not be really related to creatures, either God can be unsurpassable in value without being really related to creatures, or else God can be surpassable in value (analysis of "not needing to be really related" and of "being surpassable/unsurpassable in value").

1.4. God cannot be surpassable in value (analysis of "God").

1.5. Therefore, if God need not be really related to creatures, God can be unsurpassable in value without being really related to creatures (conclusion from 1.3 and 1.4).

1.6. But if God can be unsurpassable in value without being really related to creatures, creatures can not make a value difference to God (contrapositive of 1.2).

1.7. If creatures can not make a value difference to God, then God can not be really related to creatures (contrapositive of 1.1).

1.8. Therefore, if God need not be really related to creatures, God can not be really related to creatures (conclusion from 1.5, 1.6, and 1.7).

1.9. Either, then, God can be really related to creatures, in which case God also must be so related, or God need not be really related to creatures, in which case God also can not be so related (conclusion from and contrapositive of 1.8).

2.0. The second reason I judge the position to be untenable is not philosophical but properly theological: from the standpoint of what I take to be an adequate Christian systematic theology, it contradicts a necessary implication of the Christian witness of faith. Consider the following argument:

2.1. Each and every creature, being consummated as well as created by God, makes a value difference to God—its consummation by God consisting precisely in

---

20. Cf., e.g., Farrer, *Reflective Faith*, 178–91; Morris, *Anselmian Explorations*, 124–50.

God's giving it to make such a value difference (necessary implication of the Christian witness).

2.2. But if each and every creature makes a value difference to God, God can not be unsurpassable in value without being really related to creatures (1.2).

2.3. If God can not be unsurpassable in value without being really related to creatures, God must be so related (1.4).

2.4. Either, then, a necessary implication of the Christian witness is false or else God not only can be really related to creatures, but also must be so related (conclusion from 2.2 and 2.3).

100

What Is the Role that Properly Belongs to God—and to Creatures?

The role that properly belongs to God is to make whatever else there is or ever can be both really possible, in fact as well as in principle, and really real and ultimately significant. To make all things really possible is to determine the general outlines, or "grand design" (as distinct from the "details"), of anything and everything that ever actually happens. To make all other things really real and ultimately significant is to allow each thing partly to determine itself and other things as well as God's own everlasting actuality. (I owe my use of the distinction here between "grand design" and "details" to Franklin Gamwell.)

What, then, is the role that properly belongs to creatures of God, individually and collectively? This role is to determine the "details," as distinct from the "grand design," of what actually happens, including what actually happens to God. Within the general outlines determined by God alone, the creatures have the role of determining how the more or less determinate possibility determined by God is to become still more fully determinate actuality in and through their own creaturely decisions.

I contend that these two roles are inalienable and nonexchangeable. It is as impossible for God not to play the role that properly belongs to God and to play the role that properly belongs to creatures as it is for creatures not to play the role that properly belongs to them and to play the role that properly belongs to God. Just as it is the creatures' role to be patient of God alone playing God's role—the name for such patience at the human level, where it can and must be, in the first instance, a matter of free and responsible self-understanding, being "faith" (*fides*), which is to say, "trust" (*fiducia*) and "loyalty" (*fidelitas*)—so it is God's role to be patient of creatures alone playing the role that is theirs—the name for such divine patience toward human beings, and, specifically, sinful human beings, being "grace" (*favor*).

101

On Nature and Grace

God is by nature gracious toward God's creatures, so God's creatures are by nature graced by God.

And this is so not merely in one respect, but in two: (1) in God's *creating* creatures, by so acting that anything that becomes actual has already become possible in fact as well as in principle, and that there is always a relatively ordered world of other actors, of the being and activity of all of which God is *the* sustaining *conditio sine qua non*; and (2) in God's *consummating* creatures, by ever and again so reacting to the being and activity of all the other actors in the world as to incorporate their being and activity creatively into God's own.

Creatures, therefore, are by nature graced by God not merely in one respect, but in two, in keeping with the traditional theological concept of the "double gratuity" of God's grace: (1) in their *being created* as creatures, in that there is some world in which they can be and act that is no more their own doing, either individually or collectively, than that this world always has a certain relatively stable order that allows for the possibility of more good than evil being realized through their own being and activity; and (2) in their *being consummated* as creatures, in that, being creatively incorporated into God's own being and activity, they are thereby delivered from their bondage to decay, from the meaninglessness of not making a difference to anyone or anything more enduring than themselves.

But there are creatures, specifically, who are so created as to be capable of understanding their creaturehood and therewith of understanding, in principle, all that either is or could be, which is to say, themselves, others, and the whole that is God. Being created as such self-understanding, all-understanding creatures is itself a matter of being graced in a special way, even as the creation of such creatures may be said to be a special act of creation (though hardly "an act of special creation"). Included in this special grace of creation is the grace of being created by nature with an "obediential potency" (Karl Rahner), or a capacity for "original righteousness" as well as for "original sin" (Reinhold Niebuhr). This explains why any creatures so created are also graced with a special grace of consummation, in that they are also always confronted with the gift and demand of actualizing their obediential potency, or their capacity for original righteousness, instead of that for original sin. In this way, their consummation by God always already confronts them in every here and now with the gift and demand of obedient faith in God's creating-consummating grace.

But more than that, wherever the decisions of creatures are such as to actualize God's will as regards either creation or consummation, there is a further instance of special grace, whether of creation or of consummation. The will of God as regards creation is that the local orders that creatures themselves establish through their own being and activity should conduce to actualizing the fullest potential of each and all. In the case of self-understanding, all-understanding creatures such as human beings, God wills that this also be the case with the social and cultural orders that they have the distinctive freedom and responsibility to create. The will of God as regards consummation in their case is that God's consummation of all things not only be accepted by each of them through her or his own obedient faith, but also be attested, witnessed to, implicitly as well as explicitly, its being attested implicitly by anything they do to promote actualizing the fullest potential of all others as themselves. The event of such attestation or witness to the grace of consummation is itself an event of that grace—the decisive such event being the decisive re-presentation of the special grace of consummation of human beings, indeed, of all rational beings, and hence itself the decisive event of God's consummating grace.

In what sense, if any, would I affirm the so-called double gratuity? I would affirm God's gratuitous creation of all concretes other than God in the sense that, although God could not be God without *some* concretes other than God—God's own concreteness, like any concreteness, necessarily involving real internal relations to other concretes—no concrete to which God has a real internal relation is necessary absolutely to God's being or existence as God, but is necessary, if at all, only relatively to some particular *de facto* state of God. Thus, whereas any concrete other than God could not be concrete at all except for God, God could and would be God without any other concrete whatsoever, provided only that there were *some* concretes without which God would not and could not be God.

Beyond this, I would affirm God's creation of Godself through God's gratuitous consummation of all concretes other than God. Although God could not be God without somehow relating Godself adequately to any other concrete as and when it becomes real, and no other concrete could itself be really real or abidingly significant except for God's thus somehow relating Godself to it, the specific act of self-relation by which God relates Godself to each and every concrete is not essential, either to God or to the concrete itself. In this sense, God's consummation of all concretes is even more gratuitous than God's creation of them, which *is* essential to any of the other concretes even though none of them is essential to God.

Whereas God need not create any concrete other than God, provided only that God creates *some* concretes other than God, any concrete other than God needs to have been created by God, since otherwise it would not be a concrete at all. But not only does God not need to consummate any other concrete in just the way in which God in fact does consummate it, no other concrete needs to be consummated by God in just the way in which God consummates it, provided only that there is *some* way in which God does so.

∾

What about the other, related distinction between "the natural and the supernatural"? The natural is to the supernatural, arguably, rather as abstract structure is to concrete event. Just as a concrete event includes its abstract structure, so the supernatural includes the natural.

Let us say, for example, that actualizing an authentic self-understanding, in the sense of an existential understanding of oneself, others, and the whole whose presuppositions and implications, metaphysically and ethically, are true and right, is concrete event relative to the abstract structure constituted by these same presuppositions and implications as disclosed by existentialist analysis. As such, accordingly, the event itself can be said to be supernatural, or a matter of grace, relative to its abstract structure that is natural.

Of course, even the event itself is "natural" insofar as *what* it is, as a *possibility*, is as much a matter of metaphysical and ethical analysis as are its necessary presuppositions and implications. If certain metaphysical beliefs are true, then a certain self-understanding is both possible and alone authentic; and so, too, if certain ethical beliefs and actions are right, one both can and should understand oneself in one way instead of any other and further act accordingly. To this extent, there is nothing supernatural about an authentic self-understanding, because, as Rudolf Bultmann rightly says, an authentic self-understanding is simply the "natural" understanding of human existence. But as an *actuality*, as an actual event of understanding one's own existence, it is not just natural but also supernatural, in that it is concrete event, and so more than, because inclusive of, its abstract structure.

∾

If I argue, as I do in the foregoing passage, that the natural is to the supernatural rather as abstract structure is to concrete event, how can I also argue, as I do elsewhere, that the natural is to the supernatural as some is to all, or part is to whole?

I can argue for both conclusions consistently by remembering and applying the insight that, not just one, but "[t]wo of the several distinctions in logical-ontological type are evidently fundamental to all the others: that between *subjects* and *objects*; and that between *the one, extraordinary, everlasting individual* and *the many ordinary, transitory individuals*." But, significantly: "Neither of these fundamental distinctions . . . is such as to constitute a dualism. In both cases, the two sides of the distinction do not simply stand alongside one another, but rather are so related that one side includes, or, in Hegelian terms, 'overlaps,' the other. Thus subjects include objects, and, in the same way, the one and only extraordinary, everlasting individual includes all the many ordinary, transitory individuals" (see thesis 8 of note 58, "Logical-Ontological Type Distinctions").

In sum: subjects transcend objects; and *the* (unsurpassable) subject transcends all other (surpassable) subjects, whether events or individuals, as well as all objects that are merely objects.

102

On Providence

Any possible kind of world necessarily involves a multiplicity of individuals, each making its own free decisions. And the idea of a multiplicity of individuals each making its own free decisions necessarily implies an element of chance in what comes to pass.

Nor can it be otherwise simply because one of the individuals involved is rightly said to be God, in the sense of the one universal individual whose power as compared with the greatest conceivable is absolutely unsurpassable—i.e., such that not only no other individual but not even this individual itself could possibly surpass it. If individual x freely decides to do a, while individual y freely decides to do b, the result of their decisions, if both are effective, is the occurrence of ab, which itself, however, is not freely decided, but simply occurs, having been freely decided as such by neither x nor y. And this remains true even if x or y is the universal individual God, or if God is yet a third individual Z whose free decision to do C is distinct from both x's and y's to do a and b respectively—unless, of course, "free decision" is merely verbal because it refers to nothing of the kind in its application to particular individuals, the universal individual being not only the sole *universal* cause of all things, but their *only* cause—period.

In short, divine providence cannot eliminate the element of chance except by eliminating the free decisions of the many individuals other than God that any possible world also always involves. The only conception of providence that would exclude every element of chance would also exclude all other decision-making individuals, which means, simply, all other individuals, a non-decision-making individual being a contradiction in terms. But, then, absurdly, providence, being without any world of other particular individuals, wouldn't have any creatures to provide for.

But what can providence do if it cannot simply eliminate the element of chance? It can limit the scope of chance by so ordering the world of other particular individuals, or creatures, that the risks of their freedom, and so also of chance, are fewer than the opportunities of their freedom. Otherwise put: the providence of God is God's own free decision that the ratio of opportunity to risk from the free decisions of the creatures is optimized—in the sense that the opportunities for good resulting from their decisions could not be better than they are as compared with any risks of evil that could result.

As for justifying the ways of providence, it is properly accomplished, not in the usual way, by futilely attempting to show that such evils as occur are really goods in disguise, but rather by showing that and why the same multiplicity of free decisions that makes possible or probable any evils that occur is equally necessary to making any goods that occur possible or probable.

∽

What is to be said about the widely prevalent religious view that moral commitment makes no sense unless the world is such that "absolute justice" will eventually be done—understanding by "absolute justice" a state of affairs in which there is an exact proportion between the past deeds of a person, good or bad, and her or his eventual condition of weal or woe?

The first thing to be said is that this notion of "absolute justice" is evidently incompatible with the very nature of reality conceived as genuinely "social"—in the sense that, while the being of everything is in part determined by the being of other things, no thing (not even God) can completely determine the being of any other. If all things are social in this sense, so that everything is in part self-determined, in part other-determined, by others that are themselves one and all in part self- as well as other-determined, there is and must be an irreducible factor of chance in existence simply as such. Why? Because what actually happens is always the product of multiple causes, so that, given this essential sociality of existence, no one, not even One having the unsurpassable power attributed to God, could possibly guarantee an exact proportion between past deeds and eventual condition that so-called absolute justice supposedly requires. Given genuine freedom or self-determination on the part of every member of a society, there is an unavoidable risk of evil in the sense of the consequences of some members' actions not harmonizing with those of other members; and by the same token, there is an irreducible factor of chance—and insofar, "injustice." Therefore, the only conditions under which "absolute justice" could be realized are conditions under which real sociality, and hence real existence, would be impossible. Any supposedly social situation, in this world or any other, where "absolute justice" would be realized, would be an intrinsically *non*social situation, and so not really a social situation after all.

So the notion of "absolute justice" involves a self-contradiction—essentially the same self-contradiction involved in any other set of assertions that at once postulate a social situation—for example, between Creator and creatures—and yet imply that the situation cannot be really or conceptually, but at most verbally, "social." The Creator, being omnipotent, is tacitly supposed to have, or is held accountable for having, all the power there is, instead of having all the power that any one individual could conceivably have consistently with there being other individuals who also have some power—or, in other words, consistently with the situation between Creator and creatures being the genuinely social situation it purports to be. But if the notion of "absolute justice" is implicitly self-contradictory in the same way, its eventual realization cannot be made a necessary condition of moral commitment without making moral commitment itself similarly self-contradictory and, therefore, senseless.

Nor is this the only serious problem with the whole notion that moral commitment doesn't make sense unless "absolute justice" will eventually be done in the distribution of rewards and punishments. Another problem is with the underlying supposition that, if moral actions are to be meaningful, they somehow require external sanctions in the form of proportionate rewards and punishments. But anyone who does not love God and her or his neighbors as her- or himself for their own sakes, does not love them—period. And if she or he doesn't love them, what reward could she or he, in a moral sense, deserve? Anyone who needed a reward wouldn't deserve it, and anyone who deserved a reward wouldn't need it, love of others for their own sakes being its own—and only morally necessary—reward. And could anyone ever be persuaded to love others anyhow by the promise of eventual reward or the threat of eventual punishment? If the promise or threat worked, would she or he really love God and her or his neighbors as her- or himself, or only behave *as if* she or he loved them in order to cop the reward or evade the punishment?

It's all too clear that external sanctions neither have nor can have anything to do with properly *moral* commitment, whatever role they may play—and quite properly play—in controlling the behavior of sinful, self-centered human beings. Insofar as rewards or punishments are necessary to secure good behavior, just human laws and enforcement procedures should by all means be devised to provide them—but only with the clear recognition that conformity to rules is one thing, the behavior morality demands, something else.

103

Qualified Pluralism/Synergism

Like any other philosophy properly so-called, a process philosophy is a more or less reflective self-understanding that is comprehensive in scope and generally secular rather than specifically religious in constitution. As such, it properly includes, although it is not exhausted by, both a metaphysics and an ethics, which is to say, both a theory of ultimate reality in its structure in itself and a theory of how we ought to act and what we ought to do because of the structure of ultimate reality in its meaning for us.

The metaphysics that this self-understanding implies, and that a process philosophy therefore properly includes, is in every sense anti-dualistic, being in one sense monistic, in another sense a qualified pluralism. It is monistic in the sense that it recognizes but one transcendental concept, or set of such concepts, in which anything that is concrete and singular can and must be conceived as such, simply as concrete and singular. Thus, for a process metaphysics, there is only one kind of ultimate subjects of predication, and no difference between any one such ultimate subject and any other amounts to an absolute difference in kind, whether it be a merely finite difference between one and another part of reality or even "the infinite, qualitative difference" between the all-inclusive whole of reality and any of its included parts. Even the integral whole of reality as something concrete and singular is so in literally the same sense in which this must be said of anything else that is more than a mere aggregate or an abstraction. This is why *the* transcendental concept for a process metaphysics is precisely "process," in the sense that to be anything concretely and singularly real is to be "a process," either an event or an individual, an instance of becoming or process, or an ordered sequence of such instances, each of which is an emergent unity of real, internal relatedness to all the things that have already become in the past—together with, of course, everything that they, in turn, necessarily presuppose—which then gives itself, along with all of them, to all the other such emergent unities that are yet to become in the future.

And yet, if a process metaphysics is in this way attributively monistic, it is at the same time substantively pluralistic, albeit in a qualified sense. It is substantively pluralistic insofar as it recognizes many ultimate subjects of predication. Although anything concrete and singular is either an instance of becoming or an individual sequence of such instances, all of ultimately the same kind as any other, there are an infinite number of these instances, each an emergent unity of real, internal relatedness ontologically different from all the others. Above all, there is the unique ontological type-difference between, on the one hand, the self and all others as all mere parts of reality and, on the other hand, the all-inclusive whole of reality of which they are but the parts. Even as each fragmentary becoming is ontologically different from every other, so each of them severally and all of them together are ontologically different from the integral becoming of the whole.

But the distinction between part and whole is unique; and for this reason, the pluralism of a process metaphysics, real as it certainly is, is also qualified. Although "part" and "whole" are indeed correlative concepts in that each necessarily implies the other, the symmetry between their two referents presupposes an even more fundamental asymmetry between them. While there could not be an integral becoming of the whole without the fragmentary becomings of the parts, any more than there could be the fragmentary becomings of the parts without the integral becoming of the whole, what the whole as such necessarily implies is not just these parts or those, since all of its parts, unlike itself, are merely contingent rather than necessary, but only some parts or other. Alternatively put, the whole implies that the intensional class of parts have at least some members and so not be a null or empty class. On the other hand, what each and every fragmentary becoming necessarily implies is not merely some whole or other (since the idea of more than one whole of reality is patently incoherent and absurd), but rather the one and only necessarily existing whole: the integral becoming of which all fragmentary becomings are contingently occurring or existing parts, and but for which none of them would be possible, either in principle or in fact, or either be real or have any abiding significance.

Characteristic of a process theology, so-called, in distinction from a process philosophy, is the understanding of God, the self, and the world that it explicates in concepts and terms convergent with, whether or not derived from, those of a process metaphysics. A defining feature of this understanding is its interpretation of "God" as properly referring to the one strictly universal individual, and hence to the integral whole of reality, whose many parts are properly distinguished as including "the self" and "the world." If this interpretation is monistic enough to bear a certain resemblance to pantheism, it is nevertheless distinctively different from positions that traditionally have been so designated. By distinguishing, as a process philosophy does, between the abstract identity of the whole, as the one individual sequence of integral becomings, and the concrete reality of these becomings themselves, each in itself and as an ordered sequence thereof, a process theology is able to assert the sole necessary existence of God in contrast to the radically contingent existence of everything other than God, thereby maintaining the unique ontological difference between God, on the one hand, and the self and the world, on the other. To this extent, it is undoubtedly more like traditional theism in its classical forms than any traditional form of pantheism, although the pluralism it asserts in thus distinguishing God from the self and the world is like that of the process metaphysical theory with whose concepts and terms its own are convergent in asserting only a qualified pluralism. God is indeed asserted to be ontologically different from everything else, but everything other than God, whether the self or the world, is held to be *absolutely* dependent on God, whereas God is only *relatively* dependent on it, being dependent on it for neither existence nor essential identity as God, but only for the concrete content of God's integral becoming insofar as it is internally as well as externally related to any and all fragmentary becomings.

I contend that just such a qualified pluralism as a process theology explicitly asserts is also necessarily implied by the Christian witness of faith, and specifically by its distinctive stress on both divine and human agency, as well as creaturely agency generally. As the Protestant Reformers rightly insisted, this witness affirms that we are saved *by* grace alone *through* faith alone. Thus it is sharply different from any monergistic understanding of grace, according to which faith is somehow so created in us by God's gracious action that we are saved without any free and responsible action of our own.

But the question remains whether this difference warrants the familiar interpretations of Christian witness as necessarily implying synergism. My answer is that, if the Christian understanding of grace and freedom is to be described as "synergistic" at all, it is so only in much the same way in which a process theology's understanding of God, on the one hand, and the self and the world, on the other, may be said to be "pluralistic," which is to say, it is at most a *qualified* synergism, in that it asserts a certain symmetry between grace and freedom only by at the same time presupposing an even more fundamental asymmetry between them. It asserts that there is indeed a difference between God's gracious acceptance of all things and our acceptance of God's acceptance through obedient faith, which is our own free and responsible act and not any act of God. But it also presupposes that, whereas God would be a gracious, all-accepting God, even if we never so much as existed, we could no more exist in faith than exist at all, except for the radical prevenience of God's grace.

In short, if the Christian understanding of grace and freedom is synergistic, it nevertheless bears enough of a resemblance to monergism to be at most a *qualified* synergism and to imply a metaphysical understanding of God, on the one hand, and of the self and the world, on the other, that (like process theology's) is at most a qualified pluralism.[21]

---

21. Cf. Ogden, "Process Theology"; also Ogden, *Doing Theology Today*, 109–22.

104

The Agency of God

1. Although "the agency of God" is a topic that may fall to be considered in pursuing different inquiries, our interest in it here, in this and the following theses, arises out of the inquiry distinctive of Christian systematic theology.

2. This means, among other things, that we can discuss our topic adequately only by putting two closely related, but logically distinct, questions to everything that not just we but Christians generally have thought and said on it: first, the question of whether it is appropriate to Jesus Christ because or insofar as it either is the witness of the apostles or substantially agrees with their witness as attested by Scripture and tradition; and, second, the question of whether it is credible to human existence because or insofar as it substantially agrees with "the 'right' philosophy" as attested by human culture and religion in general.

3. Because the Christian witness to which we put these questions is constituted explicitly as such by some formulation or other of the twofold assertion that Jesus is the Christ of God and that God is the God of Jesus Christ, the proper procedure for us to follow in formulating any statements about the agency of God is to explicate the understanding of God, and thus of strictly ultimate reality, necessarily implied by this twofold constitutive assertion.

4. Central to any such explication is the symbol of God as "nothing but love" (Luther), or as "pure, unbounded love" (Charles Wesley), and thus as the one strictly universal individual who both loves and is loved by all others as well as self, and who as such is unsurpassably good, wise, and powerful, and at once the sole primal source of all things and their sole final end.

5. Thought and speech about the agency of God, like many, although not all, of the other things that Christians have to think and say about God, are plainly symbolic rather than literal in meaning.

6. For the purposes of our discussion, we may assume that ordinarily the word "agent" means someone who acts or has the power and/or the right and the responsibility to act; and that the word "agency," accordingly, means the capacity, condition, or state of being an agent in this sense, and hence is roughly synonymous with the word "action."

7. "The agency of God," then, we may provisionally define as the capacity, condition, or state of being the unique agent that God is as "sheer love," or "pure, unbounded love," and thus as the universal individual; and so the phrase is more or less

synonymous with "the action of God," where the word "God" is understood to refer to just this unique agent.

8. As the action of boundless love, and thus of the universal individual, the agency of God, comprehensively understood, pertains to the love of God both reflexively, in relation to Godself, and nonreflexively, in relation to others.

9. The love of God reflexively, in relation to Godself, is the agency of God *ad intra* that constitutes God as essentially triune: God the Father being the primordial unity of God as both loving Godself and loved by Godself, God the Son being God as loved by Godself, and God the Holy Spirit being God as loving Godself, in their primordial difference—from one another and from their primordial unity.

10. The love of God nonreflexively, in relation to others, is the agency of God *ad extra* that constitutes God as essentially the sole primal source and the sole final end of all things, and therefore as *the* Creator and *the* Consummator and also *the* Savior.

11. The agency of God as the Creator, Consummator, and Savior pertains in each case to two closely related, but nonetheless distinct, types of divine action: first, that which is immediately and directly God's own action, whether as the Creator of all things, or as the Consummator thereof, or as the Savior of women and men as well as of any other rational beings; and, second, that which is God's own action only mediately and indirectly, since it occurs only through one or more of God's creatures or in cooperation with their immediate and direct action as creatures.

12. As the Creator of all things, God acts immediately and directly to establish a world of creatures so ordered as to allow for the possibility of more good than evil being realized through the actions of the creatures themselves; as the Consummator of all things, God acts immediately and directly to accept any world of creatures into God's own unending life, thereby bringing the creatures' lives to completion by allowing them to make a difference to something infinitely more enduring than themselves; and, finally, as the Savior of women and men and of any other rational beings needing to be saved, God acts immediately and directly to restore to them the possibility of obedient faith, notwithstanding their having fallen into sin by actualizing the possibility of disobedient unfaith instead.

13. But in all three respects, as the Creator and the Consummator and also the Savior, God's own immediate and direct action can be fully realized only through God's creatures or in cooperation with their own action.

14. Thus, in creating human beings in such a way as to establish optimal limits of their action as creatures, God acts so that only good shall be actualized rather than evil; but whether (or to what extent) good instead of evil is actualized depends not only on God's action as the Creator, but also on the actions of women and men as obedient creatures of God.

15. In a somewhat different way, God acts as the Consummator of human beings so that they accept God's acceptance of them even now in the present, thereby participating already in God's consummation of their lives and giving expression to

it by all that they think, say, and do; but, again, whether (or to what extent) God's consummation of women and men is thus accepted by them depends on their own immediate and direct action of obedient faith and witness.

16. In both cases, however, we may quite properly speak of the creatures' action as the mediate and indirect action of God insofar as God's own immediate and direct action as the Creator and the Consummator is met with a cooperating action on the part of the creatures; for not only is God's action in that event the strictly necessary condition of theirs—except for which it neither would nor could be at all or have any abiding meaning—but their action, being cooperative with God's, also serves to realize God's end.

17. Beyond these two cases of God's mediate and indirect action as the Creator and the Consummator, there is the third case of such action that can and must be distinguished—namely, the case of God's mediate and indirect action as Savior, where some creature is so experienced by a woman or a man or another rational being who has already fallen into the sin of unfaith that she or he or it is thereby restored to the possibility of faith, thus fully realizing the end of God's action to save all women and men and any other rational beings, and to establish valid means of salvation to that end.

18. This third case of God's mediate and indirect action is concretely instanced by the effective use of any valid means of salvation: not only the secondary means of word and sacraments, or even the primary means of the visible church as such, but also, and above all, the primal means of Jesus Christ himself, through whom the end of God's action that all women and men and any other rational beings be saved is decisively re-presented as the gift and demand of obedient faith.

19. As for any other cases of God's agency such as are sometimes classified as "divine interventions," we may well question whether thinking and speaking of such are any longer either appropriate or credible in the present theological situation.

20. This is not to say that so-called divine interventions are ruled out simply because, according to the supposed implications of a modern scientific picture of the world, God could not intervene in the ordinary course of events; on the contrary, one may reasonably assume that any God who is "sheer love," or "pure, unbounded love" (and therefore the universal individual who is unsurpassably good, wise, and powerful), certainly could and would thus intervene if there were any good and sufficient reason to do so.

21. But it is not easy to see how any of us could ever be in a position to determine whether or not there were such a reason; and in any event, such thinking and speaking of divine interventions as Christian systematic theology has to consider can be accounted for both more appropriately and more credibly by reducing them to one or the other of the three cases previously considered of God's mediate and indirect action or agency.

NOTEBOOKS

What is meant by "an act of God"? I mean either: (1) something immediately and directly done by God, whether as Creator-Emancipator of all things or as Consummator-Redeemer thereof; or (2) something done by God mediately and indirectly through, or in cooperation with, one or more creatures, whereby either God's immediate and direct act as Creator-Emancipator and/or Consummator-Redeemer is carried out by the corresponding act of a creature, or else one creature is so experienced by yet another creature capable of self-understanding and moral freedom as to re-present God's immediate and direct act as gift and demand to that other creature. This may be further unpacked as follows:

As Creator-Emancipator of all things, God immediately and directly acts to establish the fundamental rules or "laws" of natural order, in the sense of the optimal limits of creaturely action. This means that an essential prior decision in the past of every creaturely act is the immediately past decision of God whereby the optimal limits of all creaturely acts are ever again reestablished. This implies, of course, that the creature's creation, involving its own act, is in part *self*-creation. Even so, God's part as *the* Other in the self-creation of every creature is decisive and is God's act alone; that there is always some world, and that this world always has an order in which the ratio of opportunities for good to risks of evil through creaturely acts is always favorable, is due utterly and completely to the creative-emancipative act of God. On the other hand, as Consummator-Redeemer of all things, God immediately and directly acts to include all other action in God's own ongoing self-creation as God. Thus all that comes to be through creaturely action is a prior decision to which God responds in God's present consummative-redemptive choice to create Godself.

But now, in both respects, both as Creator-Emancipator and as Consummator-Redeemer, God's immediate and direct act depends on the acts of God's creatures if it is to be fully carried out. In acting as Creator-Emancipator to establish optimal limits of creaturely freedom, God acts so that good shall be actualized instead of evil. But whether, or to what extent, good instead of evil is in fact actualized is a function of creaturely action as well as of the act of God. However, because or insofar as a creature so acts in response to God's creative-emancipative act as to actualize good instead of evil, its act, being the carrying out of God's action, is, indirectly and mediately, God's own act. In a somewhat different way, God acts as Consummator-Redeemer so that any creature who is capable of doing so should so respond to God's consummative-redemptive act as to participate already in the present in God's future consummation-redemption of all things. Moreover, God's consummative-redemptive act itself has the power to bring about the faithful acceptance of it, through which such participation alone takes place. So, at any rate, do those confess whose faith in God's consummation-redemption is experienced to be grounded in that very consummation-redemption—somewhat as those whose trust in another human person is experienced to be grounded, not in themselves, but, as they say, in the trustworthiness of that person her- or himself. In this sense, and for this reason, the faith that is the creaturely act of accepting God's own immediate and direct act as Consummator-Redeemer is itself an act of God, albeit through (or in cooperation with) the free act of a self-understanding creature capable of such an act of faith.

But if faith is, in this way, God's act, so too is the witness of faith, insofar as it gives expression to the faith that corresponds to God's act as Consummator-Redeemer. Through, or in cooperation with, the free act of a self-understanding creature capable of bearing witness to God's immediate and direct act as Consummator-Redeemer, God also acts mediately and indirectly.

Beyond these several ways in which God may be said to act mediately and indirectly as Creator-Emancipator and/or Consummator-Redeemer, there is still another way. The point of reference here is not a creaturely act corresponding to God's act, or conforming to its purpose, but rather a creaturely experience of a distinctive sort— namely, an *understanding* experience through which some other creature is understood to re-present God's own immediate and direct act as gift and demand. If, for whatever reasons, one creature is so experienced by another self-understanding creature that this other creature thereby understands God's gift and demand as Creator-Emancipator and/or Consummator-Redeemer, then the creature so experienced, like the experience itself, is properly said to be God's act—albeit, again, God's mediate and indirect act through God's creature.

Obviously, it is this last way in which God acts mediately and indirectly that is most significant for christology, although not only for christology. The point of reference so far as the christological assertion is concerned is not a creaturely act corresponding to God's act either as Creator-Emancipator or as Consummator-Redeemer—i.e., as the actualization either of good or of faith, or even as the re-presentation of the possibility of faith. Rather, it is an understanding experience on the part of one creature through which another creature is experienced as decisively re-presenting God's gift and demand. In other words, the Jesus who is the subject term of the christological assertion is not "the so-called historical Jesus," viewed in some way or other in terms of *his* actualization of good or of faith or of *his* re-presentation of the possibility thereof, but rather "the historic, biblical [*sc.* apostolic] Christ," viewed in terms of *our* actualization of faith and *our* re-presentation of it as a possibility for others, also, decisively through him, by means of our witness to his decisive significance. For whatever reasons, the earliest Christians so experienced Jesus that, decisively through him, they experienced the real presence, the gift and demand, of God Godself. But this is sufficient to explain, then, why this last way in which God acts mediately and indirectly is significant not just for christology, but also for ecclesiology and sacramentology, and so for the doctrine of the means of salvation, or ultimate transformation, generally. Experiencing an act as a sacrament—whether or not it is intentionally performed as such—is a matter of one creature's so experiencing another as thereby to be confronted with the gift and demand of God as Creator-Emancipator and Consummator-Redeemer.

105

"The Glory of God"

"The glory of God," arguably, has both an abstract and a concrete meaning. God's glory, in its abstract meaning, is simply God's essence as God—what God is and has to be in order to be God at all, which is to say, absolutely unsurpassable in being and value in all the respects in which anything or anyone can be clearly and consistently conceived to be so. To believe in God with what Christian faith means by "obedient faith" is to acknowledge God's glory in this sense: to acknowledge that God is, and that this is the God that Jesus decisively re-presents God to be. It is to "let (this) God be God."

But in its concrete meaning, "the glory of God" refers to all that—although it is other than God, distinct from God, absolutely dependent on God, and so on—nonetheless finally contributes more or less to God's own actual concrete being and value, which is not only absolutely unsurpassable in all the respects in which anything or anyone can be so, but is relatively unsurpassable as well, because it is the most inclusive actual value conceivable. Although "the glory of God" in this concrete meaning is indefinitely more than God's mere essence/existence simply as God, it, too, is *God's* glory in that it is solely God who is the necessary condition of its being at all and to whom it finally belongs in all that it is.

For a Christian, then, to live to the glory of God, to give God the glory, or to glorify God is (1) to let God be God by entrusting oneself unreservedly to God and loyally serving God's cause; and then (2) to contribute as much as one can to the accomplishment of God's purpose optimally to actualize all possibilities, and all in all possibilities, that can possibly be actualized.

106

God and the Lord's Prayer

The petition of the Lord's Prayer "your kingdom come, your will be done, on earth as in heaven" evidently presupposes that (1) God's kingdom comes because, or to the extent that, God's will is done; and (2) whereas God's kingdom is yet to come, because God's will is yet to be done, on earth, God's kingdom has always already come, because God's will is always already done in heaven.

But how exactly are these presuppositions to be understood, especially if one takes seriously that "heaven," no less than "earth," is distinct from God, because it, too, is something created and consummated by God?

In my view, as in Charles Hartshorne's, the cosmic order constituted by natural law(s) is not God, but something created by God, in the sense that it comes into being and is maintained, not simply by the metaphysical essence of God as such, but only by certain contingent decisions of God—in Scripture, called "fiats": God does these things rather than those, which, in the theological sense, are completely free or gratuitous. In this sense, God wills that a certain cosmic order prevail, and God's will is *eo ipso* done, insofar as any other decisions about what is to be done or not done, and so all creaturely freedom to make contingent, and therefore similarly free and gratuitous decisions, is exercised only within the limits already set by the natural law(s) constituting this, that, or some other particular cosmic epoch. Put differently, anything that actually happens is always a further determination of a more or less determinate possibility, which (although it is also more or less indeterminate relative to the still more determinate thing that actually happens) is also more or less determinate relative to indeterminate possibility simply as such, being determined, in the first instance, by the decisions of God in establishing the natural law(s) constituting the cosmic order of the epoch in question.

This means that, in creating any actual world, God first establishes the natural law(s) constituting a given cosmic order, thereby creating a more or less determinate possible world of which any actual world is yet a further determination. It is actually determined, however, not by God's decisions, but by the decisions of the creatures themselves within the limits set by God's. Although all actual things are indeed created *by God,* they are all also *self*-created, each by itself as well as by all of the other actualities that have already been created within the cosmic order constituted by God in establishing the natural law(s) constitutive of the given epoch. But if creation by God is completed only by self-creation in this twofold sense, self-creation, for its part, necessarily presupposes God's creation of the relevant cosmic order and therewith of the more or less determinate possibility of which every fully determinate actuality is a still further determination.

My suggestion is that "heaven," in the sense in which it figures in the petition whose presuppositions we are trying to understand, be taken to refer to the more or less determinate possibility that God first creates in making any fully determinate actuality—namely, by establishing the natural law(s) constituting the relevant cosmic order. Because this more or less determinate possibility is determined solely by God, God's kingdom has always already come, because God's will has always already been done in "heaven," which, in this respect, is significantly different from "earth." I would further suggest that by the term "earth," in the sense presupposed by the petition, we properly understand fully determinate actuality, which is always self-created in the twofold sense previously explained as well as created by God. Because anything actual, being in part self-created, cannot be determined solely by God, there is always the possibility that on earth God's will has yet to be done—namely, by each fully determinate actuality in determining itself and the other actualities that remain to be created, also by themselves as well as by God.

By thus taking account both of God's constituting cosmic order through establishing natural law(s)—thereby unilaterally creating "heaven"—and of every actuality also being self-created in a twofold sense—by other actualities as well as by itself, thereby multilaterally creating "earth"—I have, in effect, confirmed Hartshorne's observation, "Always, there is a mixture of (1) providence, (2) good or bad chance, and (3) one's own self-management, good or bad, these three. . . . [T]his must be so, and in any possible world state. Providence makes life's gamble possible. It does not play the game for us."[22]

It remains to reflect that "earth" and "heaven," so understood, are closer in meaning to what the Nicene Creed speaks of respectively as "the visible" and "the invisible" (or "the seen" and "the unseen") than they are to "the earth" and "the heavens" referred to in Genesis 1:1. There seems little doubt that what this passage, and Scripture more generally, means by "the heavens" is the dome of the sky above us, with its sun and moon, stars and planets, somewhat as though they were all located on the inside of an inverted cup viewed by someone looking up at it from the plane on which the cup rests. But if this were to be taken as the meaning of "heaven" in the petition whose presuppositions we are considering, it would effectively assert that, while God's kingdom has always already come, because God's will has always already been done, in the sky and among the so-called heavenly bodies, this is not so on the planet Earth—which can hardly be what the petition presupposes. On the other hand, to take "heaven" in the petition to mean "the invisible" or "the unseen" makes perfectly good sense. The possible as possible, no matter how determinate, is precisely not visible or seen, or otherwise the object of our ordinary sense perception, whereas the actual as such is

22. Hartshorne, *Darkness and the Light*, 206.

typically accessible, directly or indirectly, to sense perception of one sort or another, whether or not it can be literally seen.

107

The Incarnation: After the Fall or Before It?

What does it mean to say that, "though [the Incarnation] came later than the fall, [it] was in God's purpose before it"? To answer this question, one first has to ask what God's purpose is. God's purpose, in my understanding, is to create and to consummate all things in order thereby to realize as fully as possible God's own literally infinite potentiality for self-creation. In all its *essential* aspects, this purpose cannot possibly be defeated, or even frustrated, since its realization in these respects depends solely on God's own unbegun and unending self-creation in and through the creation and self-creation of God's creatures.

But God's purpose very definitely can be frustrated and even defeated in its non-essential, or *accidental*, aspects, since in these aspects its realization also depends, in part, on the self-creations of God's creatures, all of which, precisely as creatures, have a beginning and an end. With this distinction in mind, one can appreciate the truth in Frederick Denison Maurice's claim that "the fall did not in the least frustrate the scheme of God," even while precluding the error to which this claim, left unqualified, is exposed, of making (or appearing to make) the fall and its consequences to be of no significance to God.

If God's essential purpose is ever to create Godself in and through the creation and consummation of others—themselves, in their ways, also self-created and consummative of others—this essential purpose acquires different accidental aspects contingently upon the others that God creates and consummates. Insofar as these others are self-understanding, and therefore morally free and responsible, creatures who can and must create themselves in and through their own understanding and moral freedom, God's purpose acquires the accidental aspect of creating and consummating creatures who are faced with the fundamental option of either obediently acknowledging the divine purpose and bearing witness to it for the sake of others or failing thus to acknowledge and bear witness to it. But then, God's purpose must also acquire the accidental aspect of willing that it itself be decisively re-presented, whereby this fundamental option ceases to be merely implicit, or explicated only partially and inadequately, and becomes fully—which is to say, adequately and fittingly—explicit.

Assuming, then, that the decisive re-presentation, or making fully explicit, of the divine purpose is just what is properly meant by "the incarnation," one may say that it was indeed in God's purpose before the fall, since God's essential purpose could not acquire the accidental aspect of creating and consummating creatures that are self-understanding and morally free and responsible without also acquiring the accidental aspect of willing its own decisive re-presentation, however such creatures may have exercised their fundamental option: whether so as to realize original righteousness or so as to realize original sin, and insofar to fall.

It lies in the nature of the case that there cannot be a decisive re-presentation of God's purpose unless there is some individual or community that takes it to be such. This is the truth, presumably, expressed so inadequately by all the christologies that focus on Jesus' own personal relation to God instead of keeping their attention focused unwaveringly on the decisive significance of Jesus for *our* personal relation to God.

∽

For Christians, Jesus is *the* act of God, and so the event through which God's salvation is decisively revealed. Thus the significance of Jesus for Christians is that it is by reason of their encounter with him through the church's witness that they have become certain of the saving grace of God. Conversely, the only thing that Christians mean by "Jesus" when they assert that he is the Christ—in this or any other functionally equivalent formulation—is the event that thus authorizes their certainty of God's saving grace.

Accordingly Jesus, for Christians, is not "the founder of the Christian religion," in the sense of the one *with* whom they believe in God—that being, rather, the role proper to the apostles as the first Christians, upon whose faith and witness those of all other Christians necessarily depend. Rather, Jesus is the one decisively *through* whom all Christians, including the first, believe in God, the one who is the decisive re-presentation of God's own gift and demand to us.

"Incarnation" is one way, although not the only way, of saying this—of saying, in effect, that Jesus is the explicit, primal source (more exactly, the explicit, primal, *ontic* source) of the peculiar certainty constituting Christian existence, immediate experience of Jesus as such being the explicit, primal, *noetic* source of this certainty. Insofar as the myth of incarnation involves making distinctions between the Father who sends the Son and the Son who is obedient to the Father's sending, and so on, it represents the explicit, primal source of Christian authority as though it were just one more authority among others, even if the highest. At the same time, the whole point of the doctrine of the incarnation, as distinct from the myth, and, specifically, of the *homoousion* clause of the doctrine, is to remove this implication of the myth by making clear the difference in principle between all who are sons (≡ children) of God *by adoption* and him who alone is the Son of God *by nature*.

This becomes intelligible as and when one reflects on the interdependence of the explicit and implicit primal sources of authority, or of decisive and original revelation. It is only in the light of the *explicit* source of authority, or *decisive* revelation, that the content or meaning of the *implicit* source of authority, or of *original* revelation, is made known (as true as it is and must be that, in the orders both of being and experiencing, the direction is reversed). Thus, as certain as it is that God as God ever was, is, and will be the gift and demand of existence in and for freedom, of faith working through love; and as certain as it is that this gift and demand are *the* gift and demand to all human beings as such, at least implicitly present in all human experience whatsoever, to be certain of this as Christians are certain of it presupposes specifically Christian experience of Jesus as the explicit, primal, ontic source of all religious authority or the decisive revelation of God.

One way, although, again, not the only way, of making the assertion about Jesus that such experience of him at least implies, is to speak of the incarnation.

If a word, spoken or otherwise expressed, succeeds in capturing a clear and consistent concept, thereby also disclosing some reality—actual, possible, or necessary—the event of the word's expression may be analyzed as one event in two natures. The two natures of the one event are respectively the nature of the reality disclosed by the word and the nature of the word as disclosing the reality.

To understand this is to understand why

> Jesus can be truly asserted to be the Christ, or any of the other things that Christians appropriately assert or imply him to be, if, and only if, the possibility of self-understanding that he explicitly authorizes as the authentic understanding of ourselves in relation to ultimate reality is, in truth, our authentic self-understanding—which is to say, is, in truth, the self-understanding that is always already authorized at least implicitly by our existence as such, through all our experience and reason simply as human beings of the meaning of ultimate reality for us.[23]

---

23. Ogden, *Understanding of Christian Faith*, 70.

108

"For These Two Belong Together, Faith and God"

In my theological understanding, God and faith belong together in the sense that "God" designates strictly ultimate reality insofar as it authorizes—appoints and empowers—our authentic self-understanding, while "faith" designates our authentic self-understanding itself insofar as, being such, it is authorized—appointed and empowered—by strictly ultimate reality.

In theistic religions, the decisive re-presentation of God and faith also belong together in the sense that "the decisive re-presentation of God" designates strictly ultimate reality's *explicit* authorization—appointment and empowerment—of our authentic self-understanding, while "faith" designates our authentic self-understanding insofar as it is decisively, and therefore explicitly as well as implicitly, authorized—appointed and empowered—by strictly ultimate reality.

The decisive re-presentation of God is experienced as such either immediately, by those who thereby become the constitutive members of the community of faith constituted by it, or else mediately, by all other members of the same community, who can become such only through the witness of its constitutive members. In either case, the decisive re-presentation of God is experienced as such only insofar as it is experienced as explicitly authorizing—appointing and empowering—faith in the sense of our authentic self-understanding—even as God is experienced as such only insofar as strictly ultimate reality is experienced as the implicit primal source of such explicit authorization—appointment and empowerment.

The witness of the constitutive members of the community is its sole primary authority, in that any other authority in the community must be authorized by this constitutive witness. But even its authority is an *authorized* authority, deriving from the decisive re-presentation of God and, through it, from God. This means that it is experienced as such, as the sole primary authority in the community, only insofar as it is experienced as in turn explicitly authorizing—appointing and empowering—faith in the sense of our authentic self-understanding.

Consequently, the authority of the sole primary authority is limited to explicitly authorizing—appointing and empowering—faith. Of course, faith, like any other self-understanding, necessarily implies both beliefs (*credenda*) and actions (*agenda*), and one cannot bear witness to it except by somehow formulating the beliefs and somehow specifying the actions that it necessarily implies. For this reason, the authority of the sole primary authority in explicitly authorizing faith might appear to extend to explicitly authorizing particular beliefs and actions as well, in that they are necessarily implied by faith. But, recognizing as we must, that in different situations the same beliefs can be differently formulated even as the same actions can be differently specified and, conversely, that different beliefs can be similarly formulated even as different actions can be similarly specified, we can only conclude that the authority of the sole primary authority does *not* extend to the formulations of particular beliefs or the specifications of particular actions, except in the sense that it authorizes any formulations insofar as they appropriately formulate the beliefs necessarily presupposed and implied by faith, and any specifications insofar as they appropriately specify the actions that faith necessarily presupposes and implies.

There can be no question, then, of the primary authority's authorizing everything in the formulations of beliefs or the specifications of actions through which faith has found expression in particular situations in the past. As a matter of fact, there can be no question of everything being authorized, even in the formulations of beliefs or the specifications of actions in the primary authority itself. Because even its authority derives entirely from the primal source of authority, it is itself authorized only to the extent that the faith of which it is the witness is authorized, and its formulations of the beliefs and its specifications of the actions necessarily implied by this faith are appropriate thereto.

109

"He That Made Us without Ourselves Will Not Save Us without Ourselves"

The most obvious truth in this saying of Augustine's is that God's consummative/redemptive action makes our salvation, not actual, but only really possible. Its becoming actual requires our own faithful acceptance of God's action.

But the contrast Augustine draws between salvation and creation is misleading, insofar as God's creative/emancipative action likewise makes our creation only really possible, not actual. Its becoming actual likewise requires our own self-creative action.

Even so, Augustine is right that God makes us without ourselves to the extent that God's role in creative/emancipative action is unsurpassable and dependent upon no one and no thing. That there is some world for us and all our fellow creatures to exist and to act in is no more our own doing, individually or collectively, than that there is always a certain relatively fixed and stable order to the world that allows for the possibility of more good than evil being realized through our own creative/emancipative action. All this is from God, in no way anything that either we or any other creature(s) could even possibly do.

110

On Tillich's Dictum: "The End of Creation Is the Beginning of the Fall"

Without either denying that there are definite dangers in the view expressed by this dictum or claiming that Tillich himself avoids them, I think it may nevertheless be defended, insofar as creation is, in its own way, a co-operative and social act. All creation is and must be, in some respect, *self*-creation, so that creation by others, even the unique, infinitely, qualitatively different case of *all* things being created by God alone, does not and cannot exclude each of these things, also (in some way) creating itself. To this extent, any creature of God is *eo ipso* the creature of its own as well as of God's and the antecedent world's creative activity. As Tillich puts it, "being a creature means both to be rooted in the creative ground of the divine life and to actualize one's self through freedom."[24]

Among the other implications of this is that God could not—*logically* could not—create a world that did not also involve the self-creation of each of the creatures constituting that world. If a creature actually exists as more than a mere possibility, it does so only in and through the exercise of its own creativity as well as through the creativity of others, whether the antecedent world of fellow creatures or God. The conclusion is unavoidable, then, that the biblical and orthodox picture of the original creation in paradise can be the picture only of a possibility, not of an actuality. It is, indeed, a picture of what, given the being and activity of God, is possible and will also become actual, provided only that creaturely, and specifically human or moral, freedom is exercised in accordance with the will of God and not contrary to it.

But, of course, this still does not justify Tillich's dictum. Provided that what one means by "the fall" is our human exercise of our moral freedom so as to actualize our possibility of "original *sin*," instead of our other possibility of "original *righteousness*," one cannot say, as Tillich does, that "creaturely freedom is the point at which creation and the fall coincide," if one means thereby that any exercise of "creaturely freedom" is *eo ipso* "the beginning of the fall" as well as "the end of creation." Why not? Well,

24. Tillich, *Systematic Theology*, vol. 1, 256.

first of all, because "creaturely freedom," properly understood, is an indefinitely more general concept than "human freedom," or "moral freedom" more generally, and it is solely the second, much more specific concept that is involved in the notion of "the fall" as clarified above. There may be, of course, some kind of an analogy between the actualization of original sin through the (mis)exercise of human or moral freedom and the consequences of the exercise of creaturely freedom more generally. But there cannot be more than an analogy—and, frankly, it's not at all clear to me whether the conditions necessary to support even an analogy are present. Then, second, even the actualization of the possibility of original sin is an *option* of human or moral freedom, and therefore by no means identical with any exercise of such freedom. To be human or moral is not *eo ipso* to be fallen, although it certainly is to be faced with the "fundamental option" of either standing or falling, of either authentic or inauthentic existence. This must be insisted on, even if every human or moral being who has ever existed has, in fact, misused her, his, or its freedom in an inauthentic, sinful way. Were that to be so, one could indeed say that human or moral freedom is the point at which the creation and the fall coincide. But that would be then a strictly *factual*, or ontic, statement, in no sense a modal, or ontological, statement.

So there is falsity as well as truth in Tillich's dictum as it stands. Its truth is quite simply that even creation involves the creature as well as the Creator, and that the creation of human or moral beings involves the exercise, not only of divine freedom, but of human or moral freedom as well. For this reason, there is a sense in which Augustine's famous dictum, "He that made us without ourselves will not save us without ourselves," expresses the reverse of what should be said. For "the end of creation," if not its beginning, is *eo ipso* cooperative, social, "synergistic," while consummation, at least, is nothing of the kind—although salvation in the proper sense, as distinct from consummation, certainly is, if only in a qualified sense. We are saved *by* grace alone, but not without ourselves, because we are saved *through* faith alone.

111

"One Truth Is Clear: Whatever Is, Is Right"

If this statement of Alexander Pope's, the title of this note, was true in the most obvious sense in which to take it, the very concept of being "right" would be meaningless. If nothing can be meaningfully said to be "wrong," nothing can be meaningfully said to be "right," either. Moreover, if Pope's statement were true in the same obvious sense, any properly moral choice would be absurd. Do as you'd please, but the result would be the same: just right. Whatever you did, it would be exactly as it should be. So serving God, or doing the good and what is right, would come down to doing whatever you happened to do. No matter what you did, you couldn't fail to serve God, or to do the good and what is right.

The conclusion seems unavoidable, then, that Pope's statement can be true, if at all, only in some sense other than the most obvious sense in which to take it. It is credible only if it is taken to apply to the real, not at the level of *actuality*, but rather at the level of *possibility*—more exactly, possibility in fact—and therefore also, of course, at the level of *necessity*. At the level of actuality, "whatever is" includes the results not just of the always and necessarily right decisions of the one universal individual properly called "God," but also those of all the relevant particular individuals, any of which may always be "wrong" as well as "right," and that not only "morally," at the level of "Man," in Pope's terms, but also, "naturally," at the level of what he distinguishes as "Nature." There is always the possibility, in other words, of "natural evil," as it is traditionally called, as well as "moral evil."

So, although "whatever is, is right" is not true but false in the most obvious sense in which it can be taken (i.e., as applying to the actual), still whatever is eternal, necessary, and metaphysical is right, there being nothing else it could be coherently said to be. Moreover, whatever is temporally, contingently, factually not right, but wrong, whether merely naturally or also morally, is itself a product of a cosmic process and a part of a cosmic whole, all of whose most fundamental laws—temporal, contingent, and factual as well as eternal, necessary, and metaphysical—are themselves right and only right.

༄

I do not find it at all surprising that Abraham Lincoln should have confessed to thinking that Alexander Pope's "Essay on Man" "contained all the religious instruction which it was necessary for a man to know" (so the English traveler, George Borrett reported, according to Douglas Wilson).[25] After all, Pope's religious views are largely convergent with Lincoln's own, provided one resists exaggerating the differences between Lincoln's later, so-called new religious position/understanding and his earlier one. This is true, at any rate, so far as Pope's religious views can be determined from what he himself seems to have thought of simply as a "system of Ethics," consisting of a consideration "of the Nature and State of Man" in a fourfold respect: "the Universe," "Himself as an Individual," "Society," and "Happiness."

The convergence is nowhere more marked than in Pope's line, "One truth is clear, 'Whatever is, is Right.'" But at many other points as well, it is only slightly less striking—whether Pope's own deep egalitarianism ("Equal is Common Sense, and

---

25. Wilson, *Lincoln's Sword*, 257.

Common Ease") or his insistence that the end, as the beginning, of all "Faith, Law, Morals" is "Love of God, and Love of Man."[26] I find it particularly interesting that Lincoln seems very close indeed to Pope's understanding of true religion and government as alike having originated in the principle of "love," while superstition and tyranny both have their origins in the principle of "fear."[27]

~

Edward Carwardine speaks of "Lincoln the limited fatalist." His warrant for this, presumably, is Lincoln's long-time partner, William Herndon, who allegedly reported Lincoln' concession that "the will to a very limited extent, in some fields of operation, was somewhat free"—indeed, that humans "had the capacity to 'modify the environments' which shaped them."[28]

If this is a fair understanding of Lincoln's "fatalism," it would appear that such determinism as he implies is a relative, or qualified—not an absolute, or unqualified—determinism. But, then, the difference between his determinism and a relative, or qualified, indeterminism such as my own may be largely, if not entirely verbal. After all, if Hartshorne is right that the freedom of a creature's decision may be thought of as like the numerator one of a fraction, the denominator of which is the number of all the free decisions preceding it, then all creaturely freedom, including all moral freedom, is, to say the least, unimaginably slight.

My guess, however, is that Lincoln's "fatalism" is best thought of, not as implying metaphysical determinism, nor even a relative, or qualified, determinism/indeterminism, but simply as expressing a profound faith in the ultimate meaning of life and a keen sense of our human vocation—and of his own personal vocation—to play our proper part in actualizing that meaning. Otherwise put: Lincoln was a religious person, in the deepest sense, not because he accepted any specific answer to the religious question, and much less because he ever did so dogmatically and uncritically, but because he was profoundly concerned with *asking* the religious question, and therefore in *seeking* an answer to it, never doubting its "basic supposition" in common human faith or failing to keep the "basic commitment" implied in asking it. He deeply believed that, far from everything being permitted, everything is a part of a whole that is, at bottom, moral, and that it is up to any self-understanding part, such as himself, or any of his fellow human beings, to understand oneself accordingly and earnestly seek to play one's role in actualizing the fundamentally moral purpose of the whole. In this connection, I cannot but think that the testimonies by his contemporaries that come closest to accurately describing his "religion" are those by Isaac Cogdal, who asserted that "his mind was full of terrible enquiry—and was skeptical in a good sense," and

---

26. Pope, *Poetical Works*, 269, 277.
27. Pope, *Poetical Works*, 265–56.
28. Carwardine, *Lincoln*, 43–44.

by Joshua Speed, who, in Carwardine's words, "was certain that over the years Lincoln 'was a growing man in religion,' advancing from religious skepticism in the 1830s to serious Christian inquiry in the White House."[29] I would, of course, want to underscore "terrible *enquiry*" in the one testimony, and "Christian *inquiry*," in the other, just as I would respectfully suggest that even what Carwardine calls Lincoln's "new religious understanding," or "new religious position," is more properly thought of as a *philosophical* faith, if not, possibly, a political faith, than as a specifically religious, not to say a properly Christian, faith.

This interpretation fits well, certainly, with all the other observations by Lincoln's contemporaries that he was, above all, a deeply moral man. True, morality is one thing, and politics something else; both are distinct from religion, and from the underlying faith in the ultimate meaning of life that is the basic supposition of any religion as well as of any morality or politics. In any case, what is constant in Lincoln's thinking, as I make it out, is his profound concern with truth and justice—with doing them as well as with knowing them—and with the faith in the ultimate significance of life that this concern necessarily presupposes. Everything else, I suspect, is variable, including his God-talk, which, as often as not, seems to function heuristically, as a way of expressing the basic faith in the ultimate meaning of life necessarily presupposed by his practical as well as theoretical concern with truth and justice.

Incidentally, there are places where Lincoln clearly assumes that *what is to be* (i.e., justice) is determined by *what is* (i.e., truth). To the petitions of a delegation of visiting clergymen, he responds, "I must study the plain physical facts of the case, ascertain what is possible and learn what appears to be wise and right."[30]

All in all, then, Douglas Wilson's evident tendency to play down the differences between Lincoln's earlier religious views and his later ones—his "new religious position"—seems to me preferable to Carwardine's tendency to play them up—being guided in this, perhaps, by writers like Mark Noll and Allen Guelzo.

∽

It occurs to me that to argue as I do in answering the question of where God is in tough times that "God is where God is in all times, tough or not tough—doing what God unfailingly does in every time,"[31] is, on its face, to argue rather as Alexander Pope does, that "One truth is clear, whatever is, is right"/"Submit—in this or any other sphere"/"[T]o reason right is to submit."

I say "on its face," however, because in my understanding, as in Reinhold Niebuhr's, although perhaps not in Pope's, "whatever is" includes "things that *should* (and therefore *can*) be changed" as well as "things that *cannot* be changed." This means

---

29. Carwardine, *Lincoln*, 33–34.
30. Carwardine, *Lincoln*, 228.
31. Ogden, *To Teach the Truth*, 149.

that to obey God, and thus to submit to God as God, cannot be singular, but only dual. To act loyally and courageously to change the things that should be changed is no less to obey God, and so to submit to God as God, than to act trustfully and serenely to accept the things that cannot be changed.

"Whatever is, *is* right," in my view, then, only in the sense that, whatever is, God unfailingly does mainly two things. First, God makes whatever comes to be really possible, in fact as well as in principle; and, second, God makes whatever comes to be both really real and abidingly significant. In doing the first thing, God may be said to create and emancipate, or providentially order, all things; and in doing the second thing, God may be said to redeem and consummate all things. Because, in both cases, God's doing extends to *all* things, God is rightly said to be, in the one case, *the* Creator, and in the other case, *the* Consummator—all things other than God being in their myriad different ways also creators and consummators, but always only of *some* things, never of all.

And yet, because God is present and active in these two ways, whatever happens, our possibility as human beings of understanding ourselves and leading our lives before God is ever the same. Whatever is, we always have the same possibility that I call, following Paul, "obedient faith," which is to say, entrusting ourselves unreservedly to God's pure unbounded love and then living in unqualified loyalty to the cause of God's love, loving God with the whole of our being by loving all whom God always already loves, to whom God is always already loyal—by loving our neighbors as ourselves.

112

Human Needs and the Reality of God

When I last read Ernst and Marie-Luise Keller's book, *Der Streit um die Wunder* (The Dispute over Miracles), I was especially struck by their citing a writer, Bernhard Bavink, who speaks of human beings having a basic "causal need," or "need for causality" (*Kausalbedürfnis*), that demands to be satisfied. In context, the Kellers are concerned to clarify what they take to be "a very important concept . . . which has become indispensable for explaining natural processes in the new physics: the concept of statistical regularity." They continue:

> It is very instructive to see how this concept was formulated by physicists themselves immediately after the discovery of uncertainties. . . . One needs some explanation of this, and this case shows that the human spirit apparently

simply cannot give up a concept of something like regularity or a law of nature. Bernhard Bavink has spoken in this context of a human "causal need," or "need for causality," that has to be satisfied unconditionally. It may be said without exaggerating that, when the earlier view of a mechanically rigid law of nature at least partially broke down and no longer sufficed, one tried to satisfy this causal need with "statistical regularity." And this attempt proved happy, because it allowed uncontrollable processes to be explained *rationally*, and at least as convincingly as the earlier attempts at explanation in mechanics had explained them.[32]

Reflecting on this, I naturally thought of Rudolf Bultmann, who uses a similar term, "*Geltungsbedürfnis*," to distinguish what he takes to be yet another basic human need. Meaning literally "validation (or confirmation) need," or "need for validation (or confirmation)," it is perhaps better rendered into more recent theological English by "acceptance need," or "need for acceptance"—in something close to Paul Tillich's use of "acceptance" in his sermon, "You Are Accepted."[33] Such a need is deemed "basic," presumably, because not to have it would be one and the same with not being or living humanly at all. But, then, I realized that I had to reflect further on the connection between distinguishing two such basic human needs and the priority I have learned to give—especially thanks to Charles Hartshorne—to two arguments for the existence, or reality, of God: the argument from basic faith in a causally ordered world and the argument from basic faith in the abiding meaning or worth of life.

These arguments are alike in deserving the priority I give them because each, in its way, is a matter of making the belief in God implicit in a basic human need fully explicit as belief in God *as* God. The concept/term "God," in other words, functions to understand, or to interpret, what we cannot not believe in, given our basic needs as human beings to believe in the world as causally ordered and in our own lives as finally worth living. At that point, I was struck by the closely parallel ways in which these two basic human needs seem to have been understood in successive periods of Western history.

In an earlier period, the need for acceptance was understood, or interpreted, as meaning that, contrary to Sigmund Freud's maxim, the world *is* a kindergarten, in that God was widely expected to intervene "providentially" to manifest God's acceptance by all sorts of special favors. In roughly the same earlier period, the need for causal order was understood, or interpreted, as requiring unqualified determinism, be it theological determinism in the guise of "predestination," or (in the later part of that earlier period) metaphysical or scientific determinism.

Then, still later, as modernity became more self-critical, there increasingly appeared, thanks particularly to developments in physics, a new and different understanding of causal order as not strict or absolute, but statistical only. Whether best

32. Keller and Keller, *Der Streit um die Wunder*, 189.
33. Tillich, *Shaking of the Foundations*, 153–63.

characterized as a qualified determinism, or as a qualified indeterminism, it involves, in any case, the abandonment of unqualified determinism (as well as, I would add—for careful thinkers, at any rate—unqualified indeterminism). The order of the world, while real and fundamental, is understood to allow for a certain element of disorder, chance being as real as necessity in the general ongoingness of things. In a somewhat similar way, more and more thoughtful persons have come to agree with Freud that the world is *not* a kindergarten after all, and have significantly reduced the demands they feel justified in making on the favor of God, viewing what William James called "an effort to lobby in the courts of the Almighty for special favors" as the very acme of irreligion. Indeed, many modern persons would almost certainly feel the full force of Hartshorne's reasoning, expressed already some three-quarters of a century ago: "In its early stages religion means certainty about many things. But we now see that [she or] he is most religious who is certain of but one thing, the world-embracing love of God. Everything else we can take our chance on; everything else, including man's relative significance in the world, is mere probability."[34]

Of course, the issue between these earlier and later ways of understanding, or interpreting, our two basic needs remains deeply controversial right up to the present. From the standpoint of the later understanding, the earlier one is likely to seem more superstitious than religious, whereas for anyone still judging from the earlier understanding, the later one may well appear as, at best, something like a "soft deism," and at worst, atheism in everything but the name. But however one seeks to resolve this issue, the essential facts of the case seem clear enough: two needs basic to human life each implies, in its way, a belief that theism, in some form, makes explicit; and there have come to be two main ways of understanding, or interpreting, both needs that yield very different (in fact, incompatible) forms of theistic belief. If the one, earlier way may seem more appropriate, when judged simply by the datum discourse of traditional Christian witness and theology, the other, later way may appear to be more credible—and, as some of us hold, also more appropriate—when judged, not just by the (mythological) forms of Christian witness and theology, but also, and most importantly, by their (existential) substance, by their own understanding of human existence and its deeper presuppositions and implications.

---

34. Hartshorne, *Beyond Humanism*, 44.

113

Proofs of, or Arguments for, God's Existence

There is always an immediate, albeit dim, and all but unconscious, perception of God, insofar as there is always such a perception of the encompassing whole of reality of which we perceive ourselves and others to be parts. The reason (or the sense in which) there is a perception of the encompassing whole of reality immediately given in and with all perception is that the part is always—and is always perceived as—part of the whole. The distinction between the part and the whole is one of the two most fundamental distinctions given in experience (the other being that between the concrete and the abstract); and it, too, is of necessity always given, insofar as all experience, being either of the whole or of the part, is also an experience of the distinction between them, since the part can no more be or be experienced without the whole than the whole can be or be experienced without the part.

There is also always a basic faith in God, insofar as there is always a basic faith in such things as the order of the world or the appropriateness and validity of ideals of truth, goodness, beauty, etc., as well as the ultimate meaning or significance of life lived in accordance with, or contrary to, these ideals.

But thus to perceive God or to have such a basic faith in God is one thing, while to perceive God *as God*, or to have a basic faith in God *as God*, is something else. The function of so-called proofs of, or arguments for, God's existence is to justify perceiving God *as God* or having a basic faith in God *as God*.

Such proofs or arguments can succeed, however, only insofar as a clear distinction is made between the transcendental, and so strictly literal, idea of God as the whole, or the universal individual, and the categorial, and so merely symbolic, idea of God as the supreme person—the proofs or arguments succeeding in establishing the existence of God as conceived by the second idea only in that they succeed in establishing the existence of God as conceived by the first.

∽

I have at times hesitated to speak of "proofs" for the existence of God, as distinct from speaking, simply, of "arguments." In fact, I have on occasion implied, and even said, that we should give up speaking of "proving" God's existence. The reason for this, I have reasoned, is that any valid deductive argument is reversible, in that one need not feel constrained to accept its conclusion if one has good and sufficient reasons for rejecting at least one of its premises.

But the more I have thought about it, the clearer it has become to me that this is not a good reason for ceasing to speak of theistic "proofs." If it belongs to *any* valid deductive argument that it can always be reversed in this way, then either "proving" a conclusion means something more than testing it by giving good and sufficient reasons from which it can be validly deduced, or else one should feel perfectly free to continue speaking of proving God's existence, because any proof of it, just as of anything else, being nothing other than such an argument, is *eo ipso* reversible.

In any case, the challenge in arguing for, or proving, that God exists is to find premises so far less controversial than their denials that rejecting them is too high a price to pay for rejecting their conclusion

∽

To the existence of what God do the so-called proofs of God's existence lead insofar as they are sound, which is to say, formally valid deductions from premises that are materially true? Do they lead to the existence of the God of whom Hartshorne speaks when he says, "the word God . . . stands for an analogy (difficult no doubt) between the thinking animal and the cosmos conceived as animate"?[35] Or do they lead instead to the existence of the God who, as I put it, is the whole, the eminent or universal individual, who therefore is, or will be, really, internally—as well as logically and externally—related to all other individuals and events, whether actual or possible?

∽

Speaking of his "favorite arguments for belief [in God]"—namely, "the argument from order and the argument from what Kant called the *summum bonum* and [he calls] the rational aim: what rational beings could reasonably accept as the final purpose of their existence and activity"—Hartshorne says: "I am not saying, Unless God exists life has no meaning or rational aim and the cosmos no order. I am sure life has meaning and the cosmos order. I am saying that I can understand how there is meaning and order only by believing in God as enriched by our experiences."[36]

I take this to indicate that, in Hartshorne's view, as in mine, the beliefs that the world has order and that life has meaning are as basic or unavoidable beliefs as the belief that there is a God. Consequently, it's not the case that, unless I believe in God, I cannot believe that the world has order and that life has meaning. I can and must believe the second two beliefs simply because I exist and act at all. But I also believe in

---

35. Hartshorne, *Creative Synthesis and Philosophic Method*, 220.
36. Hartshorne, "Our Knowledge of God," 60, 62.

God because only by so believing can I *understand* at all adequately how or why there is the order and meaning in which I cannot fail to believe. Otherwise, as Hartshorne says in speaking of atheism in relation to "the regularity of nature," my beliefs in the order of the world and in the meaning of life remain matters of "a mere brute fact or blind mystery."[37]

～

All valid arguments for God's existence are a priori, since no a posteriori argument for God's existence could possibly be valid. Either an a posteriori argument would be valid, but would not be an argument for *God's* existence, or else it would be an argument for God's existence, but would *not* be valid. The distinctive thing about the so-called ontological argument is not that it is a priori, since all sound arguments for God's existence must be so, but that its premise is the transcendental idea of God itself, taken to be a clear and coherent idea.

Essential to the transcendental idea of God is that God could not possibly be surpassed and therefore must exist necessarily, since anyone or anything existing not necessarily but only contingently would be *eo ipso* surpassable, because it could be surpassed by someone or something existing not contingently but necessarily. The ontological argument for God's existence exploits *this* point. Any other sound metaphysical argument for God's existence has as its premise, directly or indirectly, some transcendental idea(s) other than the idea of God, taken to be a clear and coherent idea.

In the nature of the case, all transcendental ideas necessarily imply one another—either because they are convertible ≡ coextensive (as, e.g., are "being," "unity," "truth," "goodness," "beauty") or because they are disjunctive (as, e.g., are "concrete/abstract," "subject/object," "contingent/necessary," "relative/absolute," "effect/cause," "unsurpassable/surpassable," and so on). All other sound arguments for God's existence exploit *this* point, insofar as any transcendental idea other than the idea of God necessarily implies *this* transcendental idea, which, like all transcendental ideas, cannot fail to be instantiated.

～

The transcendental concept of God both implies and is implied by all other transcendental concepts. There are, in principle, then, two ways of arguing metaphysically to the existence of God:

---

37. Hartshorne, "Our Knowledge of God," 61.

(1) arguing from the transcendental concept of God itself; and

(2) arguing from some transcendental concept other than the concept of God, which is either convertible (≡ coextensive) or disjunctive and applies in systematically different ways both to concretes and abstracts and to God as the universal individual and all other concrete and singular things as particular individuals—whether short-term individuals, in the case of "events," or long-term individuals, in the case of "individuals" properly so-called.

∽

Why must there be metaphysical arguments for the existence of God?

It is a necessary implication of the religious idea of God as the all-worshipful or unsurpassable that "God" must be a transcendental idea, or that there is a transcendental idea of God. Therefore, since any transcendental idea is necessarily implied by any other idea, it is also necessarily implied by any other transcendental idea, from which it follows that, if the idea of God is the transcendental idea that religion itself necessarily implies it to be, there are and must be metaphysical arguments for the applicability of this idea, and hence for the existence of God. In fact, there must be as many metaphysical arguments for the existence of God as there are transcendental ideas—including the idea of God itself.

∽

If theism, properly defined, is good grammar, it cannot fail to be true, since its denial is, in any case, bad grammar, and so necessarily false. The most completely abstract general terms applicable to God are literal in that application. To be sure, there is always a difference in meaning between their application to God and any of their other applications, so that they are, in this sense, applied "analogically," instead of either "univocally" or "equivocally." But this difference itself can be stated literally.

Contrary to the negative theology, some concepts must apply to God positively as well as literally, since where there are no definite common aspects, there can be no definite contrasts either. So, for example, if God is not positively as well as literally cause or influence, God cannot contrast with all other individuals as causative or influential universally or cosmically rather than merely particularly or locally.

All of the transcendental features of reality must be features of God if God is literally being, or reality, itself. Thus God must be conditioned as well as unconditioned, potential as well as actual, relative as well as absolute, concrete as well as abstract, universal effect as well as universal cause, and so on.

God in God's essential aspect as God is neither a mere case under the transcendentals, nor yet a mere exception to them. Rather, God's essence *is* the transcendentals in their eminent, unsurpassable instantiation, as the fixed properties of a universal individual within whose actuality is a duality of perfect and imperfect cases, the former necessarily including the latter, even as the latter are necessarily included in the former.

∞

Hartshorne argues that, if discussion of the existence of God is to be properly rational, there have to be:

(1) rules or principles valid for all individuals, not excluding God, and so definitive of *individuality as such*;

(2) rules or principles valid for all individuals other than God, and so definitive of *nondivine individuality*; and

(3) rules or principles valid solely for God, and so definitive of *divine individuality*.

Beyond this, there have to be both a *criterion* for distinguishing between the second and third sets of rules or principles, and *reasons* why they have to be distinguished.[38]

I now realize that I have long made essentially the same point (without being aware I was doing so!) whenever I argued that, if talk about the existence of God is to be cognitively meaningful, not all terms can be used symbolically (≡ nonliterally), because at least some terms have to be used literally (≡ nonsymbolically), in a twofold respect: (1) in that, on either use—either to speak of God as the one and only universal individual or to speak of any particular individual as one among many such individuals—they are used literally (≡ nonsymbolically), whichever type of individual they speak of; and (2) in that, on both uses, the terms have a core of literal meaning that remains ever the same, whichever type of individual is spoken of.

Clearly, to agree with Hartshorne that there must be one set of rules definitive of individuality as such, not excluding God's individuality, is also to agree with me that there is a core of literal meaning that ever remains the same whichever type of individual is spoken of, whether the universal individual God or any particular individual that is not God. Likewise, to agree with Hartshorne that there must be two additional sets of rules definitive, respectively, of divine individuality and of nondivine individuality, is also to agree with me that, although the difference between the two types of individuality, being an "infinite, qualitative difference," can be nothing less than transcendental, each type can and must be defined literally (≡ nonsymbolically). And this is so because the criterion of the difference as an infinite, transcendental difference is the literal (≡ nonsymbolic) distinction between "all" and "some" ("none" being the remaining term of an exhaustive three-part division).

---

38. Cf. Hartshorne, *Natural Theology for Our Time*, 37.

Proofs of, or Arguments for, God's Existence

∽

Is it true, as Hartshorne claims, that the religious idea of God furnishes the sole way of construing necessary existence—as the cosmological argument has to hold if it is to conclude validly to the existence of God as religiously conceived? Yes—and no.

Yes, insofar as the "grammar," which is to say, the logic, of the religious idea of God is the logic of the universal individual, in the sense of the universal center of interaction. According to this logic, God is the one individual interacting with—acting on and being acted on by—*all* individuals (indeed, all *events*), including Godself as the universal individual, as well as all other particular individuals (and events). If what is meant by "the religious idea of God" is simply the idea of the universal individual in this austerely transcendental sense, then yes, the religious idea of God may be said to furnish the sole way of clearly and consistently construing necessary existence in literal (≡ nonsymbolic) terms.

But this is also not true insofar as "the religious idea of God" is not ordinarily understood to be the austerely transcendental idea of the universal individual, but rather the categorial idea of the supreme conscious person. Far from being the sole way of construing necessary existence, this categorial idea of God is, at best, only one way of interpreting the transcendental idea of the universal individual symbolically.

∽

To Hartshorne's metaphysical question, how can the universe be "a single existent, while it also has as its parts all other existents"? the religious idea of God, in its bare logic, can indeed give an answer—and, arguably, the only adequate answer. This it can do because the metaphysical idea of the universal individual that the religious idea of God necessarily implies does indeed suffice to explain how it is that the universe is one as well as many.

"God," however, adds more than metaphysically irrelevant "emotional (or existential!) coloring" only insofar as "God" means, simply, "the universal individual." On the other hand, "God" as the eminently conscious person *is* just so much metaphysically irrelevant emotional (or existential) coloring, whatever relevance it may be reasonably taken to have, religiously and even philosophically.

∽

A sound ontological argument for God's existence may be analyzed in terms of five main points:

General Rule: Anything that is clearly and coherently conceivable is *either* actual *or* possible (i.e., "really," or "ontologically," as well as "logically," possible).

Assumption: God, or the Unsurpassable, can be clearly and coherently conceived.

Inference: *Either* God exists and is actual *or* God is possible, ontologically as well as logically.

Argument: But God is not—indeed, cannot be—possible but not actual, because "unactualized possibility of unsurpassability" is self-contradictory and therefore meaningless.

Conclusion: Therefore, God exists because God is and must be conceived as actual.

As regards the General Rule, the point is that "meanings are logically possible only because referents are ontologically possible or actual." A meaning cannot refer merely to its own possibility or actuality; rather, it means in relation to the actuality or the possibility of its referent, of that to which it refers. This is not to say that all meanings have to refer to reality directly, but only that they must do so at least indirectly. Why? Because all other "language games" necessarily presuppose the primacy of "the real language game," where "real" arguably includes all three modes of "reality"—i.e., *the necessary* as well as *the possible* and *the actual*. Thus "subjective or logical or epistemological possibility is sufficient evidence for the disjunction: either real existence or real potency of existence."

One may argue in support of the Assumption: (1) that unsurpassability can be clearly defined in terms that do not seem to yield any incompatible consequences insofar as it is defined "neoclassically," as "modal coincidence" (better: "modal coextensiveness," or "modal all-inclusiveness"); (2) that, and more decisively, "logic and ethics inevitably make at least implicit use of the idea of unsurpassability or of perfection." "Reasoning is sound so far as it is capable of reducing the discrepancy between our knowledge and the ideal of perfect knowledge, or omniscience, and conduct is right so far as, within our capacity, our motivation accords with the ideal of wholly enlightened or perfect good will, that is, with the holiness or all-righteousness of God." If, then, the idea of perfection, or unsurpassability, were to be unclear or incoherent, the ideal to which all our striving necessarily refers would be meaningless. But this ideal cannot possibly be meaningless because "the ideal necessarily involved in all our striving cannot be given up"; and (3) that the cosmological argument supports the ontological argument at this very point. If (as the cosmological argument shows) we must admit a necessary being, and if we have no conception of a character other than perfection or unsurpassability that could render a being necessary instead of contingent, then the assumption that the concept of unsurpassability is clear and coherent is the only way to meet the demand whose validity the cosmological argument establishes.

The Argument, then, takes the form of establishing that the Unsurpassable must be so (1) in some respect(s) by all others only, in which respect(s) its unsurpassability is relative; or (2) in some respect(s) by itself as well as all others, in which respect(s) its unsurpassability is absolute. In either case, unsurpassability undoubtedly entails eternity—being without either beginning or end—since any noneternal being can be conceived only as surpassed by an eternal one; and this excludes unsurpassability's being a mere unactualized possibility. Moreover, possibility means that a transition from possible to actual can at least be clearly and consistently conceived. But it is self-contradictory and meaningless to speak of an eternal transition, or a transition to eternality—i.e., to the status of never having come to be and never ceasing to be.

So the Conclusion can be said to follow from two further premises: unactualized possibility involves a conceivable transition to existence, but no such transition could conceivably terminate in a being unsurpassable in every, if in any, respect. Or, again, nothing unactual is objectively possible unless an adequate cause of its actuality is actual, but (a) an adequate cause of an unsurpassable being must itself be an unsurpassable being; and (b) no being caused to exist by another unsurpassable being could itself be unsurpassable.[39]

∾

The soundness of the ontological argument turns on the soundness or unsoundness of a rule, supposedly admitting of no exceptions, that the relation between essence and existence is always contingent. This rule can be derived, if at all, only from an understanding of the meanings of "essence" and "existence" as such. So if we do not know whether or not the rule is sound, we do not know altogether what we mean by these fundamental conceptions. On the other hand, the ontological argument derives God's exceptional mode of existence from an analysis of *God's* "essence" (i.e., unsurpassability). If the meanings of the concepts that define unsurpassability necessarily imply existence, as they evidently do, then the above rule is shown to be valid, if valid at all, only with one unmistakable exception. Since necessity of existence is essential to God on any conception of God's essence expressed or implied more or less clearly and consistently by the axial religions, one or the other of two things has to be true: either the axial religions' conception of God, widespread as it is, violates the rule that existence is always contingent in relation to essence and is therefore sheer nonsense; or else this rule is significantly limited in its applicability by the metaphysical uniqueness of God as conceived by the axial religions, for which it is the essence of God to exist.

∾

The point of the argument for God's existence from the reality of order can be put as follows: localized interaction by itself fails to make intelligible the possibility of any order whatsoever, notwithstanding that, without some order, the concept of interaction has no meaning. Hence to deny any nonlocalized form of interaction (i.e., any form at once individual and universal) is to deny any interaction at all, which is meaningless,

---

39. The above is my reformulation of what I take to be the burden of Hartshorne, "Formal Validity." All statements quoted are his.

since "there is interaction" (and so, "there is order") is necessarily true, the alternative being nonsensical.

Following the general rule that metaphysical arguments for the existence of God are in effect "*reductio ad absurdum* arguments against alternatives or substitutes for theism," we may say that the argument from order is successful to the extent that it shows all the alternatives to be without coherent meaning in terms of our common human experience, thereby exhibiting theism as "sole residual legatee."

Specifically, there seem to be the following alternatives to the idea of God as the nonlocalized, universal as well as individual, form of interaction, without which there could be no interaction at all:

(1) there is no coordination or mutual harmony between the localized forms of interaction;

(2) there is such coordination, but there is no common subordination of all the localized forms of interaction to one nonlocalized, universal as well as individual, and hence superior, form; and

(3) there is both coordination and subordination, but the superior, superordinate form of interaction is not unsurpassable (i.e., not "worthy of inclusive devotion because supremely good").

But none of these three alternatives seems to have a coherent meaning.

Ad 1: There has to be at least enough coordination or mutual harmony between the localized forms of interaction that they do not exclude or prevent one another's existence. *Ad* 2: But then this coordination is due either to the mutual adjustment of each localized form of interaction to all the others, or else to their common subordination to a nonlocalized form of interaction. The first alternative, however, seems invalid, since it presupposes the very thing it is supposed to account for. There can be no adjustment to an environment whose members are not mutually adjusted, since, were they not so adjusted, they would not constitute an environment to which adjustment could be made. The old idea that, in infinite time, atoms would fall into all possible arrangements by chance simply begs the question, since to talk of the mere existence of atoms with definite characters maintaining themselves in relation to one another through infinite time is to speak of what in itself is already a very high degree of order. So the order calling for explanation is not accounted for but presupposed.

Ad 3: But nothing except superior goodness or value makes universal subordination to a superior power intelligible. Power inheres in that which has value to offer, in proportion to its value—the most valuable being *eo ipso* the most powerful, and vice versa.

But what of the usual objections to the argument from order? It is usually held, first, that the existence of evil—or, more broadly, dysteleology of any kind—in our actual empirical world speaks against the claim that the goodness and beauty of that world require us to think of it as a product of the unsurpassable. But to the dispute thus formulated, both parties are mistaken, since they alike assume that the argument logically is a posteriori or empirical, instead of a priori or metaphysical. The premise of the argument as formulated above has nothing whatsoever to do with the actual empirically given order of the world. Its premise, instead, is the idea of order, or of harmonious, coordinated interaction as such. The argument then seeks to show that *any* world (i.e., any even *conceivable* world) would require an unsurpassable orderer, because only if there were such would the idea of order itself be clearly and coherently conceivable in terms of our experience. Thus the point of the argument is not that, because there is nothing chaotic or unfortunate in events, the order of the world is perfect, and therefore requires a perfect, unsurpassable orderer. Its point, rather, is that, apart from such an orderer, there is no way to understand or make intelligible how there could be even such limits as there are, and, of necessity, have to be, to the confusion and anarchy implied by the notion of a multiplicity of interacting agents, none of which is unsurpassably wise and influential.

A second objection is that the argument misuses the idea of cause, since it supposes that God's ordering of the world is done in eternity, prior to, apart from, in no way influenced by, the decisions of the localized forms of interaction. Thus the unsurpassable cause is a sheer exception to the rule that concrete causes are also concrete effects, and vice versa. But this objection simply assumes the classical conception of God as exclusively cause, in no sense effect, and this conception is illogical and unnecessary. As the *concrete* cause of each event (although no cause, even the unsurpassable cause, uniquely determines its effects), God *is* effect of prior events as well as their cause. And as prior to *all* events, God is wholly abstract, merely existent, undetermined to any particular actual state. So, once classical assumptions are abandoned as mistaken, the objection fails: the universal rule pertaining to causes and effects is not violated but conformed to.

A third objection is that the argument does not exclude polytheism. But if the point of the argument is that only universal, nonlocalized interaction can explain cosmic order, the notion of a plurality of universal interactors either implies a distinction without a difference—i.e., despite the plurality of interactors there is still cosmic order—or else misses the whole point of the argument that order is, in principle, the rule of one, not many.

To sum up: the point of the argument is that all particular localized interaction requires universal nonlocalized interaction to set limits to chaos and mutual frustration.

∽

What is said, for the most part, in the preceding entries on proofs of, or arguments for, the existence of God is concerned with what are more exactly distinguished as *metaphysical* proofs or arguments. This means that they are arguments from utterly universal concepts, otherwise called "transcendentals," including—in the case of the so-called ontological argument—the transcendental concept "God" itself.

There are, in addition to all such properly metaphysical arguments, other ways of giving reasons for believing that "God exists" is a true assertion. There are, for example, what may be distinguished as *moral or ethical* arguments, insofar as they reason directly from the necessary conditions of the possibility of acting morally or ethically and therefore reason only indirectly from strictly metaphysical concepts. But there is also what I think and speak of as a properly *existential or religious* argument for God's existence. In fact, it is just such an argument, expressly identified as such, and accordingly distinguished from all metaphysical arguments, that is developed in my essay, "Concerning Belief in God."[40]

The key to this kind of religious argument is an analysis of properly existential or religious inquiry. My contention is that the question by which all such inquiry is constituted is the question about the meaning of ultimate reality for us, which is to say, the twofold question about ultimate reality as determining my authentic self-understanding—or, vice versa, about my authentic self-understanding as determined by ultimate reality. By "ultimate reality" I mean the concrete reality of my own existence as an understanding, self-understanding individual ("self") in the ultimate setting of the many other events and individuals more or less like myself ("others") and of the one strictly ultimate reality that is radically unlike all of us in being our sole primal source and our sole final end ("the whole"). Just as the self and any other are, in their ways, centers of interaction, acting on and being acted on by others and the whole, so the whole also is, in its unique way, analogously an interacting center. But whereas the field of interaction in the case of either the self or any of the others is particular or fragmentary, being interaction with *some* others only, the whole's field of interaction is universal or nonfragmentary, because it is interaction with *all* others.

Being understandingly aware of itself in this ultimate setting, if only implicitly, the self exists in a basic confidence in the all-environing whole and in a comparably basic loyalty to it and its parts. But since the self's awareness of itself is always fragmentary, it is also always questioning, and the self is compelled to ask, among its other vital questions, just how it is to understand itself, others, and the whole if it is to do so truly and authentically instead of falsely and inauthentically.

Religion in general, I hold, is the primary form of culture through which we as selves explicitly ask and answer this underlying existential question. And religious inquiry is the process of our seeking the true answer to this twofold question about the meaning of ultimate reality for us. In seeking it, we ask about ultimate reality only insofar as it authorizes or makes appropriate authentic self-understanding, even as we ask about authentic self-understanding only insofar as it is authorized or made appropriate by ultimate reality. But then, the formula for any properly existential or religious argument for the existence of God is clear enough. Given some concept of

40. Ogden, *Doing Theology Today*, 95–108.

just what is to be understood by "God," one reasons to the conclusion that strictly ultimate reality so conceived provides the best or most adequate answer to the existential or religious question about the meaning of ultimate reality for us: how we are to understand ourselves in our ultimate environment if we are to do so truly and authentically, and lead our lives accordingly.

To establish that this is, indeed, the case is the objective of all arguments for God's reality or existence, insofar as they belong to properly existential or religious inquiry. However many are the ways of developing it, there is really only one such existential or religious argument—to the effect that what we all believe, at least implicitly, if we exist humanly at all is re-presented explicitly by the existence of God so conceived and that, as a consequence, we too may believe as it gives and calls us to believe, thereby rendering our explicit understanding of ourselves both complete and consistent and providing for ourselves and others valuable means of salvation or ultimate transformation.

114

On "the *Euthyphro* 'Dilemma'"

By "the Euthyphro 'dilemma'" is meant that "either God's approval of certain states of affairs is what makes them right or good or God approves of certain states of affairs because they *are* right or good, as in Plato's *Euthyphro* (10A)."[41] Otherwise expressed: "[T]he Euthyphro question" is: "[I]s something good because God wills it or does God will it because it is good?"[42] The right response is "neither!" "'God neither obeys the moral order, nor does [God] invent it. [God] is Goodness itself, and all else that is good is good in imitation of God's nature' [so Katherin Rogers]. Hence the Euthyphro 'dilemma' is really a tri-lemma."[43]

There is a parallel argument from modal logic. "God neither invented modal truths nor is bound by them. Rather, modal truths reflect the divine nature itself. . . . [B]oth moral and modal logical considerations make it possible to reject the forced choice implied in the Euthyphro 'dilemma': there is a third option made possible in perfect being theology or philosophy of religion, the option wherein it is integral to the divine nature to *be* good and necessary, rather than [either] to (arbitraily) *invent* goodness

---

41. Dombrowski, "Objective Morality," 205.
42. Dombrowski, "Objective Morality," 209.
43. Dombrowski, "Objective Morality," 211.

and necessity or [to](dependently) *conform* to goodness and necessity."[44] Once again, according to Rogers: "'[I]t is impossible that God should command us to act in ways that are not for the best. . . . God neither creates nor conforms to the standards of value; [God] *is* the standard.'"[45]

The choice before us, then, is this: either "(1) the tradition from Hume to G. E. Moore is correct in claiming that an ought cannot be derived from an is, so that any oughts are merely the result of some decision that we make, whether individually or collectively, in which case there may be . . . intersubjectivity in morality, but not real objectivity; or (2) there is an omnibenevolent, perfect being [why not, rather, "perfect, omnibenevolent being"?] that generates in us an objective *ought* if and when we become aware of such a being."[46] With respect to the second alternative, however, we also have a choice—between classical theism, on the one hand, and neoclassical or process theism, on the other, the latter being relatively more adequate and freer of difficulties.

For all of my sympathy—as well as agreement—with Dombrowski's (and Rogers's) argument, I am also put off by it. For one thing, what he calls a "tri-lemma" is nothing of the kind, but is simply one of the ways of successfully coping with a dilemma taken together with the dilemma itself—that way, namely, generally known as "escaping between the horns." Also troubling is that some of his interpretations of process thought are insufficiently subtle or nuanced—as when he creates the impression that the very concept/term "omnipotence" is the problem, instead of clearly identifying the problem as the untenable, because self-contradictory, "meaning" commonly assigned the concept/term, implicitly if not explicitly, in the theological tradition;[47] or when he says, "in the neoclassical or process theistic view, God is *a se* or independent with respect to divine *existence* (the fact *that* God exists), but not with respect to God's *actuality* (*how* God exists)," thereby not only misleadingly implying that God's existence is, after all, a (matter of) fact but also ignoring God's *essence*—i.e., that God not only exists *a se* but also exists *as God* in the same absolutely independent way.[48]

---

44. Dombrowski, "Objective Morality," 211. On p. 205, perfect being philosophers and theologians are said to think that responses to the question of what attributes a perfect being would possess ought to drive responses to most other questions in theology and philosophy of religion. "For example, what are the implications, if any, of the logic of perfection for the claim that God exists? What are the implications, if any, of believing in a perfect being for moral theory or metaethics?; etc.".

45. Dombrowski, "Objective Morality," 213; cf. also 216: "God does not create objective moral principles, nor is God bound by them; rather, God *is* the moral standard and we are moral to the extent that we imitate divine omnibenevolence."

46. Dombrowski, "Objective Morality," 220.

47. Dombrowski, "Objective Morality," 215.

48. Dombrowski, "Objective Morality," 210.

On "The Euthyphro 'Dilemma'"

Hartshorne rightly argues that there clearly seems to be something like a universal, rational ideal—namely, being completely open in all of one's lines of communication, internal and external, with self and others, and acting accordingly.[49] But, equally clearly, this ideal could not be fully realized by any human (or more generally, any fragmentary) being. Only God, being logically-ontologically unique as the one universal, nonfragmentary individual, could and necessarily does fully realize it, in that God's lines of communication with self and with others (both of which are and must be internal only) are always and fully open. This means that a human being can challenge God's valuations and actions only by implicitly repudiating her or his own ideal of complete openness both to oneself and to all others. Also, to oppose her or his own valuations to God's would likewise be irrational, because (arguably) only God's aim and our aim as serving God's aim can relate to the future as such, *all* the future, which any rational aim must, in principle, relate to.

But is not this to derive an *ought* from an *is*? It is, indeed. But the *is* in this case is unique, its difference from everything else being nothing other or less than a difference in logical-ontological type. Neither God's existence nor God's will that creatures serve God by serving all others as themselves just happens to be the case. On the contrary, both are strictly necessary and eternal, so that God logically-ontologically could *not* will that creatures should not live for all others as themselves and inclusively for God as ideally concerned with all of them. And from *this is*, this strictly *necessary, metaphysical is*, an *ought can be* validly derived. Only what is logically-ontologically contingent can be open to negative rational criticism, since it makes no sense to think and say that what is logically-ontologically necessary and, therefore, could not conceivably be or have been otherwise ought not to be, or ought to have been other than it is. The only attitude appropriate toward the necessary is positive acceptance. Moreover, we have no reason to reject the ideal that God alone fully realizes or can realize, if it entirely agrees with our own universal, rational ideal of complete openness both to self and to all others.

But then there is a solution, after all, to Plato's problem in the *Euthyphro*. It lies in a genuinely dipolar conception of God, according to which God is at once unsurpassably absolute and unsurpassably relative. *Qua* unsurpassably absolute, God simply *is* the standard of all goodness, whether for God's own utterly free, contingent choices *qua* unsurpassably relative or for any and all choices other than God's. Moreover, even God's utterly free, contingent, and so relative choices are, in their way, unsurpassably good, and are to be positively accepted as such, because there have to be, as Hartshorne says, some "cosmic 'traffic rules,'" and the rules that God contingently enacts for the cosmos—what we commonly refer to as "natural laws"—are rules that are and

---

49. Hartshorne, "Equality, Freedom," 23–25.

must be fully in accord with the standard of goodness that God Godself *qua* absolute simply is.

115

"Perfect Being Theology" and Christology

One of the proponents of "perfect being theology or philosophy of religion" has explained it as "the Anselmian effort to think through what Charles Hartshorne has called the logic of perfection: what attributes would a perfect being possess?"[50] Hartshorne himself has argued, as, in this sense, "a perfect being philosophical theologian," that any God who existed only contingently would be "too small," or, in other words, would be "imperfect," and so a veritable *contradictio in adjecto* if also conceived to be "perfect."

I believe that I am equally entitled to argue, as a Christian systematic theologian, that a God who created and consummated, emancipated and redeemed, and insofar saved, contingently only could be similarly dismissed as "too small," and, as such, a contradiction in terms if at the same time held to be the perfect God implied by Christian faith. Because that God is the all-worshipful, unsurpassable One, "than whom—in Anselm's phrase—none greater can be conceived," that God must consummate and redeem, and also insofar save, just as that God must create and emancipate, not contingently only, but also, in another respect, necessarily. Why? Because any God who consummated and redeemed, and insofar saved, only contingently could not conceivably be unsurpassable, but would be surpassed by a God who, in another respect, did all of God's works *ad extra* necessarily as well as contingently.

And yet it is the very logic of any properly constitutivist christology, according to which Jesus Christ is understood to be, in the traditional phrase, the "meritorious cause" of salvation, or in some way to make salvation possible, to imply that God saves, just as God creates and consummates, emancipates and redeems, contingently only. I maintain, on the contrary, that any such God, far from being unsurpassable, is all too clearly surpassed by the God who does everything God does, *ad extra*, from creation to consummation, not only, in one respect, contingently, but also, in another respect, necessarily. It is the very essence of this God as "nothing but love," or "pure, unbounded love," ever to be creating and consummating, emancipating and redeeming, some world of creatures, and therefore also always to be doing whatever can be

---

50. Dombrowski, "Objective Morality," 205.

done to save any creatures that need saving, except what they must each do themselves, both for themselves and for one another.

So much the worse, then, for any properly constitutivist christology. Only a properly representativist christology belongs in a Christian systematic theology that would be, in its own way, and for its own specifically Christian reasons, "a perfect being theology."

116

The Problem of God for Christian Systematic Theology

There are different standpoints from which God can be a problem, just as there are different reasons for finding God to be problematic. In this entry, I discuss the problem of God as I see it from my standpoint as a Christian systematic theologian, and for the reasons that I myself have found relevant and important from this standpoint.

What, exactly, is my standpoint as a Christian systematic theologian, as I understand it? On my analysis, to be a Christian is to understand oneself in one's ultimate environment in a certain way and to lead one's life accordingly. It is to understand the all-encompassing whole of which one is a part, together with everything else, as neither an empty void nor an unreconciled enmity, but as a boundless, unconditional acceptance worthy at once of unreserved trust and unqualified loyalty. To lead one's life in such trust and with such loyalty is to believe and act in a way that bears a distinctive twofold witness: to the ultimate whole of reality by which we and everything else are encompassed as, in Luther's phrase, "sheer love" (*eitel Liebe*); and to the particular historical event through which ultimate reality is so revealed—the event that Christians call "Jesus Christ"—as itself of decisive significance for human existence. In short, to be a Christian is to believe in the strictly ultimate reality that some human beings call "God" as nothing but the love that Jesus decisively discloses it to be and then to bear witness by leading one's life accordingly, bearing it explicitly through the so-called sacred forms of religion, and bearing it implicitly through the other so-called secular forms of human culture.

By its very nature, then, bearing Christian witness, implicit as well as explicit, makes or implies two claims to validity that are important for understanding the standpoint of the Christian systematic theologian. Bearing witness claims to be adequate to its content and therefore to be, first of all, appropriate to Jesus Christ in that the self-understanding and life-praxis for which it calls are in substantial agreement with the faith and way of life that the event of Jesus itself decisively calls for. And bearing witness claims, secondly, that this faith and way of life are credible to human existence and so worthy of belief because they agree substantially with common human experience and reason. By "substantial agreement" in both cases, I mean simply that the agreement is not merely verbal or conceptual, but is also real, in that the self-understanding and life-praxis referred to on both sides are not substantially different, but the same.

But, of course, making or implying a claim that one's witness is adequate, and therefore both appropriate and credible, is one thing, while making or implying one's claim validly is something else. So the activity of "bearing Christian witness" itself anticipates the other—closely related and yet significantly different—activity that I understand by "doing Christian theology," and, specifically, "doing Christian *systematic* theology." Like any other form of critical reflection or proper theory, Christian systematic theology asks about the validity of certain claims made or implied by a certain life-praxis—in its case, the praxis of bearing Christian witness. But to ask critically about the *validity* of a witness borne or to be borne is always to ask, first, about its *meaning*—at least if one has any concern about criticizing either positively or negatively only what one has first taken the trouble to understand. And so the standpoint of a Christian systematic theologian is determined by asking and trying to answer, not just one main question, but two: (1) What does bearing Christian witness really mean, not only at the surface level of its *semantic* meaning, but also (and most importantly) at the depth level of its *logical kind* of meaning? Also, (2) are the claims made or implied in bearing Christian witness really valid claims: is it, as it affects to be, at once appropriate to Jesus Christ and credible to human existence? Or, if you will, is it both Christian and true?

In my understanding, then, the problem of God for the Christian systematic theologian is to formulate an understanding of the strictly ultimate reality that the concept-term "God" is, for certain human beings, a traditional way of interpreting—by means, namely, of a formulation that is at once appropriate and credible in the senses I have tried to explain. In what follows, I will say a few more things about what I understand each of these two criteria—appropriateness and credibility—to require of any such theological formulation. But I want to say, first, just a bit more about the logically prior question concerning the *meaning* of bearing Christian witness, as distinct from the further question concerning the *validity* of bearing it, which is to say, the validity of the two claims that it itself makes or implies just as and because it is bearing Christian witness.

Lying behind my attempt earlier to clarify what it means to be a Christian by speaking in such terms as "self-understanding" and "life-praxis" is a certain analysis of the depth meaning, or the logical kind of meaning, of which bearing Christian witness is a special case. On that analysis, sometimes characterized as "existentialist," bearing Christian witness answers a distinctive human question: the so-called *existential* question about the meaning of ultimate reality for us simply as human beings. Given what is and must be the case if we are to exist at all—and in that sense, what is *ultimately* real, including what is *strictly* ultimate—what are our possibilities for understanding ourselves and leading our lives as the kind of being each of us is just as and because we are human?

I cannot possibly say here all that can and should be said to clarify what it means to ask and answer this existential question. But the one thing I simply must say is this: although it is not an empirical or scientific kind of question, or even a metaphysical or ethical kind, but rather an *existential* kind that calls for an existential kind of answer, it still necessarily *implies* the metaphysical kind of question and requires that a certain answer to that question be metaphysically valid. To trust without reservation in our ultimate environment as the God and Father of our Lord Jesus Christ, and then to serve that environment loyally without qualification as the same God, are not themselves to do metaphysics or simply to believe metaphysical assertions. But unless doing metaphysics can validate the assertions that there actually is a God and that the God there is is eminently deserving of just such trust and loyalty, they are insofar illusionary.

A word of caution: I have introduced the term "metaphysics" for reasons that I take to be relevant and important. But since I have not yet further explained the term, and my understanding of how it is to be used is not the only one, I respectfully ask that, for the purposes of our discussion here, my reader take care not to confuse it with any other, different understanding. My hope is that what I shall have to say hereafter will help to clarify further how "metaphysics," on my use, is, and is not, to be understood.

I turn now to the first theological criterion of appropriateness, and to what I understand it to require of any Christian systematic theologian who would hope to satisfy it in formulating the understanding of God necessarily presupposed and implied by Christian faith and witness. I shall begin with the first of two thesis-like summary statements and then proceed to unpack it as my present line of reasoning allows.

If a theological formulation of the Christian understanding of God is to be appropriate to Jesus Christ, the metaphysics it necessarily presupposes and implies cannot be classical, but must be neoclassical, in type.

By the distinction here between "classical" and "neoclassical" types of metaphysics, I mean essentially what others who have made it have meant by it, especially my esteemed teacher, Charles Hartshorne, who, for all I know, may have also introduced it into our English-speaking discussions in philosophy and theology. In any case, I understand neoclassical metaphysics as he does, to be distinguished materially from all classical metaphysics by two chief defining characteristics: (1) its key concept-term for thinking-speaking about concrete reality as such is "process," or "becoming," rather than "being," understood classically as the more or less fixed and unchanging; and (2) it understands the concept-term "God" properly to designate one of two infinitely different, but mutually implying, forms of becoming or process—namely, the eminent or unsurpassable form defining the One, i.e., the one and only *universal* individual, as distinct from the noneminent or surpassable form common to all the many, i.e., the many *particular* individuals and events.

I hold that it is just this type of metaphysics, with its understanding of the eminent, all-encompassing whole of reality, or God, as the universal individual, that is necessarily implied by the assertion of Christian witness that God is "sheer love," or, in the similar phrase of Charles Wesley, "pure unbounded love." Provided that by "love" is meant what these traditional phrases plainly mean, it is a matter not just of one's acting on others, but also, and primarily, of allowing others to act on oneself: to be really, internally related to them, and to make a difference to how one acts on them in turn. In this sense, love is, first of all, passive, and only then active; it is, in a word, *sympathy*, and only then action based on sympathy or benevolence. And this is why, finally, the metaphysics of love can only be a neoclassical instead of a classical type of metaphysics—*and* why the God who is nothing but love can only be the universal individual who interacts with *all* things, being really, internally related to all of them, and so acted on by them just as essentially as acting on all of them insofar as they, for their part, are really, internally related to it. Not only are all concrete things necessarily related to God by real, internal relations that make an absolute difference to the things themselves, but God is also related to all things by the same kind of real, internal relations that in turn make differences to God—differences that, in God's case, are also real and not merely logical, even though they are only relative, not absolute. In other words, they are not differences as to God's existence as God and as no one else, or as to God's bare existence in *some* state or other, in relation to some world of creatures or other. They are differences only as to what God is in this, that, or the other particular state, in relation to this, that, or the other particular world. To God's existence simply *somehow*, although always and only as God and no one else, nothing whatsoever can ever make the least possible difference, whence God's eminent nonrelativity or absoluteness as well as God's eminent relatedness.

So, with respect to the first criterion of appropriateness, the problem of God for Christian systematic theology, and so for any Christian systematic theologian, is to develop a type of metaphysics that is materially neoclassical. To try to formulate the Christian understanding of God in any other concepts and terms is precisely not to formulate it appropriately—or, if you will, *as* appropriately as it can and should be formulated, given the conceptual and terminological resources now available to us. I would stress, however, that if the Christian understanding of God is to be formulated appropriately, both poles of the distinctively "dual" or "dipolar" conception of God typical of neoclassical metaphysics demand to be developed completely and consistently, without either pole being sacrificed in any way to the other. If any metaphysics of a classical type is insofar distinctively one-sided or monopolar in absolutizing being at the expense of becoming, absoluteness at the expense of relativity, and universality at the expense of individuality, a neoclassical metaphysics is careful to avoid any such one-sidedness or monopolarity. For it, God is and must be conceived as *the* Unsurpassable, and this means that God has to be as unsurpassable in being as in becoming, in absoluteness as in relativity, in universality as in individuality—as well as vice versa. If God as conceived by classical metaphysics may be said to be "too big"—too big, at any rate, for any thought that is both clear and consistent, in something like the same way in which "the greatest possible number" is "too big"—God as conceived by certain other forms of modern, nonclassical philosophy and theology may be said to be "too small," too small to be the God and Father of Jesus Christ attested by bearing Christian witness. A God, say, whose "omnipotence," or power over others, is any less than the greatest such power conceivable is not, and cannot be, that God.

Because the point I have tried to make by this brief discussion of the first theological requirement of appropriateness has been made so often before, by other Christian theologians as well as myself, I am not going to develop it any further. I will turn instead to the problem created by the other requirement of credibility. One reason I do this is the relatively greater complexity of this problem itself, and hence the difficulty of adequately clarifying it within the limits of this entry. Another reason is that my approach to handling it may very well be the most distinctive thing I have to offer to any solution to the problem of God for Christian systematic theology. Here, again, I begin with a summary statement that I will then proceed to unpack as time limits allow.

If a theological formulation of the Christian understanding of God is to be credible to human existence, the metaphysics it necessarily presupposes and implies cannot be at all categorial, but must be austerely transcendental, in type.

The obvious parallelism between this second summary statement and the first is, of course, deliberate. But there is one important difference between them signaled by my statement, not just that neoclassical metaphysics is distinguished from classical, but that it is distinguished therefrom in a certain way—namely, *materially*. The point of my second statement, then, is to say that the type of metaphysics that the criterion of credibility requires also has to be distinguished from another type *formally*. In other words, in my understanding, as I have explained it, the type of metaphysics that the Christian systematic theologian needs has to be materially neoclassical rather than classical, lest she or he be unable to appropriately formulate the Christian understanding of God as only love. But what I now have to explain is why, in my view, a metaphysics being neoclassical materially is not sufficient if a theologian also wants to formulate that Christian understanding of God credibly. If her or his formulation is to be credible as well as appropriate, worthy of belief as well as truly Christian, then she or he needs to develop a neoclassical metaphysics that is also formally transcendental rather than categorial—or, as my statement actually says, is *"austerely,"* i.e., exclusively or nothing but, transcendental, as distinct from being, in at least some way or respect, categorial. My task now is to clarify what I mean by this and why I say it.

As good a place as any to begin is with the distinction I have already used between "reality" and "*ultimate* reality," including what I further distinguish as "*strictly* ultimate reality." According to a suggestive definition of William James that I have long found useful, "reality" designates "what we in some way find ourselves obliged to take account of." Accepting this definition, I say that *ultimate* reality, then, is to be distinguished as whatever any of us, as understanding and self-understanding beings, simply have to take account of understandingly, whether or not one also understands it explicitly or thematically, and whatever else one may or may not understand. On my analysis, this ultimate reality that we find ourselves necessarily having to understand at least implicitly, no matter what, is the threefold reality of myself, others, and the whole, of which I and all others are parts. *Strictly* ultimate reality, then, is what not only we, but also anything concretely real at all would have to take account of somehow, if not understandingly, or even so much as feelingly, then at least in the completely general, utterly abstract sense of being really, internally related to it and insofar determined by it.

Now, in my view, "metaphysics" in the strict sense of the word has the task of developing, reflectively and critically, our understanding of strictly ultimate reality in this sense of the term. But I also take metaphysics to be correctly classified as a science, which, like the other main type of science, represented by any and all of the so-called special sciences, is properly abstract, concerning itself exclusively with the essential *structure* of this ultimate reality, as distinct from its content—or, as we could also say, with its essential *form* as distinct from its substance or matter. Metaphysics in a strict sense thus abstracts from absolutely everything except the unconditionally necessary conditions of the possibility of the whole and of any of its parts. But "metaphysics" may also be used in a broad sense insofar as it includes analysis of the self as well in its essential structure as a self, and so not as just one part of the whole among others, but as the unique kind of part that it is, which is to say, as a part that understands and self-understands, and is therefore further characterized by the unique form of metaphysical freedom properly distinguished as "moral."

The term I use to designate the essential structure of strictly ultimate reality in its distinguishable features is "transcendentals," whereas I use the term "existentials" to pick out the features essential to the structure of the self as "existence," in the emphatic sense designating the unique part of reality that understands and also self-understands. But in my usage, both terms designate something importantly different from what I distinguish as "categories," or "categorials." To be sure, I understand these, too, to designate more or less general (and therefore more or less abstract) features of concrete realities as distinct from concrete realities themselves. But as general and abstract as categorials may be, they are nothing like as general and abstract as transcendentals; and the essential structure of the unique kind of concrete that is the self is characterized by existential features that are, in their own way, transcendental in that they, too, transcend any- and everything merely categorial.

Another way of putting this is to say that, whereas transcendentals and existentials both, in their ways, are extraordinary or necessary features of things—of anything whatsoever insofar as it is an object of understanding and of the unique kind of thing that itself understands and self-understands, and is therefore the subject of any understanding—categorials of all kinds, whether individualities, species, genera, or categories proper, are all merely ordinary or contingent features of things. They are features of things that might never be or have been actualized at all, and from which one can abstract entirely and still have something to talk about and something true and important to say about it. Thus to be an individual in the sense of a concrete singular that changes and endures, as distinct from an event that does neither, because it can only become and perish, is to have an individuality, in the sense of certain structural features that are definitive of it as just the individual it happens to be, as distinct from all other individuals and kinds thereof. But, then, to be any particular individual is to be a member of some species, some larger, more general class of individuals, all distinguishable intensionally by certain features characterizing any of them, actual or possible, as a member of that class. And to belong to any species is also to belong, with some specific difference, to some even larger or more general class or genus, just as any genus in turn belongs, with some generic difference, to some still larger, more general class whose chief defining characteristic is what I mean by a "category proper."

As I use it, then, the term "categorial" is systematically ambiguous in both ways. It may be used not just adjectivally as a cognate of "category," but also as a noun; and it may be thus used nominatively in a broad as well as a strict sense. Used as a plural noun in the sense in which I have just used it in distinguishing "categorials" from both "transcendentals" and "existentials," it is used strictly to designate the most abstract and general kind of the ordinary or contingent features of things that I call "categories proper," as distinct from "genera," "species," and "individualities." But used nominatively in a broad instead of a strict sense, it refers to any and all of these kinds of ordinary or contingent features, from the most to the least abstract and general. So, in this broad sense, a properly individual, specific, or generic feature of a thing may be thought and said to be a categorial feature as well.

With this much clarification of terms, I hope the further distinction I have made in my second summary statement, between types of metaphysics formally as well as materially, is gradually becoming understandable. A metaphysics, I hold, is rightly said to be formally "categorial" in type in that it in some way formulates its understanding of ultimate reality, including strictly ultimate reality, in concepts and terms otherwise designating "categories," which is to say, more or less abstract and general features of things that, for all we know or are ever able to know to the contrary, are still *only* ordinary or contingent, even if they are the most abstract and general of such features that I call "categories proper." I hold, on the other hand, that a metaphysics is rightly distinguished as "transcendental" insofar as it concerns itself solely with the features of things that are, in different senses, extraordinary or necessary, thereby abstracting entirely from any features that, being ordinary or contingent, are rightly distinguished as "categories" or "categorials." Because my terms for these extraordinary or necessary features of things are respectively "transcendentals" and "existentials," and because "existentials," also, as I have said, are, in their way, transcendental, even if only relatively, not absolutely so—i.e., relatively, not to anything simply as such, but only to anything that understands and self-understands—I distinguish the metaphysics that I hold to be required by systematic theology's second criterion of credibility simply as "transcendental," and "*austerely* transcendental" at that.

But why must the metaphysics necessarily presupposed and implied by any adequate formulation of the Christian understanding of God be formally transcendental as well as materially neoclassical? The answer, of course, as I have indicated, is because no Christian systematic theological formulation can be fully adequate to its content unless it is credible as well as appropriate, and because no formulation presupposing or implying a formally categorial metaphysics, even a metaphysics that is materially neoclassical, can possibly be credible, however appropriate it may be. Just why this is so can now be brought out sufficiently for present purposes by returning to the neoclassical concept of God as "the universal individual."

If, as I have argued, God, understood from a Christian standpoint, is "sheer love," or "pure unbounded love," and if love, whatever else it is, is sympathy, then it must be true metaphysically that God is at once an individual and universal. An individual, metaphysically understood, is a concrete singular distinguished as such from the other main type of concrete singular called "an event," by being a sequence of events that changes and endures, whether or not it also becomes and perishes. A particular individual is particular just because, having both a beginning and an end, it does become and perish even as it changes and endures, whereas the universal individual, being precisely universal, and therefore without either beginning or ending, changes and endures without becoming and perishing, as all other concrete things do, whether they be singulars or aggregates. But to say that God is nothing but boundless love is to say more than that God is an individual so understood, even if the one and only universal individual. It is also to say, or imply, that God is, in some sense, a *person*—even if the only eminent or unsurpassable person. It at least implies this because, as we ordinarily use "love," it is a concept-term belonging to the conceptuality-terminology in which we think-speak, not about what I distinguish as "strictly ultimate reality," i.e., extraordinary or necessary things, but about the very special kind of ordinary or contingent things that we distinguish as "persons," which is to say, fully developed or adult human beings and, possibly, by more or less remote analogy, the relatively few other ordinary and contingent beings sufficiently like human beings to interact with others with something like human sympathy. One thinks of how we commonly regard infants, say, or of dog owners, who typically love their pets as capable of loving them back.

But this is to say that "love" and "person" do not properly designate transcendentals or existentials, but *categorials*, and a relatively less general and abstract kind of categorials at that—or, to put it another way, they designate a relatively more specific and concrete kind of categorials than genera and categories proper. And this means that the more we say or imply when we say that God "loves" and therefore is a "person," indeed, "the eminent or unsurpassable person," is not, and cannot be, a properly metaphysical more. It is not saying or implying anything more *metaphysically* than we already say when we assert, in strictly transcendental terms, that God is the universal individual that uniquely interacts both with itself and all other individuals and events, being really, internally related to all of them, even as all of them are really, internally related to it.

But if the more we say is not a metaphysical more, what sort of more is it? It is a properly *symbolic* more of the sort that is familiar enough from the Christian religion, and, it would appear, from many, if not all, other religions, as distinct from metaphysics. Whereas metaphysical assertions necessarily involve only one stratum of meaning, and are therefore credible, if they are credible, literally or nonsymbolically, many if not most religious assertions typically involve *two* strata of meaning: the properly metaphysical stratum that they necessarily presuppose and imply if they are at all credible, and the distinctively religious stratum of meaning of these assertions themselves, which, though not metaphysical, serve to interpret certain metaphysical assertions nonliterally or symbolically. So, if one says as a metaphysician that God is the universal individual in the sense previously explained, one asserts something that is credible, if it is so, literally or nonsymbolically. I say it is credible literally or not at all, because being the universal individual is not a matter of degree, of more or less, but of all or none. One either is or is not the one and only universal individual, just as one either is or is not one of the many merely particular individuals instead. But if, on the other hand, one says or implies as a Christian, or as some other kind of theistic religious believer, that God is the eminent or unsurpassable *person*, one asserts something, which, if it is credible at all, can be so only symbolically or nonliterally, in the same way in which saying, "The Lord is my shepherd," can be credible only as a symbolic or nonliteral assertion, because it, too, is a matter of more or less, not of all or none.

But is it really credible in the *same* way? Or is there something to be said for the contrary view of Hartshorne and the Christian systematic theologians who would agree with him in holding that there is a relevant and important difference between the two cases? In this view, to assert or imply that God is a shepherd is to speak not just symbolically, but, in the traditional theological and philosophical term, "metaphorically." By contrast, to assert or imply that God is the eminent or unsurpassable person is indeed to speak symbolically, but not just metaphorically. Although to say or imply that God is a person is to use a term ordinarily used to designate certain categorial features of things, "person" is different from "shepherd" in that it may also be used to designate certain of their transcendental features. This it may do, so the argument goes, because there is a legitimate, utterly generalized sense of the term "person" in which it designates certain features of any concrete singular whatsoever that is metaphysically an individual, and so a certain *sequence* of events, as distinct from *an* event. In this utterly generalized sense, then, as distinct from the sense of "person" when it is used only of fully developed human individuals or, possibly, of their more or less remote analogues, God may be said to be a person, which is to say, the one and only eminent or unsurpassable person, in an admittedly symbolic and yet more than merely metaphorical sense of the term.

But now, fully allowing, as I do, that this distinction between "symbolic" and "merely symbolic," or "metaphorical," may indeed be made thus verbally or conceptually, I do not think that this can serve to vindicate any categorial metaphysics as a viable solution to our problem, not even a materially neoclassical or "process" metaphysics such as Hartshorne's "panpsychist" or "psychicalist" idealism. Why not? For the various reasons I have given elsewhere and at length in a number of discussions.[51] For our purposes here, these reasons may all be summarized, in effect, by saying that it is simply impossible ever to know whether or not this verbal or conceptual distinction is also real operationally. By this I mean that there is no possible way to tell in any actual case whether or not a term admittedly used symbolically is not merely so used and therefore used metaphorically. True as it may be that, if the term has, in addition to its ordinary meaning, what Hartshorne speaks of as a legitimate completely generalized meaning, it is not just categorial, and so is only a metaphor, the question remains unanswered whether, in any given case, a term really has any such completely generalized meaning, or whether it even makes sense to say that it has. Simply to assert that it has, as Hartshorne does repeatedly, without ever clearly and consistently specifying the variables that any possible value of them, even a completely generalized value, would somehow have to instance, is insofar not to answer this question but only to beg it. I conclude, therefore, that, for all he ever shows—as distinct from merely asserts—to the contrary, to say symbolically or nonliterally that God is a person, even if the eminent or unsurpassable person, is indistinguishable logically from saying merely metaphorically that the Lord is a shepherd, even if the eminently or unsurpassably good shepherd.

But this is to say that, absent a demonstration that and how any such otherwise categorial term may be used with the utterly general, transcendental meaning that Hartshorne claims it also has—i.e., what he sometimes speaks of paradoxically as its "almost categorial" meaning![52]—any claim that it has such a meaning is insofar an empty claim and, therefore, not credible but incredible. No claim can ever be credible in the sense of worth believing that is either so unclear or so inconsistent that whether

---

51. See especially Ogden, *Doing Theology Today*, 187–209; and Ogden, "Process Thought"; as well as note 78, "Analogy."

52. Hartshorne, *Creative Synthesis and Philosophic Method*, 154.

or not it is true cannot possibly be determined, not even in principle. Consequently, any metaphysics that is at all categorial, whether idealist or materialist, psychicalist or physicalist, and however appropriate it may otherwise seem to be for formulating the Christian understanding of God, is insofar incredible and so more a liability than an asset for the Christian systematic theologian. All that is required from her or his standpoint, although it most certainly *is* required if any such formulation is to be credible as well as appropriate, is what I mean by "an austerely transcendental metaphysics."

This implies, of course, that she or he must also be prepared—pending any such counter-demonstration—to give up Hartshorne's contention that there are three strata of meaning in religious discourse (see his essay by the same name) by agreeing with Paul Tillich and countless others that there are really only two: the stratum of *literal* meaning proper to the metaphysical assertions that any credible religious discourse necessarily implies; and the stratum of *symbolic* meaning proper to much religious discourse itself, insofar as it, too, affects to be credible. But if this further implies that the Christian systematic theologian must then frankly acknowledge that even the most distinctive assertion of Christian witness that God is nothing but boundless love cannot be credible literally, but only symbolically, then there is still no reason why she or he should falter—not, at any rate, if the metaphysics that her or his formulation of the Christian understanding of God necessarily implies is not only formally austerely transcendental, but also materially neoclassical, which is not the case, by the way, with Tillich's thoroughly classical formulation. If her or his formulation is also neoclassical, then not just some, but *all*, of the metaphysical conditions, necessary to the distinctive assertion of Christian witness being symbolically credible, can be met. It will no longer have to be "only a symbol" because it is an inapt symbol, but can be used to express symbolically, and aptly, the same truth that any adequate metaphysics will express literally.

117

Reflections on Acts 10:34–35

"Then Peter opened *his* mouth, and said, Of a truth I perceive that God is no respecter of persons: But in every nation he that feareth him, and worketh righteousness, is accepted with him" (Acts 10:34–35, AKJV).

"Then Peter began to speak to them: 'I truly understand that God shows no partiality, but in every nation anyone who fears him and does what is right is acceptable to him" (Acts 10:34–35, NRSV).

"*Petrus aber tat seinen Mund auf und sprach: Nun erfahre ich mit der Wahrheit, daß Gott die Person nicht ansieht; sondern in allerei Volk, wer ihn fürchtet und recht tut, der ist ihm angenehm*" (Acts 10:34–35, *Die Deutsche Bibel*, Luther's translation).

∾

34. *I perceive of a truth*—More clearly than ever from such a concurrence of circumstances. *That God is not a respecter of persons*—Is not partial in His love. The words mean, in a particular sense, that He does not confine His love to one nation; in a general [sense], that He is loving to every man, and willeth all men should be saved.

35. *But in every nation he that feareth him, and worketh righteousness*—He that first reverences God, as great, wise, good; the Cause, End, and Governor of all things; and, secondly, from this awful regard to Him, not only avoids all known evil, but endeavours, according to the best light he has, to do all things well. *Is accepted of him*—Through Christ, though he knows him not. The assertion is express and admits of no exception. He is in the favour of God, whether enjoying His written word and ordinances or not. Nevertheless, the addition of these is an unspeakable blessing to those who were before, in some measure, accepted: otherwise, God would never have sent an angel from heaven to direct Cornelius to St. Peter.[53]

∾

"In one thing we agree[:] that he who feareth God, and worketh righteousness shall be accepted of him and his Faith cannot be wrong whose life is in the right" (Abigail Adams to Louisa Catherine Adams, April 15, 1818).[54]

∾

"I know of no Philosopher, or Theologian, or Moralist ancient or modern more profound; more infallible than Whitefield, if the Anecdote that I have heard be true.

"He began; 'Father Abraham!' With his hands and Eyes gracefully directed to the Heavens as I have more than once seen him; 'Father Abraham, who have you there

---

53. Wesley, *Explanatory Notes*, 434–35.
54. Hutson, *Founders on Religion*, 90–91.

with you?' 'Have you Catholicks?' No. 'Have you Protestants?' No. 'Have you Churchmen?' No. 'Have you Dissenters?' No. 'Have you Presbyterians?' No. 'Quakers?' No. 'Anabaptists?' No. 'Who have you then?' 'Are you alone?' No.

"'My Brethren! You have the Answer to all these questions in the Words of my Text, "He who feareth God and worketh Righteousness, shall be accepted of him"'" (John Adams to Thomas Jefferson, December 3, 1813).[55]

∞

To be noted, first, is the important difference between saying that one who fears God and does what is right *is* so and so, and that she or he *shall be* so and so. Significantly, both the Authorized (King James) Version and the New Revised Standard Version, and also Luther and Wesley, translate "is," whereas the Adamses and Whitefield say "shall be."

Then, second, it is indefinitely more important to recognize that being "accepted" *by*, *of*, or *with* God, or being "acceptable" *to* God, may be one thing, whereas being—as Luther translates—"pleasing" to God may well be something else. I should wish to argue, indeed, that, although all things are acceptable to God because they are, in fact, always already accepted by God simply as God unconditionally, not all things are pleasing to God or affirmed by God, who, being all good, is pleased, takes pleasure in, or affirms only good things.

Finally, and most significantly, the line of thought developed in Acts 10:34-35 is required to be generalized further so as to apply, also, to the level of "the higher ecumenism," which is to say, to the relations that obtain, or should obtain, not just between different Christian confessions, denominations, and sects, but also between different religions, non-Christian as well as Christian. At this level, too, those who are pleasing to God (here Luther's translation brings out an important nuance) are those who fear God and do what is right. Or, in order to overcome the limits of the whole, specifically monotheistic, "Abrahamic" way of thinking and speaking, they are those who trustingly acknowledge their own fragmentariness and then loyally serve only the one strictly ultimate, integral whole of reality of which they and all other things are parts. They are, in short, those who, through whatever means, sacred or secular, religious or philosophical, exist and act authentically, realistically, in keeping with things as they are, instead of at cross-purposes with them.

∞

I have long distinguished "two senses of decisiveness," one of which I accept as appropriate to Jesus Christ, the other of which I reject. Thus I argue already in *Christ*

---

55. Hutson, *Founders on Religion*, 91.

without Myth that "[t]he New Testament sense of the claim 'only in Jesus Christ' is not that God is only to be found in Jesus and nowhere else, but that the only God who is to be found anywhere—*though he is to be found everywhere*—is the God who is made known in the word that Jesus speaks and is. In this sense, the words of Luther are correct exegesis: '*Und ist kein andrer Gott.*'"[56]

But it has occurred to me only lately that there is another, evidently closely related, distinction that may help—in certain contexts, at any rate—to clarify or explain my long-standing distinction. I refer to the distinction between experiencing or knowing *x* and experiencing or knowing *x* as such. That the only God who is to be found anywhere is the God who is decisively re-presented through Jesus in no way entails that this God is to be found only *as* the God whom Jesus decisively re-presents. If God, by definition, is and must be everywhere, and, in the case of beings capable of self-understanding, also is and must be known somehow by any such being in its knowing anything whatsoever, it is entirely possible that God is and must be known somehow by all such beings, even though this God is known *as* God—as *this* God—only through Jesus, mediately if not immediately. Indeed, it is only by tacitly making just this distinction that I as a Christian could ever even begin to accept the exclusivistic statements that so many of my fellow Christians unthinkingly allow themselves to make.

Moreover, if sin is understood as it should be, as presupposing prior knowledge of the truth that its nature as sin is to suppress; and if, as Christian tradition teaches, it is in this sense that all human beings are sinners, the only consistent inference is that all human beings always already know and must know the truth that, as the sinners they are, they all naturally suppress. But it would be absurd to infer that they all know and must know this truth "as it is in Jesus." The truth they do indeed always already know, and must know, in order to be the sinners they all are, but they do not all know, nor could they all know, this truth *as* the truth that Jesus decisively reveals.

I cannot but think in this connection of John Wesley's gloss on Acts 10:35: "*Is accepted of him*—Through Christ, though he knows him not. The assertion is express, and admits of no exception. He is in the favour of God, whether enjoying His written word and ordinances or not." "*Through Christ, though he knows him not*"—which is to say, exactly, "Through Christ, though not *as* through Christ."

∽

For over half a century, I have felt myself in profound agreement with H. R. Niebuhr's statement that a Christian is not one who "has become a member of a special group, with a special god, a special destiny, and a separate existence." No, a Christian is one who, "through the mediation and pioneering faith of Jesus Christ . . . has become

---

56. Ogden, *Christ without Myth*, 144; cf. also the discussion of two different understandings of Christian exclusivism in Ogden, *Faith and Freedom*, 85–91.

wholly human, has been called to membership in the society of universal being, and has accepted the fact that amidst the totality of existence he is not exempt from the human lot."[57] But, as the years have passed, I have realized that there is indeed an apparent tension, or lack of harmony, between my so whole-heartedly embracing Niebuhr's statement, on the one hand, and my usual analysis of what is distinctive about the call to be a Christian, on the other.

There is no question that, as I am accustomed to analyzing it, to be called to be a Christian is to be called to be more than "wholly human," more than to be a member of "the society of universal being," more than to accept "the fact that amidst the totality of existence [one] is not exempt from the human lot"—more than, in a phrase, to exist as an authentic human being. But "more" here, I submit, does not have its common connotation of "better," or "more nearly perfect," and so on. On the contrary, "more" in this case has everything to do with *means* and nothing to do with *end*—everything with *re-presentation* or *manifestation,* and nothing with *presentation* or *constitution.*

For this reason, one may even insist that "more" here may always be really "less," insofar as, in itself, without the end to which it is but the means, the presentation that it but re-presents, the constitution that it but manifests, it is (as John Wesley says of all outward religion) "lighter than vanity itself, yea . . . when used, as it were, in the place of [advancing inward holiness], an utter abomination to the Lord."[58]

So, once the apparent tension is reflected on, it is just that: apparent. The distinction remains between the substance or reality of which all culture, including religion, is but a form and all the various cultural forms themselves, sacred as well as secular, through which that substance or reality is more or less adequately re-presented or manifested. Put differently, in more traditional terms, religion as a "cultural system" (Clifford Geertz) belongs entirely to "this world," not to "the other world" of which all culture, sacred as much as secular, is at most but a re-presentation or manifestation.

And that, of course, is why there is no temple to be seen in the heavenly city (Rev 21:22), and why—as is brought out so well in John Adams' anecdote about George Whitefield—there are no differences between confessions, denominations, or sects among those gathered together with Father Abraham, and why—generalizing its point still further—there can be no differences between religions, either, in "the society of universal being."

---

57. Niebuhr, *Radical Monotheism and Western Culture,* 60.
58. Wesley, *Works of John Wesley 1,* 379.

118

On the *Optio Fundamentalis*

What, exactly, is "the *optio fundamentalis*," the fundamental decision that decides a human being's life on earth and in eternity?[59]

If one says, as Christians find it natural to say, that it is the decision of faith in God's prevenient love for all of us and of returning love for God and for all whom God loves, the formulation is still too narrow—assuming, at any rate, that "God," "faith," and "love" are all used in their specifically Christian, or even their generically theistic, senses. This means, among other things, that it will not do to advise Christians who wish to bear witness to their faith (to whatever extent they can do so, given the experience and assumptions of those to whom they wish to bear it) that they should strengthen such persons in their faith in and love for God even if they cannot yet give them full communion with Christ and his church.

The truth is that even talking about faith in and love for God is but one way among others of more or less adequately formulating the fundamental human decision, not that decision itself. In terms of Pope John XXIII's distinction, it, too, belongs to "the form in which [faith] is clothed," as distinct from "the content of faith."

If one really opens oneself to strictly ultimate reality at the deeper level of one's fundamental decision, one also opens oneself implicitly both to the meaning of strictly ultimate reality for us and to who- or whatever is sent or appointed to re-present it; and in accepting strictly ultimate reality in its meaning for us, one already accepts implicitly who- or whatever decisively re-presents this meaning. In this sense, or for this reason, Christians may say of anyone who is thus open and accepting that she or he exercises a *votum implicitum Christi sive ecclesiæ*.

There are three aspects of the act of thus really opening oneself to strictly ultimate reality and accepting it in its meaning for us. First, one orders one's entire existence to strictly ultimate reality in its meaning for us. Augustine speaks in this connection of "the love of God extending to the contempt of self," while Thomas Aquinas speaks of an "ordering of the whole life to its due end." One may also speak with Piet Fransen of "a completely free and dynamic orientation of one's whole life to the fullness of

---

59. Cf. Fransen, "How Can Non-Christians Find Salvation."

reality, the centre of which is God," or with John Hick of a transformation from "self-centeredness to God- or Reality-centeredness."

Second, this fundamental decision at the transcendental level of self-understanding necessarily expresses itself in some form of personal witness at the categorial level of life-praxis—of what we think, say, and do, or what we believe and enact—both secular and religious, given the possibilities and limitations of one's personal situation as a human being. Fransen calls this second aspect, "personal creed." Although the process of thus expressing one's fundamental decision through personal witness is guided by strictly ultimate reality itself in its meaning for us (whence talk of the *lumen fidei*, or *sensus fidei*), it also occurs of necessity through our own creatureliness and sinful historicity, which always allow for misinterpretations as well as correct interpretations. Thus, although "the light of faith," or "the sense of faith," may itself be infallible, it is also merely implicit, and our interpretations accordingly are not controlled by any revelation, fallible or infallible, that is explicit and decisive.

Third, then, there is the communal witness (in Fransen's terms, the "ecclesiastical creed," or, as I would prefer to say, the "ecclesial creed"). This communal witness has three main forms: (1) the particular form of the communal witness of a religious community that is taken to be *formally normative* or canonical; (2) other forms of the communal witness of the same religious community that are *substantially normative* when judged by its formal norm or canon; and (3) the communal witnesses of other communities, secular as well as religious, that, in their different ways, are also *more or less substantially normative* when judged by that same formal norm or canon.

If anyone who, in making an authentic fundamental decision, is *eo ipso* open to strictly ultimate reality in its meaning for us is thereby also open to and already implicitly affirms anyone who, or anything that, truly re-presents this meaning—if this is so, then, anyone, presumably, who understands her- or himself authentically is not only implicitly, or "anonymously," a Christian, but also implicitly, or "anonymously," a Buddhist or a Hindu or a Muslim, or anything else insofar as it re-presents substantially the same meaning and is religiously or existentially significant precisely because it does so. If I as a Christian believe, and must believe, that anyone who understands her- or himself authentically is "anonymously" a Christian, this need not preclude my allowing that anyone, including myself, may at the same time also be implicitly a Buddhist or a Hindu or a Muslim, or anything else provided only that it expresses substantially the same existential truth: the same self-understanding/understanding of existence that Christians hold to be re-presented decisively through Jesus Christ.

Reinhold Niebuhr argues that the Hebrew prophets identified "the real problem of history." But in point of fact, the problem identified by the Hebrew prophets is but one particular form of the problem identified, in one way or another, by prophets of all the axial religions as *the* human problem. This is the problem that human beings universally tend to understand themselves only in the inauthentic mode of *misunderstanding* themselves, and they do this not merely because they are fragmentary beings whose insights are always only partial and fallible, but also because they turn away from the original, if only implicit, insight always already given them, choosing instead, freely and responsibly, to live in darkness rather than light. Thus, according not only to the Hebrew prophets but also to all the prophets of the axial religions generally, human beings are universally in need of ultimate transformation: from an inauthentic—because false and unrealistic—self-misunderstanding to an authentic—because true and realistic—self-understanding. What is wanted, they all attest, is an ultimate turning by each and every human being from self-centeredness to reality-centeredness, from love of self to love of reality as such.

There are only two possibilities: either we are here to serve the all-encompassing whole, or it is here to serve us. The question "Is the part for the whole, or is the whole merely for the part?" is not an incidental one. It is *the* question, once we set aside our natural self-centeredness and look at life, as we say, objectively.[60]

Our original call to obedience, to be the human beings we really are, is to exist both *gratefully from* the community of all others to whom we are related and *benevolently for* them. This means that we are to appropriate every opportunity they provide, not in order to pursue our own self-chosen interest or to cultivate our own self-chosen virtue, but in order to make our maximal contribution to the same "beloved community" by optimizing the opportunity of all its members to make their own maximal contributions.

The fundamental decision is the same for each of us: whether so to trust in the encompassing whole of reality that one is both free *from* all things—oneself and all

---

60. Hartshorne, "Modern World and Modern View."

others—and free *for* them; and then to be loyal to the whole by being loyal to all its parts, accepting all others as oneself and thinking and acting accordingly.

Bibliography

Adams, E. M. "The Philosophical Grounds of the Present Crisis of Authority." In *Authority: A Philosophical Analysis*, edited by R. Baine Harris, 3–24. Tuscaloosa: University of Alabama Press, 1976.

Adler, Mortimer J. *How to Read a Book: The Art of Getting a Liberal Education.* 6th ed. New York: Simon & Schuster, 1960.

Apel, Karl-Otto. "Types of Social Science in the Light of Human Interests of Knowledge." *Social Research* 44 (1977) 425–70.

Ashworth, E. Jennifer. "Medieval Theories of Analogy." https://plato.stanford.edu/archives/fall2017/entries/analogy-medieval/.

Berger, Peter, and Thomas Luckmann. *The Social Construction of Reality.* Garden City, NY: Anchor, 1966.

Bochenski, Joseph M. *Autorität, Freiheit, Glaube, Sozialphilosophische Studien.* Munich: Philosophia, 1988.

Boff, Clodovis. *Theology and Praxis: Epistemological Foundations.* Translated by Robert R. Barr. Maryknoll, NY: Orbis, 1987.

Bultmann, Rudolf. *Glauben und Verstehen 2.* Tübingen: Mohr/Siebeck, 1952.

———. *New Testament and Mythology and Other Basic Writings.* Translated and edited by Schubert M. Ogden. Philadelphia: Fortress, 1984.

Carwardine, Richard. *Lincoln: A Life of Purpose and Power.* New York: Vintage, 2007.

Chemnitz, Martin. *Loci Theologici II.* Translated by J. A. O. Preuss. St. Louis: Concordia, 1989.

Christian, William A. *Meaning and Truth in Religion.* Princeton: Princeton University Press, 1964.

Cohen, Morris R., and Ernest Nagel. *An Introduction to Logic and Scientific Method.* New York: Harcourt, 1934.

Collingwood, R. G. *An Autobiography.* Reprint, London: Oxford University Press, 1944.

———. *Faith and Reason: Essays in the Philosophy of Religion.* Edited by Lionel Rubinoff. Chicago: Quadrangle, 1968.

Copleston, Frederick. *A History of Philosophy II: Medieval Philosophy: Augustine to Scotus.* London: Burns, Oates & Washbourne, 1950.

———. *A History of Philosophy III: Ockham to Suarez.* London: Burns, Oates & Washbourne, 1953.

Coreth, Emerich. *Metaphysik: Eine methodisch-systematische Grundlegung.* 2nd ed. Innsbruck: Tyrolia, 1964.

Dalferth, Ingolf U. "'In God We Trust': Trust, Mistrust and Distrust as Modes of Orientation." In *Trust, Sociality, Selfhood*, edited by Arne Grøn and Claudia Welz, 135–52. Religion in Philosophy and Theology 52. Tübingen: Mohr/Siebeck, 2010.

Dewey, John. *Human Nature and Conduct: An Introduction to Social Psychology*. New York: Modern Library, 1930.

Dombrowski, Daniel A. "Objective Morality and Perfect Being Theology: Three Views." *American Journal of Theology and Philosophy* 29 (2008) 205–21.

Duns Scotus, John. *Philosophical Writings: A Selection*. Translated and edited by Allan Wolter. Indianapolis: Hackett, 1987.

Farrer, Austin. *Reflective Faith: Essays in Philosophical Theology*. Edited by Charles C. Conti. Grand Rapids: Eerdmans, 1974.

Fransen, Piet. "How Can Non-Christians Find Salvation in Their Own Religions?" *Christian Revelation and the World Religions*, edited by Josef Neuner, 67–122. London: Burns & Oates, 1967.

Gamwell, Franklin I. *The Divine Good: Modern Moral Theory and the Necessity of God*. San Francisco: HarperSanFrancisco, 1990.

Goodwin, George L. *The Ontological Argument of Charles Hartshorne*. AAR Dissertation Series 20. Missoula, MT: Scholars, 1978.

Hahn, Lewis E., ed. *The Philosophy of Charles Hartshorne*. LaSalle, IL: Open Court, 1991.

Hartshorne, Charles. "Analogy." In *An Encyclopedia of Religion*, edited by Vergilius Ferm, 19–20. New York: Philosophical Library, 1945.

———. *Anselm's Discovery*. La Salle, IL: Open Court, 1965.

———. "Anthropomorphic Tendencies in Positivism." *Philosophy of Science* 8 (1941) 184–203.

———. *Beyond Humanism: Essays in the New Philosophy of Nature*. Lincoln: University of Nebraska Press, 1969.

———. "Cause." In *An Encyclopedia of Religion*, edited by Vergilius Ferm, 133–35. New York: Philosophical Library, 1945.

———. "Charles Peirce's 'One Contribution to Philosophy' and His Most Serious Mistake." In *Studies in the Philosophy of Charles Sanders Peirce. Second Series*, edited by Edward G. Moore and Richard S. Robin, 455–74. Amherst: University of Massachusetts Press, 1964.

———. *Creative Synthesis and Philosophic Method*. London: SCM, 1970.

———. *Creativity in American Philosophy*. Albany: State University of New York Press, 1984.

———. *The Darkness and the Light: A Philosopher Reflects upon His Fortunate Career and Those Who Made It Possible*. Albany: State University of New York Press, 1990.

———. *The Divine Relativity: A Social Conception of God*. New Haven: Yale University Press, 1948.

———. "The Divine Relativity and Absoluteness: A Reply [to John Wild]." *Review of Metaphysics* 4 (1950) 31–60.

———. "Equality, Freedom, and the Insufficiency of Empiricism." *Southern Journal of Philosophy* 1 (1970) 20–27.

———. "Foreword." In *The Ontological Argument of Charles Hartshorne*, by George L. Goodwin, xi–xviii. Missoula, MT: Scholars, 1978.

———. "The Formal Validity and Real Significance of the Ontological Argument." *Philosophical Review* 53 (1944) 225–45.

———. "God and the Meaning of Life." In *On Nature*, edited by Leroy S. Rouner, 154–68. Boston University Studies in Philosophy and Religion 6. Notre Dame: University of Notre Dame Press, 1984.

———. "The Idea of God—Literal or Analogical?" *Christian Scholar* 29 (1956) 131–36.

———. *Insights and Oversights of Great Thinkers: An Evaluation of Western Philosophy*. Albany: State University of New York Press, 1983.

———. "John Hick on Logical and Ontological Necessity." *Religious Studies* 13 (1977) 155–65.

———. *The Logic of Perfection, and Other Essays in Neoclassical Metaphysics*. La Salle, IL: Open Court, 1962.

———. "Love and Dual Transcendence." *Union Seminary Quarterly Review* 30 (1975) 94–100.

———. *Man's Vision of God and the Logic of Theism*. Chicago: Clark, 1941.

———. "Metaphysics for Positivists." *Philosophy of Science* 2 (1935) 287–303.

———. "The Modern World and a Modern View of God." *Crane Review* 4 (1962) 73–85.

———. *A Natural Theology for Our Time*. La Salle: Open Court, 1967.

———. "Our Knowledge of God." In *Knowing Religiously*, 52–63. Boston University Studies in Philosophy and Religion 7. Notre Dame: University of Notre Dame Press, 1985.

———. "A Philosophy of Democratic Defense." In *Science, Philosophy, and Religion: Second Symposium*, 130–72. New York: Conference on Science, Philosophy, and Religion in Their Relation to the Democratic Way of Life, 1942.

———. *Reality as Social Process: Studies in Metaphysics and Religion*. Glencoe: Free Press, 1953.

———. "The Relativity of Nonrelativity: Some Reflections on Firstness." In *Studies in the Philosophy of Charles Sanders Peirce*, edited by Philip P. Wiener and Frederick H. Young, 215–24. Cambridge: Harvard University Press, 1952.

———. "Religion in Process Philosophy." In *Religion in Philosophical and Cultural Perspective*, edited by J. Clayton Feaver and William Horosz, 246–68. Princeton: Van Norstrand, 1967.

———. "Religious Aspects of Necessity and Contingency." In *More About God*, edited by Lewis M. Rogers and Charles H. Monson Jr., 145–61. Salt Lake City: University of Utah Press, 1969.

———. "A Revision of Peirce's Categories." *Monist* 63 (1980) 277–89.

———. "Whitehead's Differences from Buddhism." *Philosophy East and West* 25 (1975) 407–13.

———. *Wisdom as Moderation: A Philosophy of the Middle Way*. Albany: State University of New York Press, 1987.

———. *The Zero Fallacy and Other Essays in Neoclassical Philosophy*. Edited by Mohammad Valady. Chicago: Open Court, 1997.

Heidegger, Martin. *Sein und Zeit*. 7th ed. Tübingen: Niemeyer, 1953.

Holub, Robert C. *Jürgen Habermas: Critic in the Public Sphere*. Critics of the Twentieth Century. London: Routledge, 1991.

Hutson, James H., ed. *The Founders on Religion: A Book of Quotations*. Princeton: Princeton University Press, 2007.

James, William. *Some Problems of Philosophy: A Beginning of an Introduction*. New York: Longmans, 1911.

Jonas, Hans. *The Phenomenon of Life: Toward a Philosophical Biology.* New York: Harper & Row, 1966.
Keller, Ernst, and Marie-Luise Keller. *Der Streit um die Wunder: Kritik und Auslegung des Übernatürlichen in der Neuzeit.* Gütersloh: Gütersloher, 1968.
Leclerc, Ivor. *Whitehead's Metaphysics: An Introductory Exposition.* Atlantic Highlands, NJ: Humanities, 1958.
Lewis, C. I. *Mind and the World Order.* New York: Scribner, 1929.
Macquarrie, John. *Principles of Christian Theology.* 2nd ed. New York: Scribner, 1977.
McNeill, William H. *A World History.* New York: Oxford University Press, 1967.
Morgan, Robert, with John Barton. *Biblical Interpretation.* Oxford Bible Series. Oxford: Oxford University Press, 1988.
Morris, Thomas V. *Anselmian Explorations: Essays in Philosophical Theology.* Notre Dame: University of Notre Dame Press, 1987.
Mulhall, Stephen. "Wittgenstein and the Philosophy of Religion." In *Philosophy of Religion in the 21st Century*, edited by D. Z. Phillips and Timothy Tessin, 95–118. Claremont Studies in the Philosophy of Religion. New York: Palgrave, 2001.
Niebuhr, H. Richard. "Life Is Worth Living." *Intercollegian and Far Horizons* 57 (1939) 3–4, 22.
———. *Radical Monotheism and Western Culture.* New York: Harper & Brothers, 1960.
Nygren, Anders. *Meaning and Method: Prolegomena to a Scientific Philosophy of Religion and a Scientific Theology.* Translated by Philip S. Watson. Philadelphia: Fortress, 1972.
Ogden, Schubert M. *Christ without Myth: A Study Based on the Theology of Rudolf Bultmann.* Reprint, Dallas: Southern Methodist University Press, 1991.
———. "The Criterion of Metaphysical Truth and the Senses of Metaphysics." *Process Studies* 5 (1975) 47–48.
———. *Doing Theology Today.* 1996. Reprint, Eugene, OR: Wipf & Stock, 2006.
———. *Faith and Freedom: Toward a Theology of Liberation.* 1989. Reprint, Eugene, OR: Wipf & Stock, 2005.
———. *Is There Only One True Religion or Are There Many?* Dallas: Southern Methodist University Press, 1992.
———. "Must God Be Really Related to Creatures?" *Process Studies* 20 (1991) 54–55.
———. *On Theology.* Reprint, Dallas: Southern Methodist University Press, 1992.
———. "Philosophy and the Religious Life: A Reflection on Charles Hartshorne's Contribution." *Creative Transformation* 6 (1997) 28–31.
———. "Pluralism." In *The Westminster Dictionary of Christian Theology*, edited by Alan Richardson and John Bowden, 449–51. Philadelphia: Westminster, 1983.
———. *The Point of Christology.* 1982. Reprint, Dallas: Southern Methodist University Press, 1992.
———. "Present Prospects for Empirical Theology." In *The Future of Empirical Theology*, edited by Bernard E. Meland, 65–88. Chicago: University of Chicago Press, 1969.
———. "Process Theology and the Wesleyan Witness." In *Thy Nature and Thy Name Is Love: Wesleyan and Process Theologies in Dialogue*, edited by Bryan P. Stone and Thomas Jay Oord, 25–48. Nashville: Kingswood, 2001.
———. "Process Thought—A Response to John B. Cobb, Jr." In *Philosophy of Religion in the 21st Century*, edited by D. Z. Phillips and Timothy Tessin, 266–80. Claremont Studies in the Philosophy of Religion. New York: Palgrave, 2001.

———. *The Reality of God, and Other Essays*. 1966. Reprint, Dallas: Southern Methodist University Press, 1992.

———. "Theology without Metaphysics?" In *Religion and the End of Metaphysics*, edited by Dewi Z. Phillips and Mario von der Ruhr, 139–55. Religion in Philosophy and Theology 34. Tübingen: Mohr/Siebeck, 2008.

———. *To Preach the Truth: Selected Sermons and Homilies*. Eugene, OR: Cascade Books, 2015.

———. *To Teach the Truth: Selected Courses and Seminars*. Eugene, OR: Cascade Books, 2015.

———. *The Understanding of Christian Faith*. Eugene, OR: Cascade Books, 2010.

Outler, Albert C., ed. *John Wesley*. New York: Oxford University Press, 1964.

Pope, Alexander. *Poetical Works*. Edited by Herbert Davis. London: Oxford University Press, 1966.

Post, John F. *The Faces of Existence: An Essay in Nonreductive Metaphysics*. Ithaca, NY: Cornell University Press, 1987.

Prozesky, Martin. *Religion and Ultimate Well-Being: An Explanatory Theory*. New York: St. Martin's, 1984.

Rahner, Karl. *Schriften zur Theologie 7*. Einsiedeln: Benzinger, 1966.

Rorty, Richard. "Philosophy-Envy." *Dædalus* 133.4 (2004) 18–24.

Schleiermacher, Friedrich. *Der christiche Glaube nach den Grundsätzen der Evangelischen Kirche im Zusammenhang dargestellt*. Edited by Martin Redeker. 7th ed. Berlin: de Gruyter, 1960.

Scholz, Heinrich. *Metaphysik als strenge Wissenschaft*. Darmstadt: Wissenschaftliche Buchgesellschaft, 1965.

Sheehan, Thomas. *Making Sense of Heidegger: A Paradigm Shift*. London: Rowman & Littlefield, 2015.

Streng, Frederick J. *Understanding Religious Life*. 3rd ed. Belmont, CA: Wadsworth, 1985.

Tillich, Paul. *Gesammelte Werke 5: Die Frage nach dem Unbedingten, Schriften zur Religionsphilosophie*. Stuttgart: Evangelischer, 1964.

———. *The Shaking of the Foundations*. New York: Scribner, 1948.

———. *Systematic Theology*. Vol. 1. Chicago: University of Chicago Press, 1951.

Toulmin, Stephen. *An Examination of the Place of Reason in Ethics*. Cambridge: Cambridge University Press, 1950.

Wesley, John. *Explanatory Notes upon the New Testament*. Reprint, London: Epworth, 1954.

———. *The Works of John Wesley 1: Sermons*. Edited by Albert C. Outler. Nashville: Abingdon, 1984.

Whitehead, Alfred North. *Adventures of Ideas*. New York: Macmillan, 1933.

———. *Modes of Thought*. New York: Macmillan, 1938.

———. *Process and Reality: An Essay in Cosmology*. Edited by David Ray Griffin and Donald W. Sherburne. New York: Free, 1978.

Wieman, Henry Nelson. *The Source of Human Good*. Chicago: University of Chicago Press, 1946.

Wilson, Douglas. *Lincoln's Sword: The Presidency and the Power of Words*. New York: Knopf, 2006.

Wittgenstein, Ludwig. *Zettel*. Edited by G. E. M. Anscombe and G. H. von Wright. Frankfurt: Suhrkamp, 1967.

Index of Names

Adams, Abigail, 318
Adams, E. M., 28
Adams, John, 318–19, 321
Adams, Louisa Catherine, 318
Adler, Mortimer J., 22
Apel, Karl-Otto, 41, 176
Aristotle, 43, 107–9, 171, 188
Ashworth, E. Jennifer, 172

Barton, John, 73–74
Bavink, Bernhard, 289–90
Berger, Peter, 12
Bochenski, Joseph M., 23–25, 102, 150–51, 153
Boff, Clodovis, 106
Bultmann, Rudolf, 9, 31, 65, 67, 76, 82, 85, 89, 150, 264, 290

Carwardine, Richard, 287–88
Chemnitz, Martin, 240–41
Christian, William A., 69, 112
Cohen, Morris R., 213
Collingwood, R. G., 17, 27–28, 111–12
Copleston, Frederick, 171, 241
Coreth, Emerich, 123–24

Dalferth, Ingolf U., 243
Devenish, Philip E., xii
Dewey, John, 42, 259
Dombrowski, Daniel A., 303–4, 306
Duns Scotus, John, 101, 171–72

Eckhart, Meister, 234–35, 241

Farrer, Austin, 260
Fransen, Piet, 71, 322–23
Freud, Sigmund, 290–91

Galileo, 43
Gamwell, Franklin I., xii, 86, 88, 261

Geertz, Clifford, 66–68, 78, 228, 321
Goodwin, George L., xii, 36, 182
Guelzo, Allen, 288

Habermas, Jürgen, 17, 21, 41, 176
Hahn, Lewis E., 182
Hartshorne, Charles, v, 8, 9, 33, 36, 39–40, 44, 57, 86, 90–95, 97–98, 101, 104–5, 108, 110, 112, 119, 124, 126–34, 137–38, 142, 144–46, 152, 154, 167–69, 172, 174–75, 181–82, 184, 186–87, 189–91, 198–99, 201, 203–7, 211–19, 224, 228, 230–32, 236, 242–43, 246, 249, 252, 255, 257, 277–78, 287, 290–91, 293–94, 296–97, 299, 305–6, 309, 315–17, 324
Hegel, G. W. F., 165, 173, 265
Heidegger, Martin, 43, 58, 106, 118, 139–40, 143, 157–59, 163, 182, 192, 222, 252
Holub, Robert C., 41
Humboldt, Wilhelm von, 12
Hutson, James H., 318–19

James, William, 8, 15, 51, 291, 312
Jefferson, Thomas, 319
John XXIII, Pope, 322
Jonas, Hans, 10

Kant, Immanuel, 136, 171, 176, 293
Keller, Ernst, 289–90
Keller, Marie-Luise, 289–90
Kierkegaard, Søren, 66, 218, 241, 243, 247, 250
Knox, John, 65

Leclerc, Ivor, 107–8
Lewis, C. I., 45
Lincoln, Abraham, 288
Luckman, Thomas, 12
Luther, Martin, 271, 307, 318–20

Index of Names

Macquarrie, John, 330
Marxsen, Willi, 65, 70, 101
McNeill, William H., 11
Morgan, Robert, 73–74
Morris, Thomas V., 260
Mulhall, Stephen, 54

Nagel, Ernest, 213
Niebuhr, H. Richard, 4, 31, 320–21
Neibuhr, Reinhold, 262, 288, 324
Nygren, Anders, 26, 34, 36–40, 124

Ogden, Schubert M., 57, 64, 67, 74, 78, 87, 104, 111, 113–14, 136, 210, 214, 219–20, 237, 239, 241–42, 253–54, 270, 281, 288, 302, 316, 320
Outler, Albert C., 67

Parker, DeWitt, 130
Paul, St., 65, 72, 232–39, 289
Peirce, C. S., 44, 130, 138, 167–70, 174, 198, 200–203
Phillips, D. Z., 54
Plato, 202, 303, 305
Pope, Alexander, 285–88
Post, John F., 102
Prozesky, Martin, 135–36

Rahner, Karl, 262
Rorty, Richard, 43

Russell, Bertrand, 32, 130
Schleiermacher, Friedrich, 70
Scholz, Heinrich, 154
Scrimgeour, Andrew D., xii
Sellars, Roy Wood, 130
Sellars, Wilfrid, 2, 130
Sheehan, Thomas, 58
Streng, Frederick J., 67, 70

Tillich, Paul, 9, 65, 68, 232–33, 251, 284–85, 290, 317
Toulmin, Stephen, 99

Vishio, Alexander F., xii

Wesley, Charles, 271, 310
Wesley, John, 67, 318–21
Whitefield, George, 318–19, 321
Whitehead, Albert North, 12, 14, 40, 44, 46–47, 55–56, 58, 85, 89–90, 104, 107–8, 110–12, 125, 128, 130, 139, 143, 148, 154, 161, 168, 181–84, 188–90, 198–200, 211, 219, 228, 230, 235–37, 255, 257–58
Wieman, Henry Nelson, 12–14
Wilson, Douglas, 286, 288
Wittgenstein, Ludwig, 46–47, 54–55, 95, 99–100, 125, 143, 154, 259

www.ingramcontent.com/pod-product-compliance
Lightning Source LLC
Chambersburg PA
CBHW080118020526
44112CB00037B/2769